One Golden Moment

The 1984 Olympics Through the Photographic Lens of the Los Angeles *Herald Examiner*

By David Davis

Foreword by Paul Gonzales

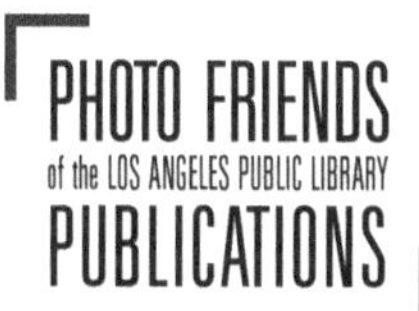

Dedication

To the photographers of the Los Angeles *Herald Examiner*
and those photographers whose work appears in these pages.

All proceeds from the sale of this book will be donated to Photo Friends of the Los Angeles Public Library, a non-profit organization that supports the LAPL's photo collection.

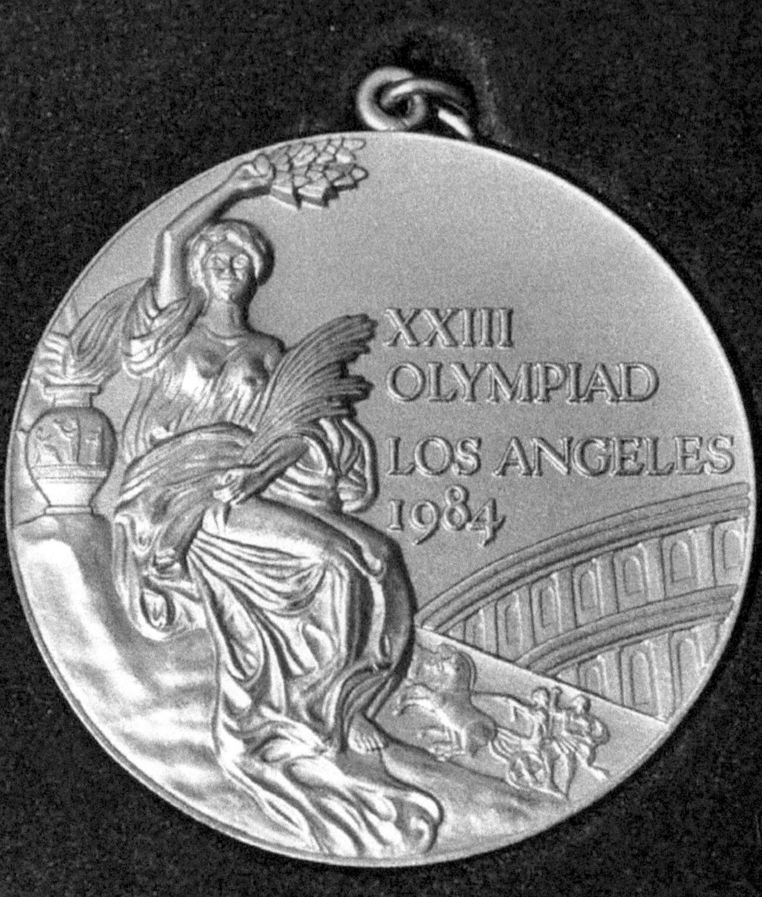
XXIII
OLYMPIAD
LOS ANGELES
1984

Contents

Opposite: **The 1984 Olympic gold medal, gilded with 6.5 grams of 24-karat gold.**

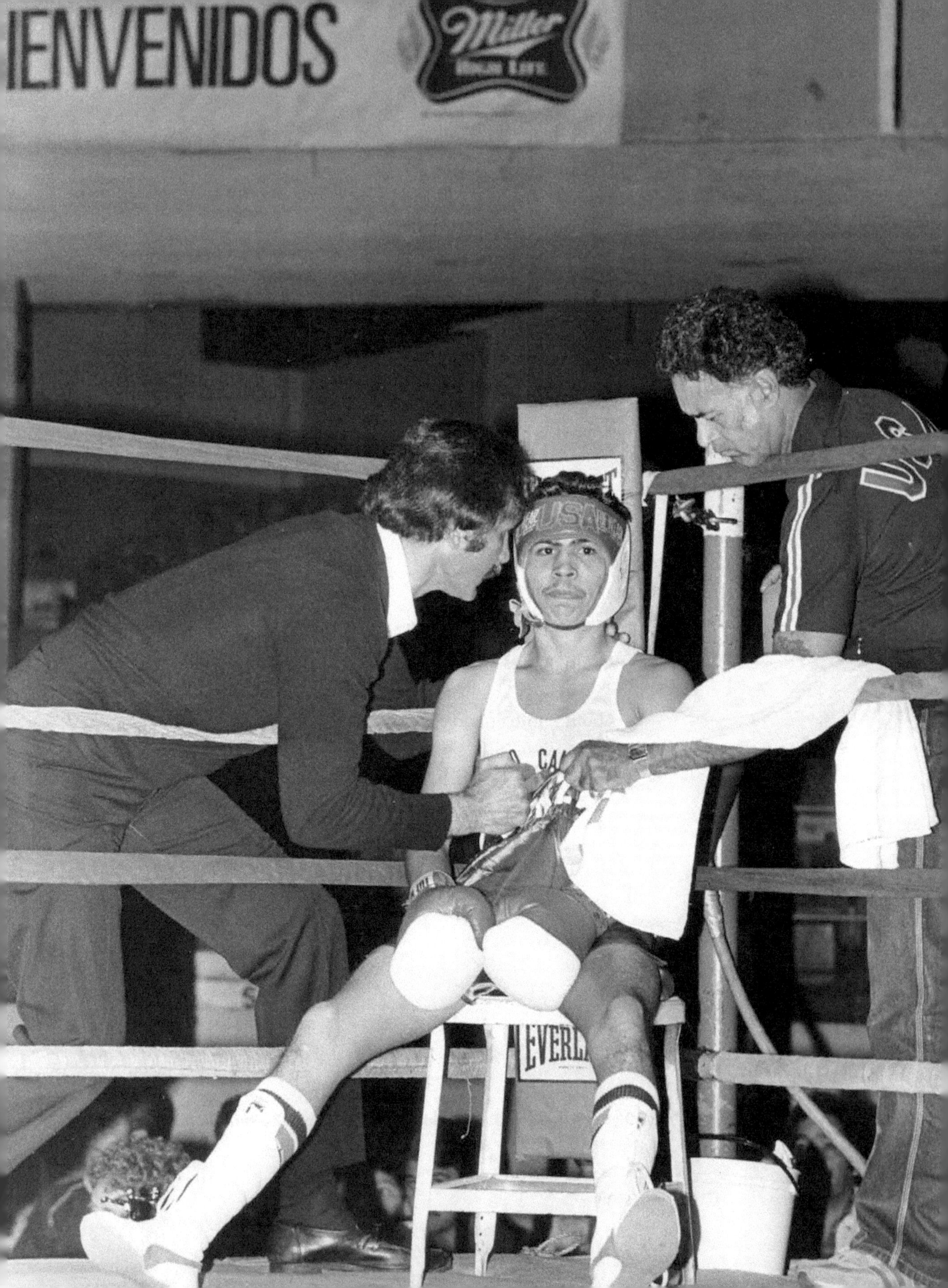
IENVENIDOS
Miller
USA
EVERL

Foreword

By Paul Gonzales

Paul Gonzales was a member of the 1984 U.S. Olympic boxing squad, a stalwart class that included Evander Holyfield, Mark Breland, Pernell "Sweet Pea" Whitaker, Virgil Hill, and Meldrick Taylor. American boxers won nine gold medals and 11 total medals in a competition that was somewhat compromised due to the absence of the Cuban, Russian, East German, and Bulgarian boxers because of the boycott.

Hailing from East L.A., Gonzales had a stellar amateur career, winning ten consecutive Los Angeles Golden Gloves championships. He faced the "local hero" hype leading up to the 1984 Olympics, but he overcame that pressure, as well as several injuries, in defeating four consecutive opponents and winning the gold medal in a walkover over Italy's Salvatore Todisco.

Gonzales was just 20. With his victory, he became the first Mexican-American boxer to win an Olympic gold medal and the first American to win in boxing's light flyweight division. Described by one journalist as "a scrawny-looking guy—106 pounds of flesh and bones and lightning," he was awarded the prestigious Val Barker Trophy as the outstanding boxer of the 1984 Olympic tournament.

Now 52, Gonzales lives in Montebello and works as a supervisor for the Los Angeles County Department of Parks and Recreation at the Eastside Eddie Heredia Boxing Club.

I was born in Pecos, Texas, the town made famous by Judge Roy Bean. My family moved to L.A. when I was a kid. After my parents split, my mom took us to live in the Aliso Village housing projects in Boyle

***Opposite:* Paul Gonzales listened to his longtime trainer, Al Stankie (*left*), in a pre-Olympic bout. (Jim Ober)**

Heights. She was a single mom on welfare who raised us seven kids.

There were a lot of gangs at the time. I was in the Primera Flats *clika* since I was 9. We would fight gangs that were in the neighborhood or other gangs that came around. It was rough. My cousin was stabbed in the neck in a fight. He died in my arms.

I myself was hit in the back of the head when I was sitting in the back seat of a car. I was maybe 13. One of my homeboys used tweezers to pick the shotgun pellets out of my scalp. Another time, some guy tried to punk me and pulled a knife. We got in real close and he stabbed me. Everybody jumped in to grab it away. The guy fell, my sister bit the guy's hand, the knife fell out. He got up, and I knocked him out. That was it.

I was always an athlete. I played football and baseball at Roosevelt [High School]. I was taking martial arts as well and got into karate. We used to watch Bruce Lee movies.

Boxing was what got my fire burning. I started boxing when I was about nine. An LAPD cop named Al Stankie caught me fighting in Pecan Park [in Boyle Heights]. He threw me down and made a challenge: "If you want to fight for medals and trophies and forget all this gang junk, come down to the Hollenbeck police station. We got a boxing club downstairs in the basement. I dare you."

Me being a curious kid, I said, "I'll take him up on that."

I ended up sneaking in the back door, where they took the prisoners in, so nobody would see me and call me a snitch. My heart was beating real fast. I heard noise downstairs in the basement. I heard the speed bag going. I peeked in. Another officer—Al's partner, Ray Mayo—he saw me. He said, "You! Get over here!" He put the gloves on me and took me over to the heavy bag. I started hitting the heavy bag, and I was in love.

We were cramped at Hollenbeck. They had a ring in the center. They had a heavy bag, a speed bag, and a little area where you could jump rope. That was it. But we loved it. What did we know? We all came from the projects.

Al's a motivator. He makes you believe. And, because he believes in you, you believe in him. The connection we had was phenomenal. If he told me I could walk through a wall, I'd walk through a wall. Not a problem.

Alexis Arguello [the Nicaraguan champ nicknamed "The Explosive Thin Man"] was my idol. I loved his style: Straight-up puncher-boxer. I was the same way—lanky but strong. I could punch and knock people out.

My drive for the Olympics started in 1976. I was young, but I watched the U.S. team in Montreal: Sugar Ray Leonard, the Spinks brothers, Howard Davis. In those days, ABC and Howard Cosell made you a star. Watching the Games and looking at the Olympic rings—it was so beautiful. Oh, man, I got the Olympic bug! I told myself, "I want this. I want to go to the Olympics."

That became my dream. I had people doubting me. They said, "Yeah, yeah, sure, sure. You're just a kid from the barrio." Al kept saying, "Son, you can do this. Conceive it, believe it, achieve it."

After I made the U.S. Olympic team, we went to train at the Abercrombie Ranch in Gonzales, Texas. My name, my town, right? See, it was meant to be!

I can't really say I was disappointed that the Cubans and the Russians weren't coming. People forget we fought all those dudes prior to the Games. I fought the 1980 Olympic gold medalist, Shamil Sabirov [from the USSR], and I beat him. I spanked him. I fought Silvio Valdes [from Cuba], and I beat him. What else did I have to prove?

There was a lot of pressure being the hometown guy. If I didn't get the decision, I could go back to Aliso Village in a bus. Al kept my mind focused on what I had to do. He had all these affirmations. He'd say, "C'mon, son. Strong, healthy, free from sickness, injury, fatigue." "Punches don't hurt you—nothing hurts you. You're indestructible." "You're gonna do it."

All the boxers stayed at the Olympic village at USC. Robert Shannon and Steve McCrory were my roommates—all the little guys were in one room. They had all the food you could eat, but I couldn't eat nothing. All I could do was smell. It was starvation. I had to weigh 105 pounds—not 106—so I had to lose an extra pound.

I didn't go to the Opening Ceremony. My first fight was the next day, and if I had went, I would've been dead. It is so tiring and draining because you're out there standing in the heat for hours. So, we watched the whole thing on TV.

The way I psyched myself up was, whoever I was fighting, I pretended that I was fighting them in their country. If you were from Great Britain, I was fighting you in London. I didn't want to coast. I didn't want to leave any doubts in the judges' minds about winning.

All of the bouts were tough. My first fight was against the Korean, Kwang-Sun Kim. That's when I broke my hand, when I hit him on the head. I felt it right away. The guy that really impressed me was Jose Marcelino

Bolivar, from Venezuela, because he was so fast and slick. He was giving me different angles. William Bagonza—the guy from Uganda—had long arms. They were so long I couldn't believe it!

My biggest obstacle really was injuries. I was fighting with a broken right hand, a hyperextended right elbow, a dislocated right shoulder, and a broken right toe. I tried to block it out of my head. I cried. I prayed. I was hurting. I bit a hole in my mouthpiece because it was so painful. I basically was fighting with one hand. I was just using my left.

Before the finals, we had one day off to rest. I went to look at the tape of my opponent, Salvatore Todisco [from Italy]. He was fast, but he came straight at you. I was salivating because there was nothing going to stop me. I was going all out. I was excited, but I didn't let myself get too confident.

I didn't find out he was injured until I got in the ring and saw him with a cast on his hand. They came over and raised my hand. I was more stunned than anything. I was like, "Is this really happening?" But I was happy. A gold medal is a gold medal. Whether you fought to win it or you won it on a walkover, it's a gold medal.

When I went up on the podium at the Sports Arena, I was carrying the Mexican flag and the American flag. A lot of people took offense to that, and I don't know why. I was not disrespecting the United States. I'm American all the way. I was showing my race, my heritage, and who I am. I was representing. I told myself I wasn't going to cry, but when I saw my mother I lost it.

The first thing I did afterwards was get into a police car with Al Stankie, and we drove over to the Hollenbeck Youth Center. All the kids and fans and family and friends were waiting 'cause they just saw me on TV. We went there to celebrate with them and show them the gold medal and say, "Yeah, I did it. I'm just a little kid from the projects and here I am representing the United States. You can do it, too."

During the Olympics I got to see other events. I saw diving because it was right outside our window. I'm concentrating on what I got to do, I look out the window, and I see this Greek god flying through the air. Greg Louganis! That guy flew like a bird! Perfect 10! He was awesome!

The Closing Ceremony—that was beautiful. We're walking through the Coliseum, all of us, and who picks me up and puts me on his shoulders? Rowdy Gaines, the gold medal-winning swimmer. He carried me around the whole Coliseum on his shoulders. I only weighed like 100 pounds.

I keep my gold medal in a safety deposit box these days. It's the highlight of my life besides my son. Look where I came from: I lifted myself from nothing. I took my family from welfare to something. I went from the projects to the podium. ★

—As told to David Davis

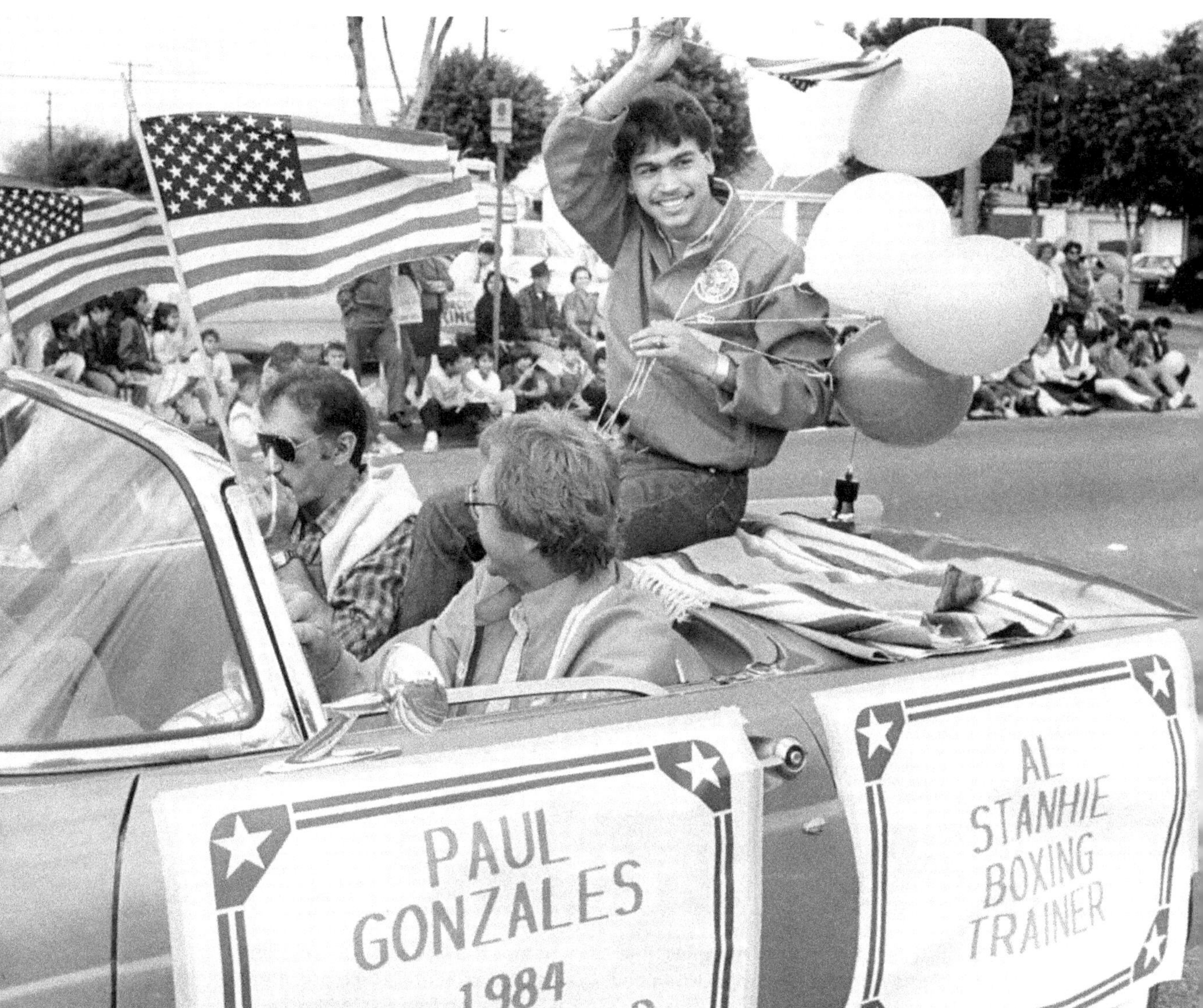

Paul Gonzales waved to the crowd at a parade in the City of Commerce one year after the Games. (The name of his trainer is misspelled on the car.) (Mike Sergieff)

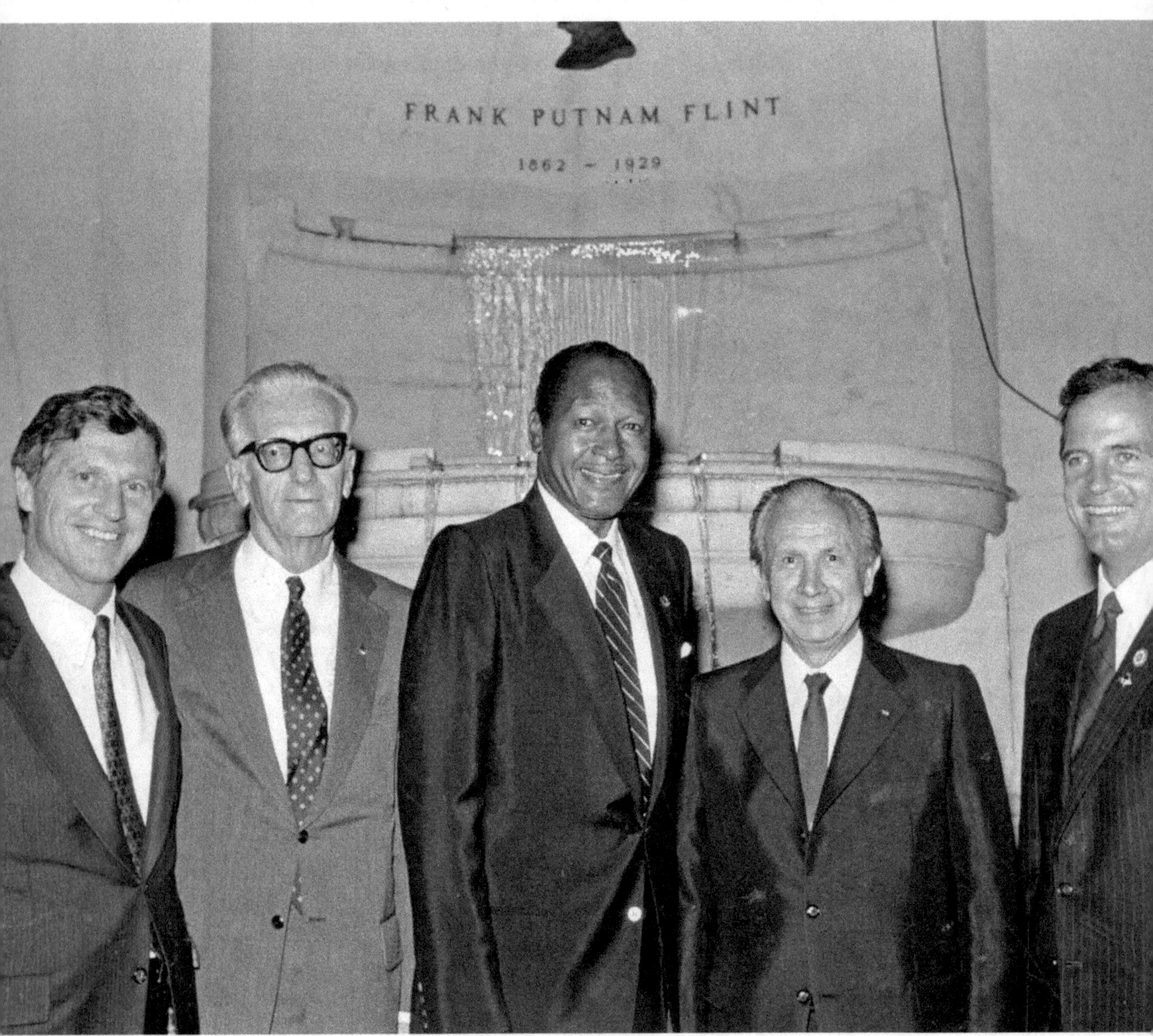

The brain-trust of the 1984 Olympics, just days before the Opening Ceremony: (*from left*) Los Angeles Olympic Organizing Committee executive vice president Harry Usher, LAOOC chair Paul Ziffren, Los Angeles Mayor Tom Bradley, International Olympic Committee president Juan Antonio Samaranch, and LAOOC president Peter Ueberroth. (Guy Crowder)

Introduction

By David Davis

In the late 1970s, as cities around the world prepared to bid for the right to host the 1984 Summer Olympic Games, the Olympic Movement was in deep trouble.

The 1968 Mexico City Olympics were marred by the Tlatelolco massacre of untold numbers of student and innocent bystanders. In 1972, Palestinian terrorists killed 11 members of the Israeli delegation during the Munich Olympics. Some 22 nations boycotted the 1976 Montreal Olympics over South Africa's apartheid policy, and the host city incurred a staggering debt estimated at $1.5 billion.

When the International Olympic Committee (IOC) called for candidates to bid for the 1984 Summer Olympics, only two cities expressed interest: Tehran and Los Angeles. And, after Tehran dropped out of the bidding process, L.A. was left to carry the flickering Olympic torch.

Los Angeles had hosted the Summer Olympics in 1932, at the height of the Great Depression. Those Games were a resounding success, highlighted by the wondrous feats of Babe Didrikson, Eddie Tolan, and Buster Crabbe; the introduction of an Olympic village for the athletes; the first use of the photo-finish camera for track events; and the construction and expansion of the Los Angeles Memorial Coliseum.

But that was a very different era—women athletes were given few opportunities to compete and only 37 nations participated—and a very different Los Angeles.

From the start, the 1984 Olympics were out of the ordinary. Led by Mayor Tom Bradley, the city of Los Angeles negotiated a unique arrangement with the IOC involving the structure and management of the Games. These were to be the first privately organized and privately financed Olympics, with the entire risk assumed by the newly created Los Angeles Olympic Organizing Committee (LAOOC) and the U.S. Olympic Committee. Headed by San Fernando Valley-based business executive Peter Ueberroth, the LAOOC adopted a no-frills philosophy to hold down expenses: they did not build gaudy new venues or Olympic villages and relied on vast legions of volunteers. They raised revenue by signing a limited number of corporate partners to lucrative sponsorship deals.

Still, as the Opening Ceremony neared, naysayers predicted disaster. Freeway traffic would be hellacious; Southern California's smog would suffocate the athletes and visitors; the cost of hosting the Games would bankrupt L.A.; a terrorist action would kill innocent people; the corporate presence would create a joyless, consumerist mood. Meanwhile, a boycott by the Soviet Union and their allies loomed, in retaliation for the U.S. boycott of the 1980 Moscow Olympics after the Russian invasion of Afghanistan.

Over an idyllic 16-day period, from July 28 through August 12, Los Angeles proved the doubters and the cynics wrong. Athletes from a record 140 nations, including the People's Republic of China in its first appearance at the Olympics since 1952, competed in a record 221 events. The weather cooperated, and many businesses adjusted their schedules so that the

At the announcement of the $225 million deal with ABC-TV that provided a timely financial infusion for the LAOOC in 1979: (*from left*) IOC executive director Monique Berlioux, filmmaker David Wolper, Peter Ueberroth, and ABC Sports president Roone Arledge. (Michael Haering)

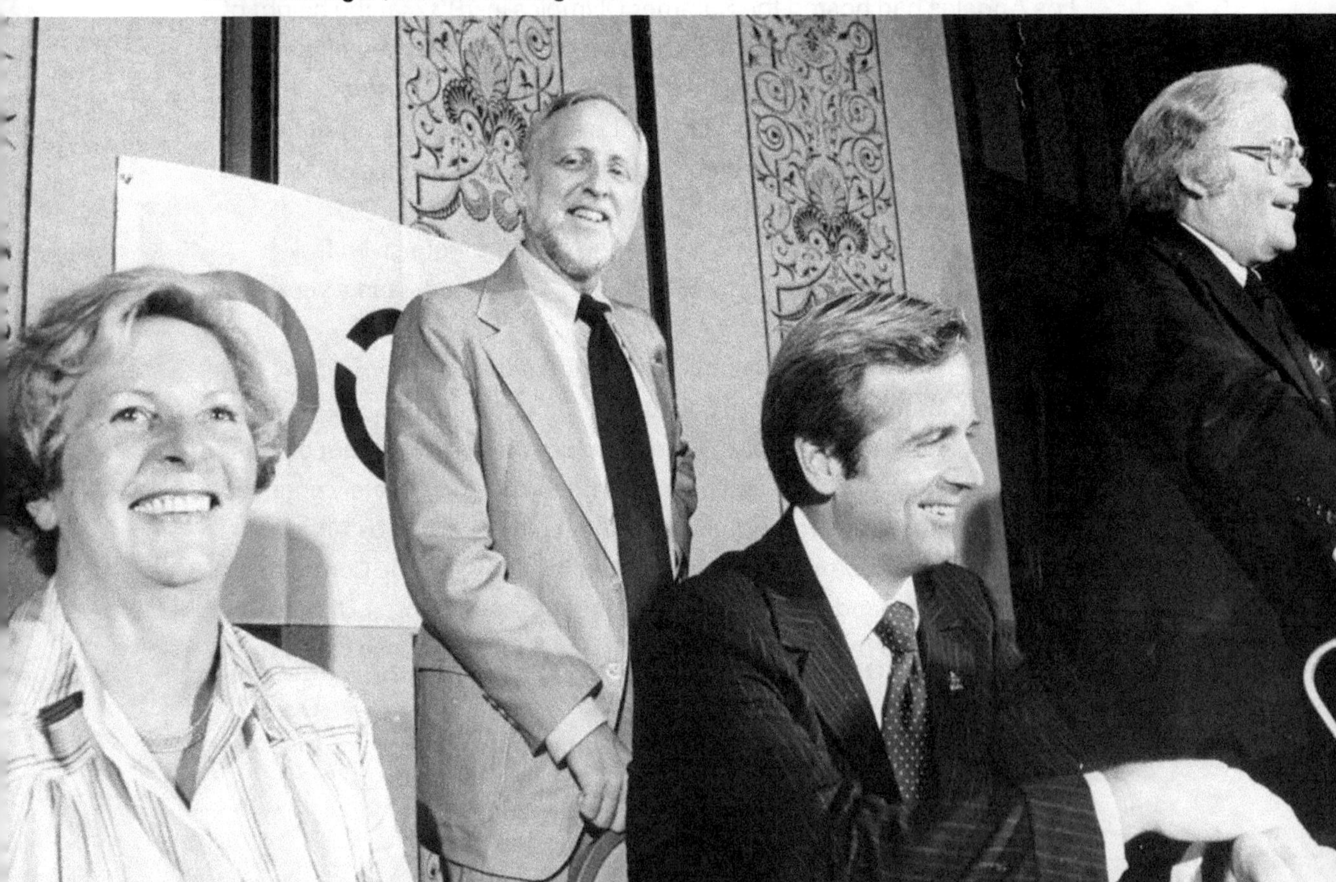

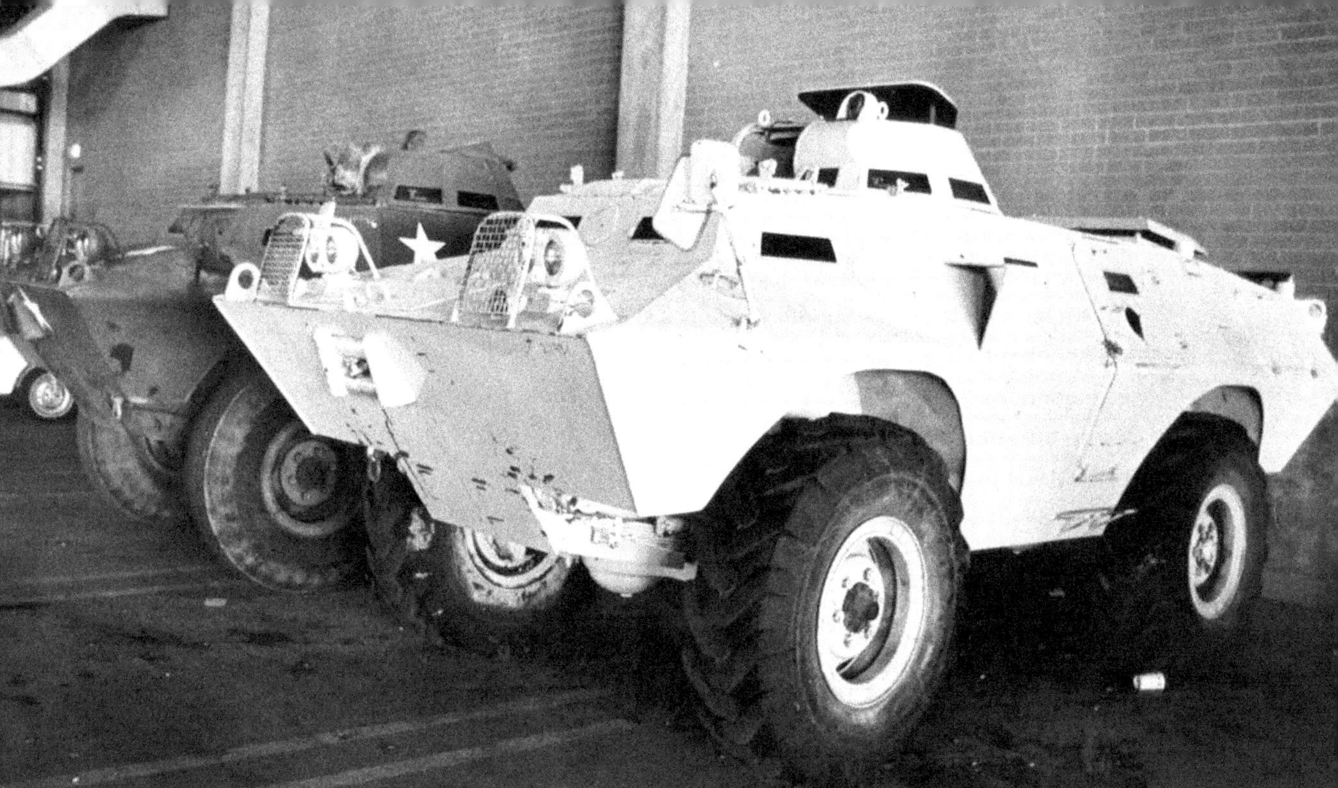

Heeding the threat of terrorism after the 1972 Munich Olympics, local law enforcement acquired armored vehicles for use during the Games. (Paul Chinn)

traffic was smooth sailing. An ambitious, well-organized Arts Festival drew appreciative crowds, and pin trading became an unofficial Olympic event. There were no acts of terrorism.

And, who could not be thrilled by the record-setting performances of Carl Lewis, Evelyn Ashford, Edwin Moses, Joan Benoit, Daley Thompson, Mary Lou Retton, Greg Louganis, Cheryl Miller, Valerie Brisco-Hooks, and Michael Jordan? Who could not despair in the heartbreak suffered by Mary Decker, Zola Budd, Gabriela Andersen-Schiess, Steve Ovett, and Evander Holyfield? Who could not notice that the 1984 Games featured a record number of events for female athletes, including the first-ever women's marathon at the Olympics, not to mention exhibition wheelchair races for disabled athletes?

That's not to say the 1984 Olympics were perfect. With the host country dominating the podium (174 total medals, including 83 gold), a discomforting jingoism surfaced. Incessant chants of "U-S-A!" echoed inside every venue, and ABC-TV's coverage was embarrassingly red-white-and-blue-sopped. Allegations of a cover-up involving positive drug tests surfaced afterwards. The boycott robbed fans of being able to watch the top Cuban,

Russian, and East German athletes compete on the track and the basketball and volleyball courts, and in gymnastics and boxing and swimming. (The real losers of the boycott, of course, were the athletes themselves.)

But it's also true that the fervor generated by the Games provided a timely boost to the U.S. after decades of turmoil, from the assassination of a president and other leaders to the Civil Rights Movement to the Vietnam War to the Arab Oil Embargo to Watergate. "By a collusion of timing and chemistry and artful television technique and happy economics, the nation fell into a spirit of coalescence and optimistic self-assertion not seen for a generation," commented *Time* magazine. "Some thought the mood was merely a self-indulgent vacation from the real world, even an orgy of narcissism on a national scale. At times the rhetoric of 'feeling good about America' bordered on the autoerotic. But the new atmosphere was alive with a great energy. The land was acrawl with entrepreneurs and Emersonian yuppies sounding the official cheer of 1984: 'Go for it!' The belief was reborn that Americans can do—well, anything."

For his achievement, Peter Ueberroth was crowned *Time*'s "Man of the Year," while Edwin Moses and Mary Lou Retton were named "Sportsman and Sportswoman of the Year" by *Sports Illustrated*.

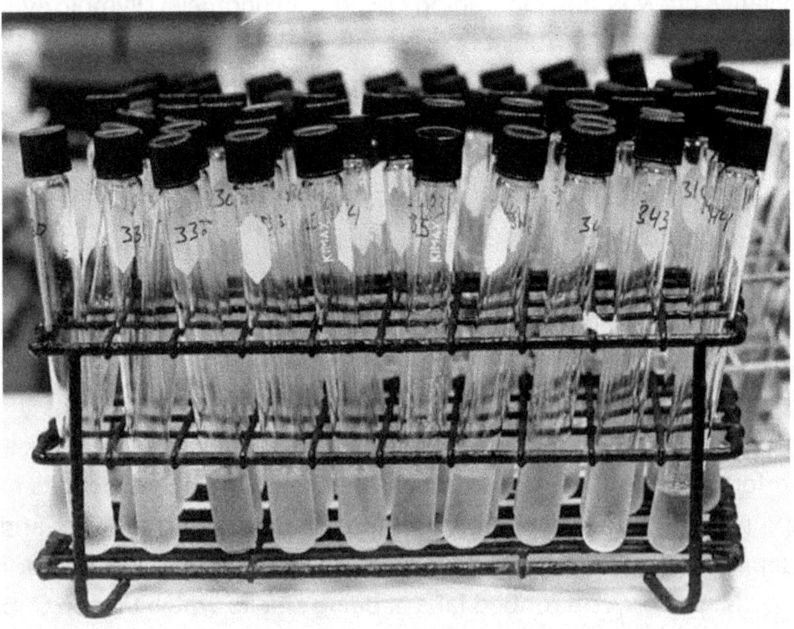

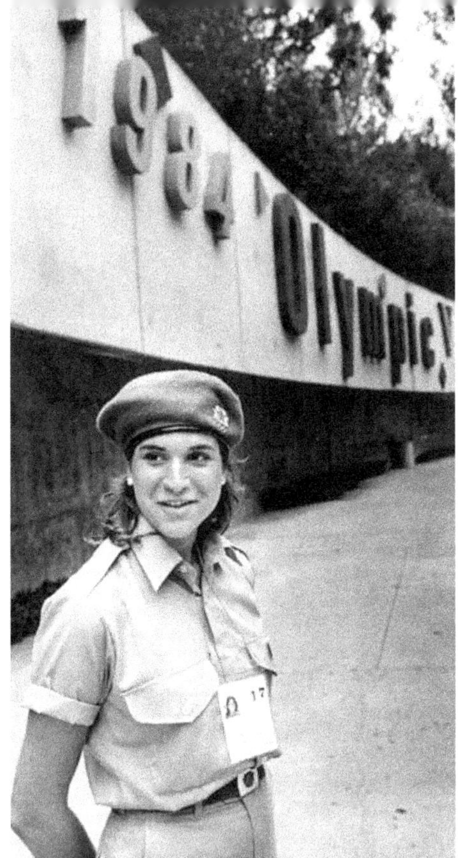

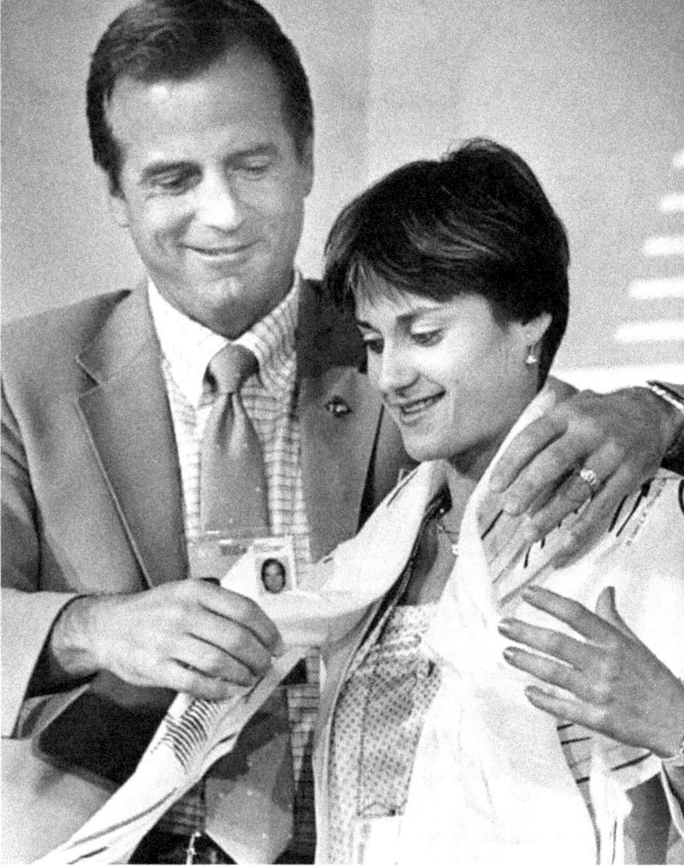

Left: **A member of the "blue beret" security force stood watch at the Olympic village on the campus of UCLA. (James Ruebsamen) •** ***Right:*** **LAOOC president Peter Ueberroth draped Olympic garb over gymnast Nadia Comaneci's shoulders at a press conference. Romania's star athlete retired after the 1980 Moscow Olympics, but her country's decision to compete in defiance of the Soviet Union's boycott was a key triumph for Ueberroth and his team. (James Ruebsamen)**

Opposite: **Officials prepared to test athletes' urine for steroids and other banned substances. (Michael Edwards)**

The legacy of the 1984 Olympics is readily apparent today. The public-private partnership created by Peter Ueberroth and his staff changed the paradigm of the Olympics such that the IOC and succeeding host cities have copied many features from L.A.'s playbook. Another legacy is linked to the surplus of $232.5 million produced by the LAOOC. Not long after the 1984 Olympics concluded, the LAOOC bequeathed 40 percent of this sum—a whopping $93 million—to create the Amateur Athletic Foundation (now known, appropriately, as the LA84 Foundation, with headquarters in the West Adams neighborhood).

This non-profit organization operates with one mission: to serve youth

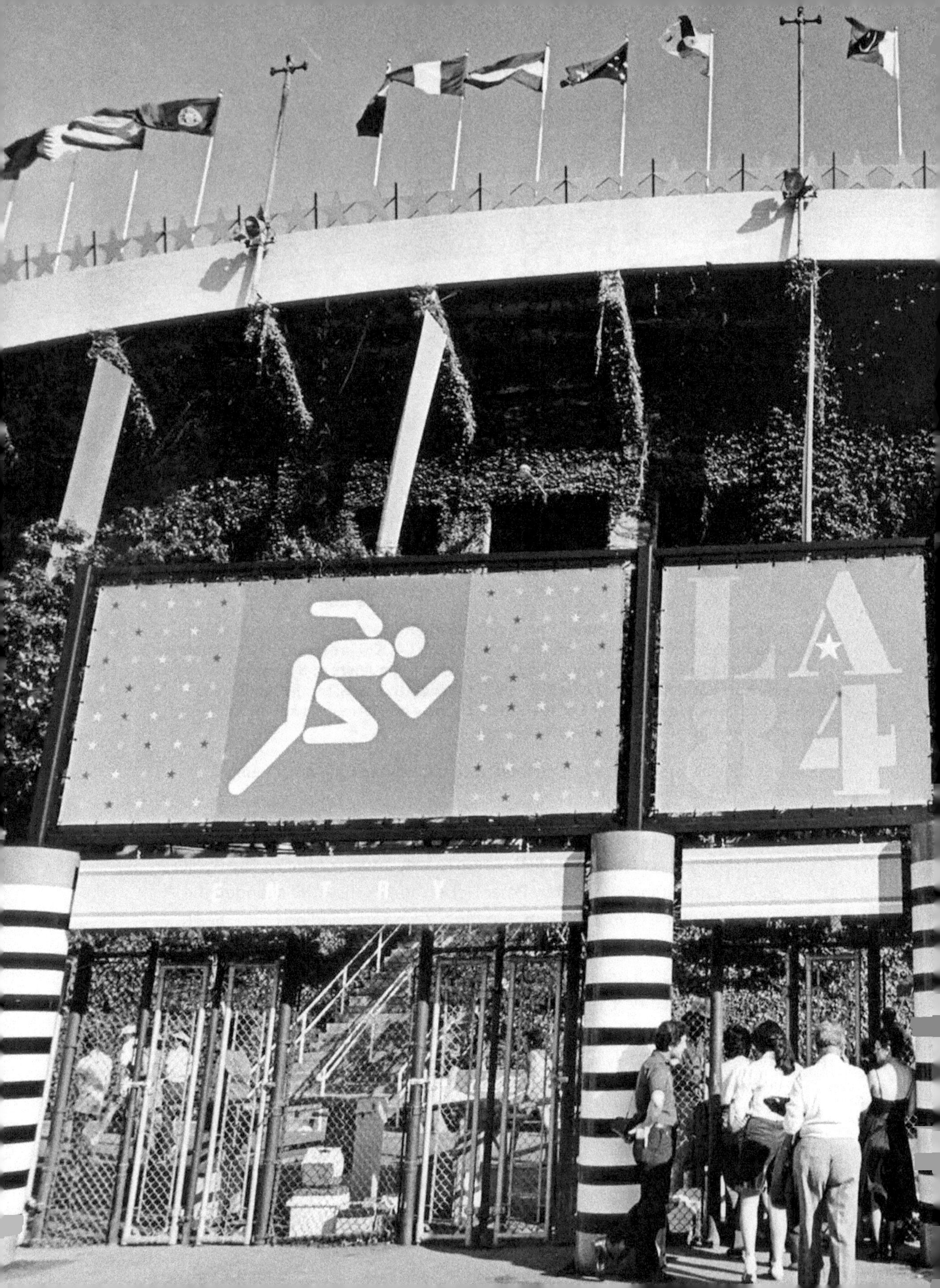
LA
ENTRY

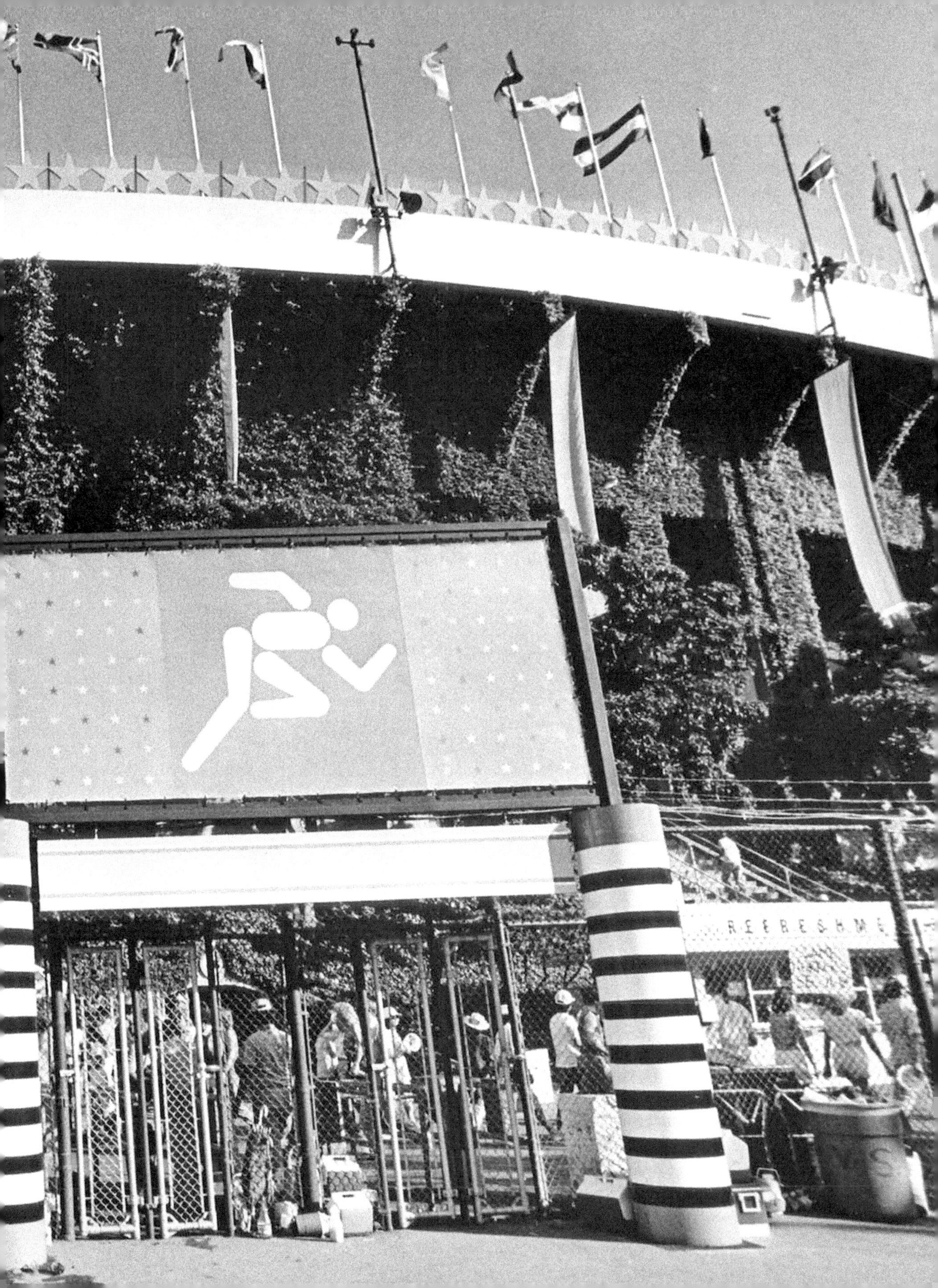
REFRESHME

through sports. Thus far, the LA84 Foundation has granted more than $220 million (and counting) to youth sports in Southern California, ranging from coaching clinics to partnering with the Los Angeles Unified School District for after-school sports teams to building soccer fields. Much of this effort supports underprivileged youth who might not otherwise be able to access such facilities or programs.

As this book goes to press, Los Angeles is vying for the right to host another Olympics, this time in 2024. The current bid trumpets several key components from 1984: curbing construction costs by using existing or soon-to-be-built venues (including the soccer stadium downtown and the football stadium in Inglewood); Southern California's glorious weather and natural resources; the connection with Hollywood's entertainment and media nexus; a loyal fan-base that supports Spartan-like Games without any outlay of public funds; and the city's rich Olympic past.

Los Angeles faces competition from Paris, Rome, Budapest, and Hamburg. The decision will be announced in 2017. ★

***Opposite and overleaf:* The unique look of the 1984 Games—featuring colorful pastels, graphics, street banners, logos and other ephemeral materials—was masterminded by designer Deborah Sussman and architect Jon Jerde. These elements helped to visually integrate the far-flung venues, including the entrance to the Coliseum and the Olympic village at USC. (Anne Knudsen)**

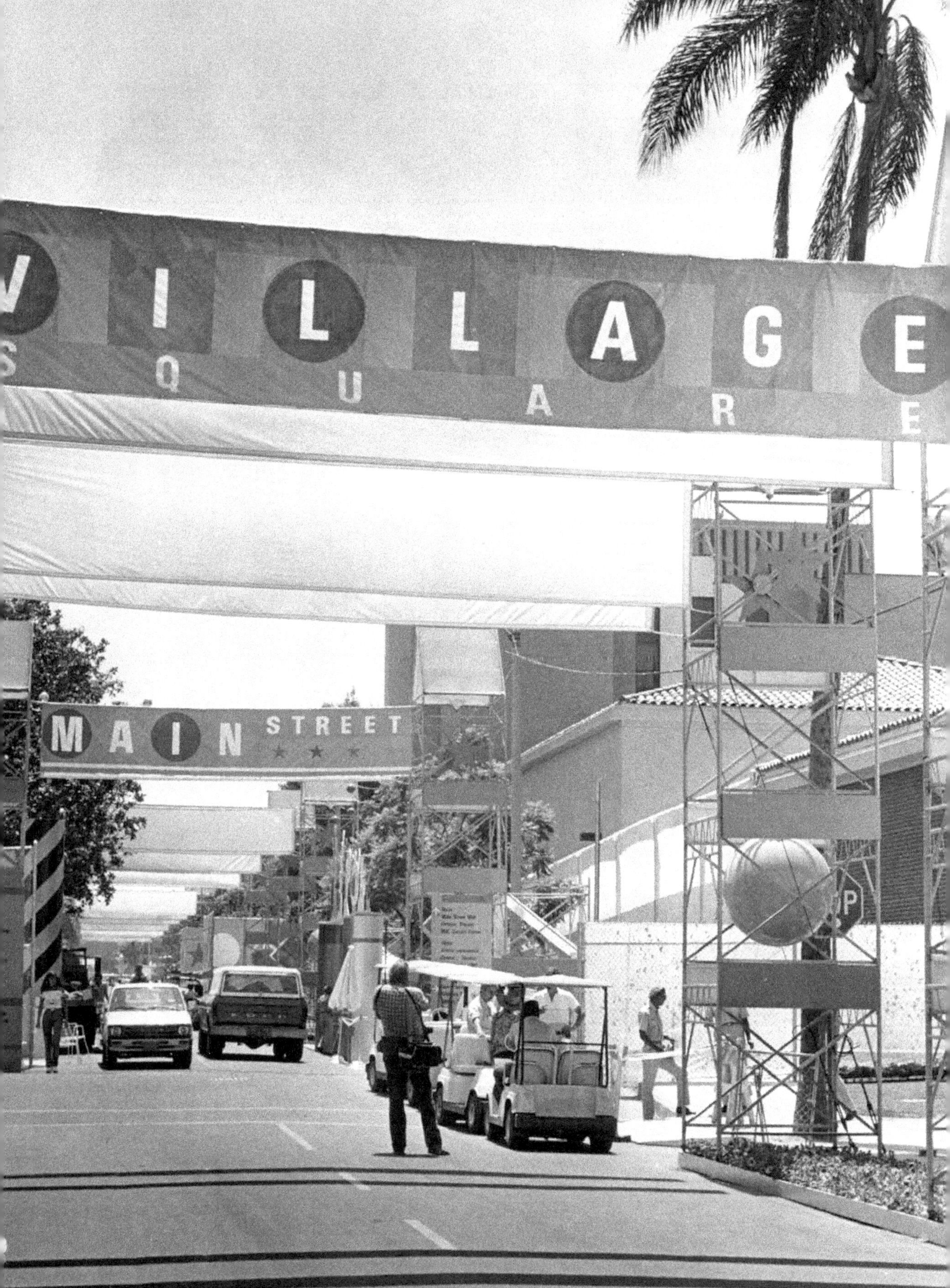
VILLAGE
SQUARE
MAIN STREET

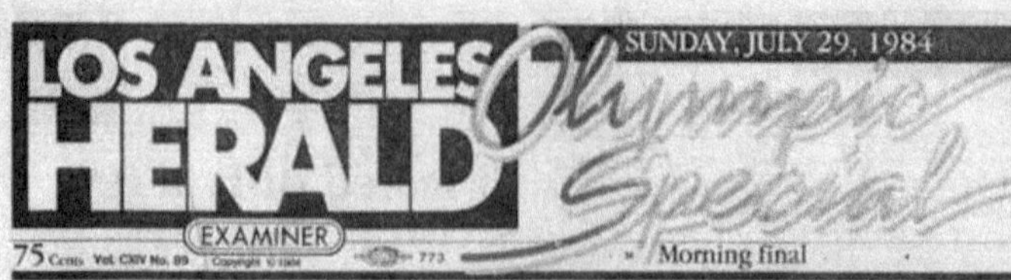

LOS ANGELES HERALD EXAMINER

Olympic Special

SUNDAY, JULY 29, 1984

75 Cents Vol. CXIV No. 89 Copyright © 1984 773 Morning final

TODAY'S NEWS INSIDE

MAYHEM IN WESTWOOD: SUSPECT & VICTIM/A-1

SUPERMARKET STRIKE ON THE HORIZON/A-2

WOW!

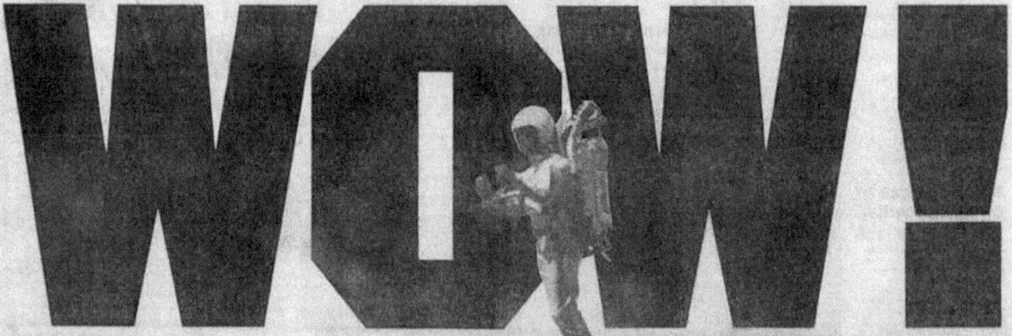

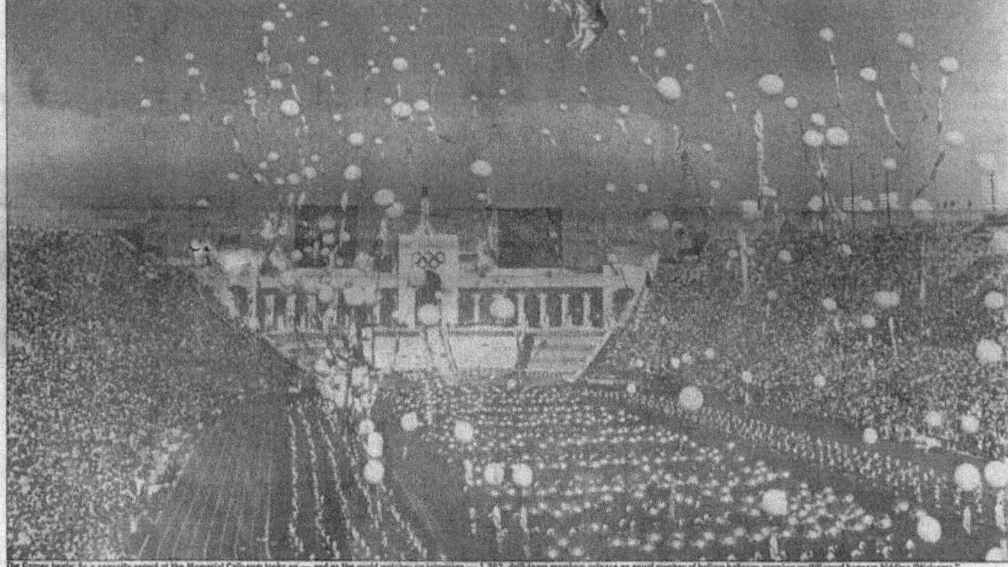

The Games begin: As a capacity crowd at the Memorial Coliseum looks on — and as the world watches on television — 1,262 drill-team members release an equal number of helium balloons carrying multilingual banners bidding "Welcome."

TODAY'S OLYMPICS INSIDE

More Olympics news in Section A

Laid back in the face of spectacle

By Diane K. Shah
Herald columnist

And so they began, the Games of the XXIII Olympiad.

They began with the ringing of church bells, the drum roll of tympani, the crackling of firecrackers. And with dark specks of helicopters circling high in a perfect blue sky.

They began with a man rocketing into the Los Angeles Memorial Coliseum, with the sound of music, the rising of balloons. And with policemen ringing the bright green grass, their backs to the field, their eyes glued to the crowd.

With thousands of security people watching over the festivities, the Opening Ceremonies of the Los Angeles Games proceeded on time and without a hitch.

Th- only unexpected development, and one that was planned that way, was the at-last revealed identity of the person who would light the Olympic Torch. The person was actually a pair: Gina Hemphill, the granddaughter of Jesse Owens, carried the torch into the Coliseum, and on her second pass around the track handed it to Rafer Johnson, the 1960 gold medal decathlete.

Johnson, who still looks in competitive shape, raced up stairs, then a very tall ladder, to reach his destination. But we are three hours ahead of ourselves here.

Unlike most crowds that turn out at the Coliseum, this one of 93,000 was in its seats when the ceremonies began precisely at 4:30 p.m., even though hours earlier traffic around the Coliseum seemed hopelessly stalled. Like most Coliseum crowds, this one was typically laid back, strangely subdued in view of the event taking place and the considerable hype it has received.

Most of the energy expended was expended near the end.

After the balloons and a welcome song, President Reagan was introduced. But in one more reminder that these Games are very much a security affair, the president was only dimly viewed through the closed windows of the press box.

Later, the windows were raised. But the president was gone.

What followed was 45 minutes of David Wolper's much-heralded entertainment extravaganza. The

Opening/Page 8, Col. 5

DIARY OF AN OLYMPIC ATHLETE

JULIE ISPHORDING

Cincinnati native Julie Isphording, 22, is a member of the U.S. Olympic team entered in the marathon. Her exclusive reports will appear every day in this section through Closing Ceremonies. Today: Opening Ceremonies.

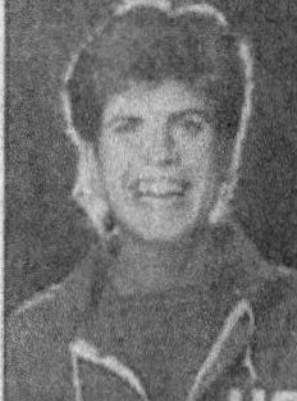

The view from the infield

How can I put what just happened into words? They'd have to invent a new language. Up until just a few hours ago, I didn't really think about what this is really all about. Now my mind is whirling.

From the moment we hit the tunnel leading onto the field and the Opening Ceremonies, the goosebumps began. They're only now starting to go away. I doubt if they'll ever disappear completely as long as I can picture what happened here last night.

The crowd began the loudest, most exciting cheer I've ever heard in my whole life as we hit the track; people were up on their feet, and seeing the look on their faces as we passed actually took my breath away. And it lasted so long! Even the celebrities in the crowd, like Brooke Shields, had tears in their eyes. It was all some of us could do to keep from getting teary.

I was glad for once to be a woman and to be short — I got to march up front, and got the best view of everything. All I could

Diary/Page 8, Col. 1

Just doing what we do best

By Joe Morgenstern
Herald columnist

It was joy to the world, a gift of incomparable music from the planet's most musical nation.

It was a blockb- ster of a show, a razzle-dazzler of unprecedented proportions, but a production predicated on a wonderfully simple idea: America doing what it does best.

We played our glorious songs,

REVIEW

danced our strong dances, hoed our exuberant hoedowns and hoked our sublime hokum.

We showed the world a thing or two about Broadway and Hollywood production values, as if it needed to be convinced, but we did it with great good cheer, rather than boastfulness. The show-biz part of the Opening Ceremonies was singularly free of pomp, given the circumstance, and rich — much richer than anyone had reason to expect — in the musical history that is every American's birthright.

Who would have thought that

Morgenstern/Page 7, Col. 4

One Golden Moment

The 1984 Olympics Through the Photographic Lens of the Los Angeles *Herald Examiner*

By David Davis

For media organizations, covering the Olympics is a massive undertaking fraught with 16-hour workdays, far-flung venues, unpronounceable foreign names, unlikely heroes and villains, not to mention obscure events that get noticed once every four years. Some have compared the experience to planning an expedition to Mount Everest. Preparation, patience, the ability to hustle and to adapt, a reliable alarm clock, and endless cups of coffee are necessities.

Consider what editors, writers, and photojournalists faced at the 1984 Los Angeles Olympics. Over 16 days, there were 221 events in 26 different sports, involving nearly 7,000 athletes (5,263 men and 1,566 women) from 140 countries. There were three Olympic villages for the athletes, one centralized press center, and nearly 30 venues throughout Southern California, sprawling from Anaheim to Long Beach to Inglewood to downtown L.A. to Arcadia to Chino to Lake Casitas.

For the photographers who worked at the Los Angeles *Herald Examiner*, there was one other element to consider: competition. They wanted to prove that their undermanned newspaper—a lively, scrappy tabloid owned by the Hearst Corporation—could compete not only with their local rival, the well-heeled Los Angeles *Times*, but also the countless global media outlets that descended on Southern California in the summer of 1984.

"You were competing against everybody, and especially whoever was on your right or left shoulder," said Dean Musgrove, the paper's assistant photo editor at the time. "You were trying to figure out how to beat them. You had to stay on your game and not be distracted, because you didn't know when something might happen."

The *Her-Ex* was granted four photography credentials for the Olympics. Photo editor Jim Roark distributed the precious passes to four young staffers—Anne Knudsen, Paul Chinn, James Ruebsamen, and Javier Mendoza—with Musgrove getting an all-important photo technician's credential.

"Jim had the foresight to put together a diverse team that was ahead of the times," Mendoza said. "There was Paul, a young Chinese-American, and Anne, a young woman, and myself, a young Mexican-American photographer."

Roark harnessed his scant resources for select events and athletes. Knudsen, 28, drew gymnastics (Pauley Pavilion) and diving (the swim stadium at USC), and focused on Mary Lou Retton and Greg Louganis. Chinn, 23, stayed busy with track and field at the Coliseum, with Carl Lewis, Daley Thompson, Evelyn Ashford, and Joan Benoit. Mendoza, a 24-year-old photojournalism student at Long Beach State, handled swimming, water polo, and volleyball—and the heroics of Michael Gross and Tracy Caulkins. Ruebsamen, 36, juggled basketball (the Forum) and boxing (the Sports Arena), shooting the likes of Michael Jordan, Cheryl Miller, and Evander Holyfield.

They tag-teamed on the all-important Opening and Closing Ceremonies and events like wrestling, weightlifting, cycling, and equestrian. Musgrove snapped photos whenever possible and served as chief courier-troubleshooter. He bought a motor scooter so that he could zip around town, picking up rolls of film from the photographers at the venues and then ferrying these to the *Her-Ex* offices downtown at 1111 South Broadway, to be processed for the next day's edition.

Their pictures complemented the crack writing in the *Her-Ex* under editor Leslie Ward, including articles and columns from Diane K. Shah, Joe Morgenstern, Bob Keiser, Pam King, Bob Mieszerski, David Gritten, Rick Sadowski, Lyle Spencer, Fred Robledo, Ben Stein, Tony Castro, and Linda Breakstone. "The *Herald*'s sports section was *the* sports section in town," Mendoza said. "Every sports fan read the *Herald* first because we had Mel Durslag, Bud Furillo, Allan Malamud, Doug Krikorian."

Like the athletes themselves, the photographers entered the arena ready for action, with two or three motorized Nikon F3 cameras around their necks and what Chinn described as "an arsenal of lenses, including 400mm f3.5, 300mm f2.8, 80-200mm zoom, and 24mm and 35mm wide-angle lenses." According to Musgrove, each photographer also carried "a Domke camera

THE FAB FOUR (Plus One)

Each day during the 1984 Olympics, the Herald's Olympic Special section brought you "One Golden Moment of the Games," a giant, full page picture of the one athletic triumph that seemed to best sum up all the action and emotion that day. We've received so many requests to reprint these extraordinary photographs that we decided to create this souvenir edition, a memento of the L.A.'s greatest summer ever.

In addition to our 16 Golden Moments, on the back page we have reproduced the front pages of all the Olympic Special sections. And below, you'll find an index to the photographs, recalling the athletes and stories behind each one. But there's a story behind these stories. They were captured on film by only *four* Herald photographers: Paul Chinn, Anne Knudsen, James Ruebsamen and Javier Mendoza.

Because media credentials for the Olympics were limited, the Herald had to make the best possible use of its four precious photographic passes to cover hundreds of events. Consequently, logistical planning extremely important.

But by working long hours against murderous deadlines, traveling to several venues each day, lugging heavy camera equipment (they had no photo assistants or runners to carry the film back to the Herald) — and with the support of many people in the newspaper's photo department who manned phones and radios, developed film and made prints — these four people somehow managed to consistently come up with what we feel were some of the best photographs of the Games. Of course, they snapped many more pictures than you see here, filling our pages daily with loads of color and black and white photos of the drama. We salute the Herald's Fabulous Four (Plus One).

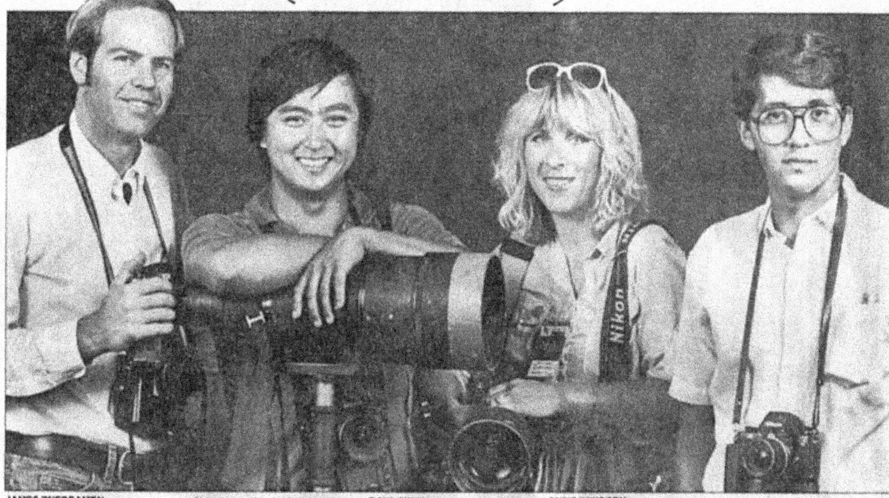

JAMES RUEBSAMEN

"I loved the idea of international competition, and wish the flavor and kinship of the Games could carry over into everyday life," says Jim Ruebsamen, 36, who was born in Santa Monica and raised in Nagoya, Japan, Arlington, Texas, and Culver City, where he now resides. Ruebsamen came to the Herald in 1981, after working for several years at other newspapers in the Midwest and Southern California. He majored in photojournalism at the University of Missouri and received a master's degree from Pepperdine University.

"Almost immediately after coming to the Herald," he remembers, "I worried about and hoped for the opportunity to photograph the Olympics when they came to L.A." And what was it like when his worst fears and dreams came true this summer? "Without a doubt, covering the L.A. Games was the highlight of my professional career," says Ruebsamen, who was at the Forum on every day of basketball competition, and also covered boxing and Opening and Closing Ceremonies. Another high point in Ruebsamen's life came just two weeks after the Games ended: He got married.

PAUL CHINN

Paul Chinn likes covering football for the Herald because it's "fast moving and very physical." But after a few days of watching superathletes like Carl Lewis whiz by at the Coliseum he admits that "track and field rapidly moved up as one of my favorite sports." Chinn, who lives in Tarzana and recently received his bachelor's degree in journalism from Long Beach State, had to be at the track every day by 7 a.m. in order to compete with hundreds of international photographers trying to stake out the best shooting spot. Armed with three cameras and a huge 600-mm lens, he would stand in the hot sun until after 9 p.m., then return to the paper to print his pictures. "It was worth it," says Chinn, whose favorite "Golden Moment" is the photo he took of marathoner Joan Benoit's triumphant finish, although he also covered wrestling, weightlifting, fencing, cycling and boxing. "One of the reasons I came to Los Angeles," says Chinn, 23, who was raised in Berkeley and began working at the Herald in 1980, "was the anticipation of photographing the Olympics. It was a once-in-a-lifetime chance. There I was, standing next to the best-known photographers in the world, and the next minute swapping f-stops with them."

ANNE KNUDSEN

Anne Knudsen used to be a ski bum in Jackson Hole, Wyoming, until, she admits, "I decided there was no future in it." So she bought a camera, enrolled in a photography class to learn how to use it, and got hooked. It is clear from her breathtaking Olympic photographs — particularly those of the gymnastics events — she needn't worry about the future. Knudsen, who is 28, is originally from Palo Alto and came to the Herald in 1979 after getting a degree in photojournalism from Long Beach State. Although she also photographed the diving and synchronized swimming events, Knudsen's favorite assignment by far was gymnastics. "Especially the women gymnasts, because they are so expressive and emotional," she says. Like the athletes, she and the other photographers were under tremendous pressure. "There was a constant high level of stress," Knudsen says, "not only to perform, but to excel. Since we're a hometown newspaper, the whole world's eyes were on us. And there was the physical pressure of trying to be on top of everything. But I like the way the Olympics brought out the best in everyone — the athletes, the people of Los Angeles and the Herald."

JAVIER MENDOZA

Javier Mendoza was born in San Luis Potosi, Mexico, but grew up in Newhall, where he learned to play water polo. Consequently, shooting the water polo competition at Pepperdine was one of his favorite Olympic assignments, he says, because he knew the most about that sport. In fact, most of Mendoza's assignments during the Games involved water (although he also covered volleyball, cycling and wrestling). He toiled every day at the USC Olympic swim stadium, and was there when the U.S. men's relay swim team beat the West Germans. It was was one of the biggest stories of the Games, but Mendoza's picture of an ecstatic Bruce Hayes, in the Golden Moment just after he had beaten Michael Gross and earned his team the nickname "Gross Busters," was not his favorite. The photo he liked the best was of the gold medalist Bobby Weaver, the little wrestler who went nuts and jumped into his coaches arms. It was a great shot, but the Golden Moment on that day instead had to be Daley Thompson, who had won the decathlon. Mendoza, 24, will have a chance to photograph many more Olympics. He became a full-time photographer with the Herald only last January, and is still a photojournalism student at Long Beach State.

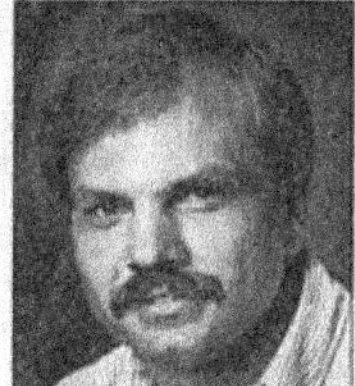

LEO JARZOMB

Proverb: He who has no Olympic credential must live by his wits. Which is exactly what Leo Jarzomb, the "Plus One" of our Olympic photographers, did. Jarzomb, 30, a Long Beach State photojournalism student, arrived at the Herald as a summer intern only a few weeks before the Games began. He was assigned to shoot the first event of the first day of the Olympics — the women's cycling road race in Mission Viejo. Since the four special Olympic photographers were busy at other events, and photographers covering the road race no special credentials, Jarzomb was told to go and get what he could. Once there, he discovered many credentialed photographers had been herded into restricted areas. Since he had no special pass, he plowed his way through the fans at the finish line and, shooting as a "spectator," got the emotional picture of the ecstatic winners, Connie Carpenter and Rebecca Twigg, after their spectacular finish. It was the first Golden Moment of the Games, and a photo the "official" cameramen would have killed for. "I only shot that one event during the whole Olympics," Jarzomb says. "It was a very pleasant experience."

bag filled with extra lenses, a strobe and extra film."

They shot almost exclusively in black and white, using Kodak Tri-X film. Chinn estimated that he shot upwards of 15-20 rolls of film daily, while for Ruebsamen the number of rolls of film shot per day "depended upon deadline times and how early or late an event might end. For some of the later events, I could only shoot four rolls because of the time element. For early events, I tried to limit my take to eight rolls."

"At the time there was no autofocus [technology]," Mendoza said, "so somebody shooting today doesn't face the same challenges that we did.

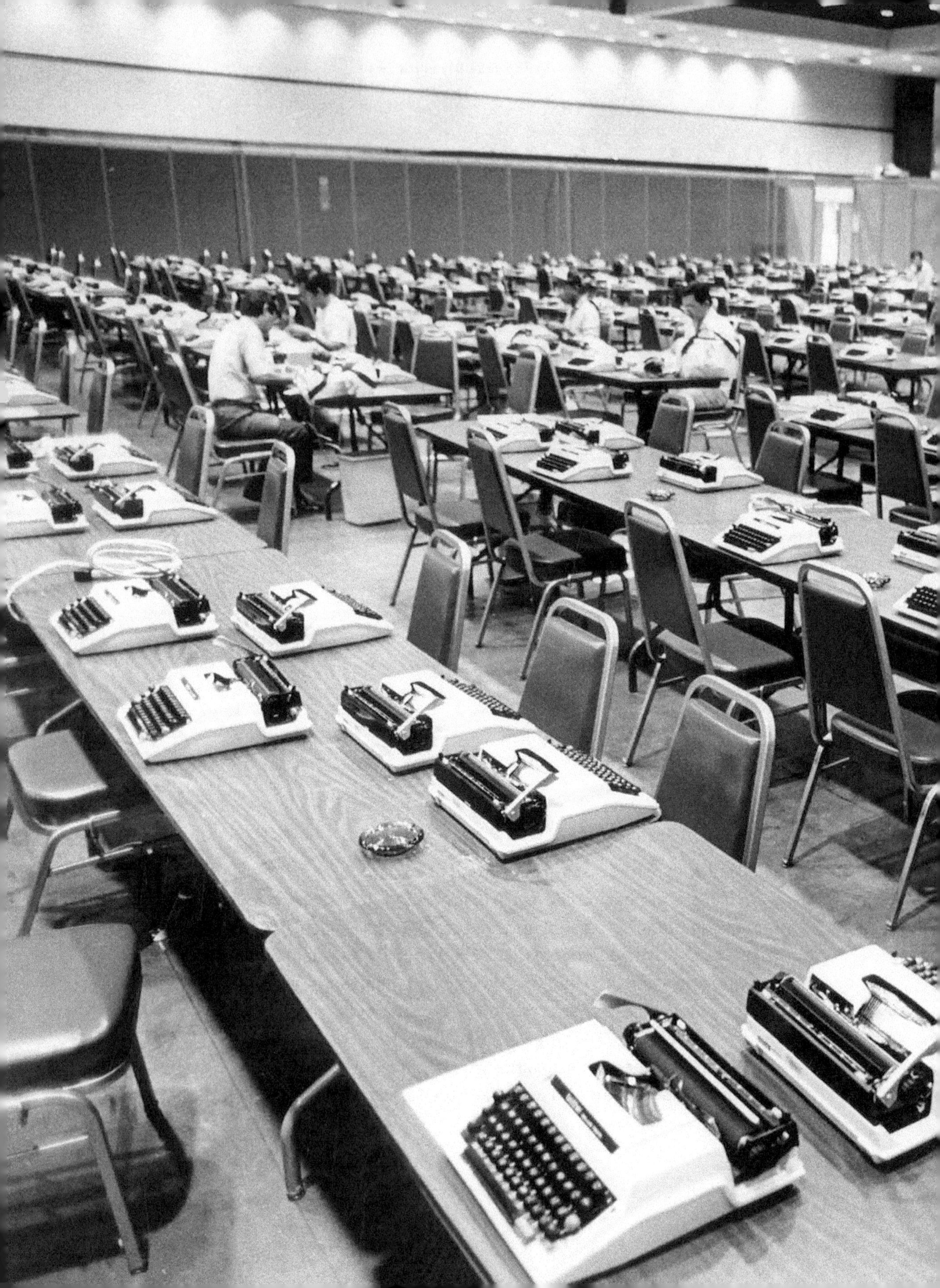

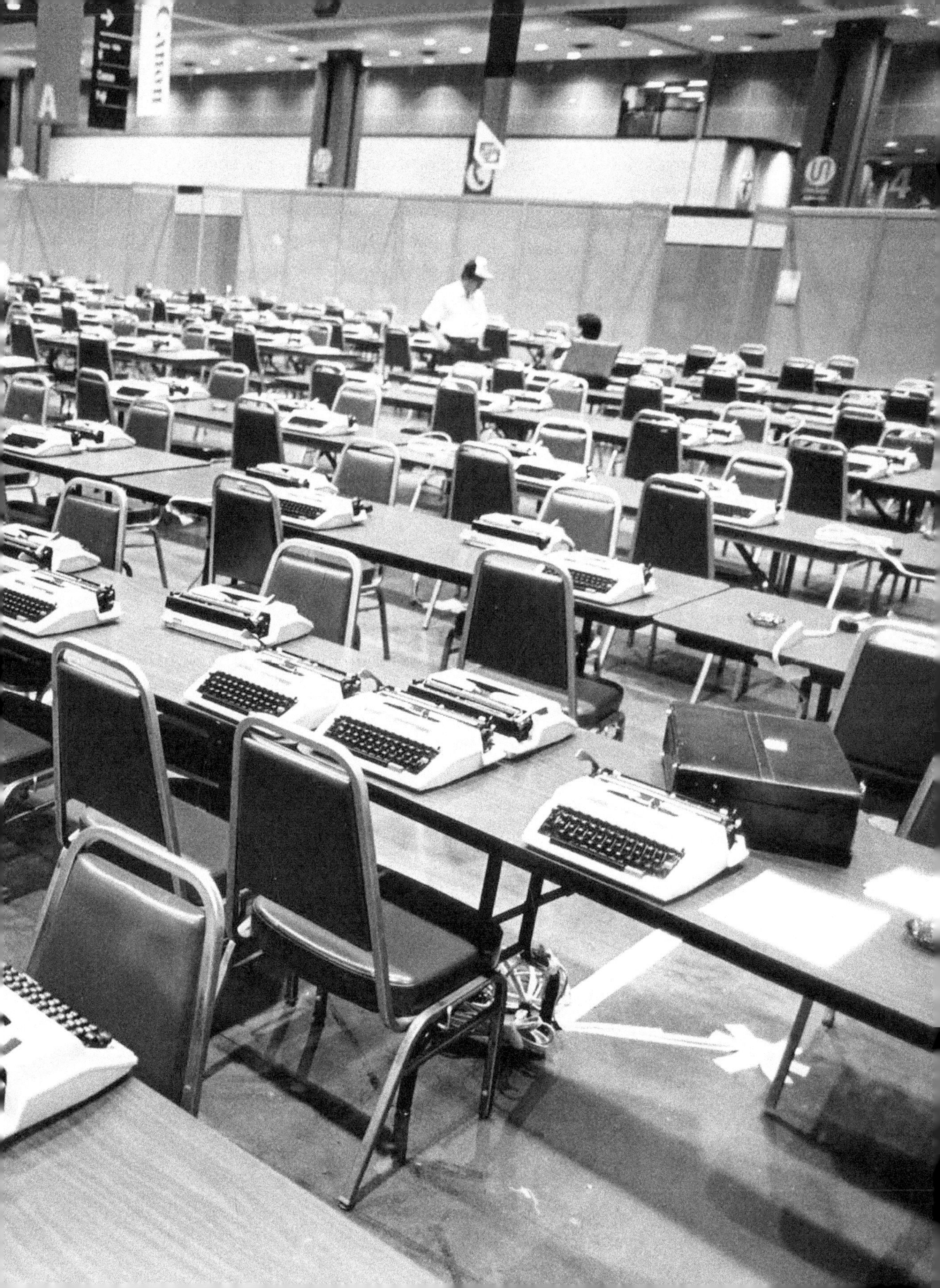

They don't have to run back from an event, develop film on deadline, and do all of that production work. Today, with digital cameras, they can shoot a bazillion shots and never run out of film. Looking back, it's like we were in the stone age, technology-wise."

Their work makes up the vast majority of the images found in this book. Other shooters affiliated with the *Her-Ex* also took pictures. Tom Zimmerman, the book's lone major contributor who did not work for the paper, was hired by the California Historical Society to document how Los Angeles was affected by the Games.

Chronicling the unfolding story of the 1984 Olympics began before the competition started. The staff covered many programs of the Olympic Arts Festival as well as the torch relay, including Mendoza's memorable photograph of former USC football star O.J. Simpson carrying the torch in Santa Monica. The picture is a poignant reminder of how the perception of a photograph and its subject can change over time.

The Opening Ceremony produced celebratory images, with the *Her-Ex* leading off with Musgrove's festive, balloon-filled photo and Chinn's monumental picture of decathlete legend Rafer Johnson lighting the Olympic cauldron. These set the visual tone for the newspaper's coverage. A simple, all-caps headline accompanied Musgrove's picture: "WOW!"

Intern Leo Jarzomb was sent to Mission Viejo on the first day of the Games to shoot the cycling action. He returned with a stunning photo of two teammates, celebrating their victory, from a perspective that no other photographer had. "Because Leo didn't have a credential, that put him in a position to get a better picture than where all the credentialed photographers were," Musgrove said. "He had to be further down the road, with the public, and that was the photo. Things work out sometimes."

Jarzomb's shot earned a full-page spread in the paper. It was part of a daily feature called "One Golden Moment," which the newspaper used to highlight the best picture from the previous day's action. "Everybody wanted

***Overleaf*: The main press center, located inside the Convention Center, readied for the world's media corps. (Paul Chinn)**

Olympic Special

LOS ANGELES HERALD

SOUVENIR EDITION

September 9, 1984

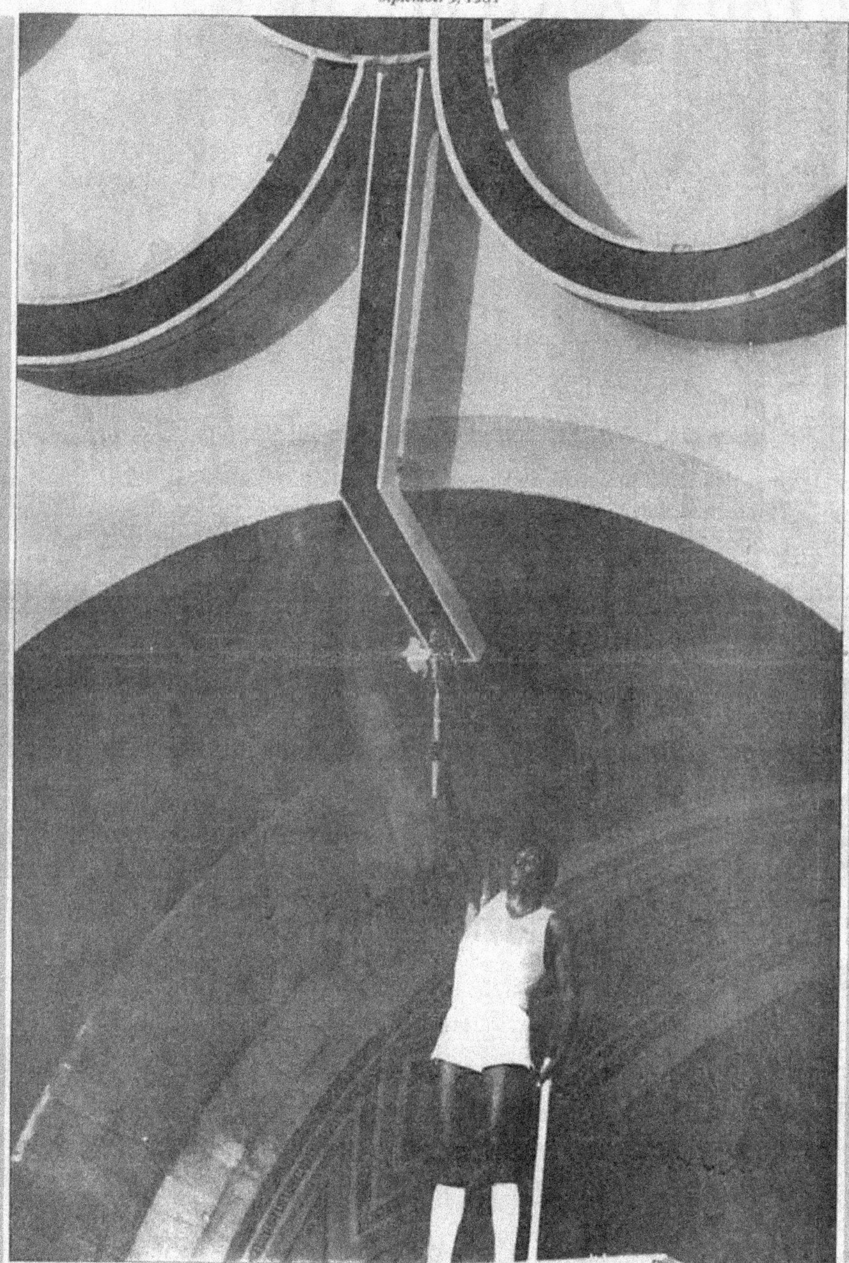

GOLDEN MOMENTS OF THE GAMES

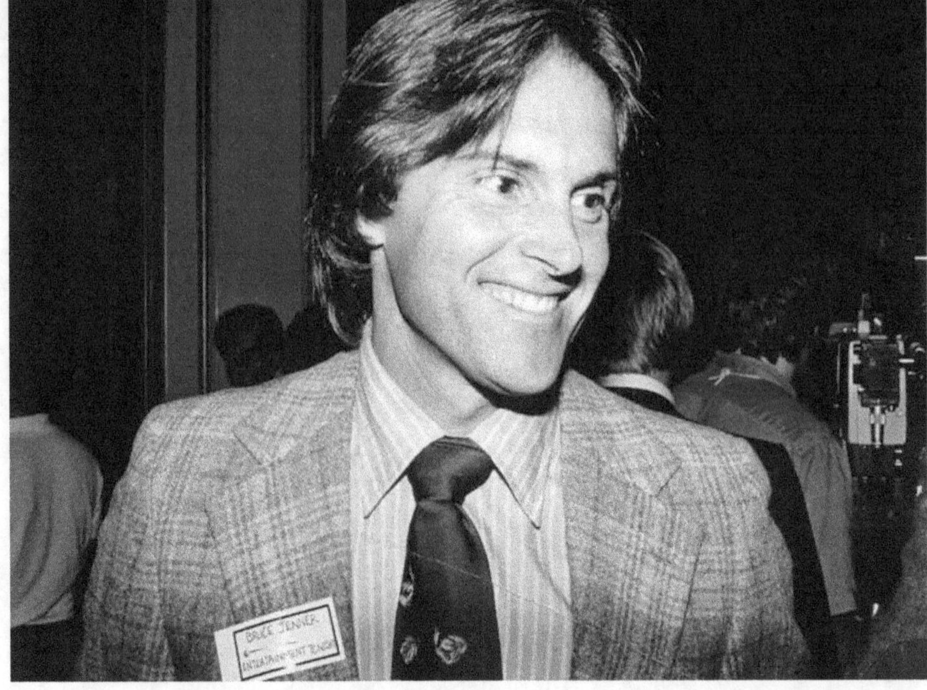

Bruce Jenner, the 1976 decathlon champ, worked as a reporter for "Entertainment Tonight." (Mike Sergieff)

to have that photo," Mendoza said. "It wasn't always the best photograph, the most technically proficient photograph. Looking back, they were the most meaningful moments—that's what they were looking for."

As the photographers re-doubled their efforts to score a coveted "One Golden Moment" picture, they captured history in the making. Ruebsamen was awed by the skills of a young basketball player named Michael Jordan, who was readying to leave college for the NBA and sign his first contract with Nike. "When Jordan got the ball and wanted to score, he was going to score," Ruebsamen said. "It wasn't like, 'Gee, I'm going to have to fake this guy and then drive by this guy.' He'd take the ball and motor by them, and those guys could only watch him go by."

Coached by Pat Summit, the U.S. women's basketball team also impressed Ruebsamen, who remembers that they "just attacked, attacked, attacked. When they played against the Chinese, it looked like they were in slow motion compared to the Americans. Cheryl Miller was at a different level in terms of strength and competitiveness. I think they would've beaten the Russians pretty easily."

Ruebsamen also recalled the pain he endured in pursuit of his craft. He was riding on the back of Musgrove's scooter, with all his gear in tow, when Musgrove let the clutch out too quickly at a red light. "He dumped me right off the back end," Ruebsamen said. "I landed squarely on my butt. But I had the presence of mind to hold onto the equipment. Dean thought he'd killed me, but I thought it was so funny. Here you are, trying to be an Olympic photographer, and you fall off a bike."

"Fortunately, neither he nor his equipment was damaged," a chagrined Musgrove said, "and I learned how to drive a little more safely."

Mendoza was a competitive swimmer and water polo player in high school, so he was overjoyed to cover aquatic events. "Those were sports that I was familiar with," he said. "I knew not only who played the sport, but how it was played. So, I really had to think about what I was trying to communicate. In photographing sports, it's always action and reaction: What are the things that are happening and how do you try and anticipate that?"

Several of his most memorable shots came outside the pool, however. He recalled an image of volleyball star Karch Kiraly celebrating after the U.S. team's gold-medal match over Brazil, and another of a pint-sized wrestler leaping into the arms of his coach. "These guys just achieved the pinnacle of what they set out to do, and I got the moment," he said. "That was cool."

Chinn learned to show up two hours before the media gates opened at the Coliseum to ensure that he got his preferred spot on the track. Said Chinn: "There was always some photographer who would try to drop in at the last minute—either stand right in front or squeeze into the pack—and we'd say, 'Hey, this isn't going to happen. Move somewhere else.' There was always that jockeying for position and holding your ground."

He witnessed many memorable moments at the Coliseum, including Gabriela Andersen-Schiess' stupor-like collapse at the end of the women's

ABC-TV officials showed off the special vehicles they employed to cover the marathon races. (Mike Mullen)

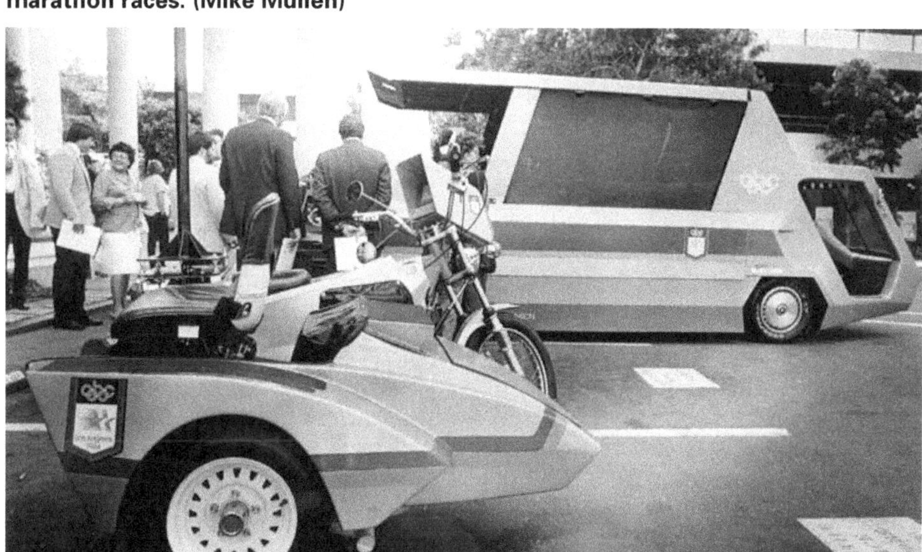

marathon. Many photographers had already left the scene, but Chinn lingered and was rewarded. "She was really struggling, but people kept saying, 'Don't touch her, don't touch her until she crosses the finish line,' because otherwise she would be DQ'd [disqualified]. That's why at the very end when she finally collapsed the medics came in and helped prop her up."

One of the most highly anticipated events was the 3,000-meter final. When Mary Decker tangled with Zola Budd and fell to the track, destroying her Olympic dreams, Chinn was standing with his camera at the finish line. "I was at the far end of the Coliseum when their collision happened," he said. "They were probably about 150 yards away. I could see them, but they were miniscule in my viewfinder."

Chinn's favorite picture is an intimate one he took of track stars Jeanette Bolden and Evelyn Ashford hugging after Ashford won the 100 meters. "That was a very emotional shot," he said. "You could look at the picture and almost think, 'Oh my god, they lost.'"

Musgrove found peaceful interludes whenever he could. "When we were done putting the paper to bed, at 1 or 2 in the morning, we'd go over to The Pantry and sit in a booth and eat breakfast," he said. "You were exhausted, but you didn't want to go home. You had this adrenaline rush and you wanted to think and reflect about what just happened and take it in. And then you'd get up early the next morning and do it again."

A focused ABC-TV camera operator at the Coliseum. (Paul Chinn)

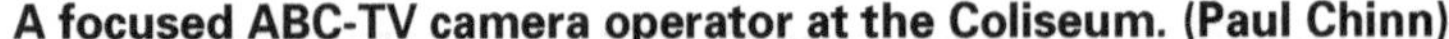

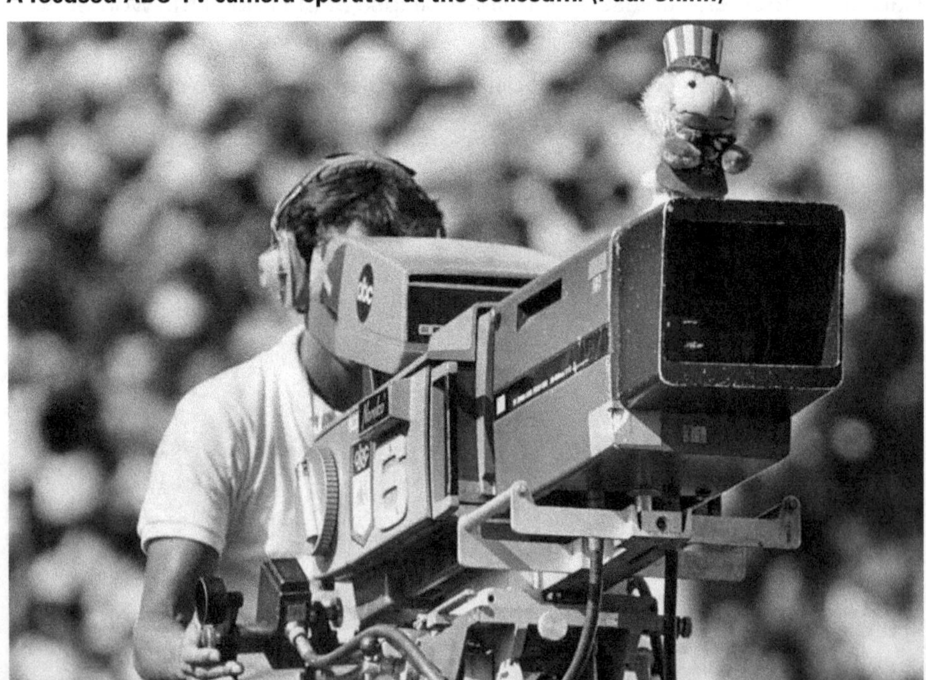

The *Her-Ex* did not have the resources or the sheer number of credentials enjoyed by the Los Angeles *Times*, which covered the Games exhaustively with their 28 photo credentials. But shot for shot, the *Her-Ex's* pictures compared quite favorably with the *Times*' work. "Wherever we would have a photographer, they would have five or six people at an event," Mendoza said. "So, the underdog element was present in almost everything that we did. As much as we liked and respected our colleagues at the *Times*, it was always you're one and they're five, and you're going to find a way to outshoot them."

As it turned out, it was the 187 color and 414 black-and-white photos published in the Orange County *Register* that resonated most dramatically. Their credentialed photographers (Rick Rickman, Brian Smith, Hal Stoelze) won the 1985 Pulitzer Prize for Spot News Photography for their coverage of the Olympics. (Bruce Chambers of the Long Beach *Press-Telegram* was a finalist for his picture of Decker's fall.)

"There's no question that the *Register* had quality pictures, but we thought our work was at least on the same level," Ruebsamen said. "We played it better, too, because we ran those full-page pictures. But they had color and great reproduction and display. That's the way it goes." [Editor's Note: the *Register* had transitioned to a full-color newspaper three years before the Olympics.]

Some 16 days after the start of the Games, the *Her-Ex* concluded its daily coverage in style, with Chinn's image of the spectacular fireworks display from the Closing Ceremony. The headline read: "THAT'S A WRAP!"

By then, the photographers were as exhausted as the athletes. "I remember Jim Roark had a post-Olympic party at his home in the Valley," Chinn said. "We were all sitting there just spent, completely drained. I think we all took a week off."

"There was a let-down afterwards," Mendoza said. "You're running on adrenaline, and then all of a sudden it comes to an end. And it's like, 'Now what?' It takes a little while to get back in the groove after you've gone through that."

"There was this anticipation about the Olympics coming to L.A.," Ruebsamen said. "We started counting down the days six months in advance: 'It's now 179 days till the Games, it's now 178 days till the Games.' It was driving me crazy. Then the Games started, and it was grueling, but then the Games ended. It was over, like that."

His final memory came in the chaotic aftermath of the Closing Ceremony, when the media transportation system broke down amid massive gridlock around the Coliseum. Desperate to make his deadline, Ruebsamen decided to walk and run the nearly four miles back to the office carrying three cameras, six or seven lenses, all the miscellaneous gear inside his camera bag, and a monopod for self-defense.

In early September, the *Her-Ex* printed a souvenir edition packed with the photographers' best photographs from the Olympics. The issue sold out quickly.

With the perspective of more than three decades, Chinn, Mendoza, Musgrove, and Ruebsamen have come to relish their experience working one of the most storied events in Los Angeles's history. (Knudsen passed away in 2013.) "It's the Olympic Games, and everything's on a competitive level," Mendoza said. "You've got the world's greatest athletes, and you've got some of the world's best photographers trying to capture those moments. What an honor for a 24-year old kid. What an amazing opportunity. That was one of the highlights of my career as a photojournalist."

"I always loved the Olympics as far back as I can remember," Ruebsamen said. "The schedule killed me, but I loved it. It was just, get out there and do what you can, and make sure you do better than anybody else."

"Before everyone was like, 'Is the traffic going to be bad? How hot is it going to be? Are we going to have smog days where it's not safe for the athletes?'" Musgrove said. "About halfway through, downtown was 76 degrees and we were like, 'This is really working out pretty cool.' The flow of everything was good."

"That was one of the greatest thrills of my life," Chinn said, "being able to cover the Olympics when I was 23 years old and just getting started in the profession. I still remember so much of it in my mind." ★

The Herald Examiner *folded in 1989, and the photographers were forced to find other jobs. In 1991, the Hearst Corp. donated the newspaper morgue—some 2.2 million photographs dating back to the 1920s—to the Los Angeles Public Library.*

LOS ANGELES HERALD EXAMINER
Olympic Special
MONDAY AUGUST 13, 1984
25 CENTS Vol CXV No. 104 Copyright ©1984
Morning final

TODAY'S NEWS INSIDE

AT LAST! ZOLA'S SIDE OF THE STORY/Page 10

REAGAN ON TAXES: 'NEVER SAY NEVER'/A-1

THAT'S A WRAP!

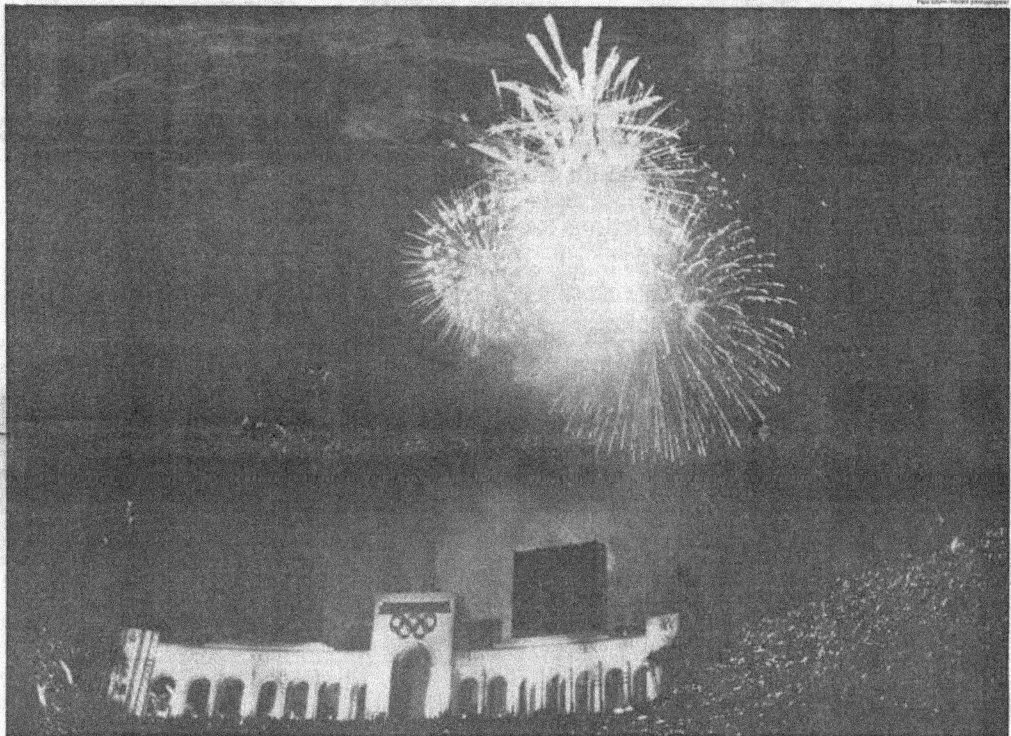

It's a whale of a show in the night sky above the Coliseum, as one of the longest and most spectacular fireworks displays ever seen anywhere blasted on and on to bring the Closing Ceremonies of the XXIII Olympiad to a show-stopping climax.

For 100,000, a Close Encounter of the XXIII kind

By Joe Morgenstern
Herald columnist

Some flames die really hard.

The Olympic Flame that emigrated to this country only three months ago went out in matchless, seemingly endless blazes of glory last night at the Coliseum.

Fireworks stupendous enough to be seen from the moon (and heard from the grave); lasers twitching across the warm summer sky; a blue St. Elmo's fire of tens of thousands of flashlights in the grandstands; a Close Encounter of the Olympic Kind (Spielbergian flying saucer dangling beneath Sikorskian flying chopper); a visitation by an extra-terrestrial from the planet of Saturday morning cartoons; and finally an all-singing, all-dancing, all-exploding show that was to questions of taste what the pyramids were to residential architecture. It was all a way of delaying the moment when the stands would be empty, the town would be depleted and the Games would be irrevocably ended.

Until the smash ending, with Lionel Richie letting the music play on, play on, while the fireworks blasted on, blasted on, the Closing Ceremonies felt like the last day of the world's greatest summer camp.

The campers were overwhelmed with joy, love and the sadness of imminent departure.

So were the counselors who coached them, and all the millions of visitors who watched them as they played their remarkable Games.

During last night's show, the classic of the Games, the marathon run was whipped together with Hollywood fun into a souffle the size of a Coliseum. Slow to rise, the production was still a wonder to behold as it reached its full proportions.

By way of prelude to the celebration (as if two weeks of competition hadn't been prelude enough), church bells of no known denomination and then trumpets of appropriately colossal volume blazed out through the vast stadium. This was at 6:45 p.m., while the marathoners were still slogging their way through the last four miles of their route. A flight of doves was also

Morgenstern/Page 7, Col. 1

INSIDE THIS SECTION

Well, L.A., we pulled the whole thing off

MELVIN DURSLAG

Now that the flame has been extinguished, it can be revealed to our Soviet visitors that the Olympic city believed to be Los Angeles actually was a set, borrowed from 20th Century Fox.

With the dismantling of the set, it can be disclosed further that the Games were staged in Fresno. The information was withheld for reasons of security.

At the Closing Ceremonies, we were set up for a smash finale featuring Mary Decker and her muscular fiance, British discus thrower Richard Slaney. In a memorable moment Friday, Slaney was seen at the Coliseum carrying off Decker.

But in the surprise ending yesterday, Decker would carry off Slaney.

It was a touch audiences would talk about for years, but it never came off — one of the few disappointments of an Olympics that could be judged, by just about any standards, as a success.

Neurotic fear spread about the world over the ability of Los Angeles to pull off these Games. There was concern over traffic, over weather, over air quality and over money.

And, God knows, fear over security reduced to nervous wrecks people on several continents. Developing such anxiety over security, in fact, the Eastern bloc stayed home.

Durslag/Page 13, Col. 1

The home team won — just like in Moscow

ALLAN MALAMUD

Like Moscow, like L.A.

The Games — and the races and the matches, too — of the 23rd Olympiad smacked of the 22nd.

The home nation, the biggest and best prepared, panned gold in record numbers while its most formidable adversary sat out the fortnight.

In case you're keeping score, the United States gold count reached 83 on closing day. Four years ago, the Soviet Union won 80.

The U.S. also took 61 silver medals and 30 bronzes for a total of 174, compared to the Soviet haul of 80-70-47 for a total of 197.

With nearly all the Soviet allies joining the boycott, Americans finished first more often than the next six leading countries combined.

"USA! USA!" was the Official Olympic Chant, and "The Star Spangled Banner" topped the music charts at most venues.

But, as ABC and other dispensers of news eventually discovered, this was also the Olympics where the Chinese enjoyed their coming-out party.

A People's Republic of China pistol expert, fertilizer salesman Haifeng Xu, was awarded the first gold medal of the Games.

It would be one of 15 for his nation, which is certain to be even more of a force in Seoul in 1988.

Malamud/Page 13, Col. 1

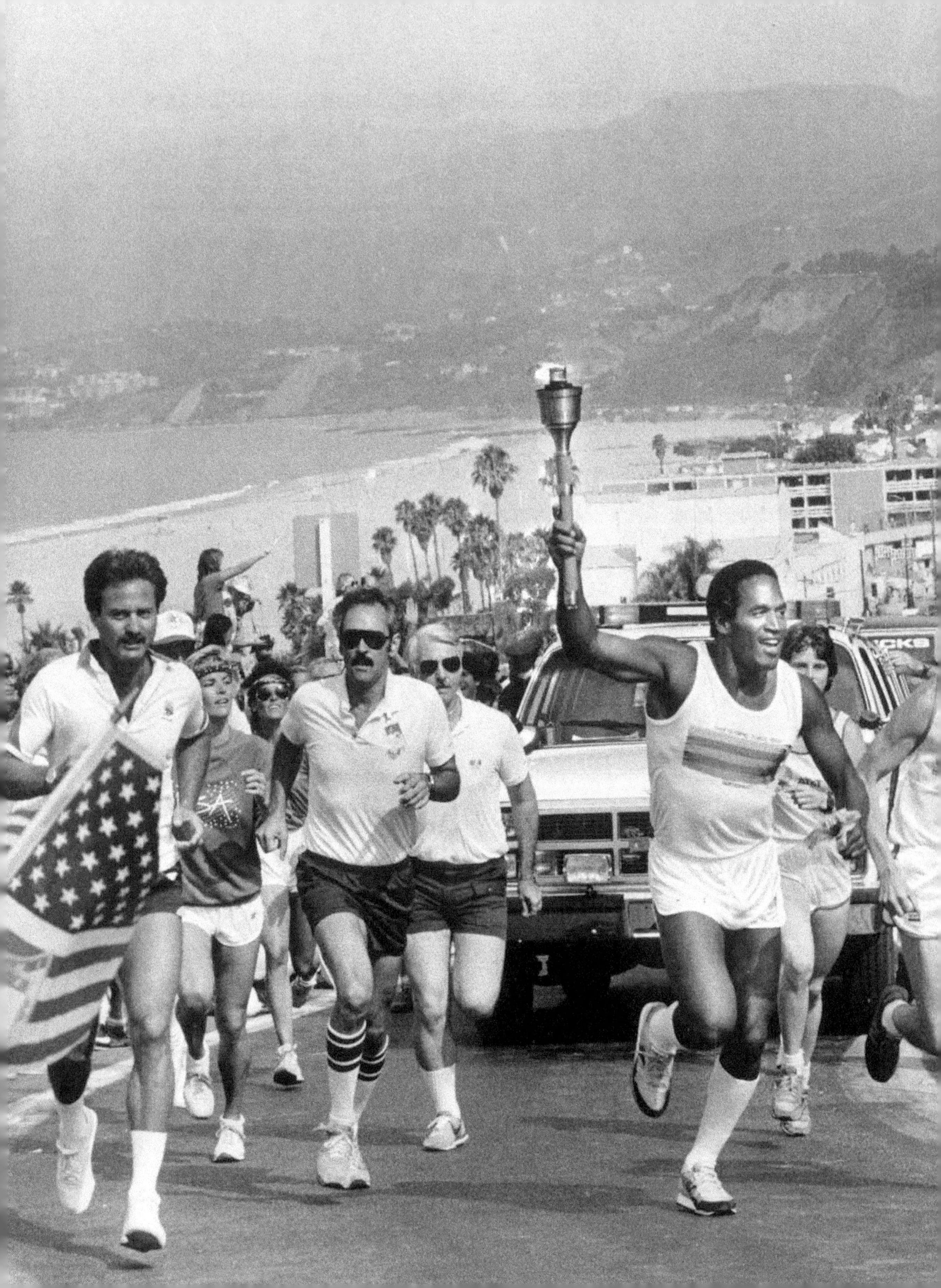

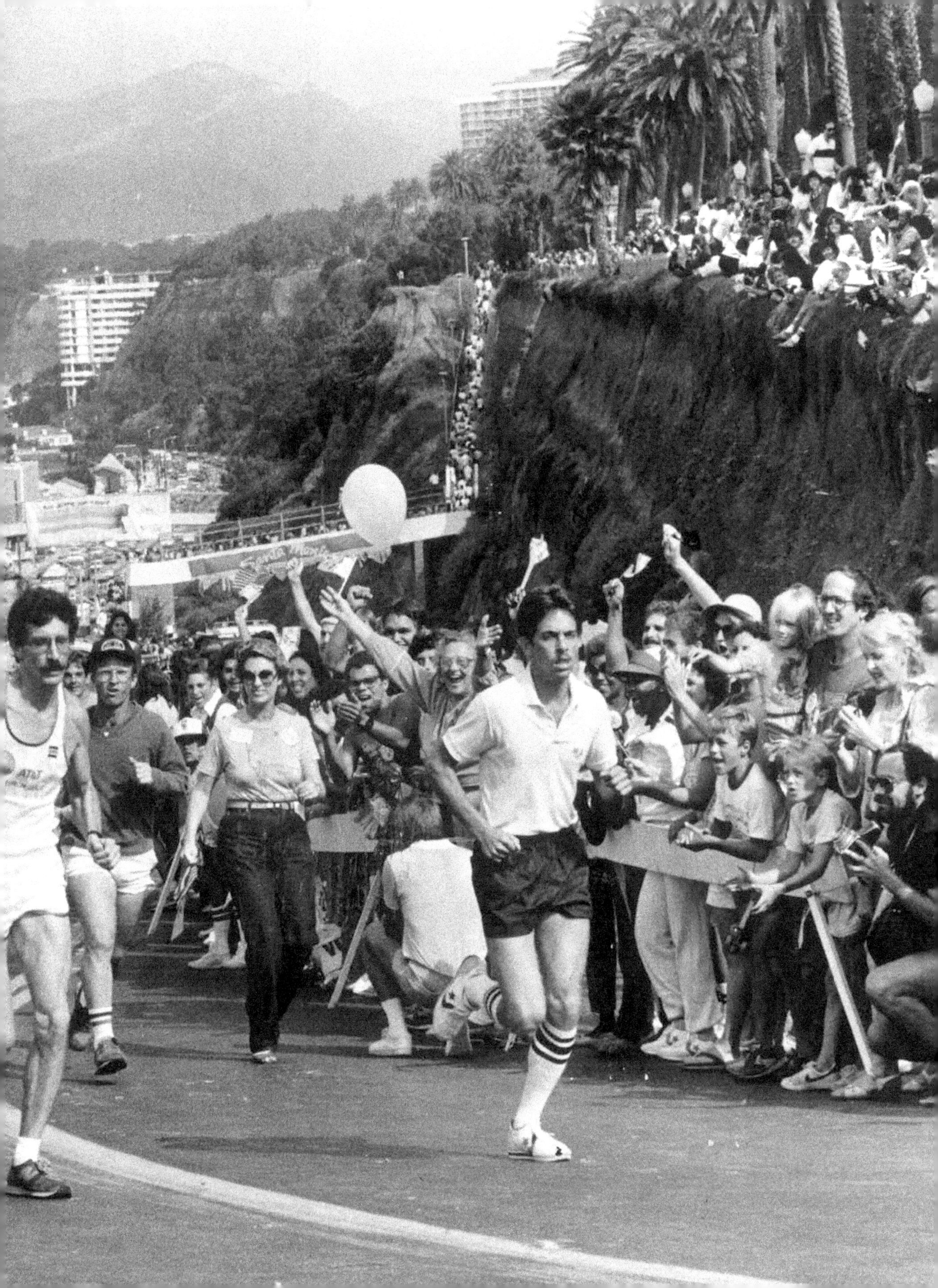
AT&T

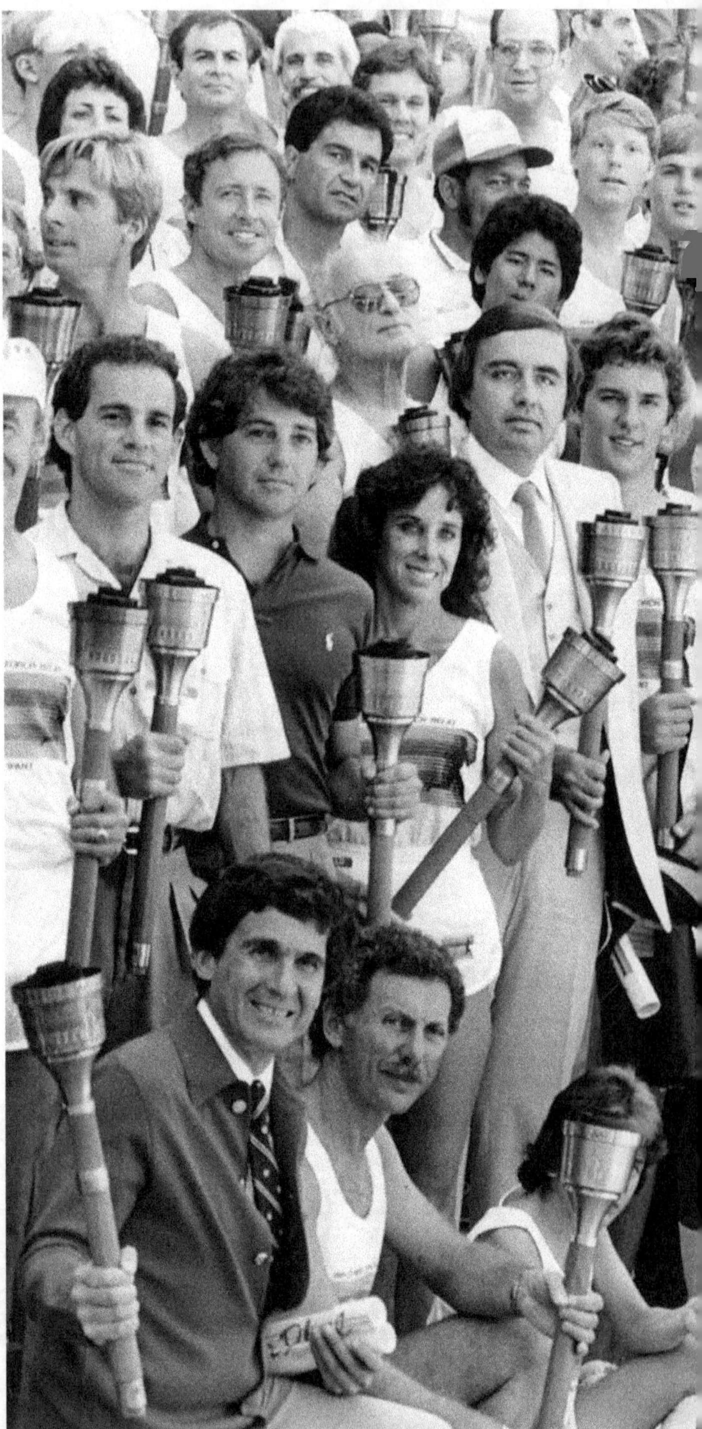

Mayor Tom Bradley stood among 300 torchbearers at City Hall. (Mike Mullen)

Overleaf: The 15,000-kilometer Olympic Torch Relay began in New York and passed through 33 states in 82 days before ending up in Southern California. Former USC football star O.J. Simpson ran with the torch in Santa Monica, accompanied by future wife Nicole Brown (*far left*). (Javier Mendoza)

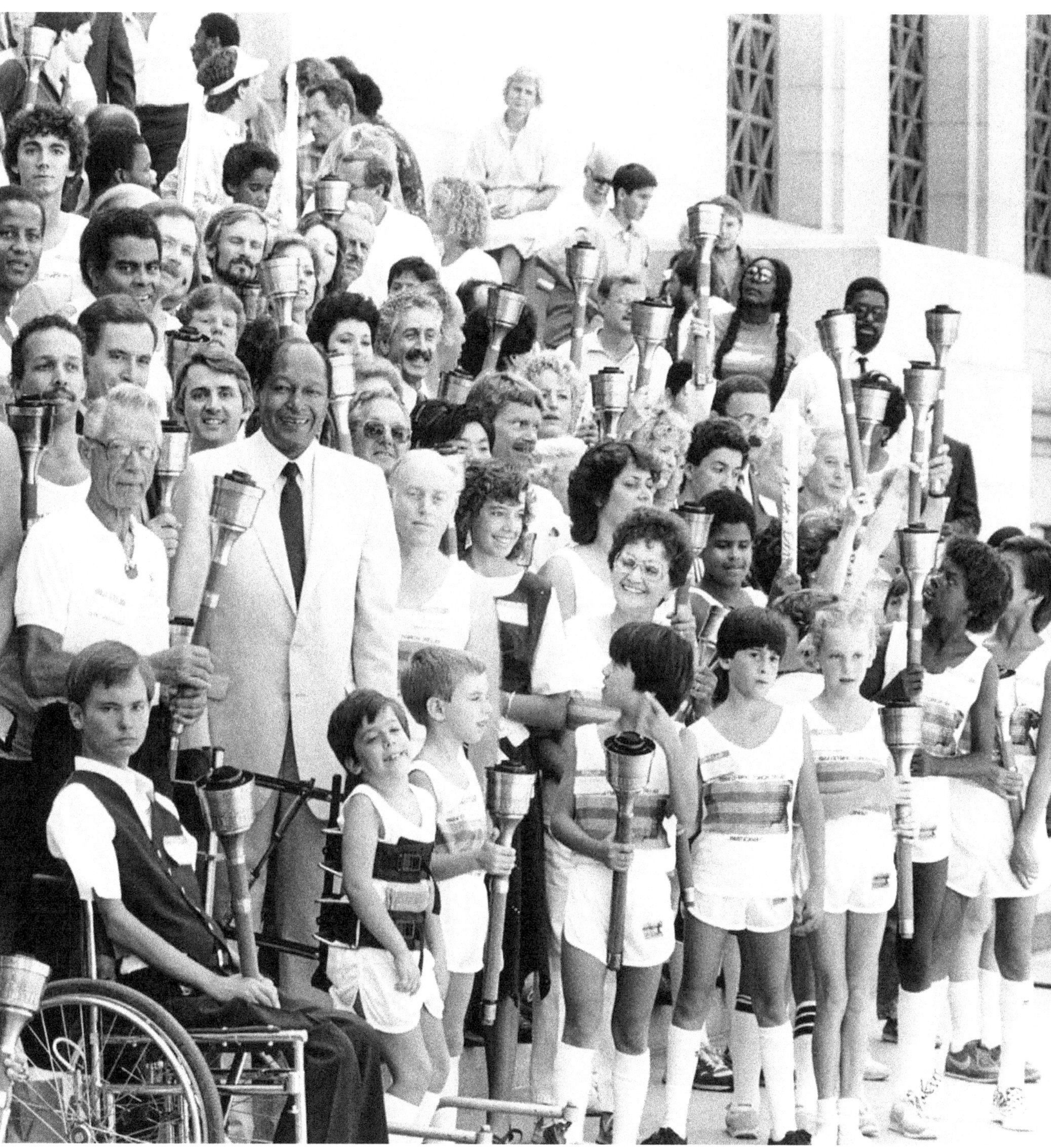

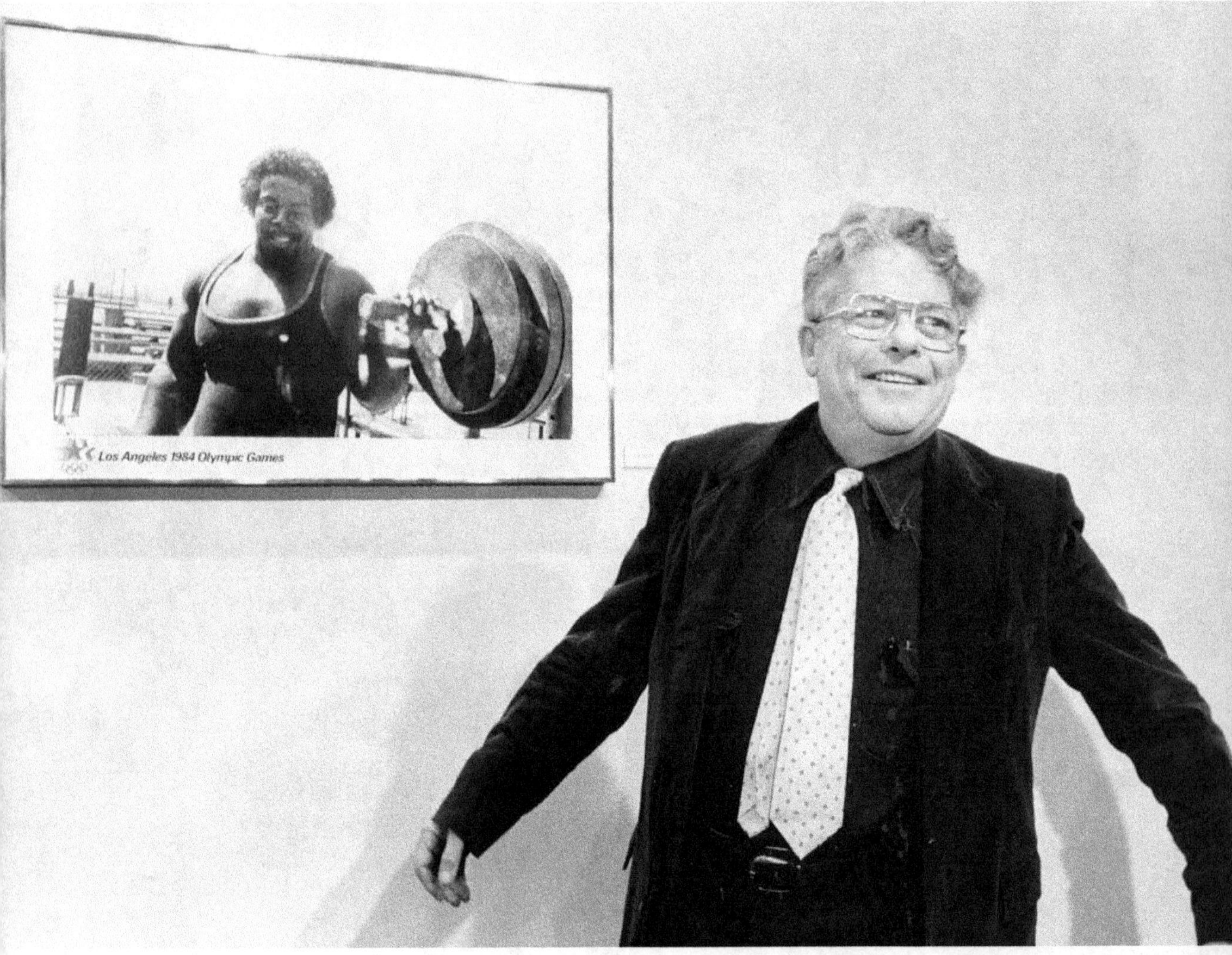

The Olympic Arts Festival, led by Robert Fitzpatrick, offered an ambitious spate of musical, dance, and visual arts programming throughout Southern California. Photographer Garry Winogrand was one of 16 artists commissioned to create a series of fine-art posters; his featured bodybuilder Bill Pettis at Venice Beach. (Paul Chinn)

Opposite: Football player-turned-artist Ernie Barnes painted five Olympic-themed works, including "The Finish." (Paul Chinn)

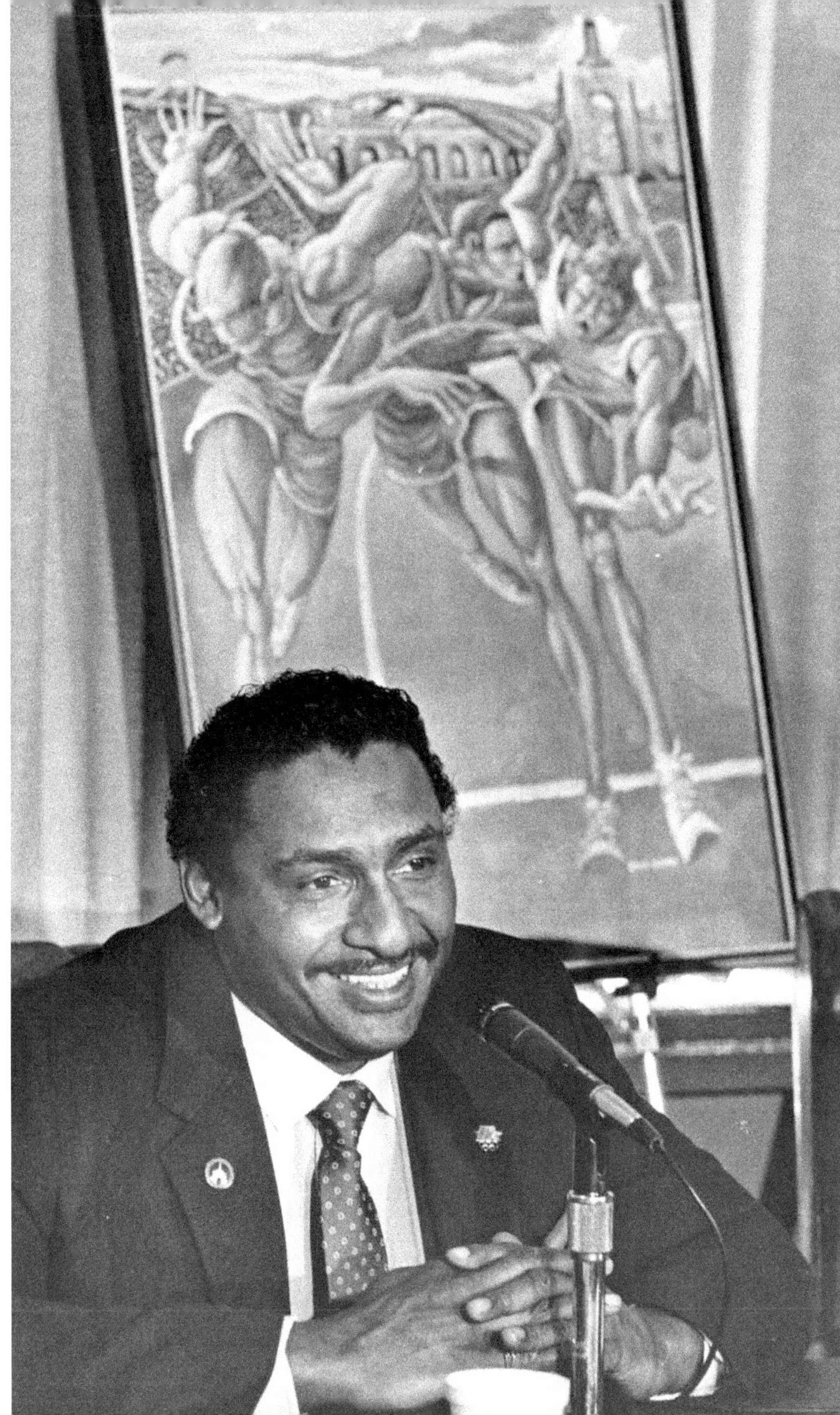

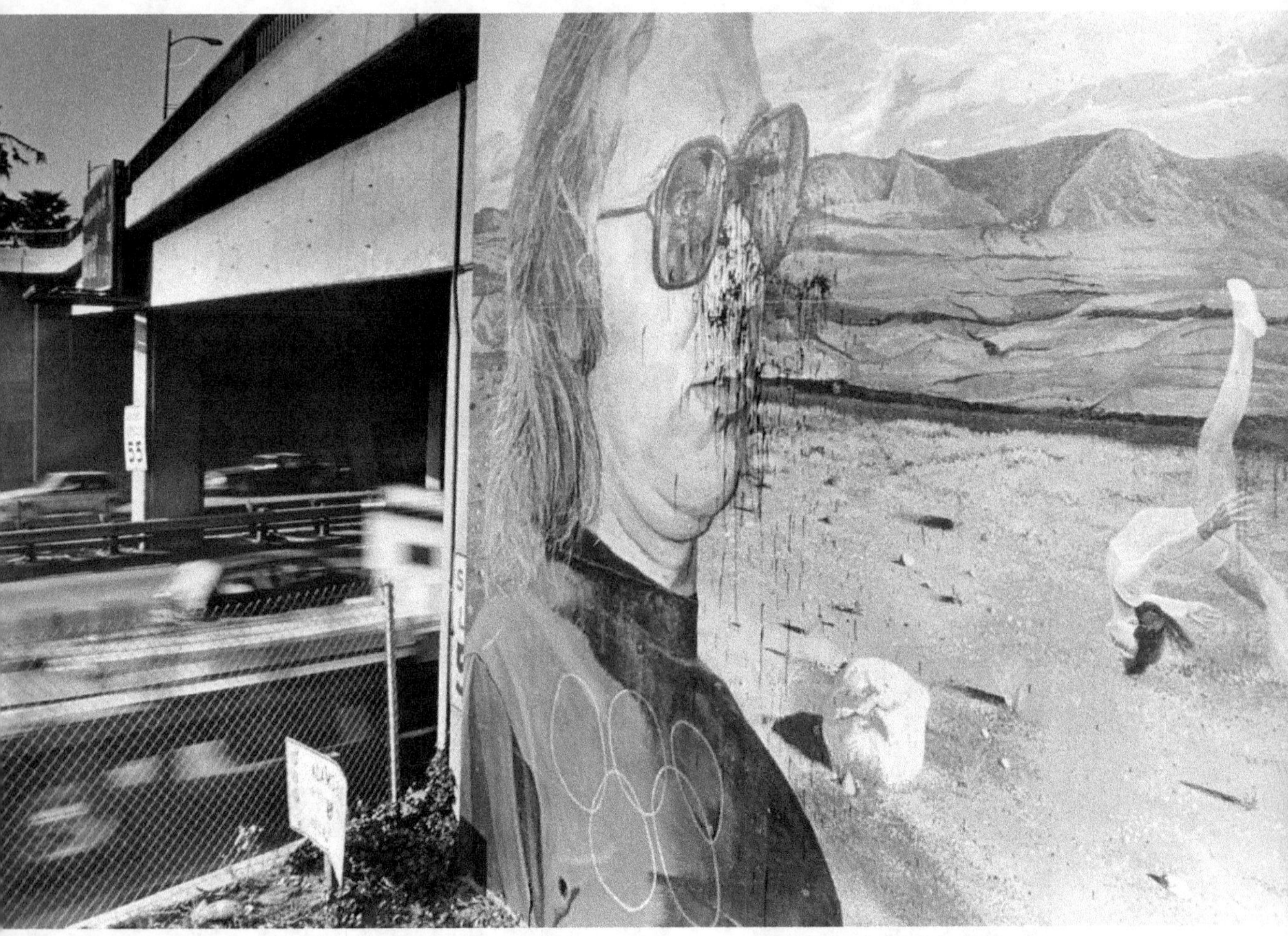

Ten artists were commissioned to paint murals; Richard Wyatt's "James and Spectators," next to the Harbor Freeway at Adams Boulevard, was defaced with paint before the Games. (Anne Knudsen)

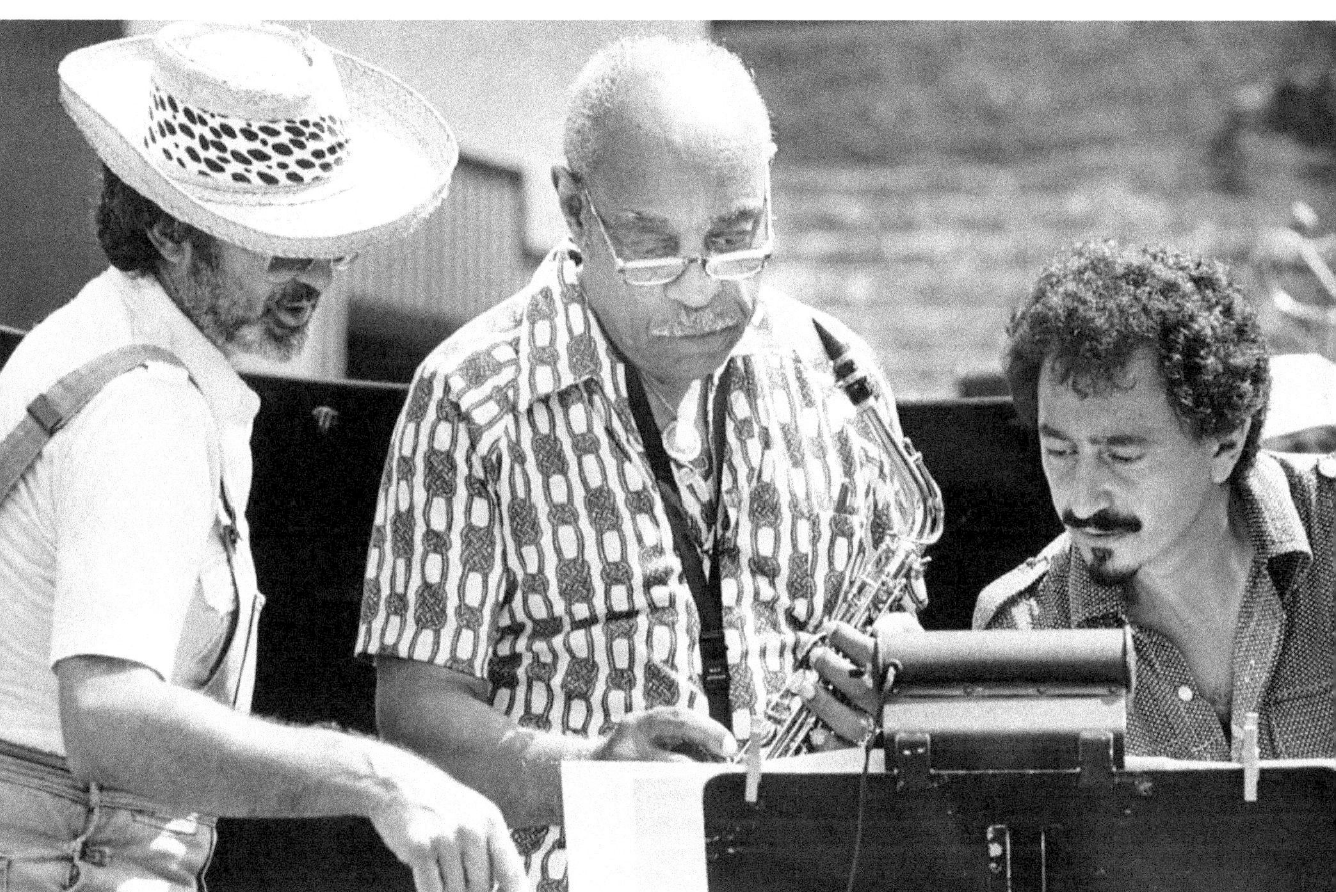

Saxophonist Benny Carter (*center*) and percussionist Tommy Vig (*right*) rehearsed with pianist Milcho Leviev before the Olympic Jazz Festival. (Lisa Hatalsky)

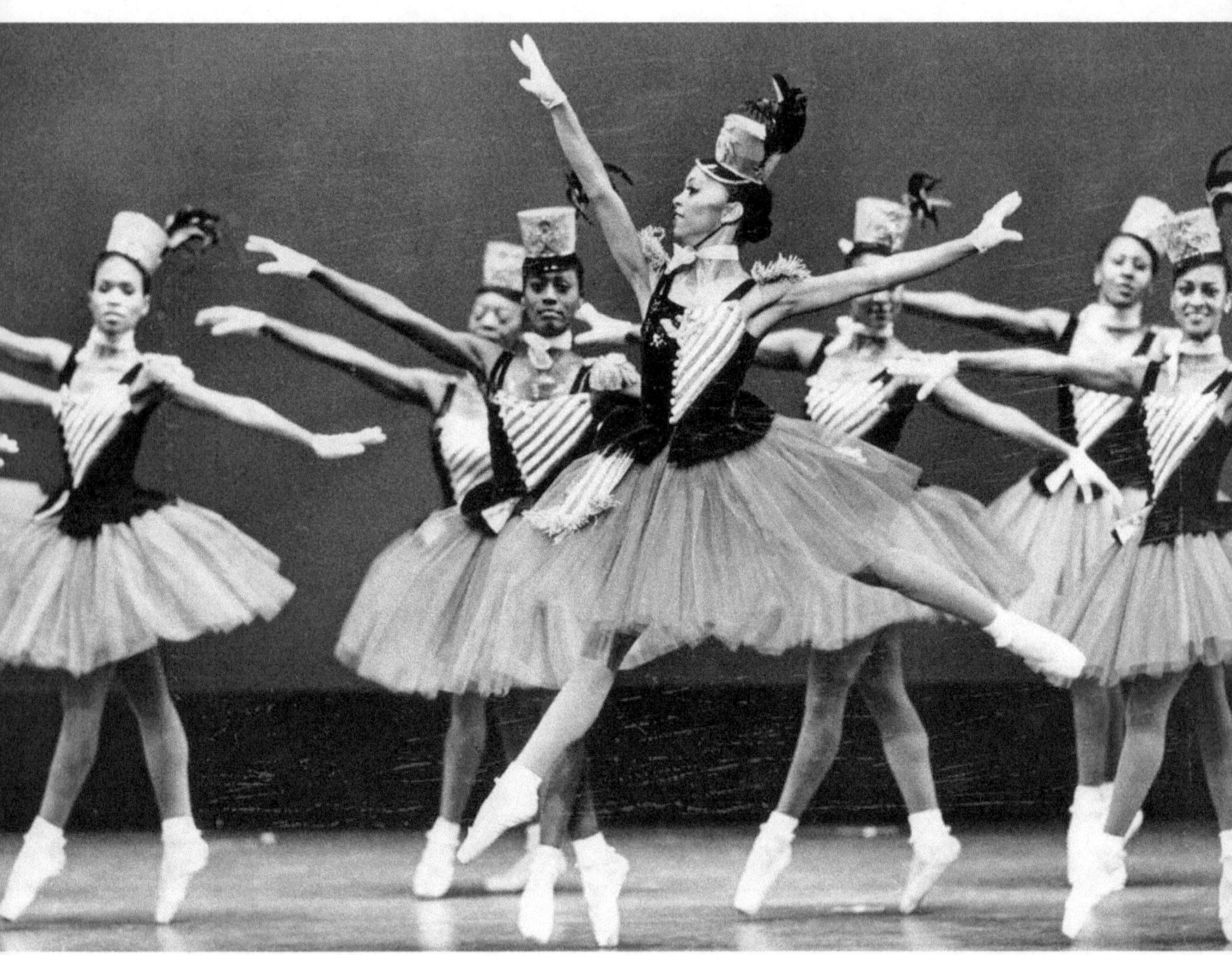

Judy Tyrus was the leader of the Corcoran Cadets in Dance Theater Harlem's "Stars and Stripes," presented at the Pasadena Civic Auditorium. (Mike Sergieff)

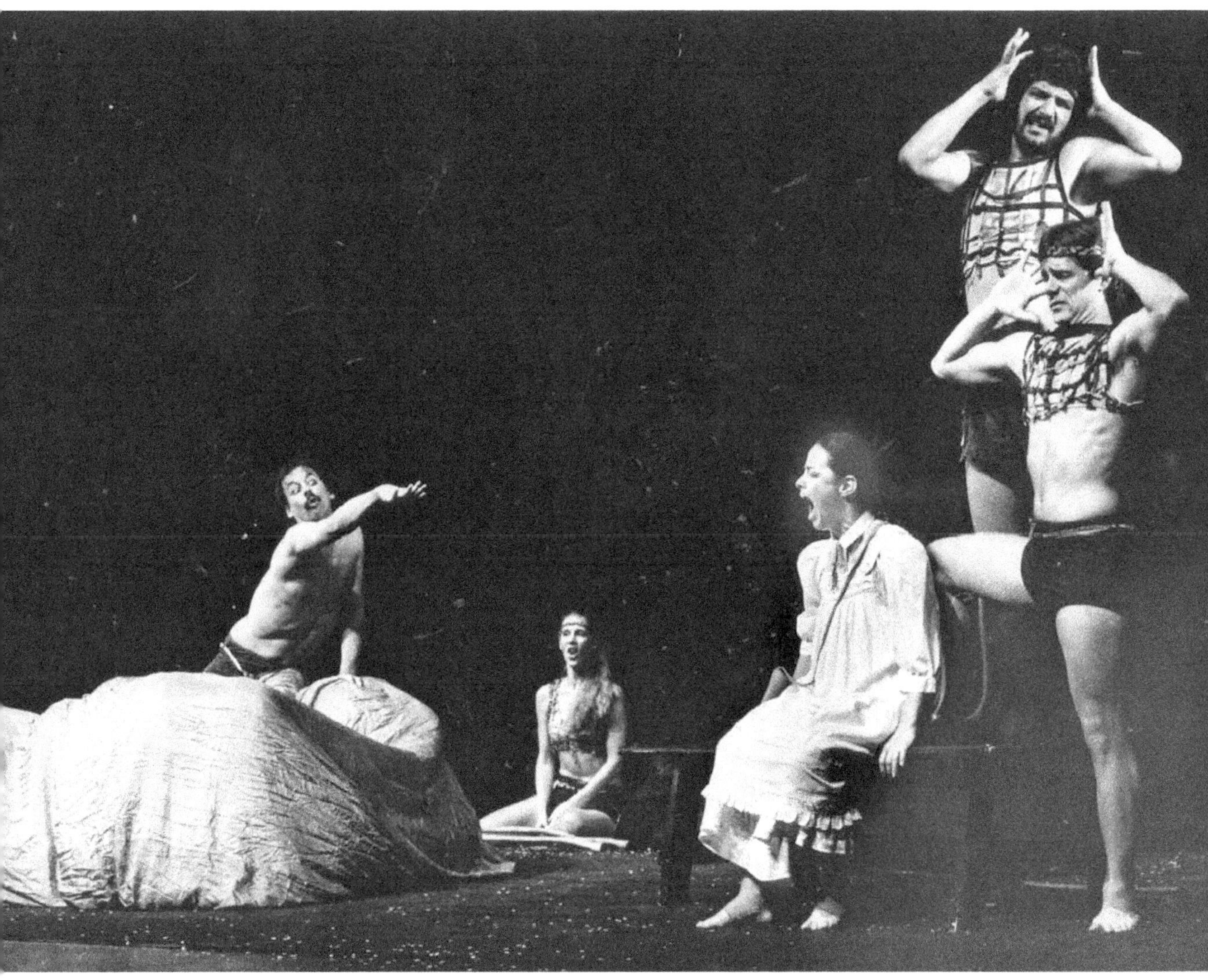

The National Theatre of the Deaf performs in one of the most poetic of all languages, American Sign Language, at UCLA's Schoenberg Hall. (Anne Knudsen)

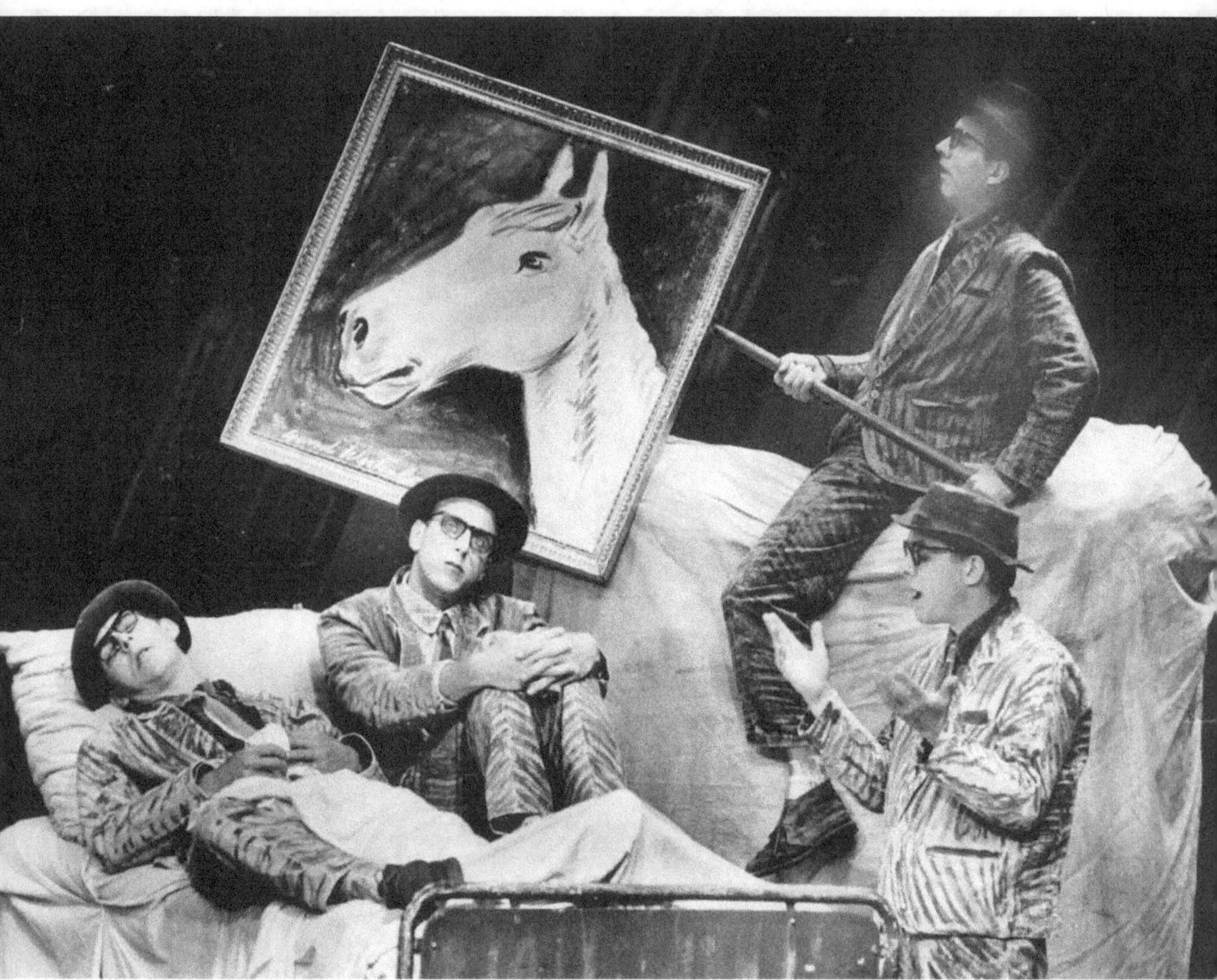

De Mexicaanse Hond presents Alex van Warmerdam's "Luisman's Law," a work with roots in dadaism and surrealism, at UCLA. (Anne Knudsen)

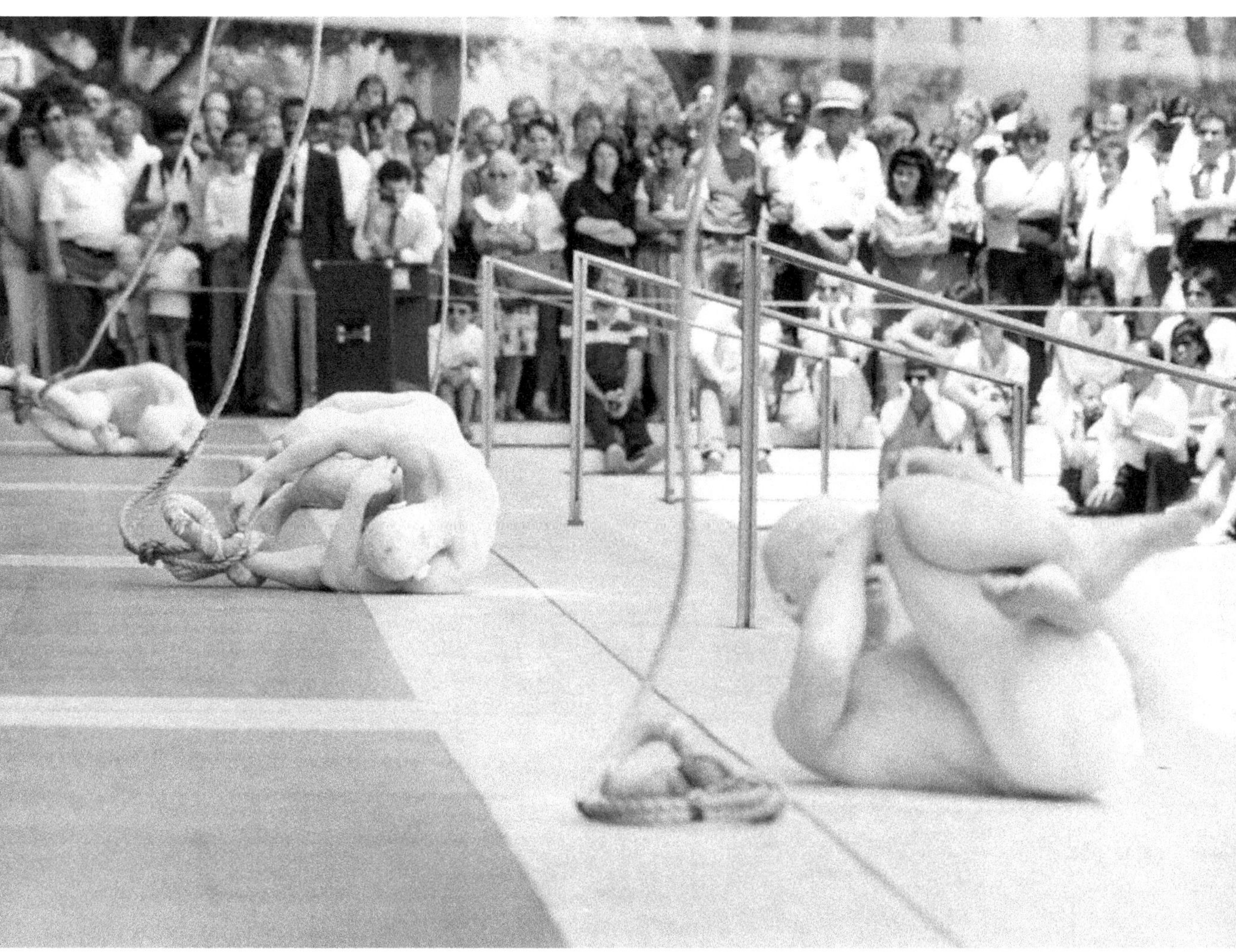

Scantily clad Japanese dancers (from butoh dance troupe Sankai Juku) gracefully untie ropes that carried them down from the roof of the Music Center. (Toru Kawana)

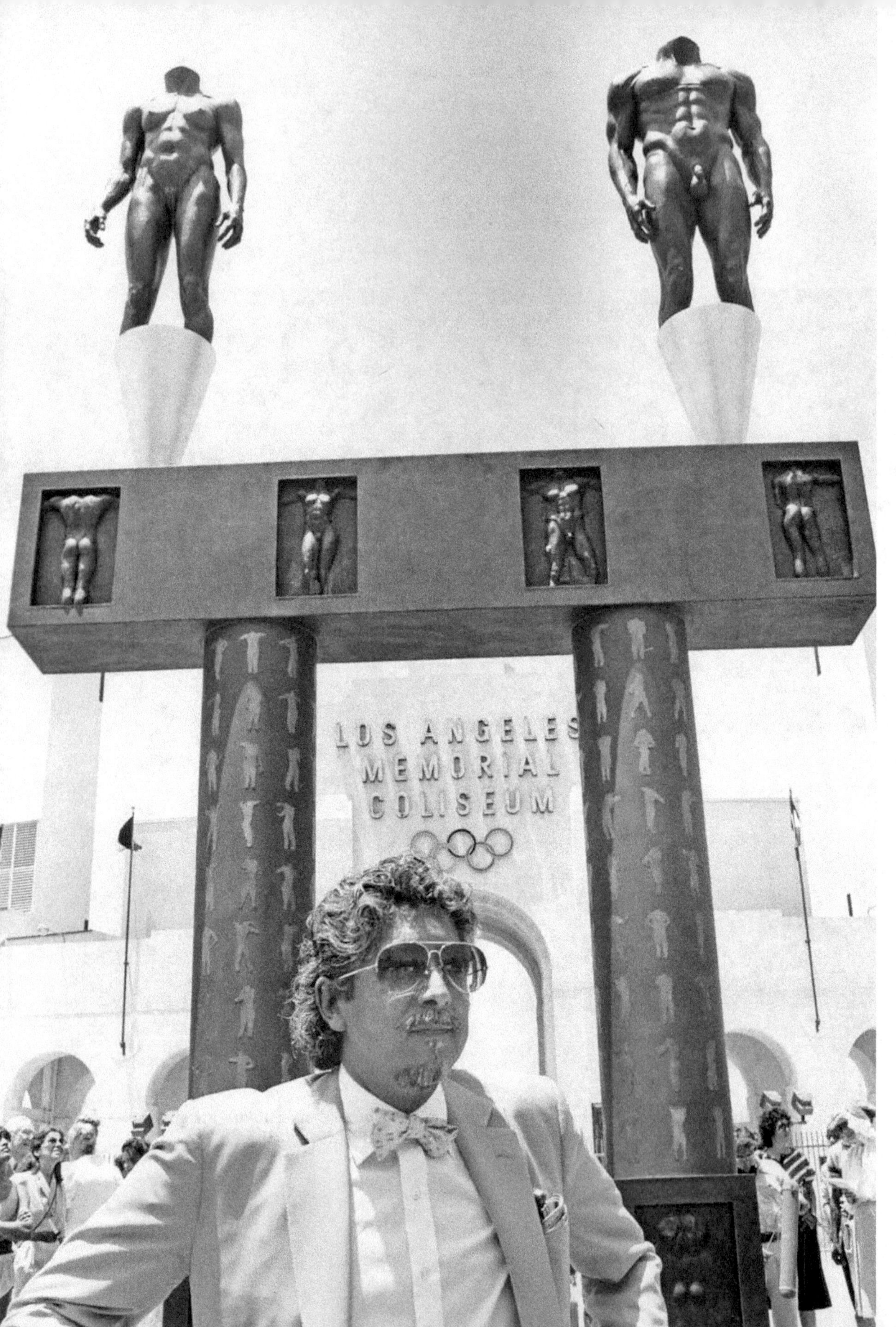
LOS ANGELES
MEMORIAL
COLISEUM

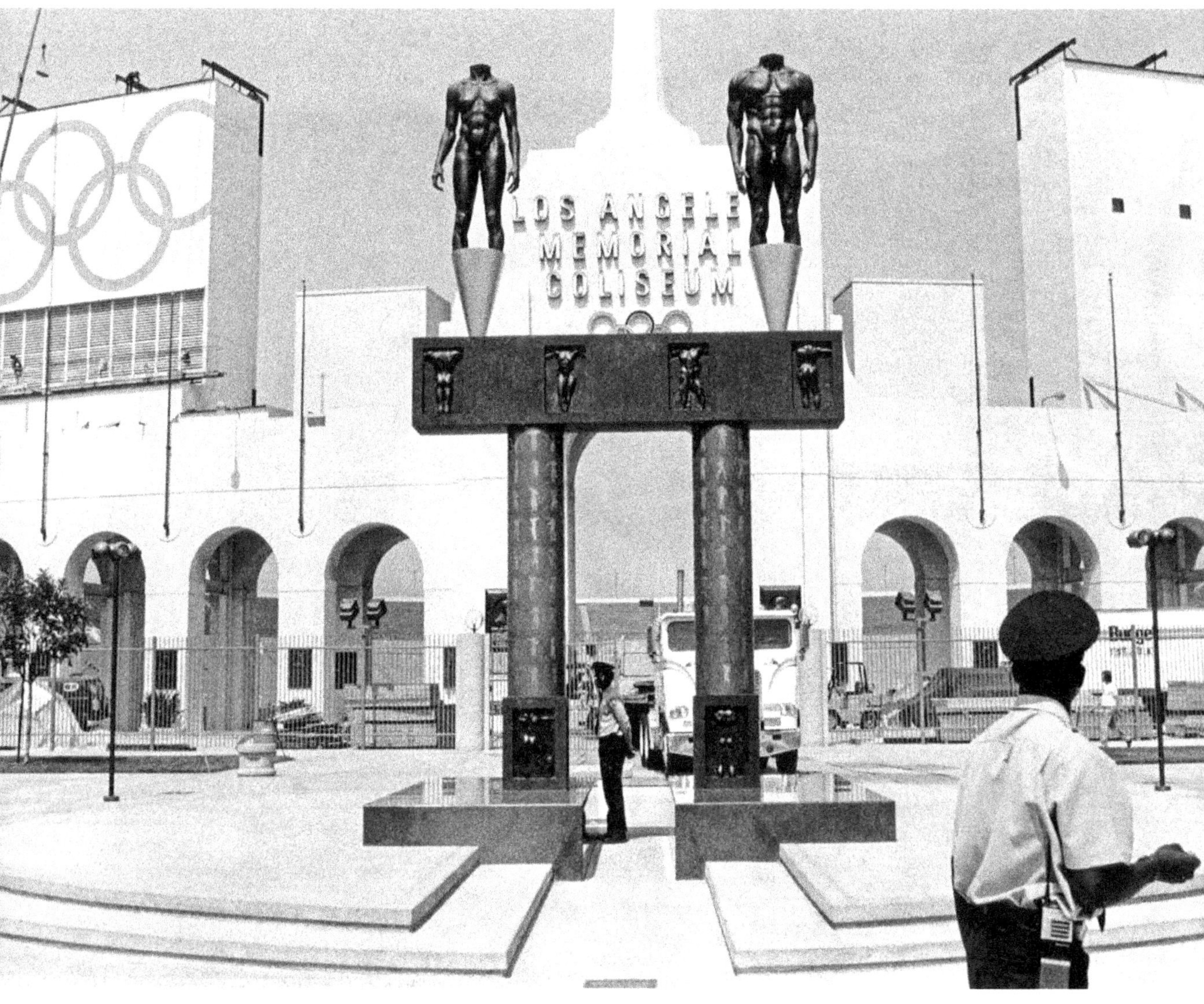

The models for the headless nudes were U.S. water polo captain Terry Schroeder and Guyanese long jumper Jennifer Inniss. The work caused controversy—and had to be guarded around the clock—but it proved to be a popular sensation and remains in place today. (Mike Sergieff)

Opposite: **Artist Robert Graham stood before his monumental bronze sculpture, "Olympic Gateway," by the entrance to the Coliseum, on the day of its unveiling. (Michael Haering)**

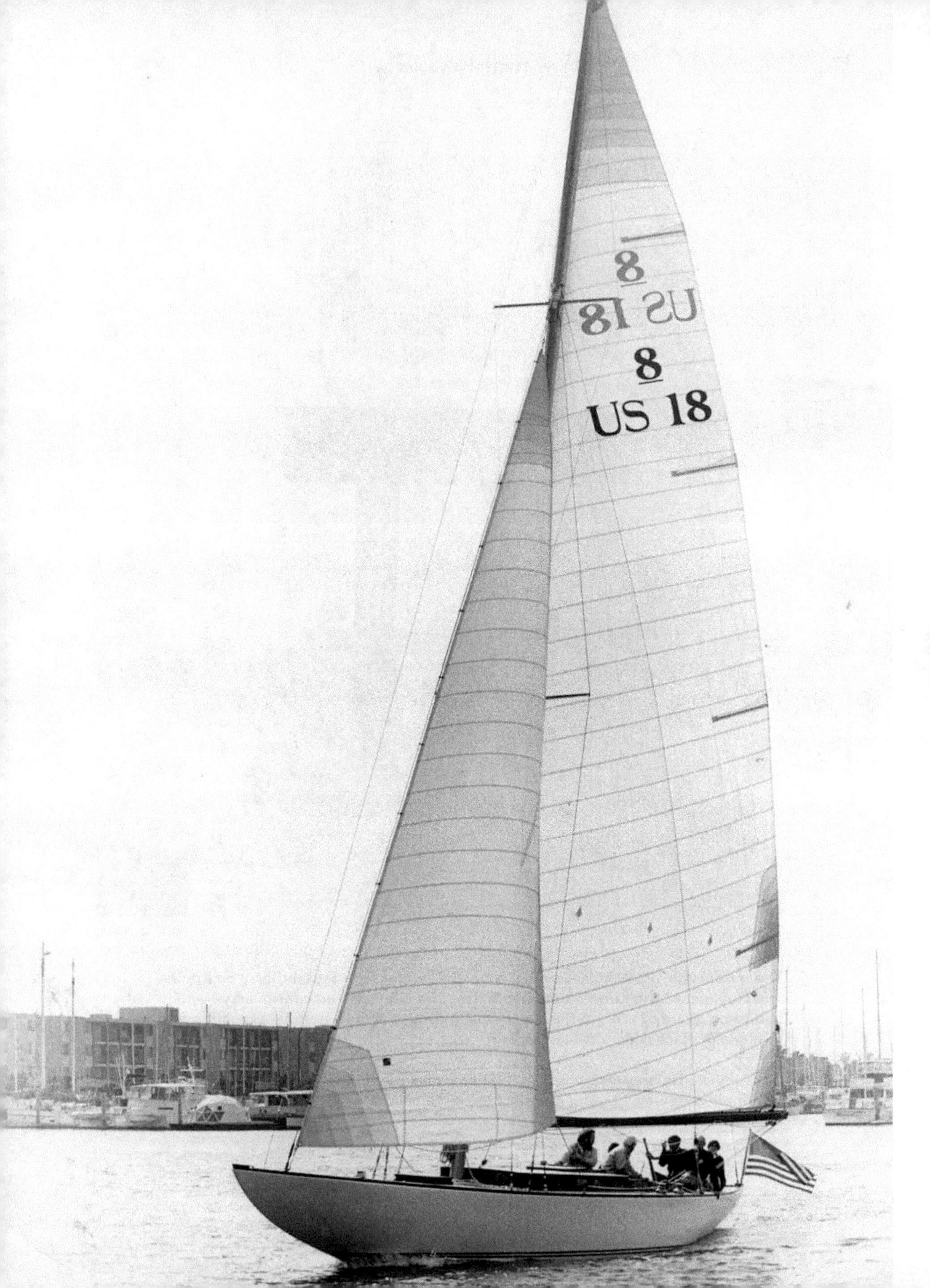
8
US 18

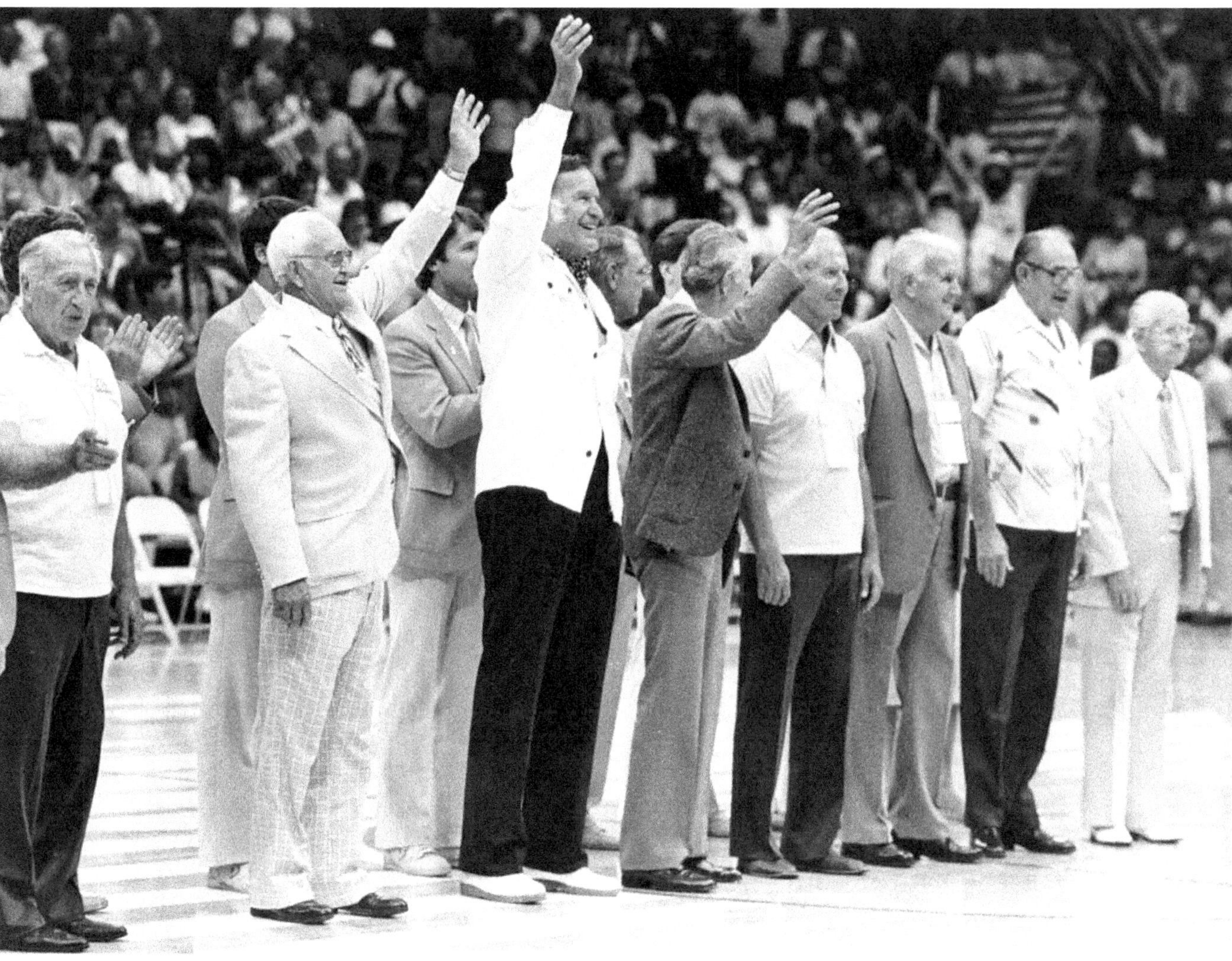

Basketball made its Olympic debut in 1936, with the U.S. represented by seven members from the Universal Pictures-sponsored team (which won the Olympic Trials), six members from the McPherson Globe Refiners, and one college student. They defeated Canada, 19-8, to win the gold medal despite playing in a driving rainstorm. Here, members from the 1936 squad are introduced at the Forum. (James Ruebsamen)

Opposite: Local organizers paid tribute to the 1932 Los Angeles Olympics in several ways. The refurbished "Angelita," the yacht piloted by Owen Churchill in 1932, was used as the flagship for the yachting competition in Long Beach in 1984, with the 88-year-old Churchill at the helm. (Michael Haering)

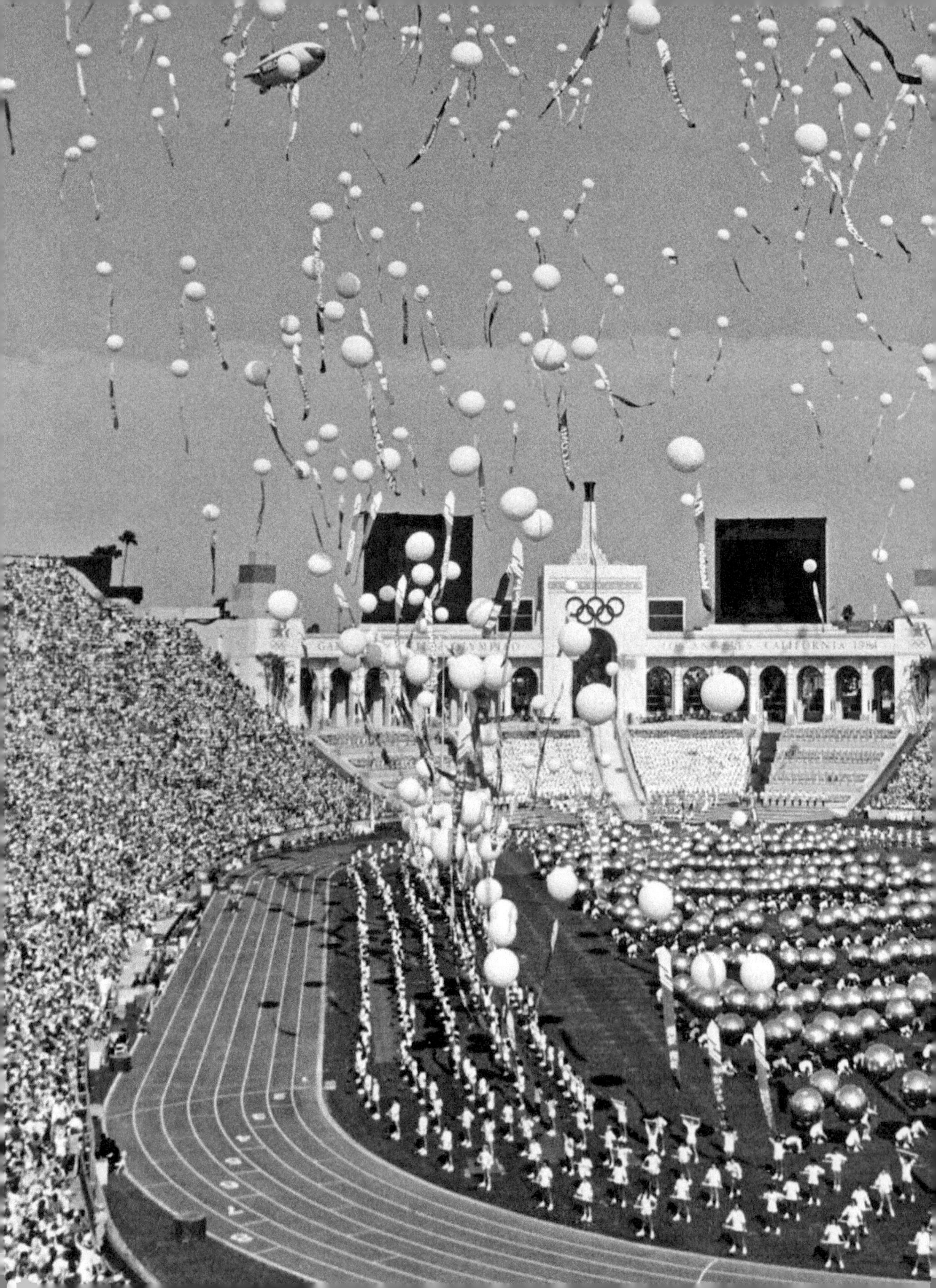
CALIFORNIA 1984

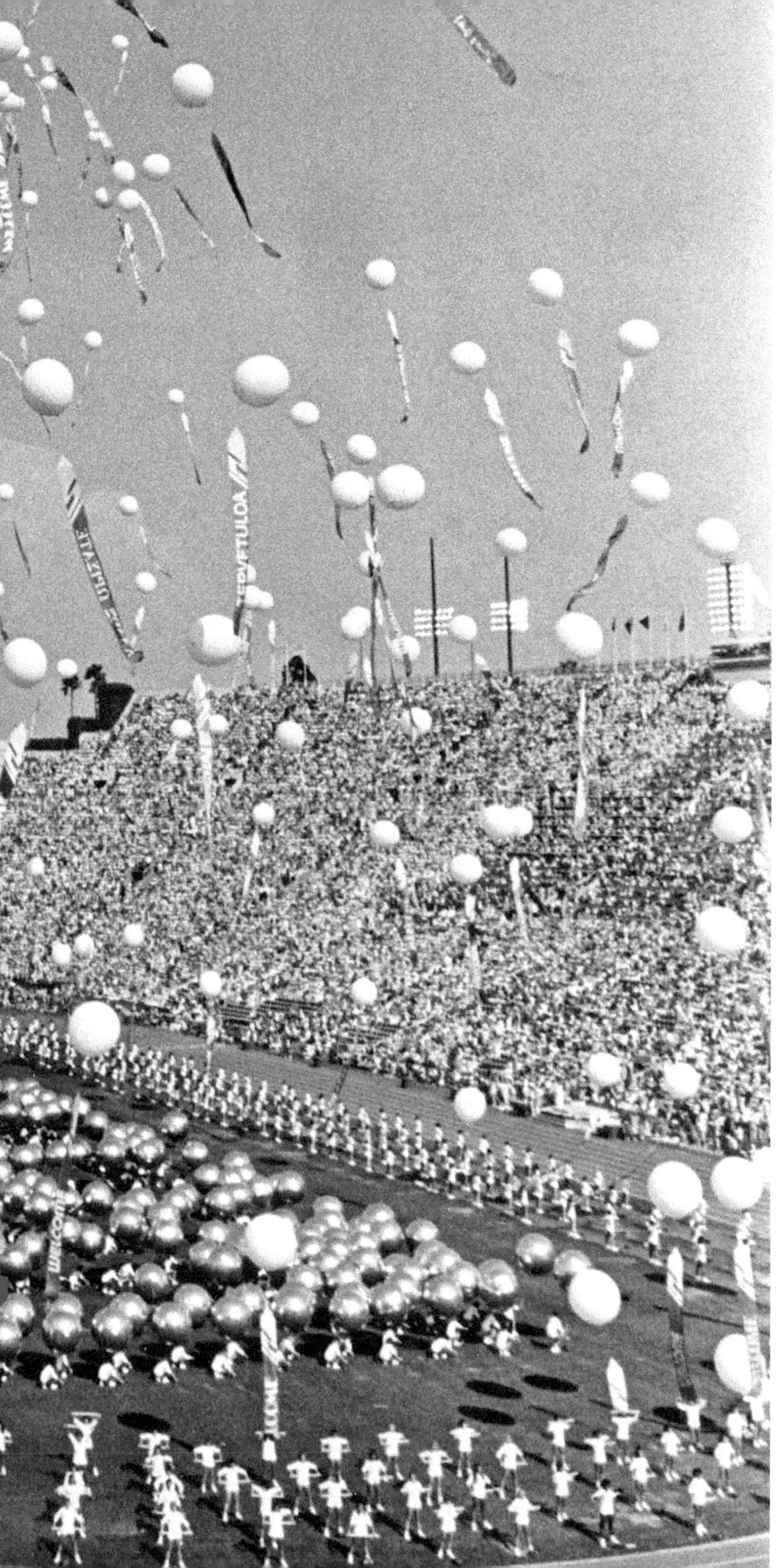

The Opening Ceremony featured balloons; compositions by John Williams, Philip Glass, and Marvin Hamlisch; performances by Etta James and a small army of dancers and musicians; the march of the athletes by nation. (Dean Musgrove)

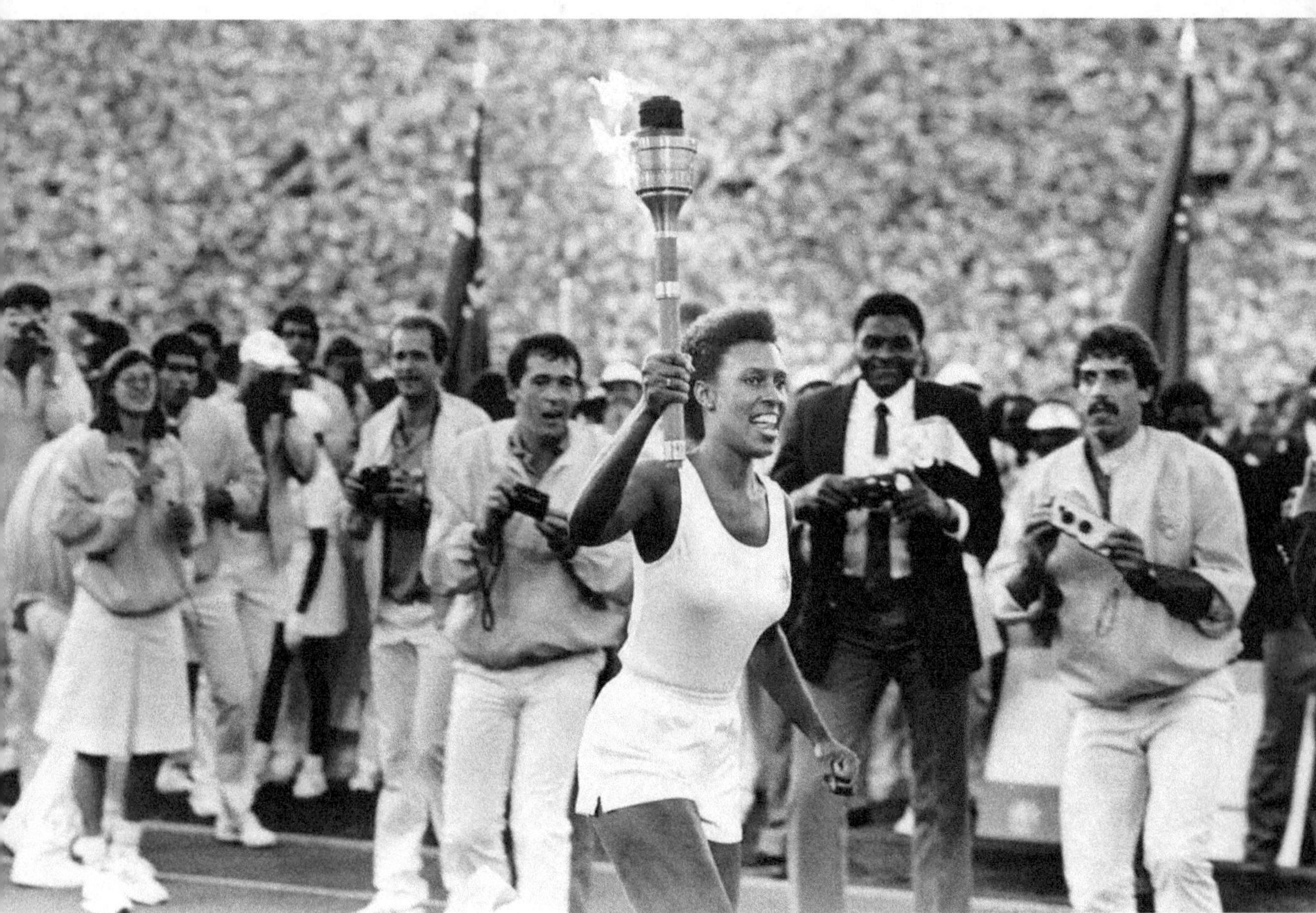

Gina Hemphill, granddaughter of Olympic legend Jesse Owens, carried the torch into the Coliseum and circled the track. (Anne Knudsen)

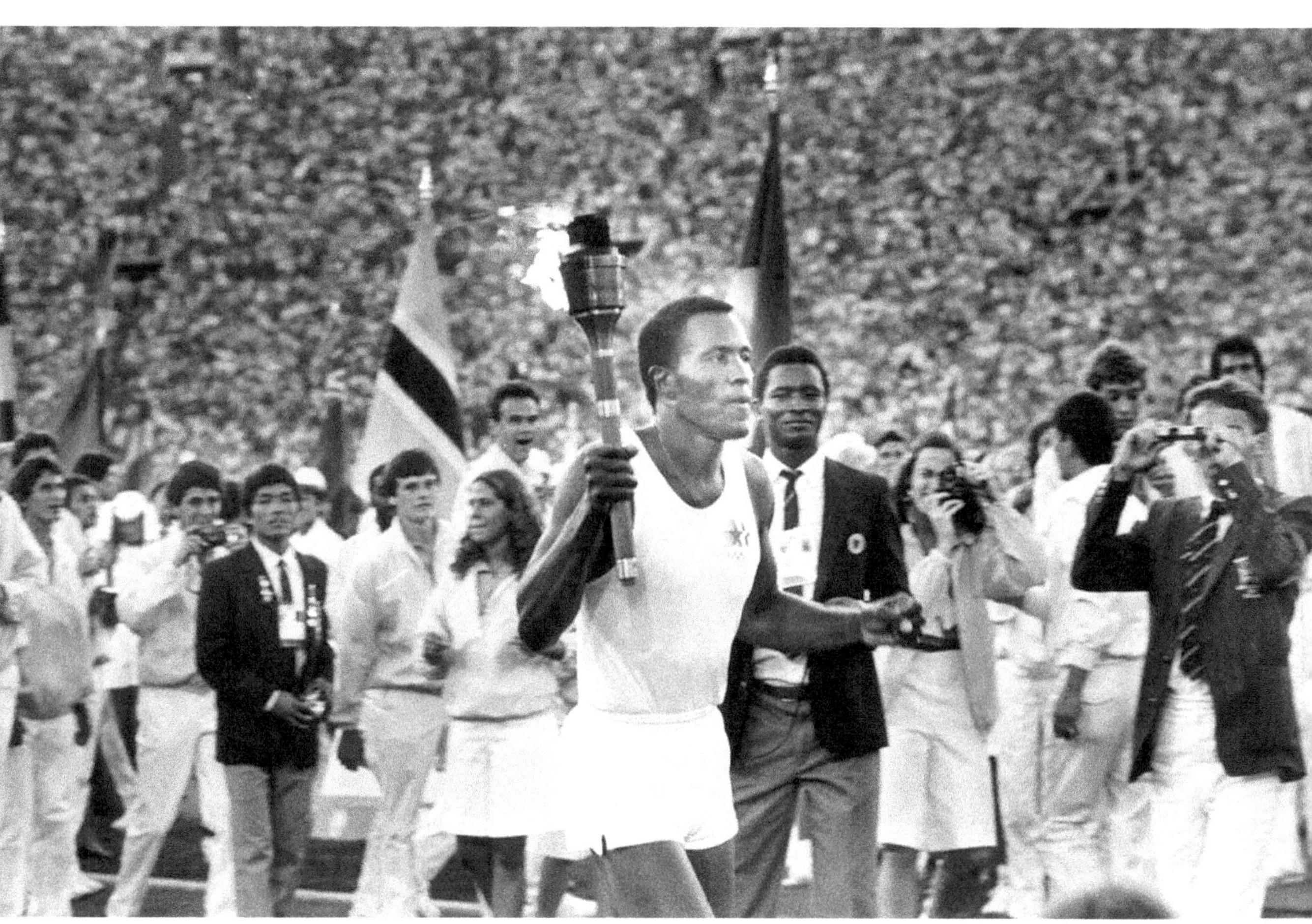

Then, Hemphill handed the torch to Rafer Johnson, decathlon champ at the 1960 Olympics. (Anne Knudsen)

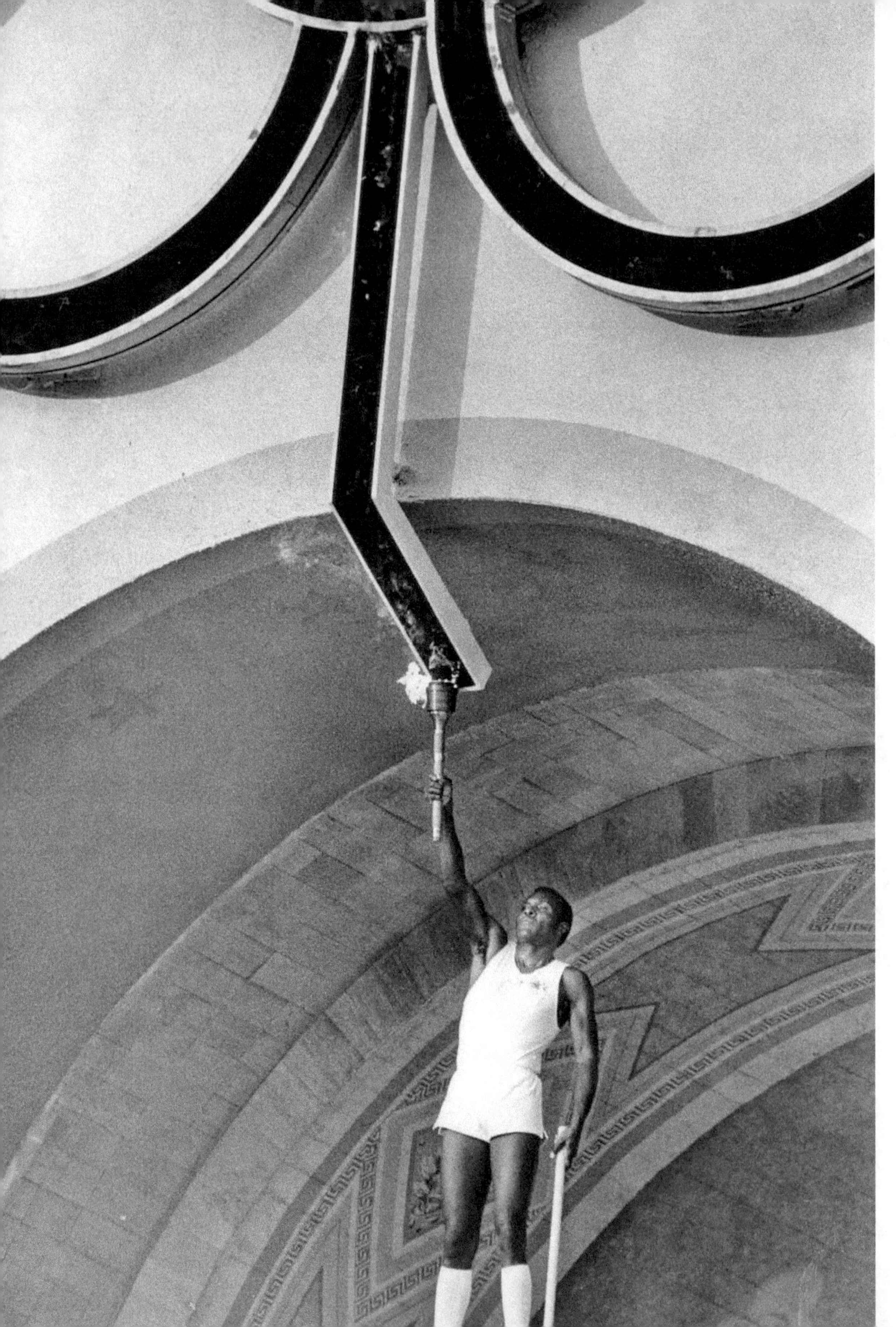

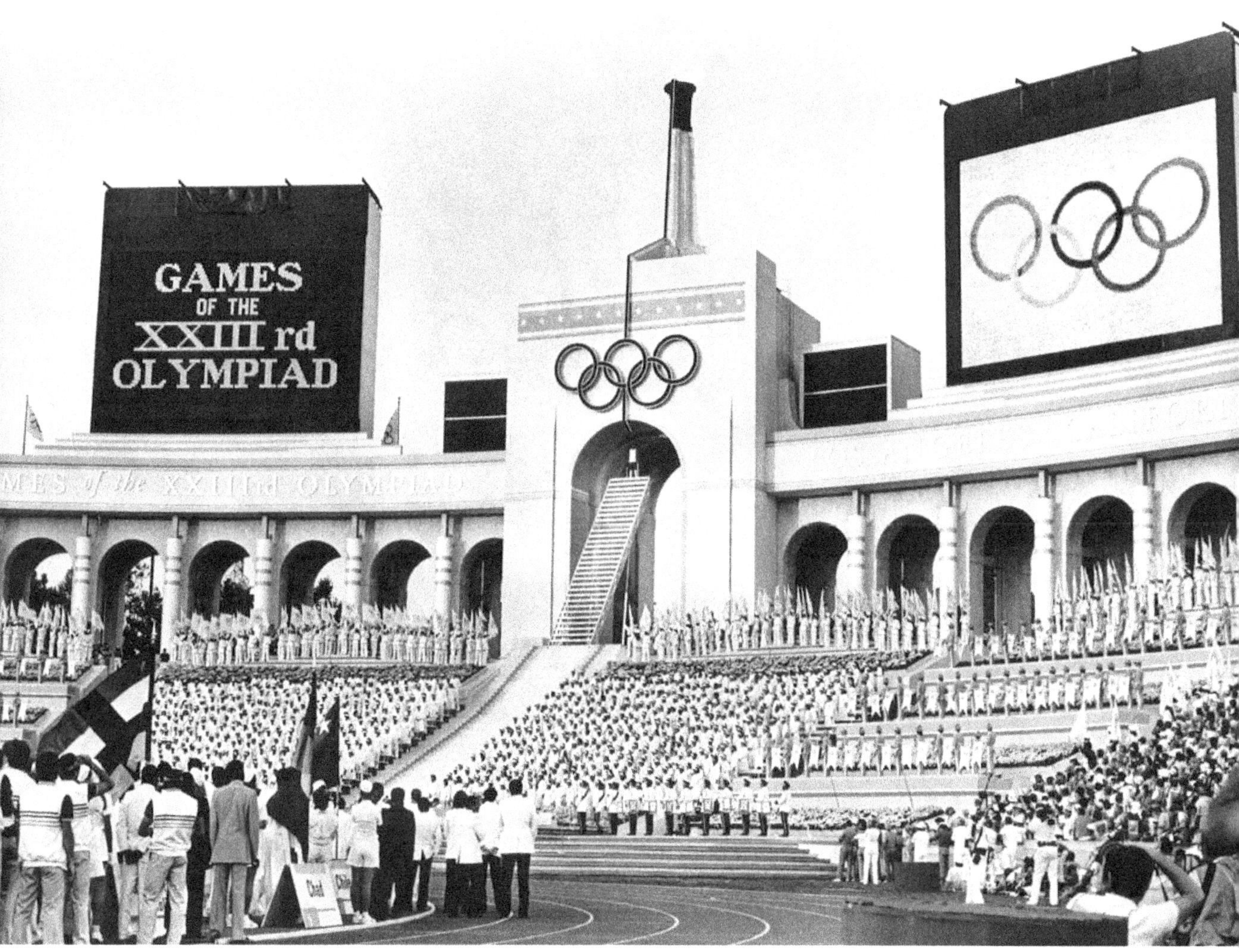

Above and opposite: **Johnson climbed 96 steps to the top of a hydraulic slip-stair by the peristyle arches of the stadium, turned and balanced himself, then ignited the Olympic cauldron. (*Above,* Anne Knudsen • *Opposite,* Paul Chinn)**

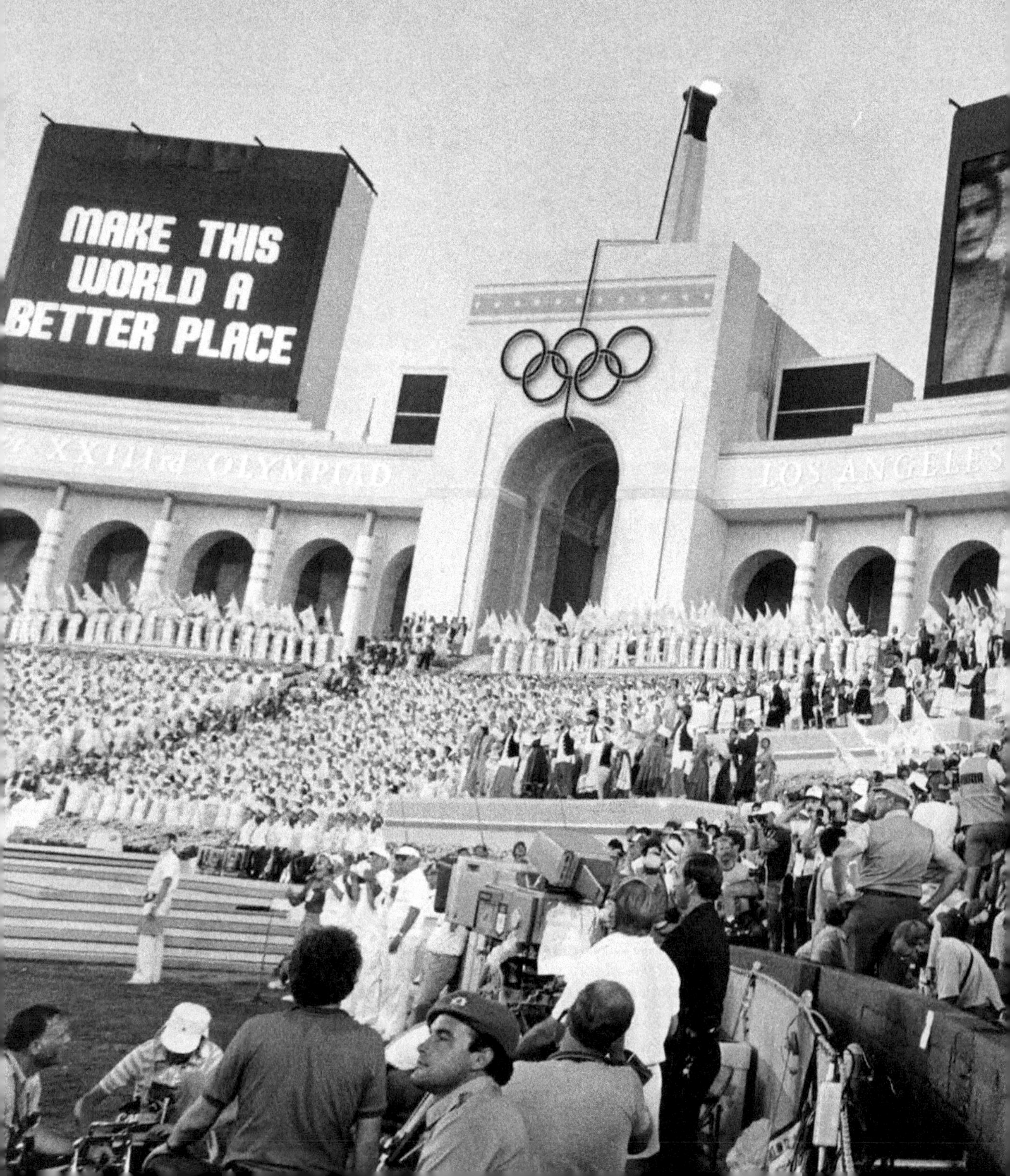
MAKE THIS
WORLD A
BETTER PLACE
OLYMPIAD

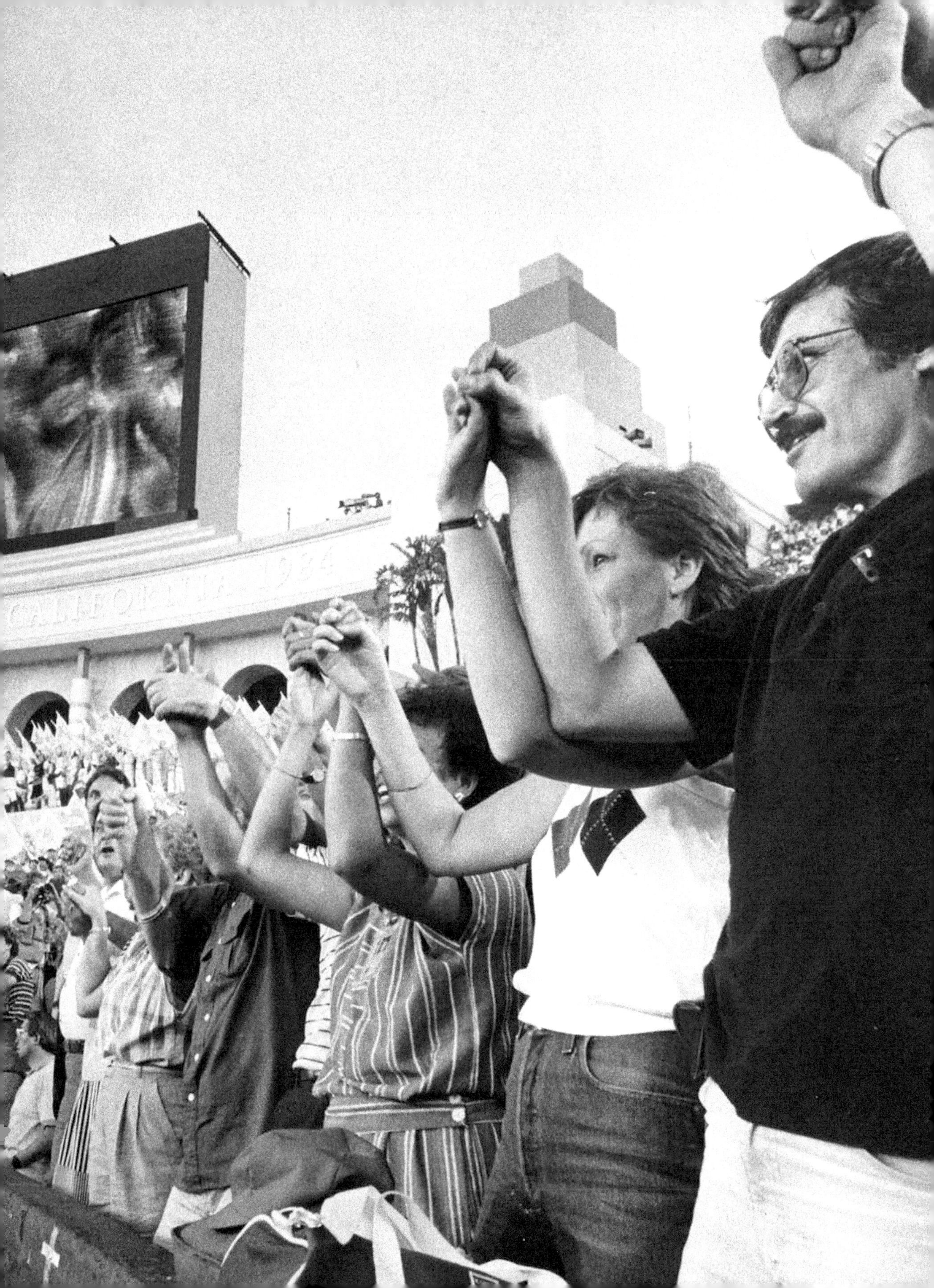
CALIFORNIA 1984

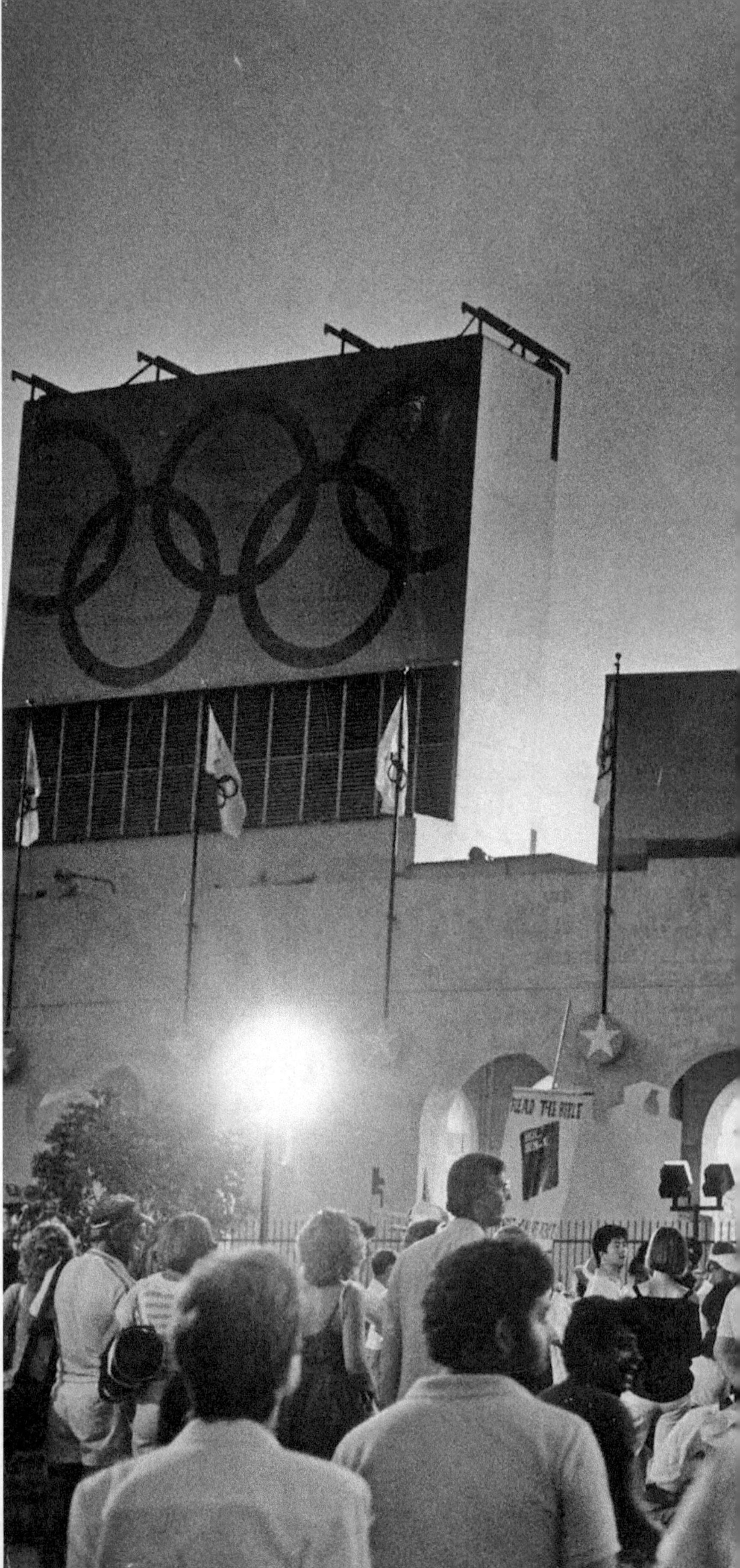

Afterwards, many of the 92,655 spectators lingered. (James Ruebsamen)

Overleaf: At the end of the grand musical overture, spectators linked hands. (Paul Chinn)

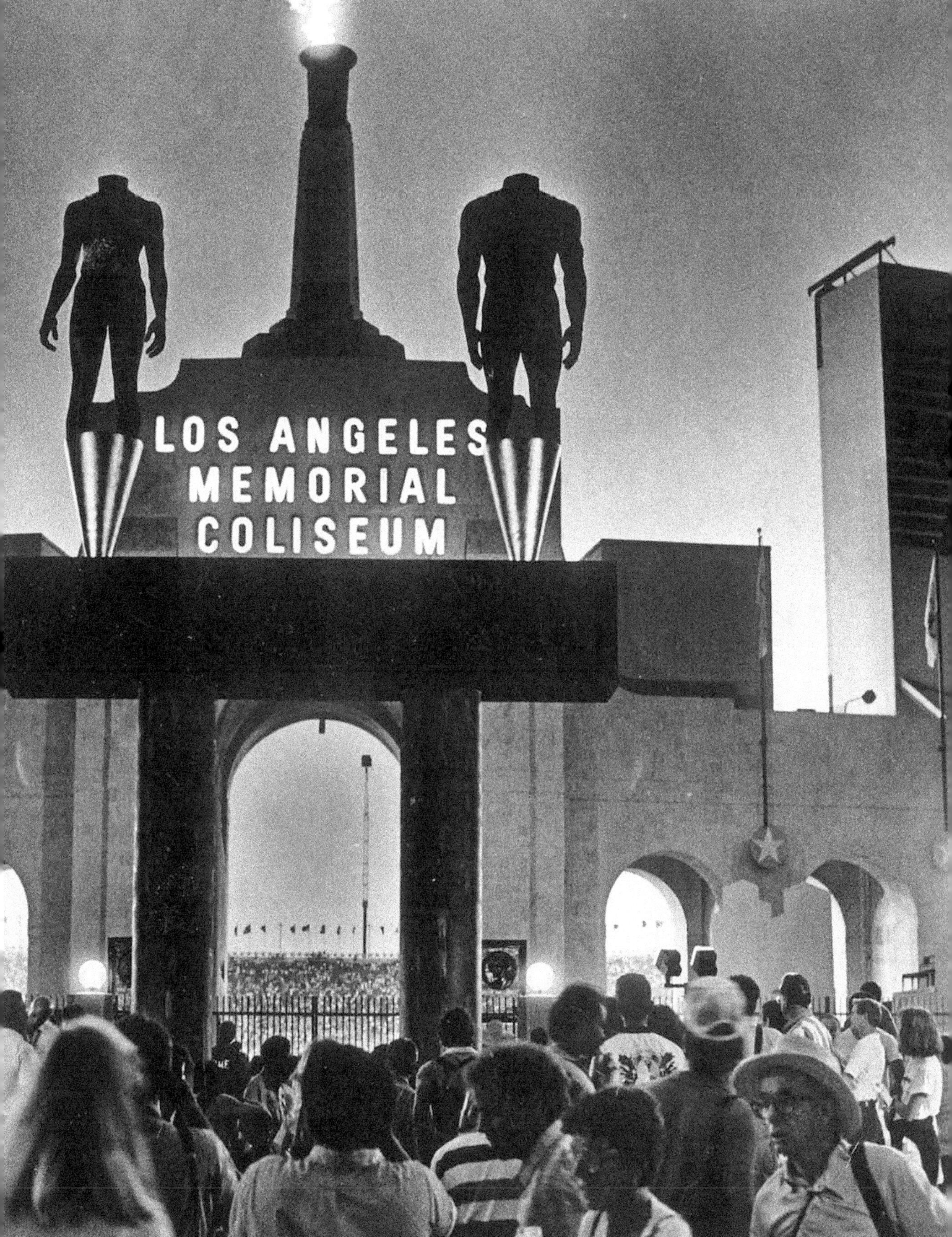
LOS ANGELES
MEMORIAL
COLISEUM

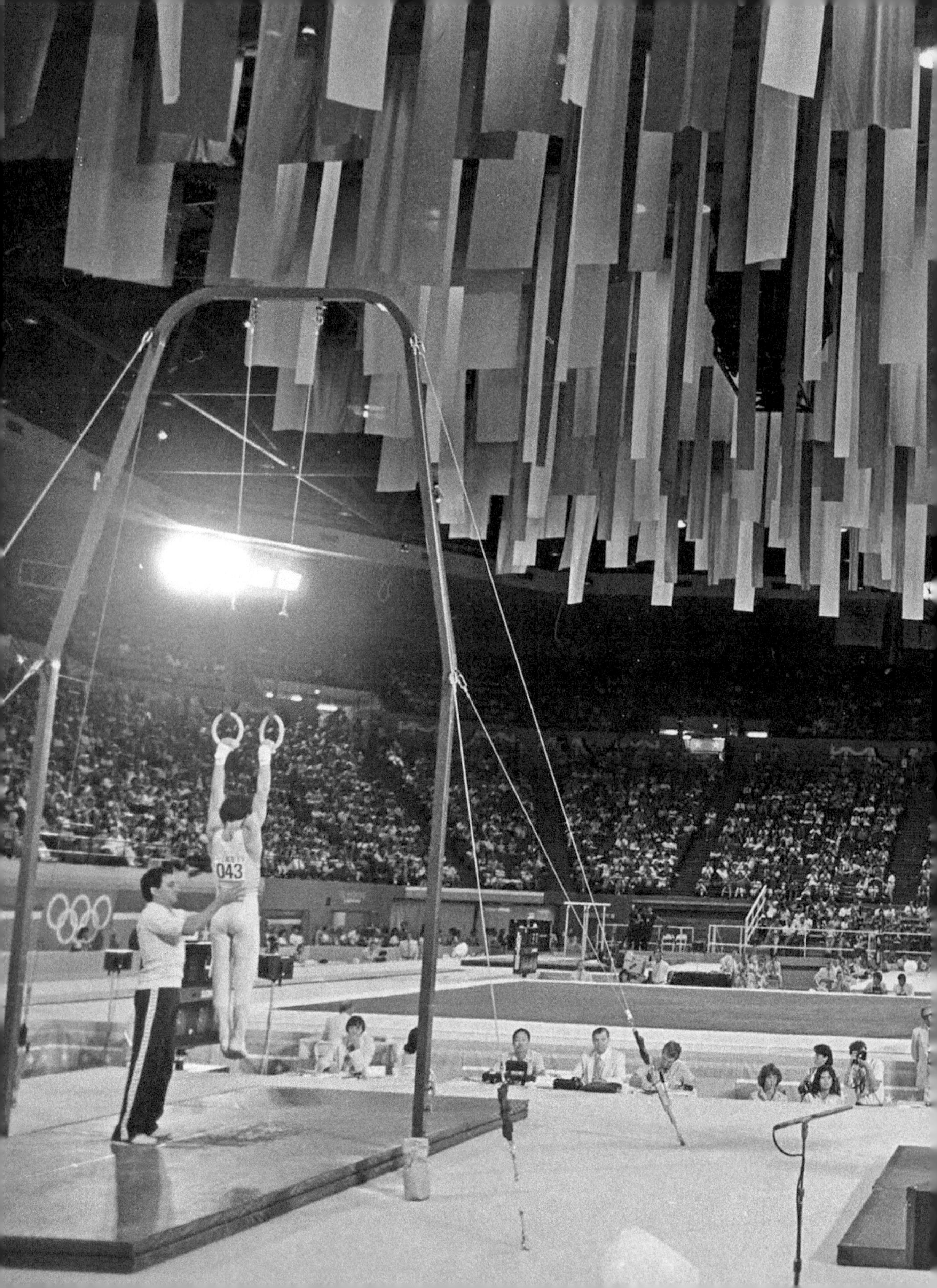
043

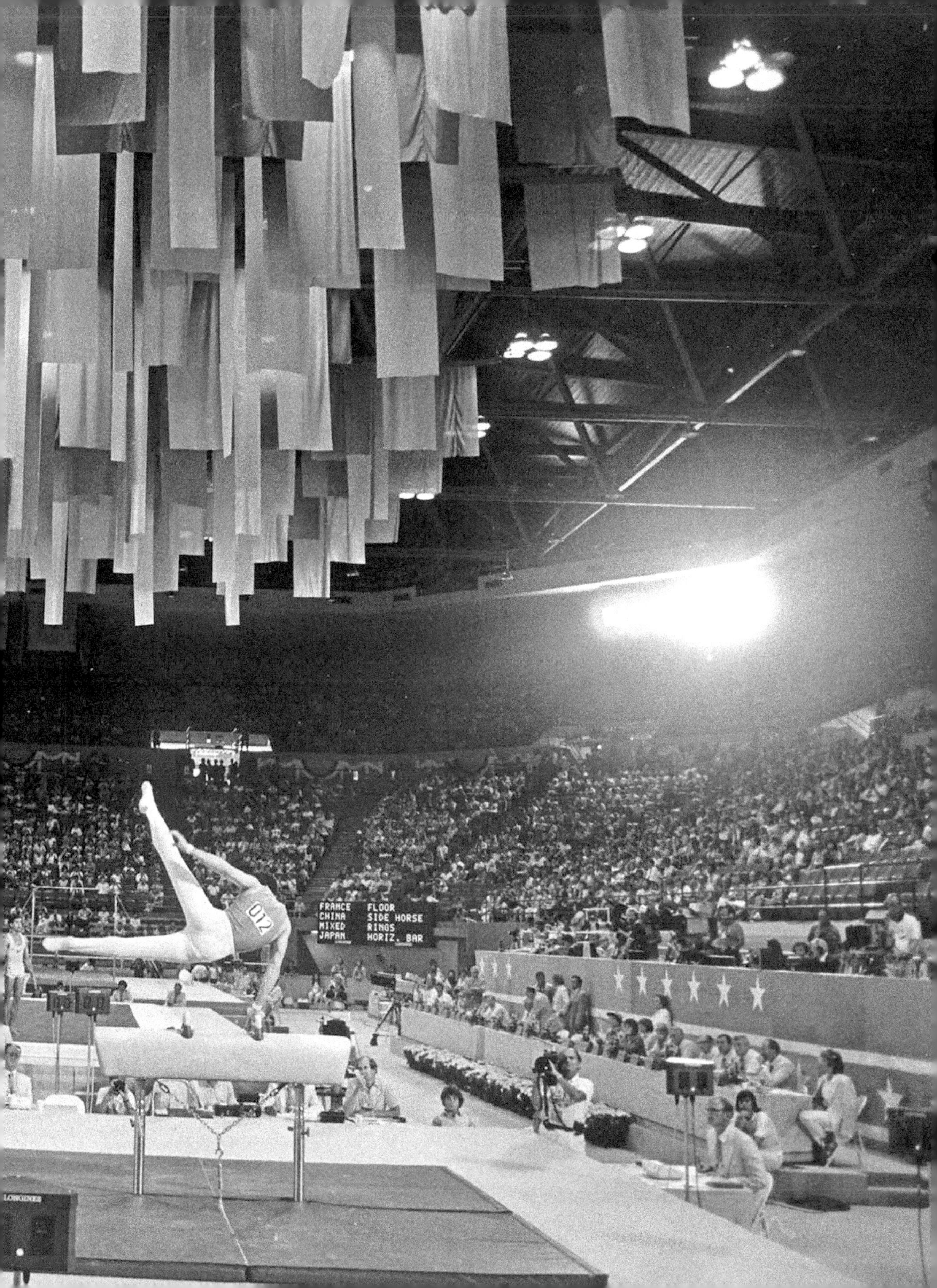
FRANCE FLOOR
CHINA SIDE HORSE
MIXED RINGS
JAPAN HORIZ. BAR
LONGINES

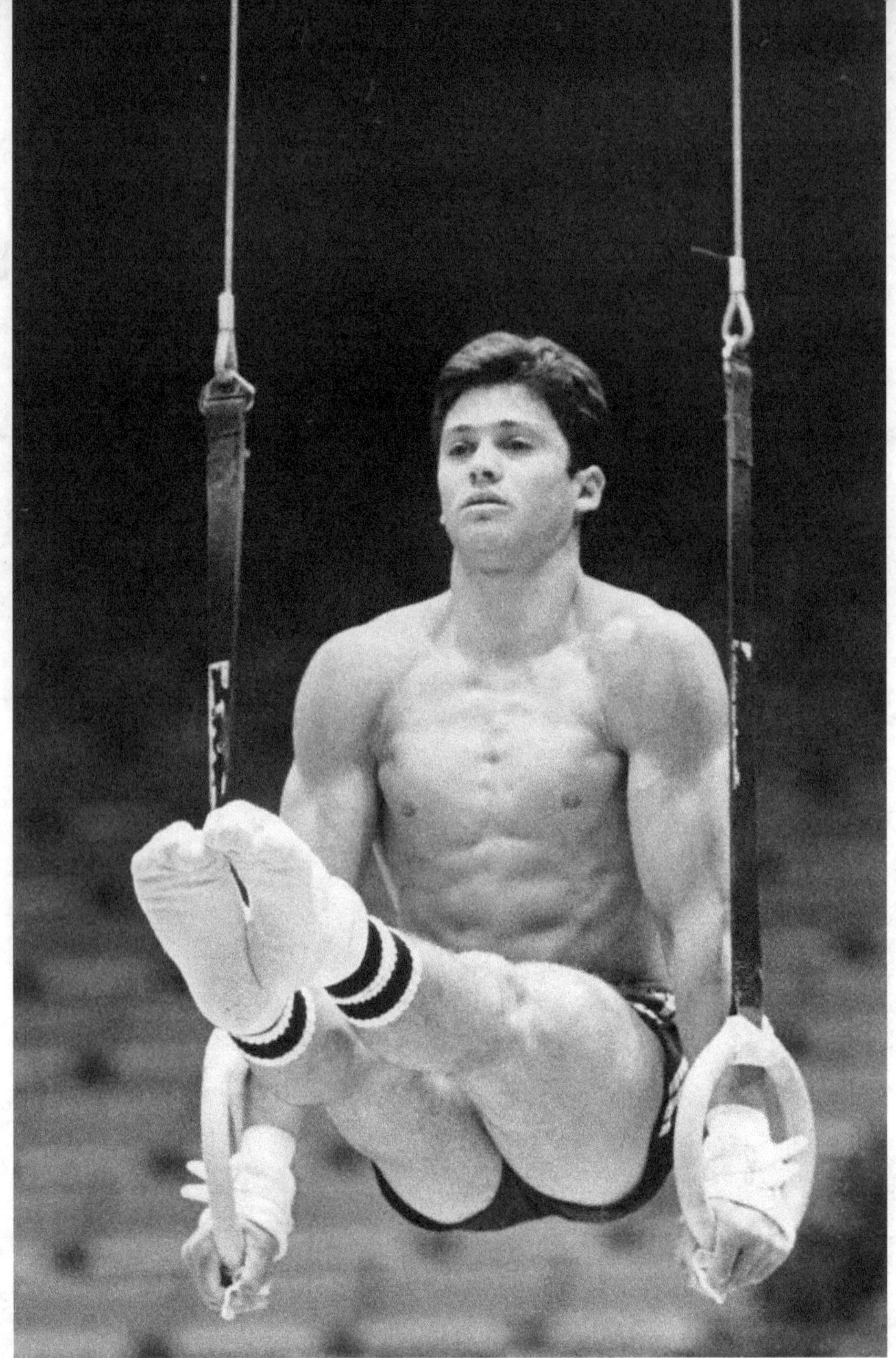

Mitch Gaylord (rings) was a crowd favorite. (*Above,* Paul Chinn • *Opposite,* Anne Knudsen)

***Overleaf:* At Pauley Pavilion, U.S. men gymnasts won the team competition over China. (Anne Knudsen)**

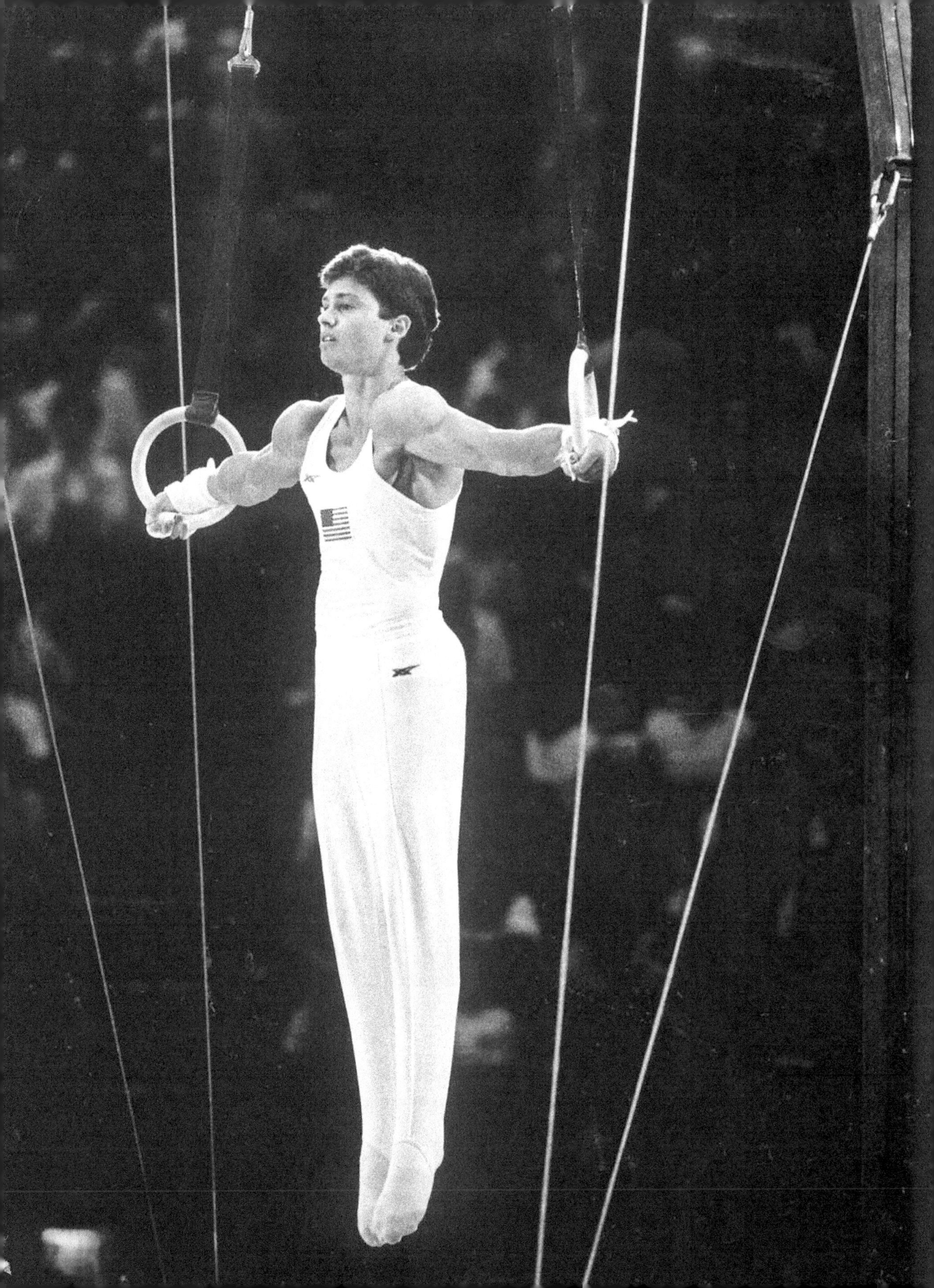

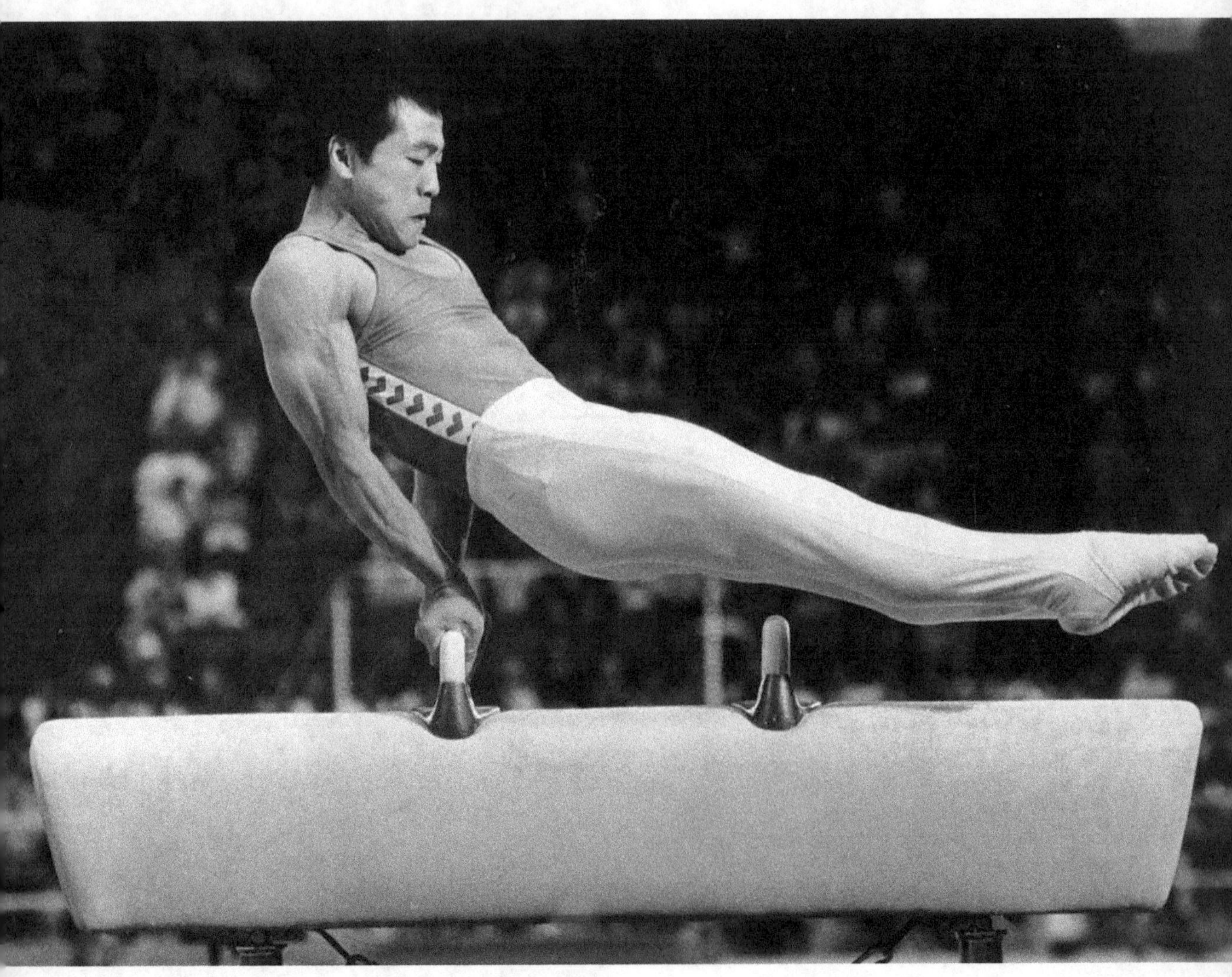

Two routines on the pommel horse: Li Yuejiu's performance (*above*) and American Peter Vidmar (*opposite*). (Anne Knudsen)

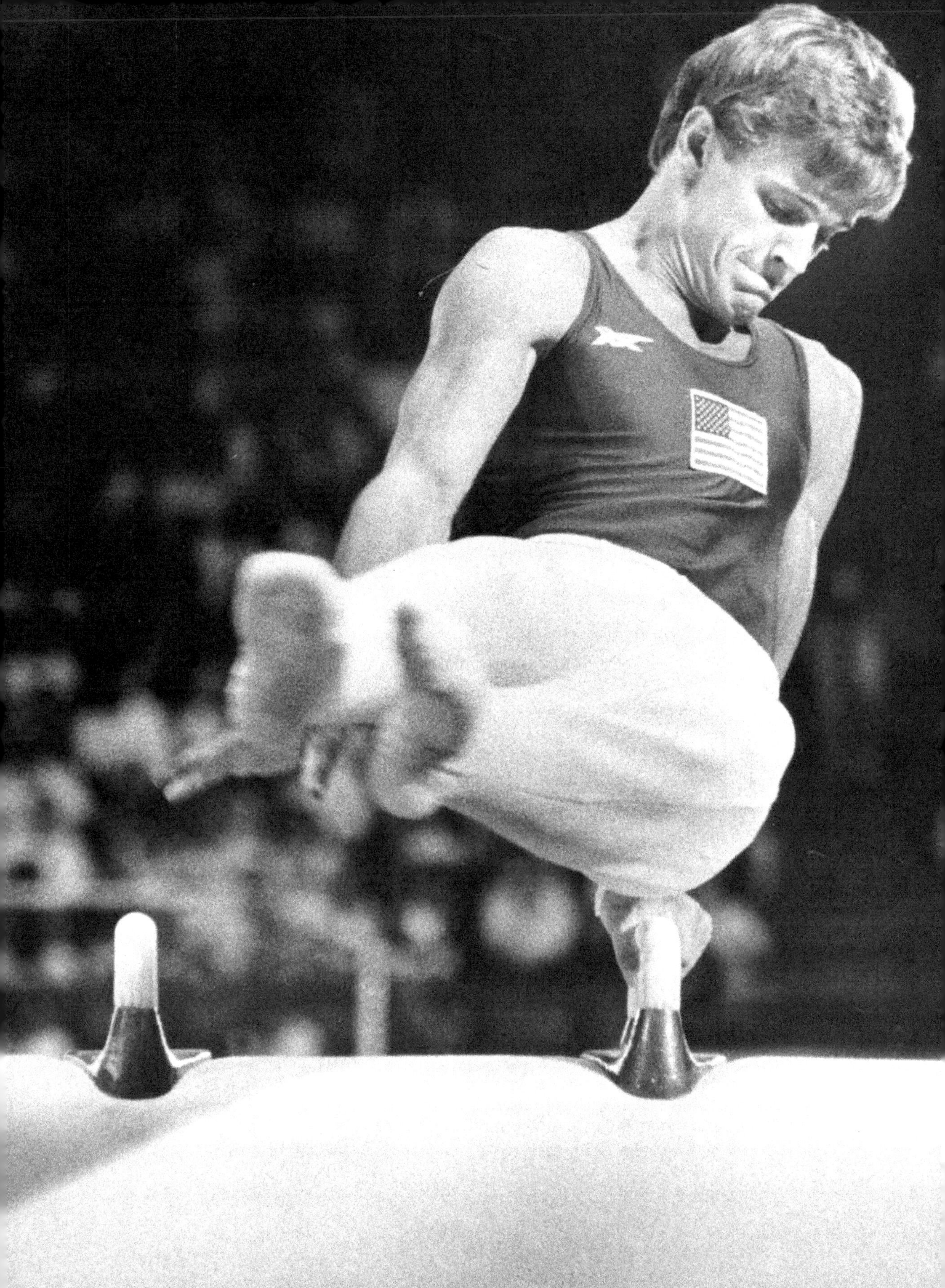

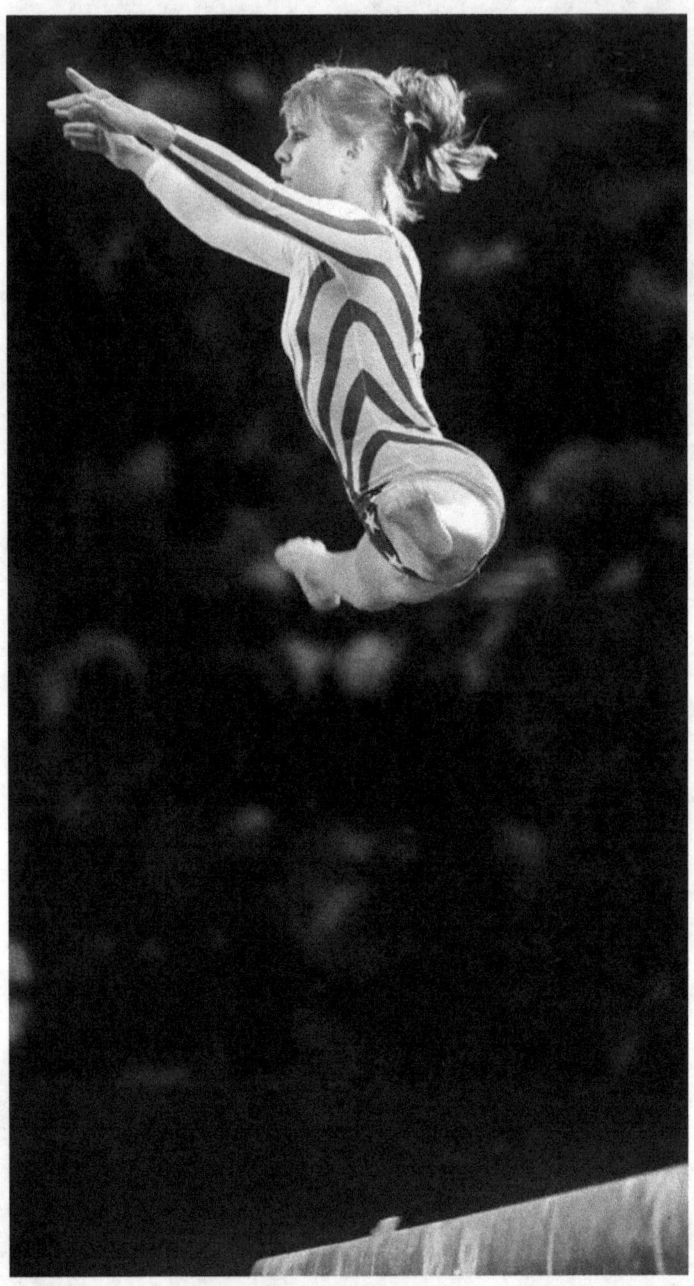

Kathy Johnson (*above*), won a bronze medal in the balance beam. Her teammate Julianne McNamara (*opposite top left and right*) tied for the gold medal on the uneven bars, took second in floor exercise, and was fourth in the individual all-around. Ecaterina Szabo (*opposite bottom*) won three individual gold medals and led Romania to victory in the team competition. (Anne Knudsen)

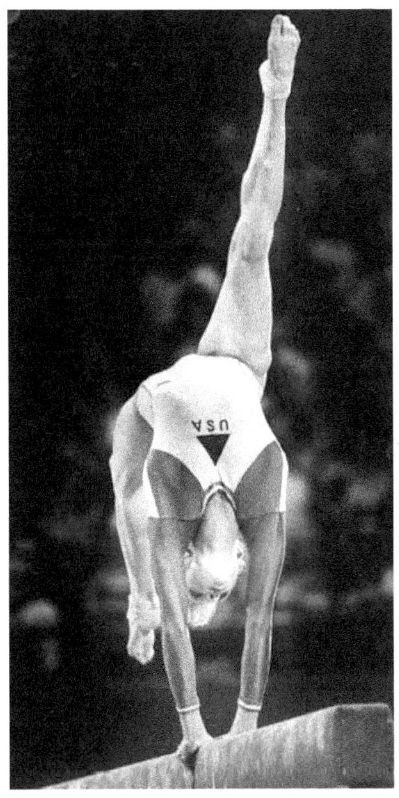
USA

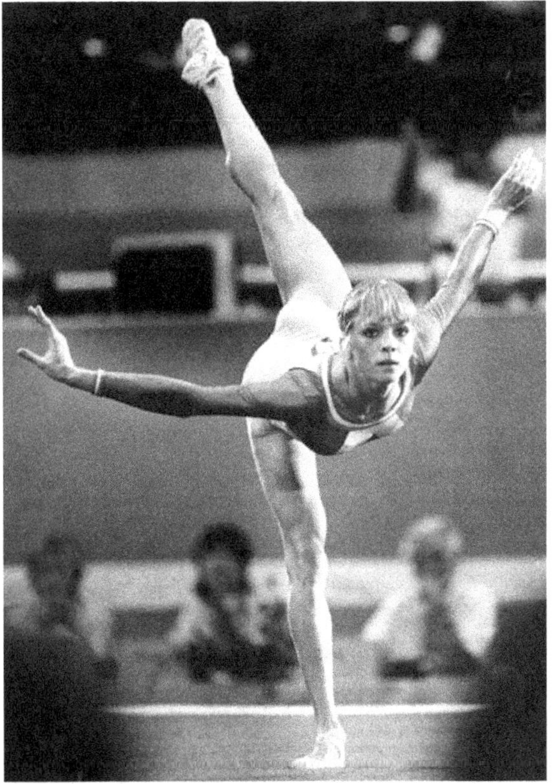

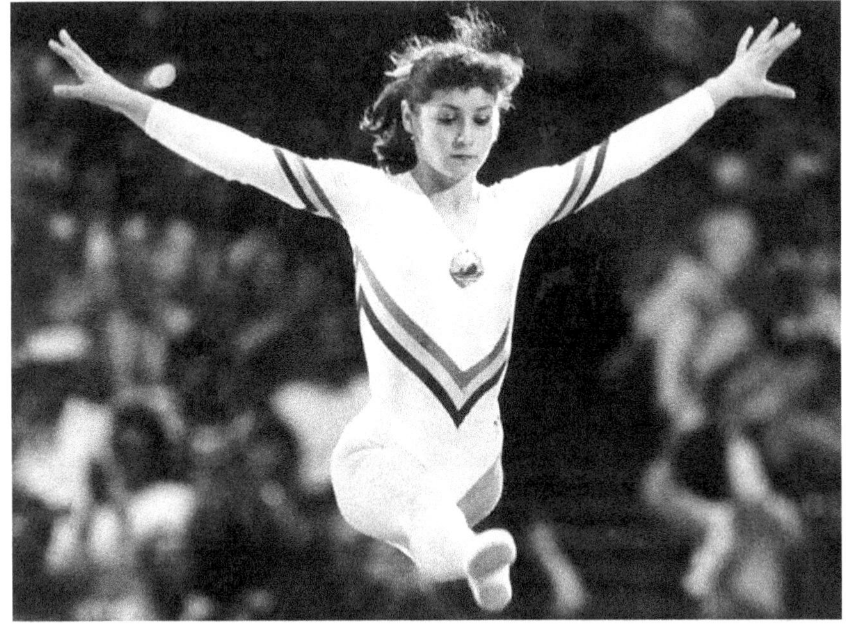

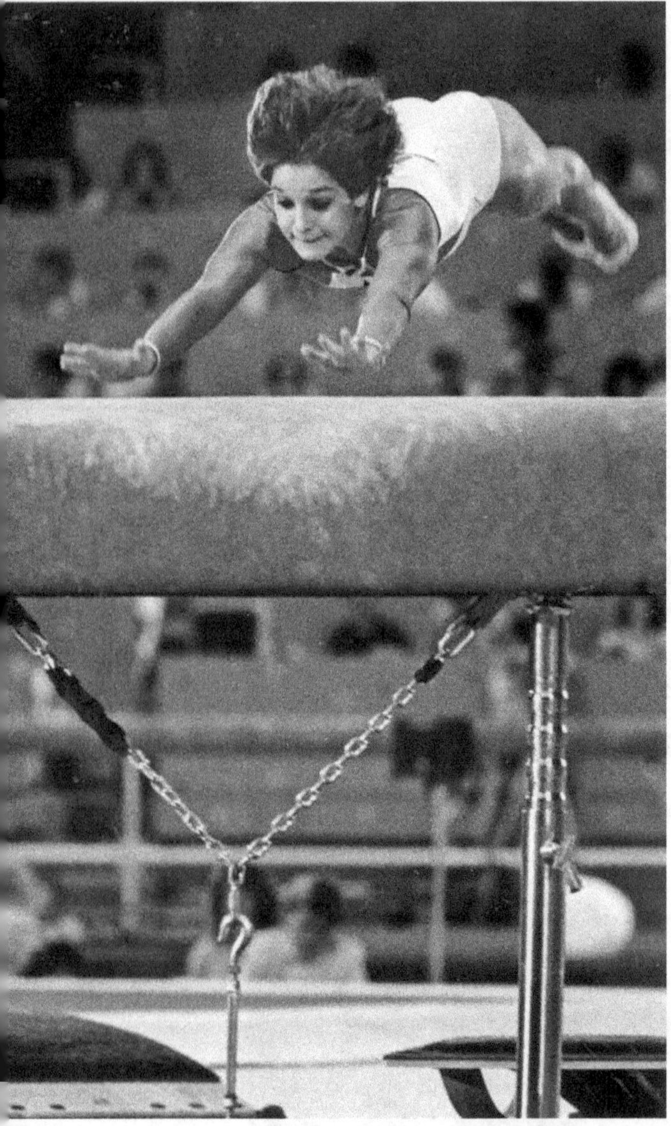

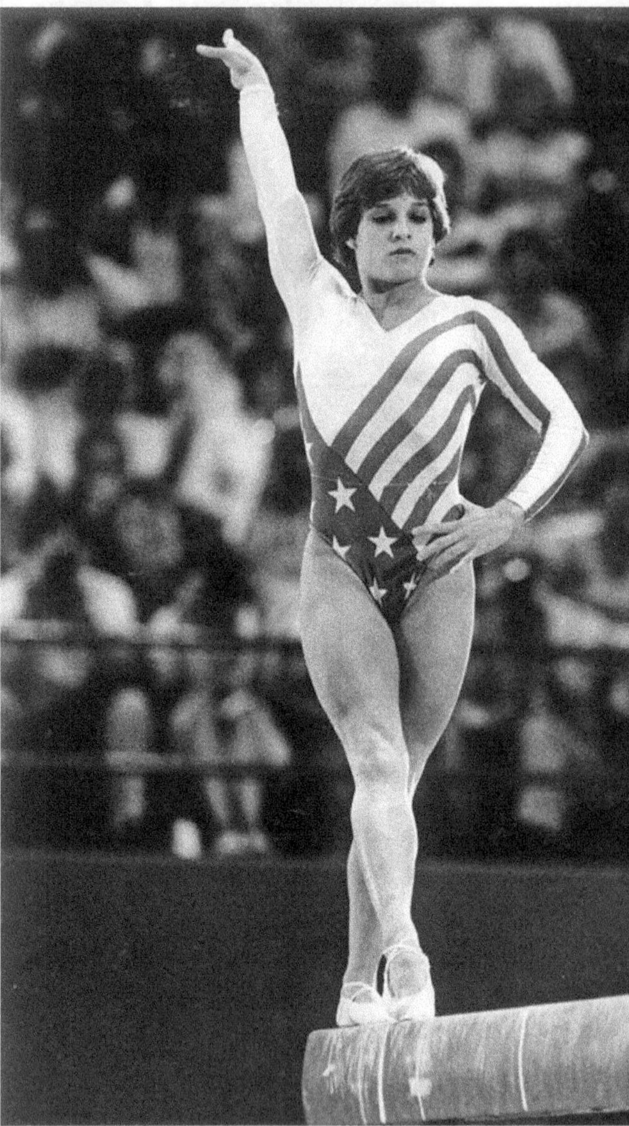

Above and opposite: **Like Olga Korbut and Nadia Comaneci before her, Mary Lou Retton emerged as an Olympic sensation. Just 16, she scored two perfects 10s and became the first U.S. woman to win the individual all-around. (Anne Knudsen)**

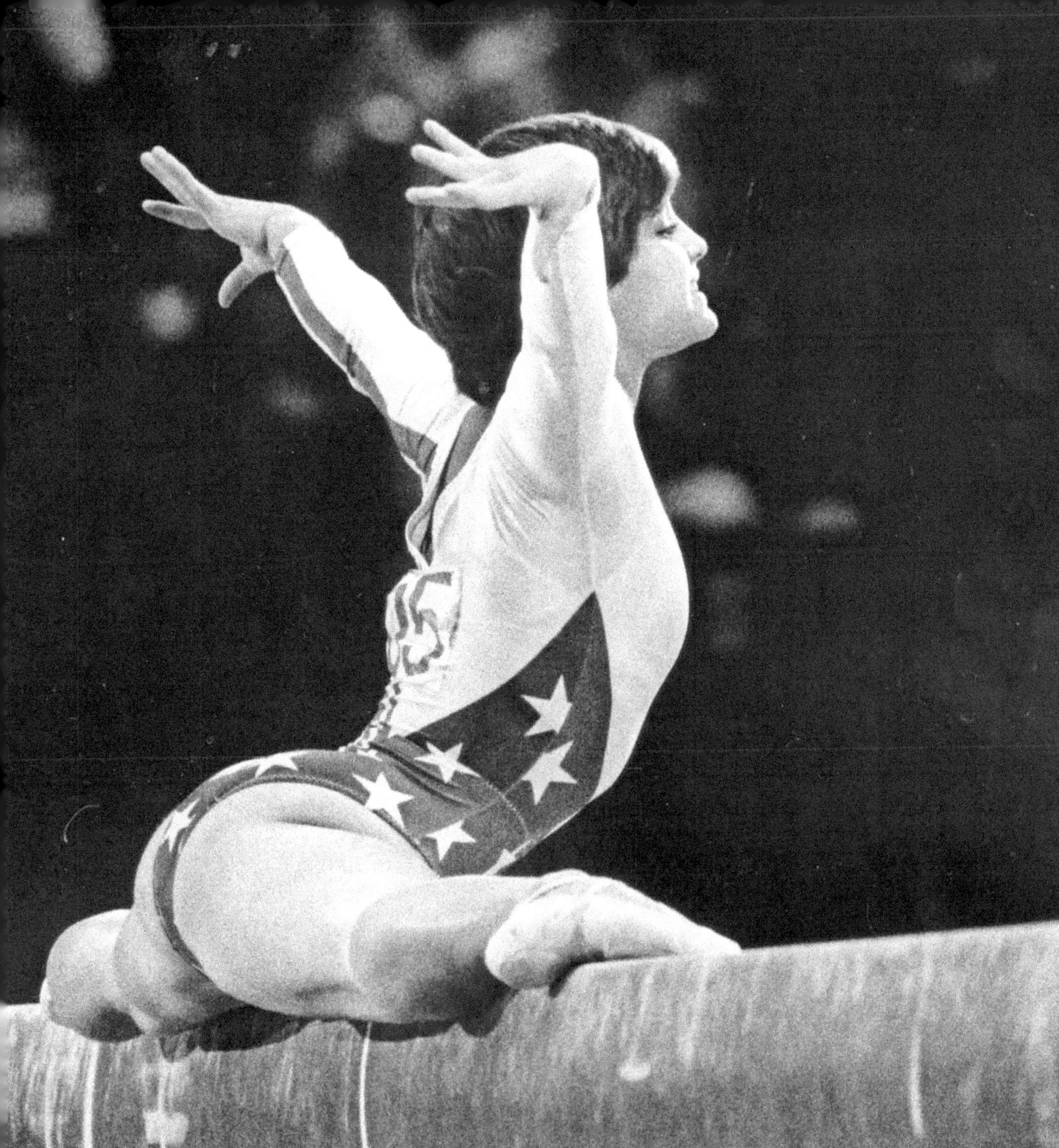

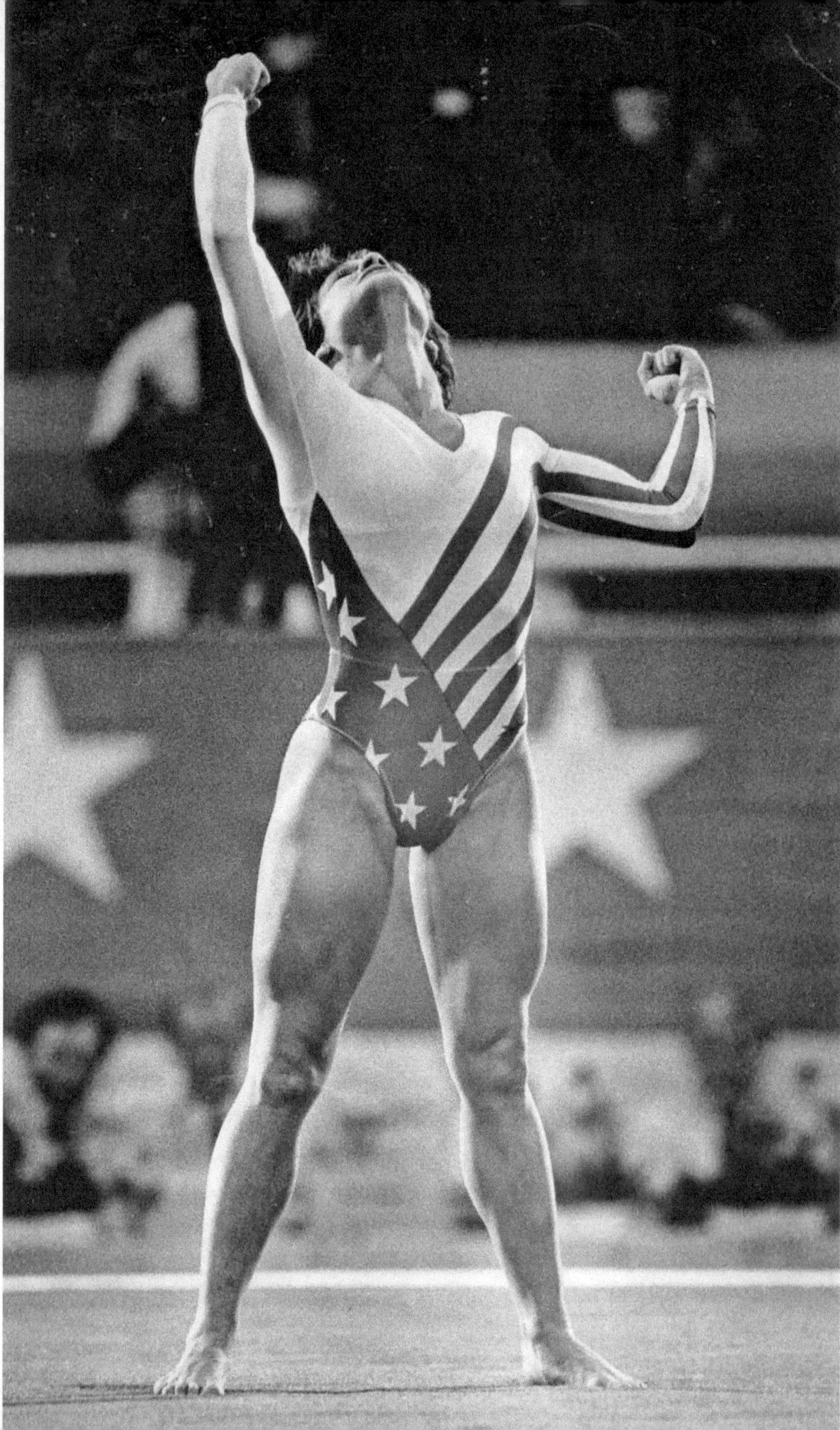

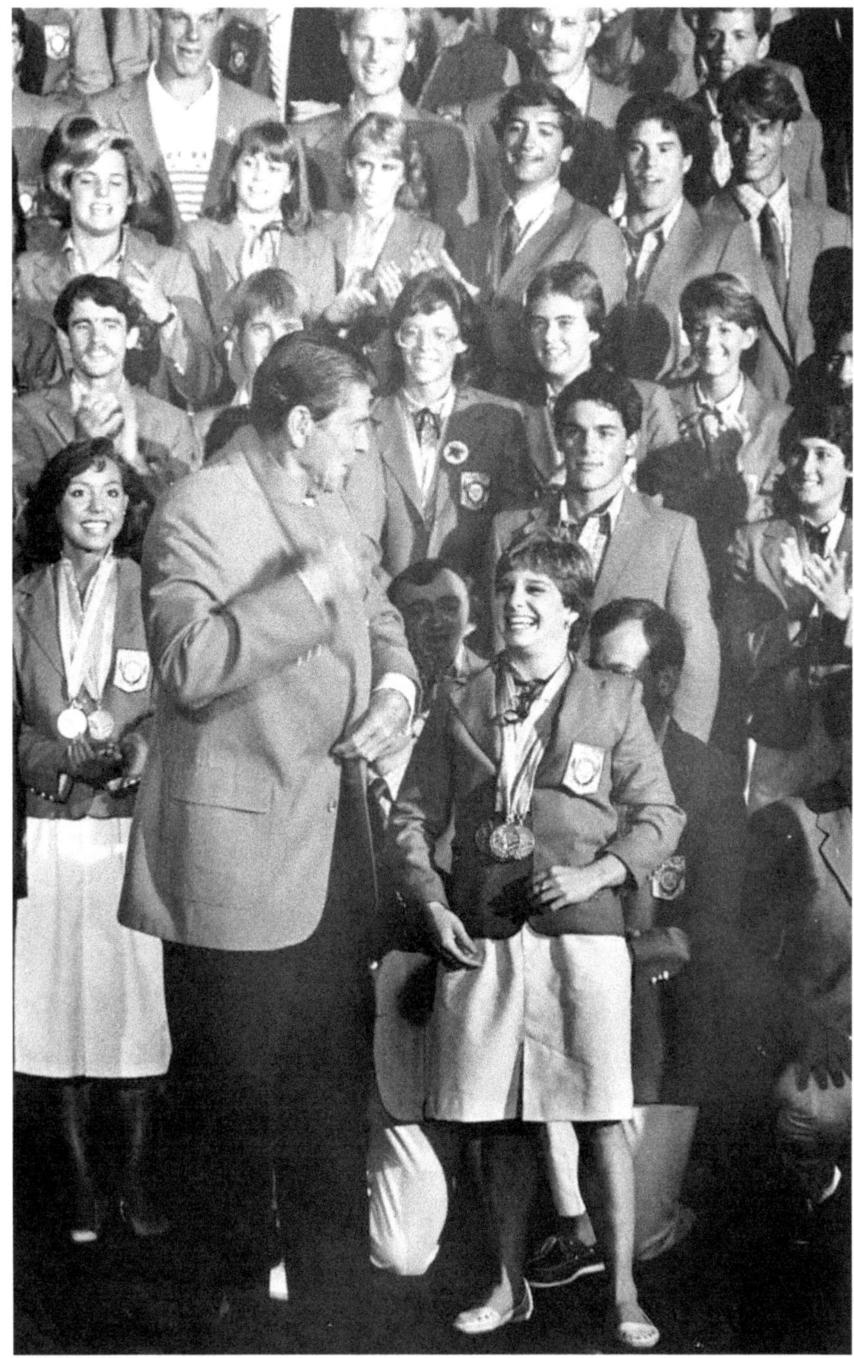

She even had time to help President Ronald Reagan with his blazer.
(*Above,* Mike Mullen • *Opposite,* Anne Knudsen)

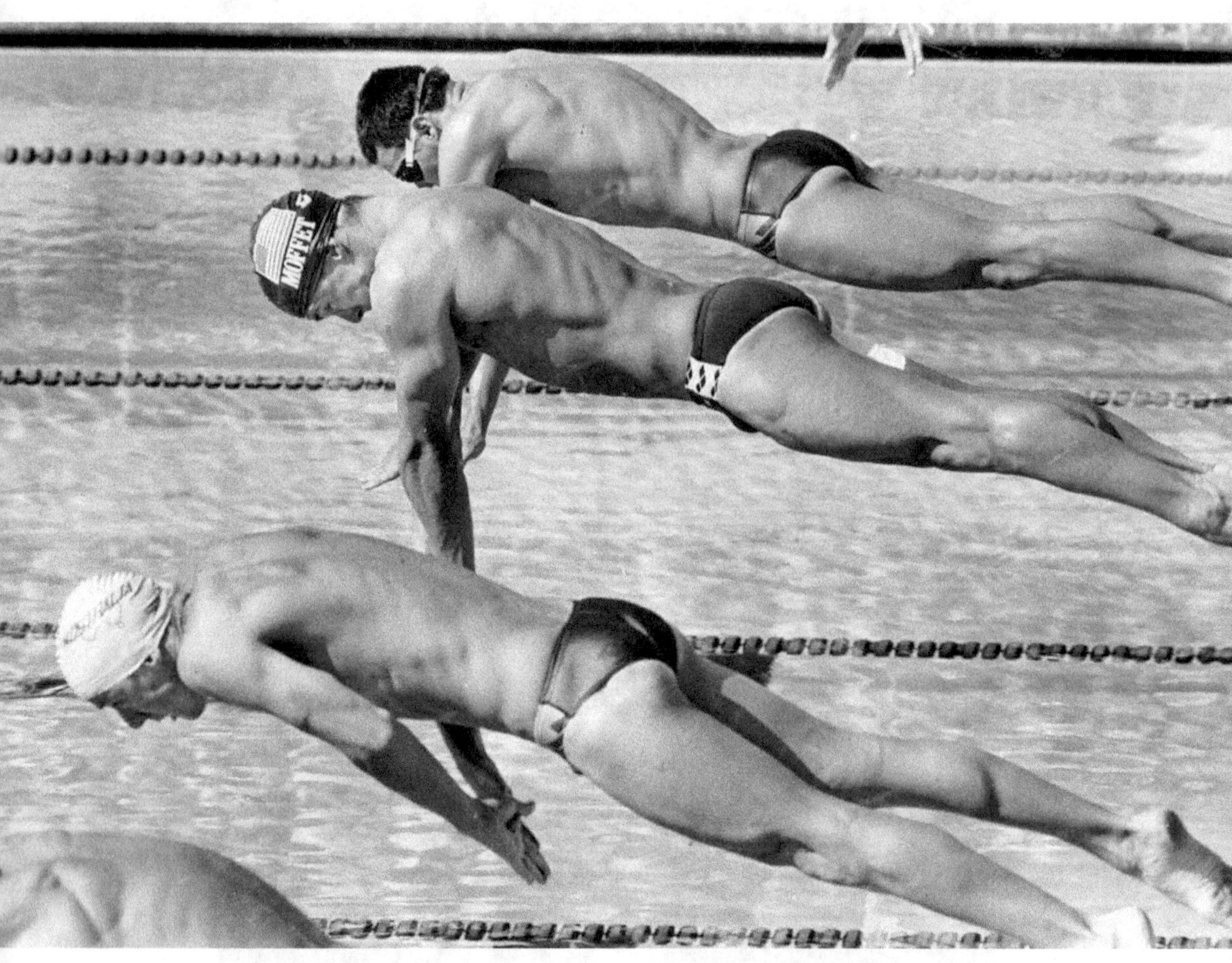

John Moffet (*center*) at the start of the 100-meter breaststroke at the Olympic Swim Stadium on the campus of USC. Moffet finished fifth. (Javier Mendoza)

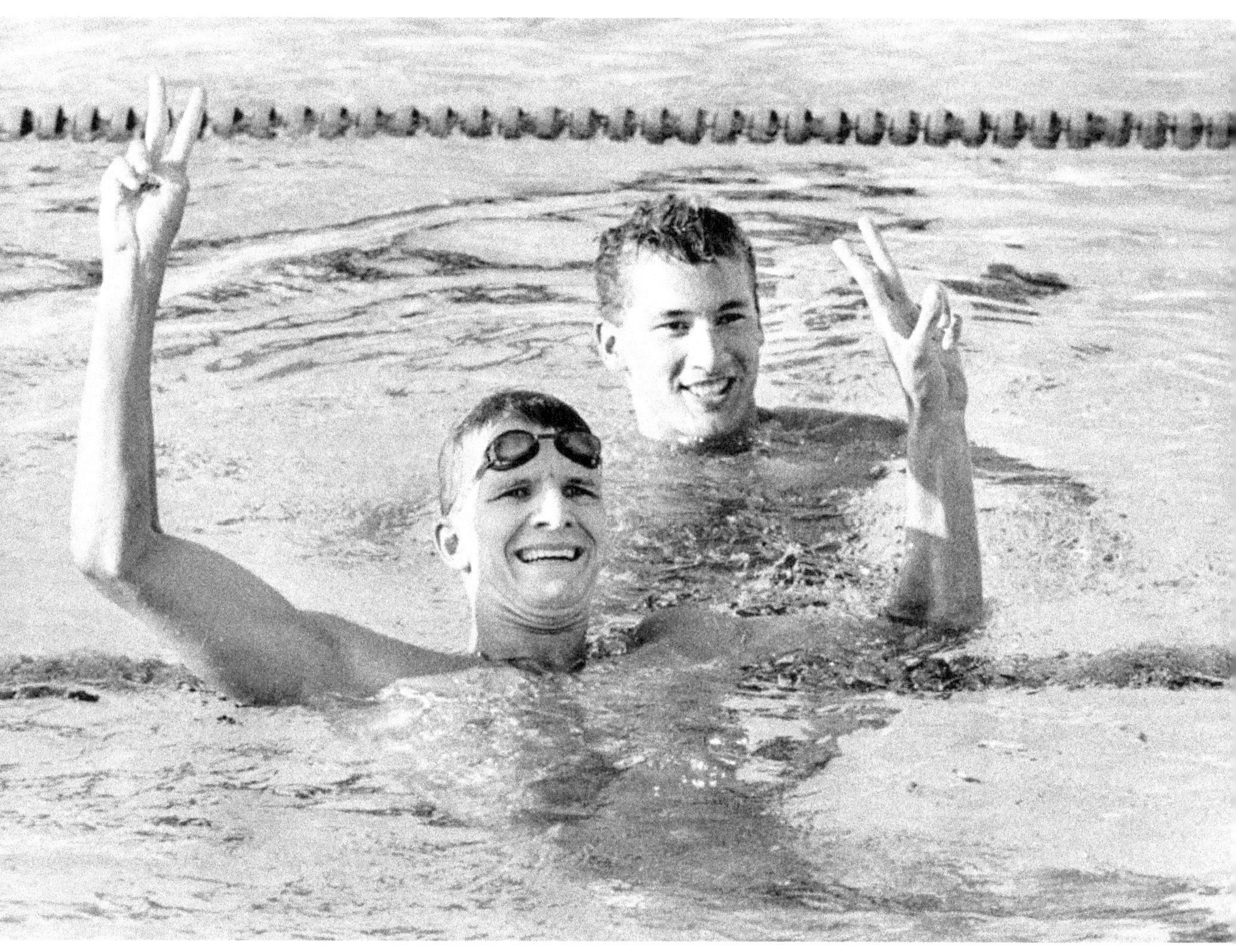

West Germany's Michael Gross (*foreground*), nicknamed "The Albatross," won two gold medals and celebrated his victory in the 200-meter freestyle. (Javier Mendoza)

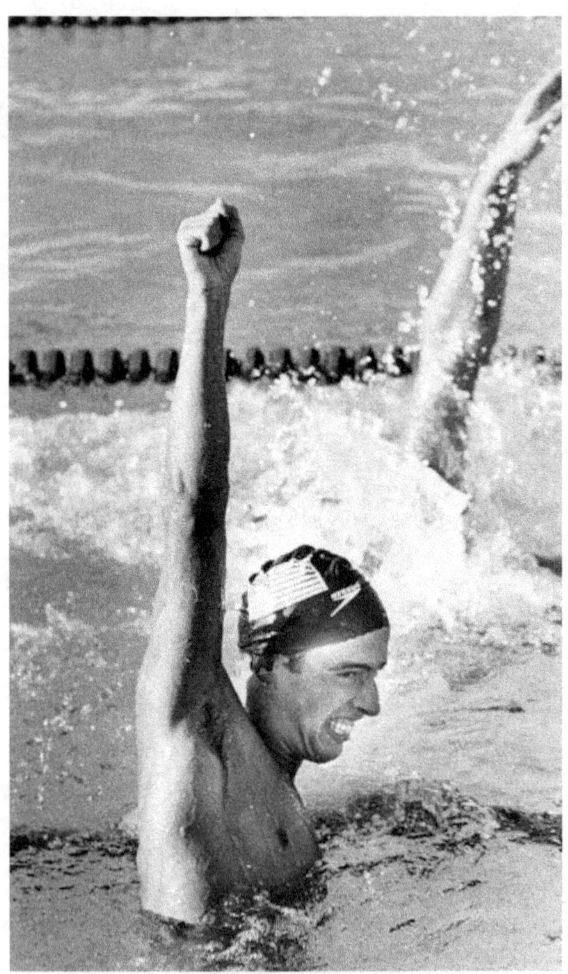

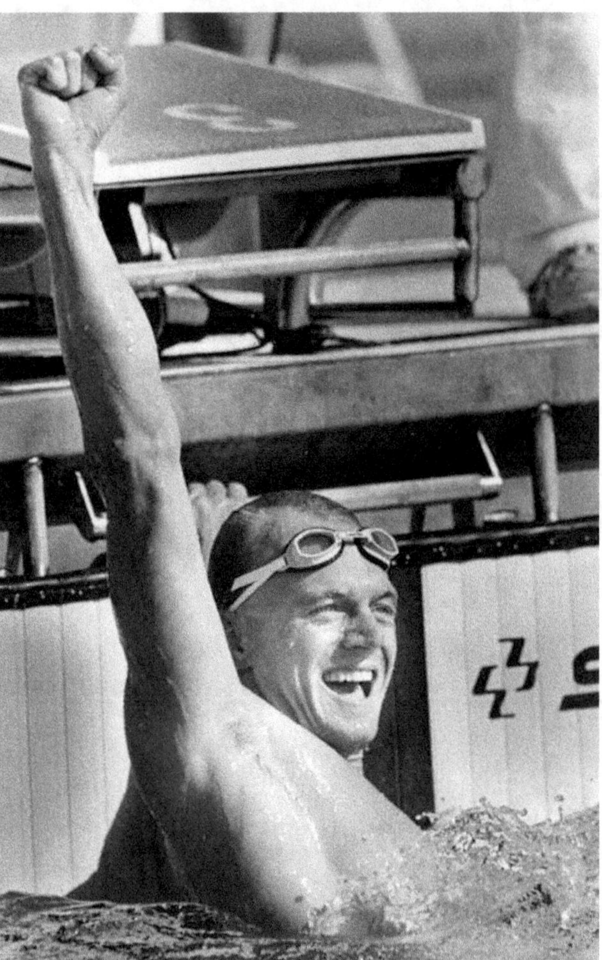

Left: **Bruce Hayes thrust his fist in the air after holding off Michael Gross in the final leg of the 4x200-meter freestyle relay for the gold medal. •** ***Right:*** **Rowdy Gaines exulted after his record-setting victory in the 100-meter freestyle. (Javier Mendoza)**

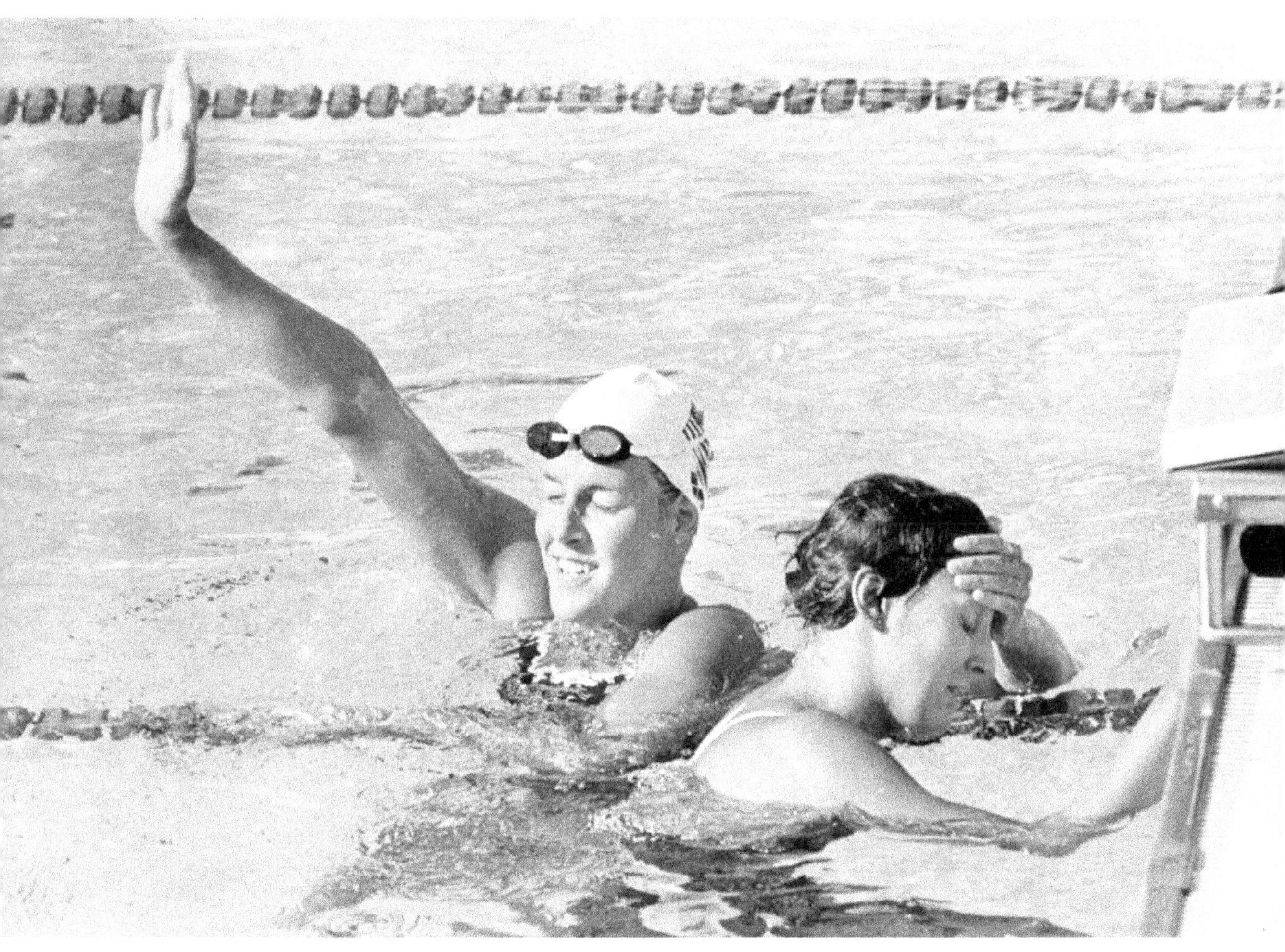

Thrill of victory, agony of defeat: Tracy Caulkins celebrated her victory in the 400-meter individual medley, while teammate Sue Heon finished fourth. (Javier Mendoza)

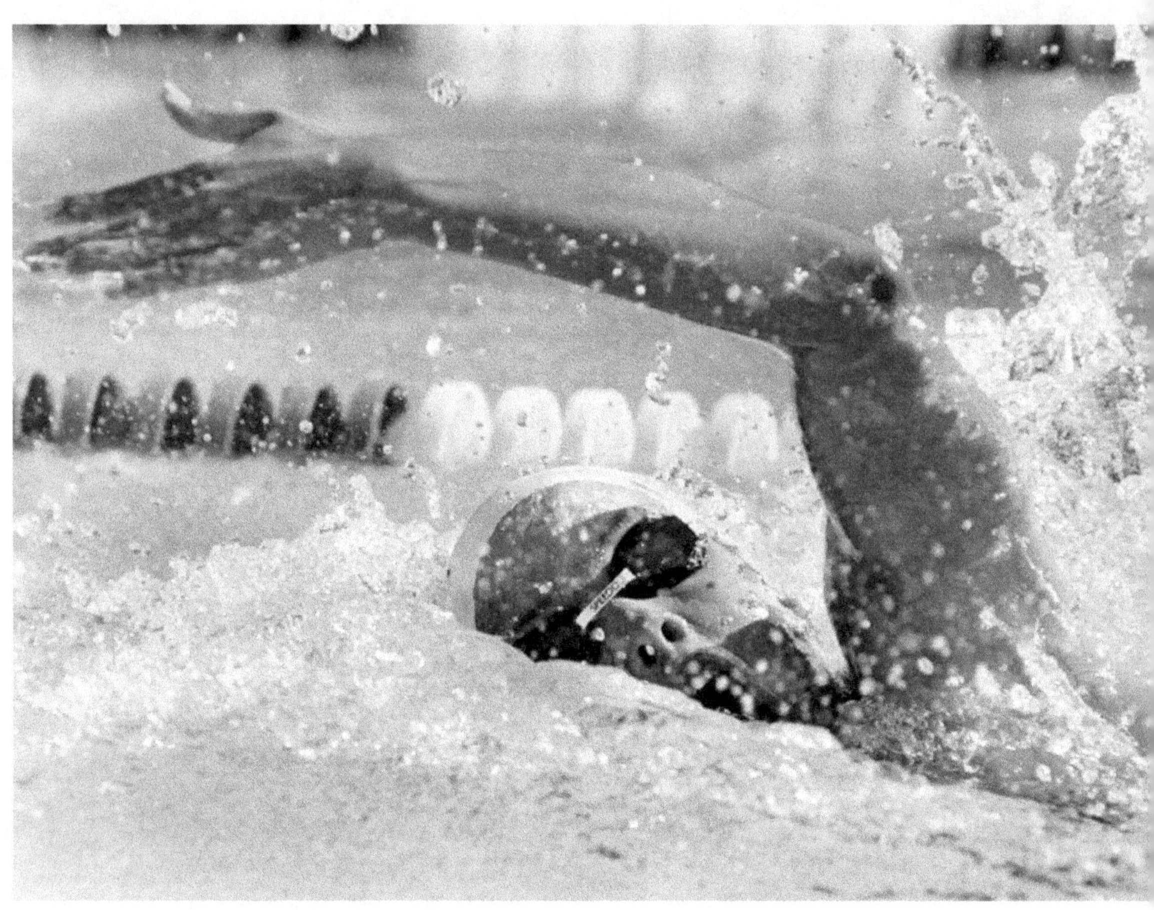

Tiffany Cohen, en route to setting an Olympic record in the 400-meter freestyle, won two gold medals. (Javier Mendoza)

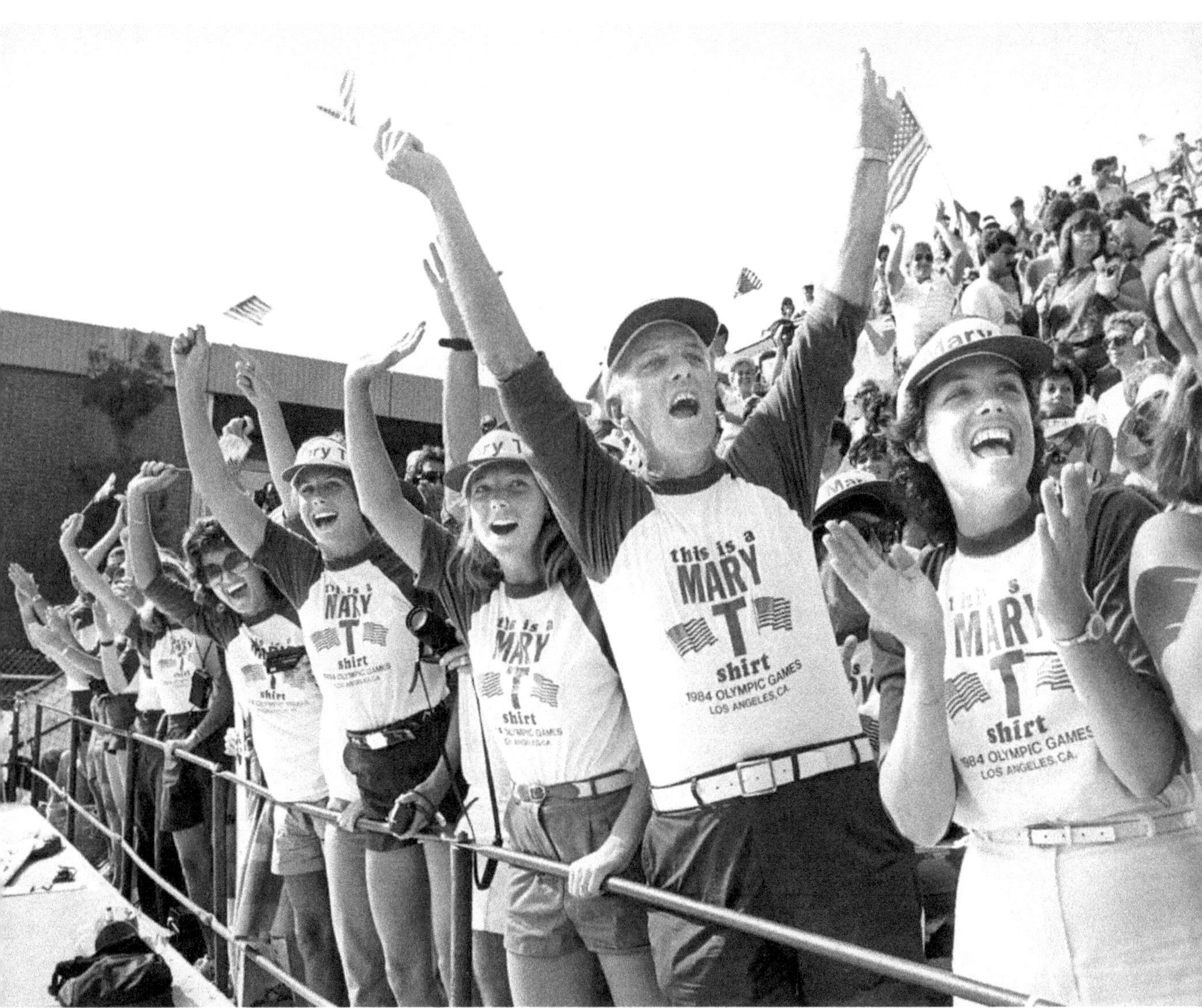

Fans of Mary T. Meagher (including her father, second from right) donned T-shirts and cheered her on to the gold medal in the 100-meter butterfly. (Javier Mendoza)

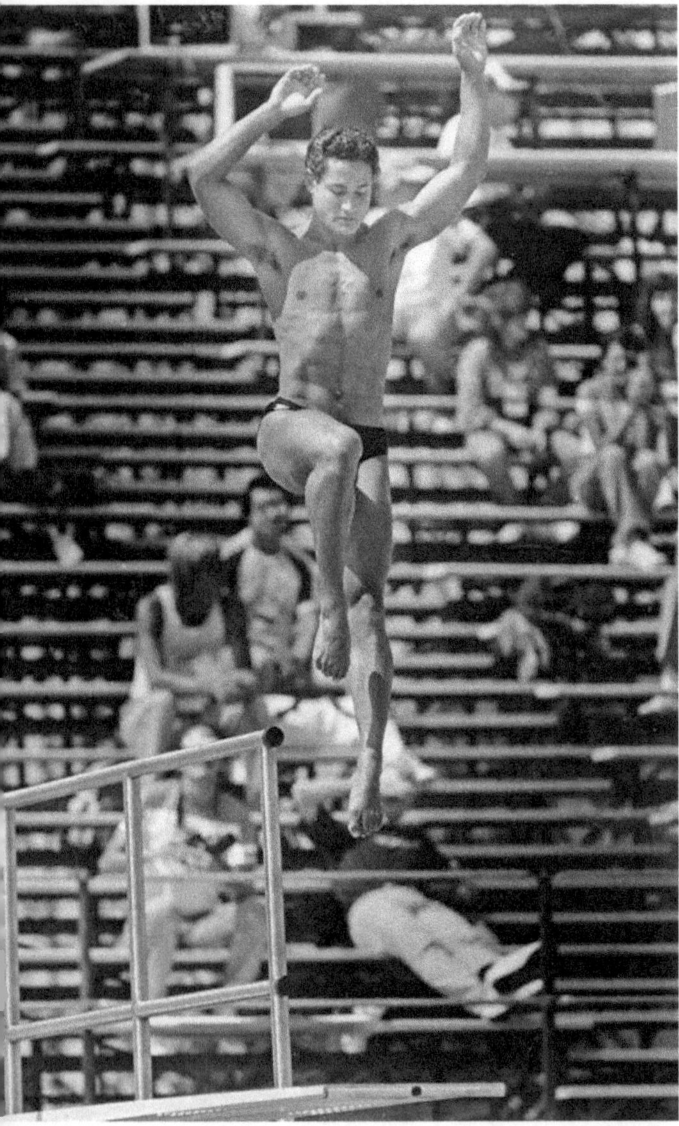

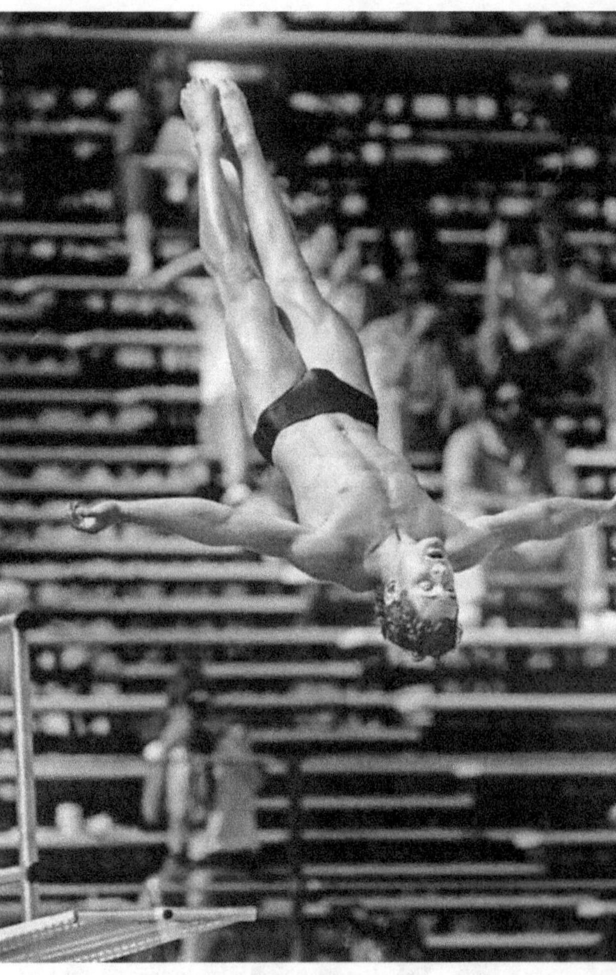

Above, opposite, page 82: **Greg Louganis dominated the diving competition, winning the gold medal in the 3-meter springboard and 10-meter platform events, leading to a tearful victory ceremony. (Anne Knudsen)**

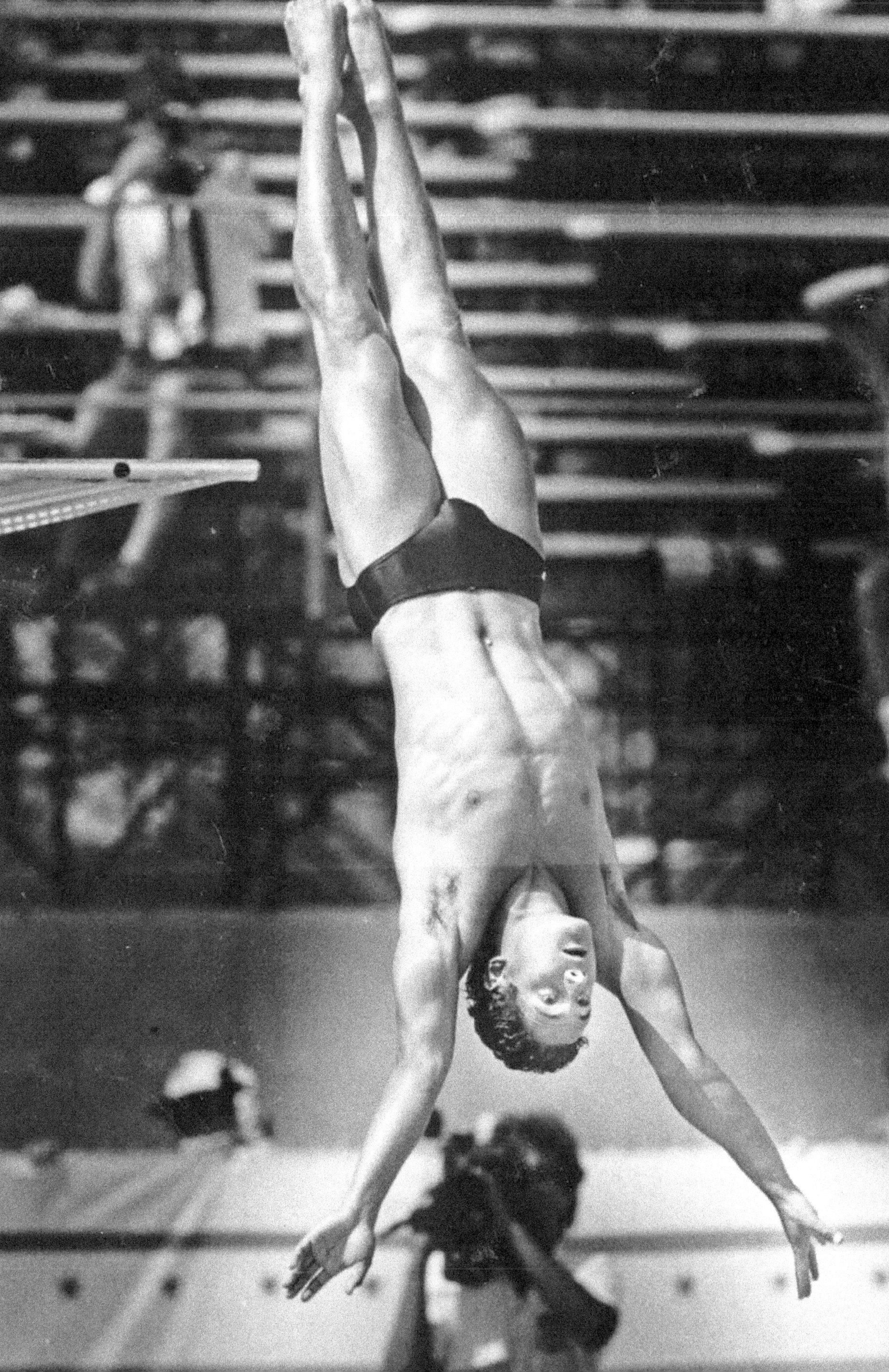

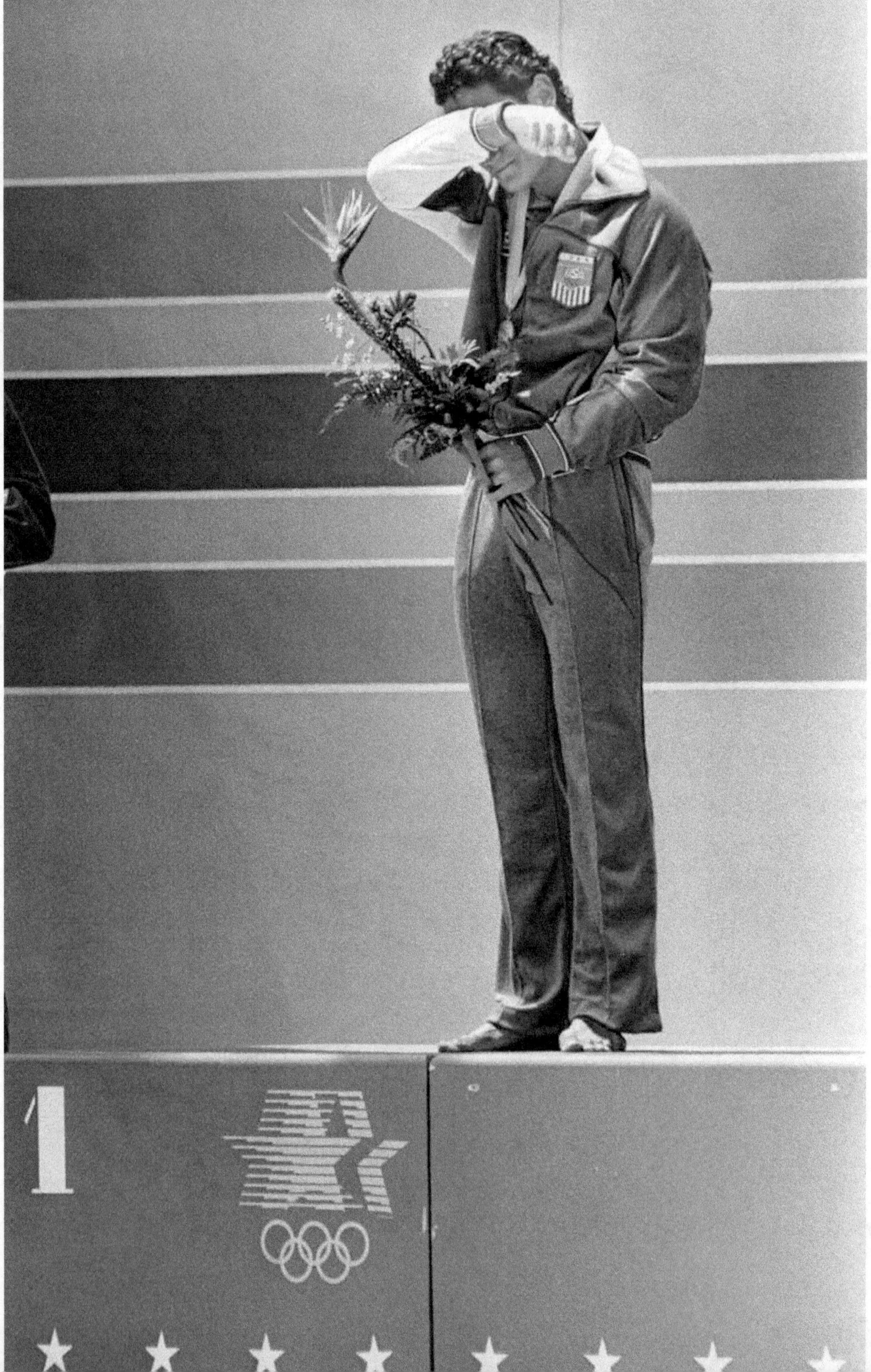
1

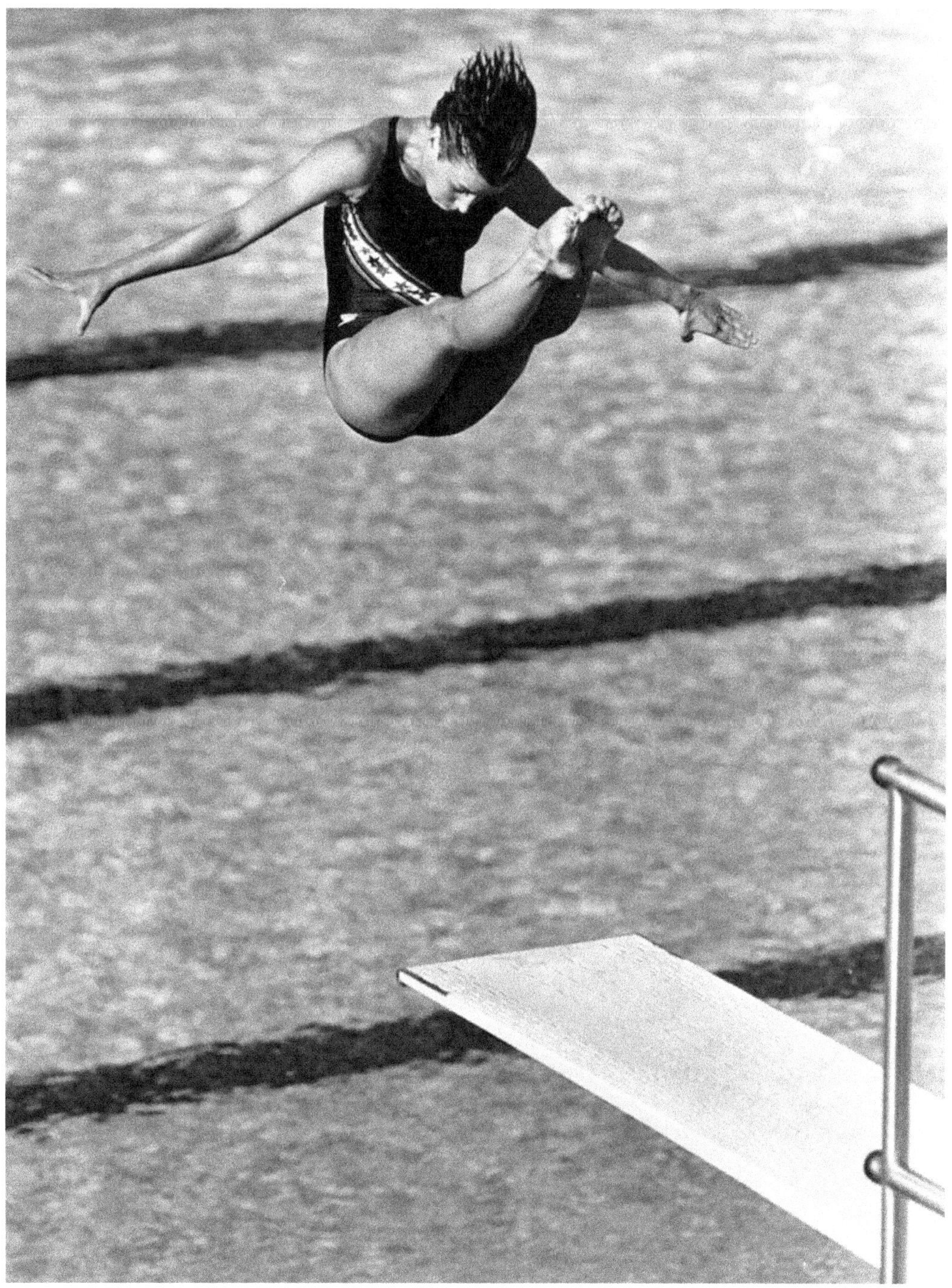

Canada's Sylvie Bernier won the gold medal in the 3-meter springboard. (Anne Knudsen)

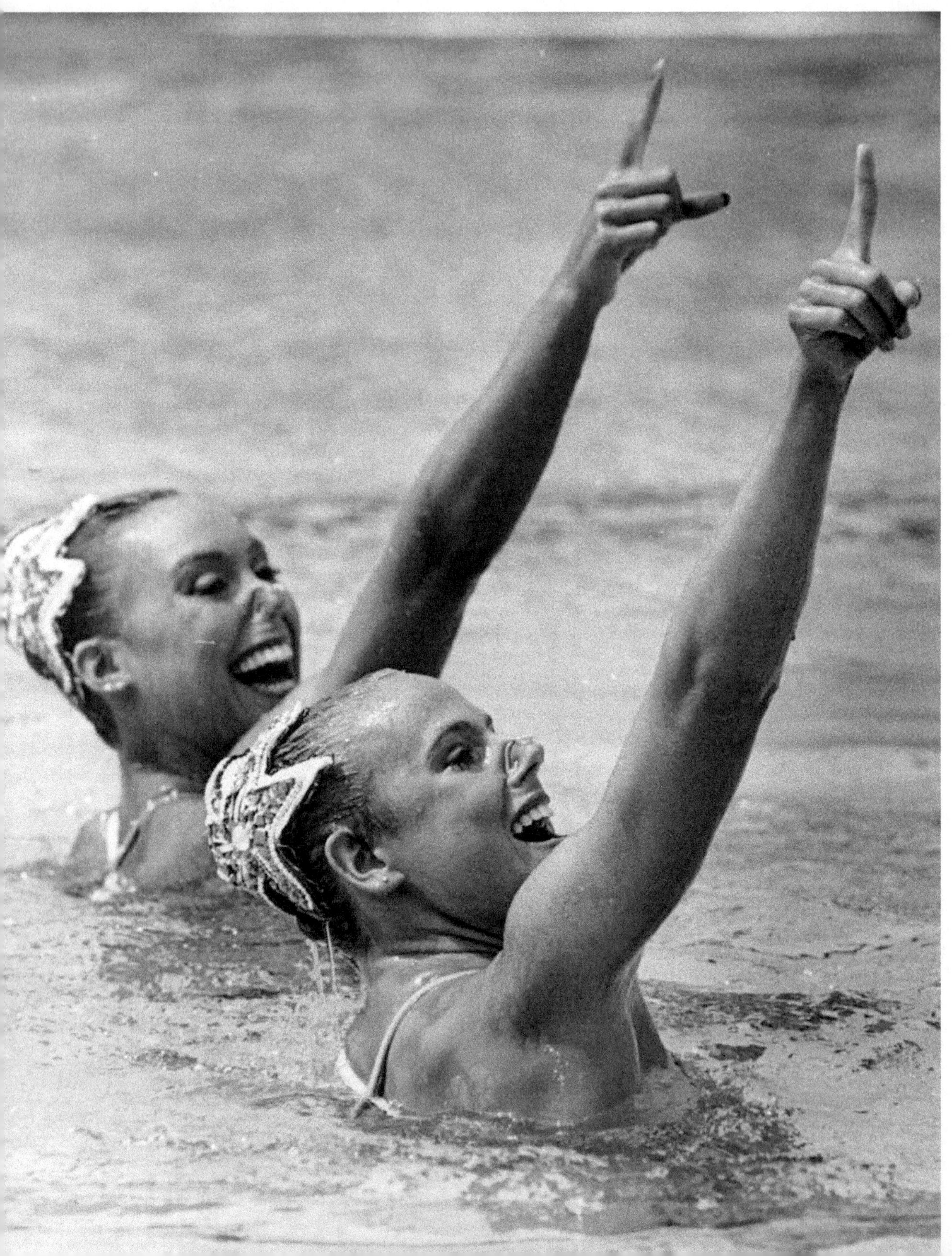

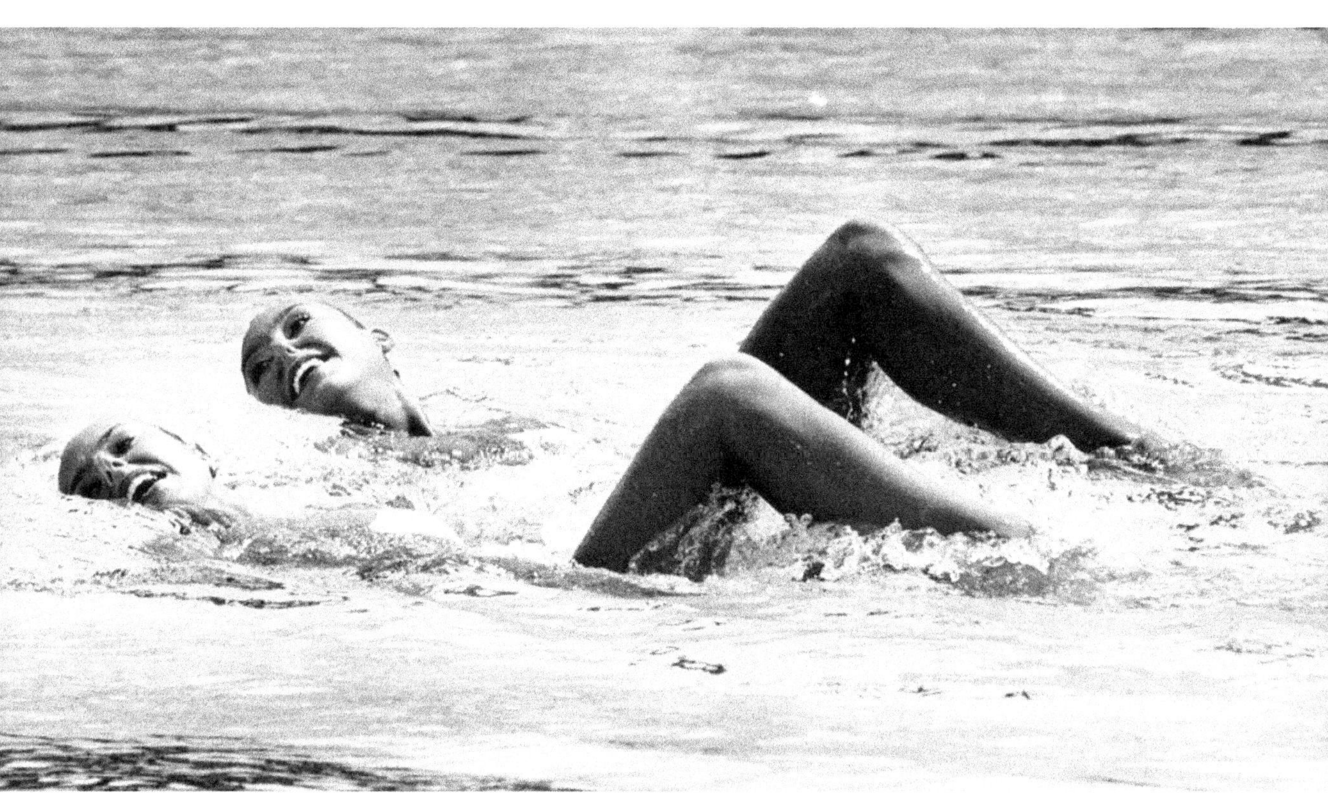

Above and opposite: Tracie Ruiz (_right_) and Candy Costie won the gold medal in synchronized swimming, performing their routine entitled "Duet."(Anne Knudsen)

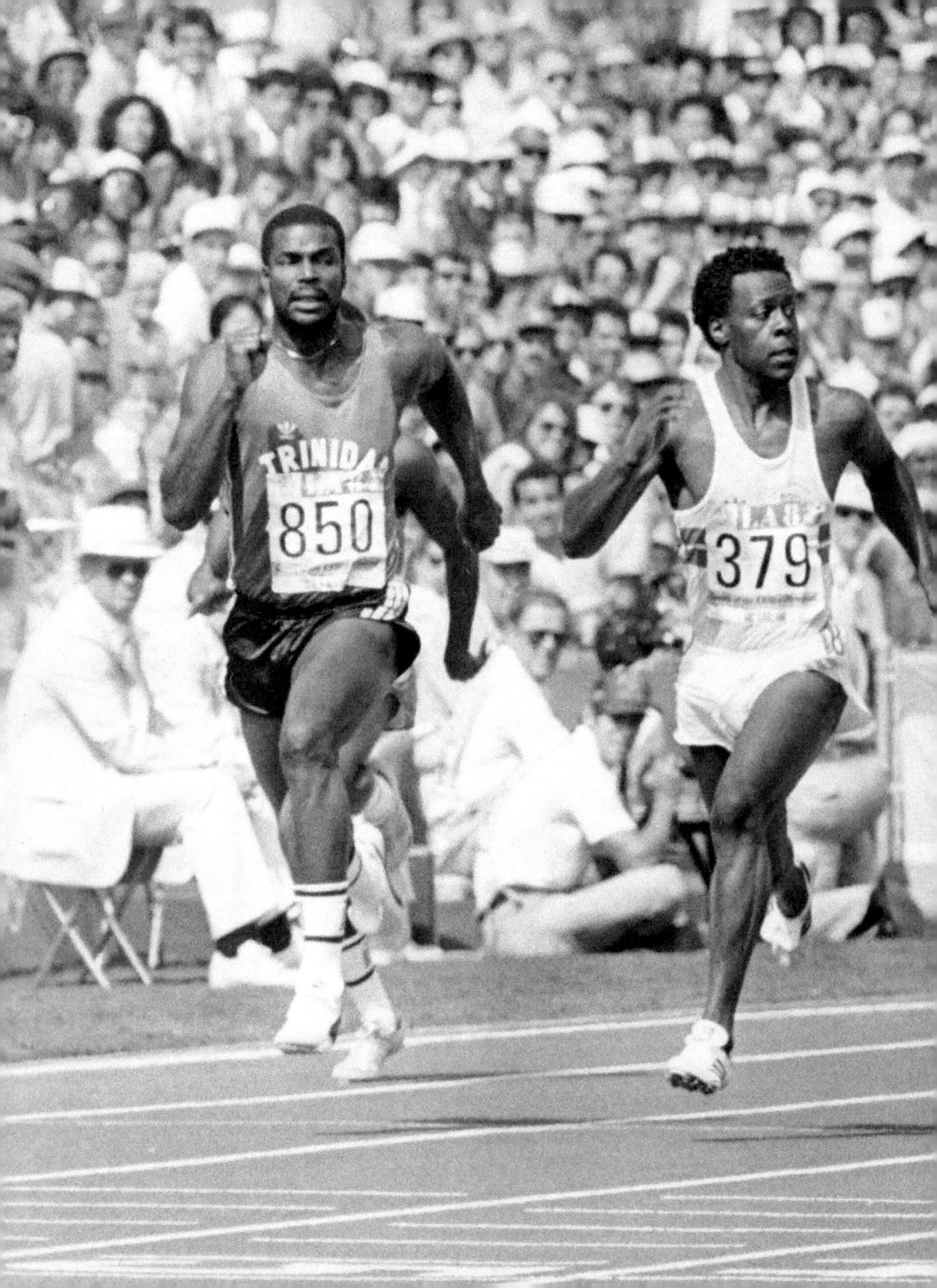
TRINIDA
850
379

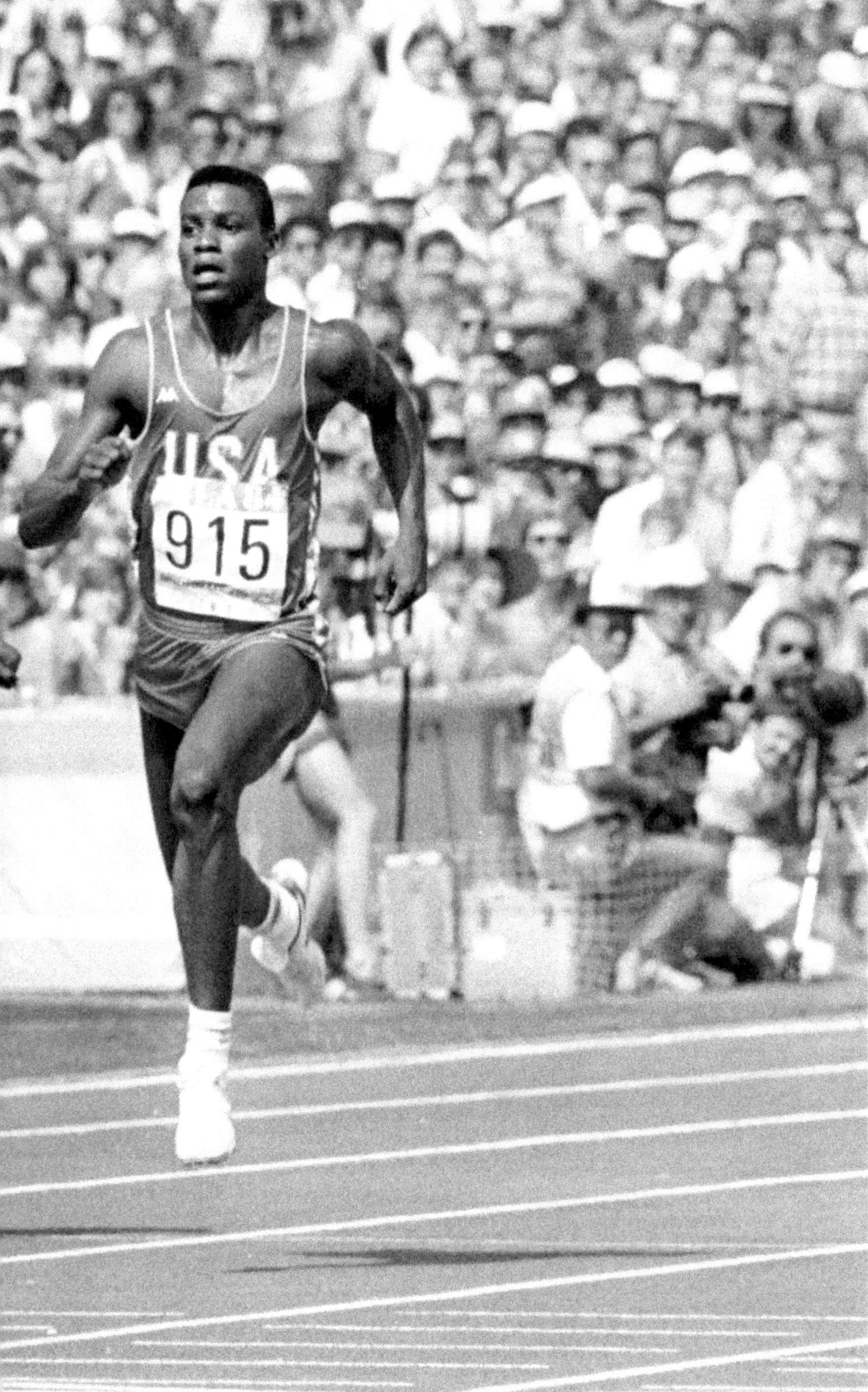
USA
915

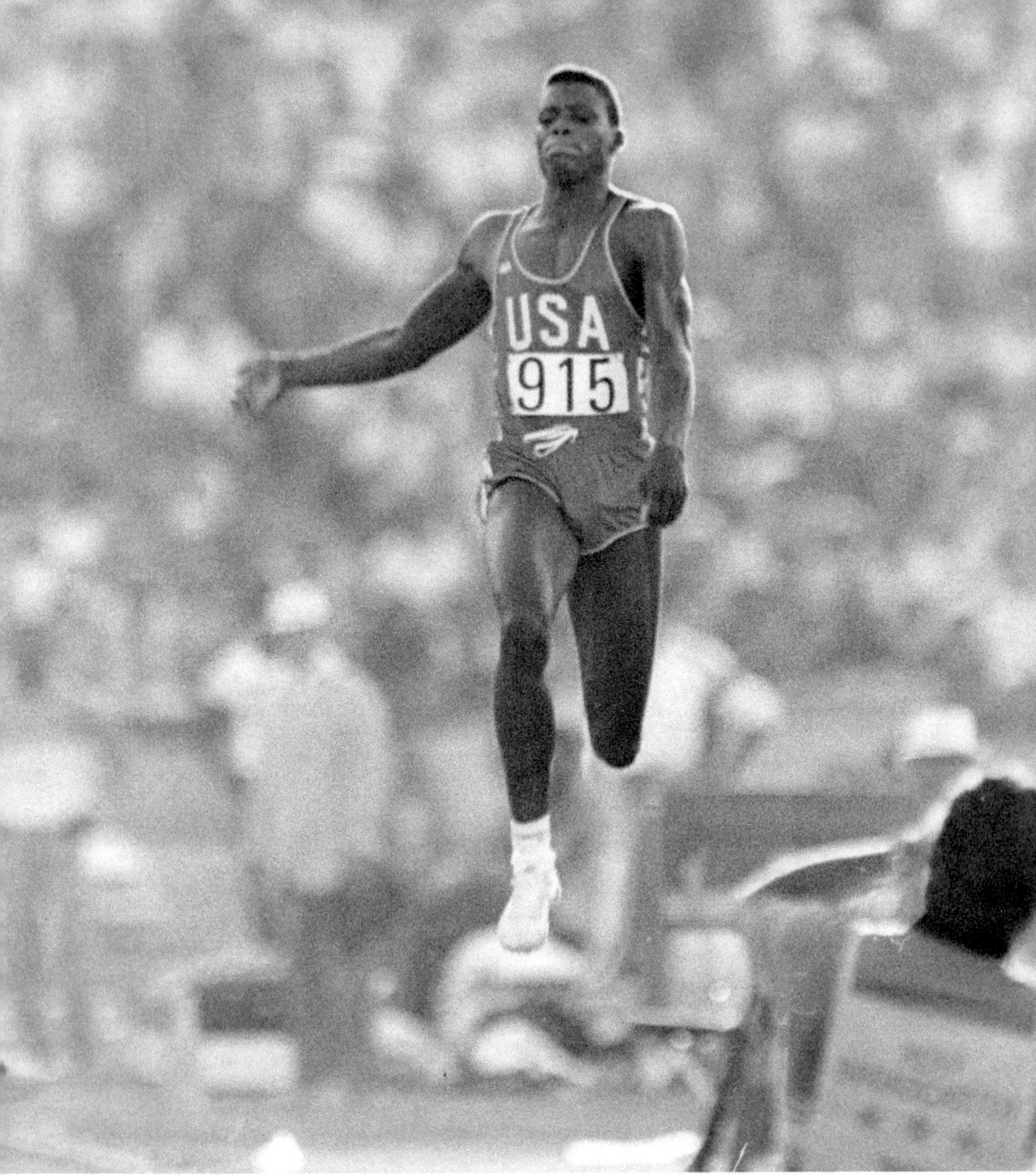

Above, opposite and overleaf: **Carl Lewis won four gold medals in four events: 100 meters, 200 meters, long jump, and 4x100-meter relay. (Paul Chinn)**

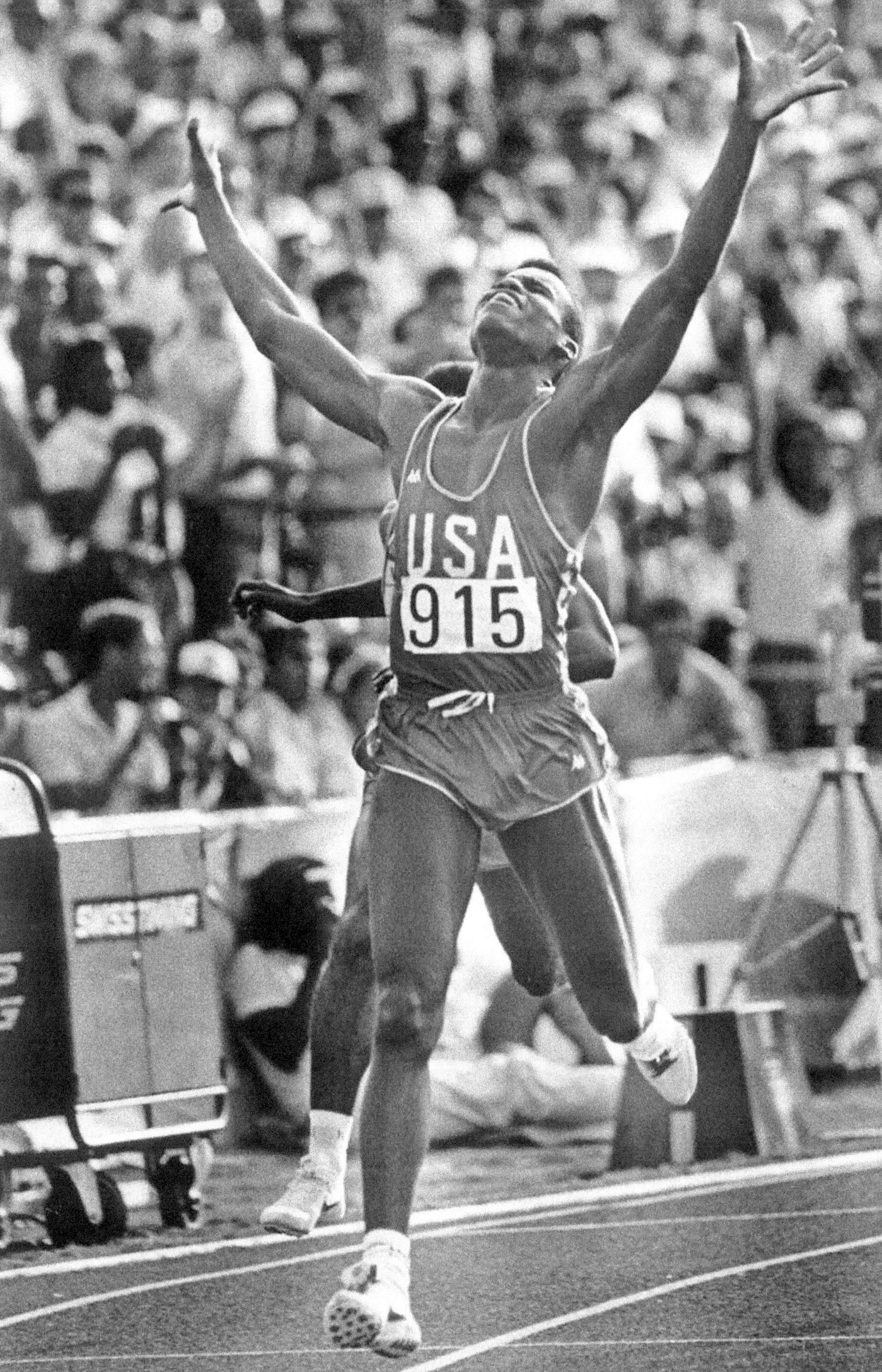
USA
915

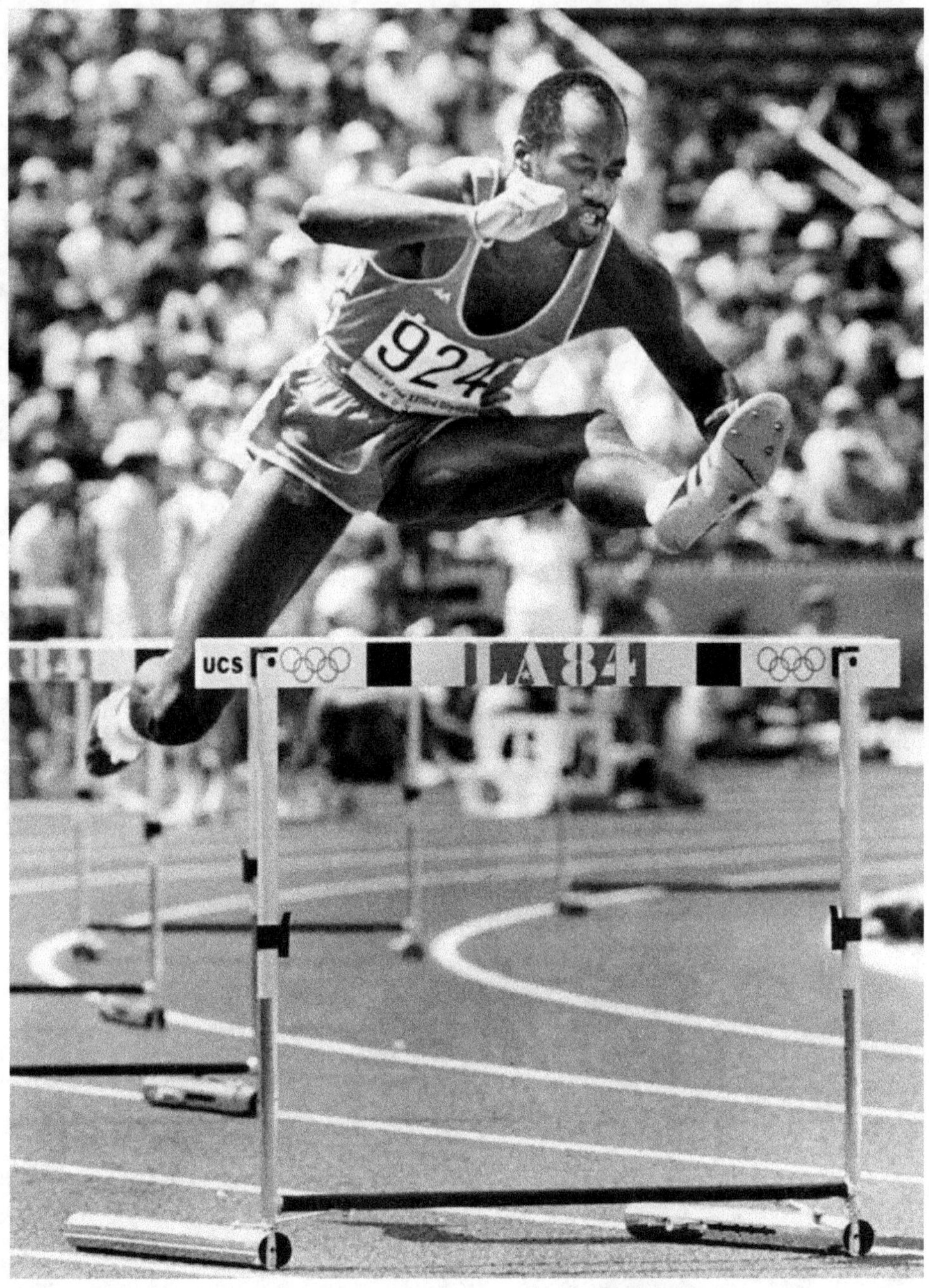

Above and opposite: **Edwin Moses extended his consecutive victory streak by taking the 400-meter hurdles. (Paul Chinn)**

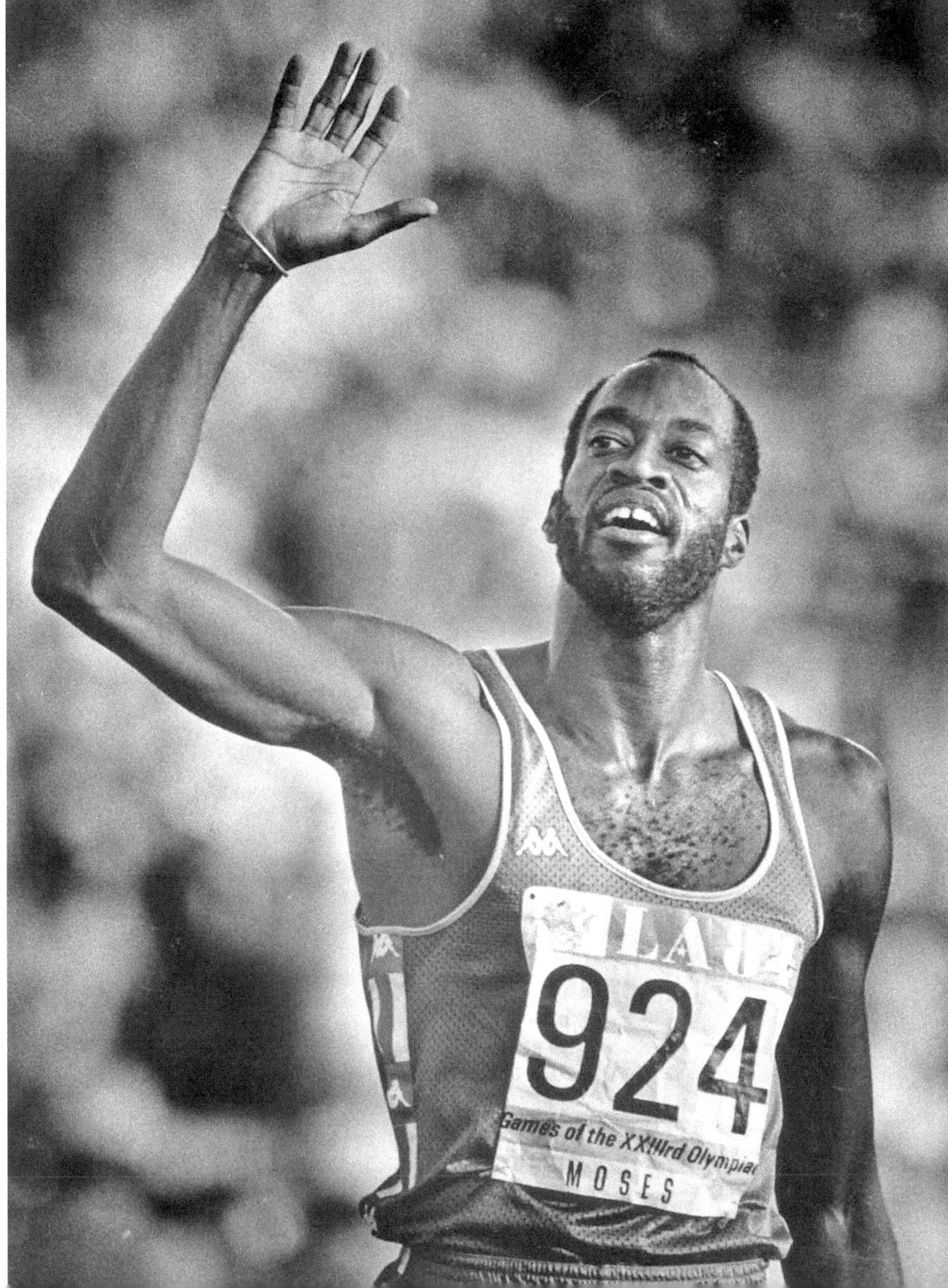
LA84
924
Games of the XXIIIrd Olympiad
MOSES

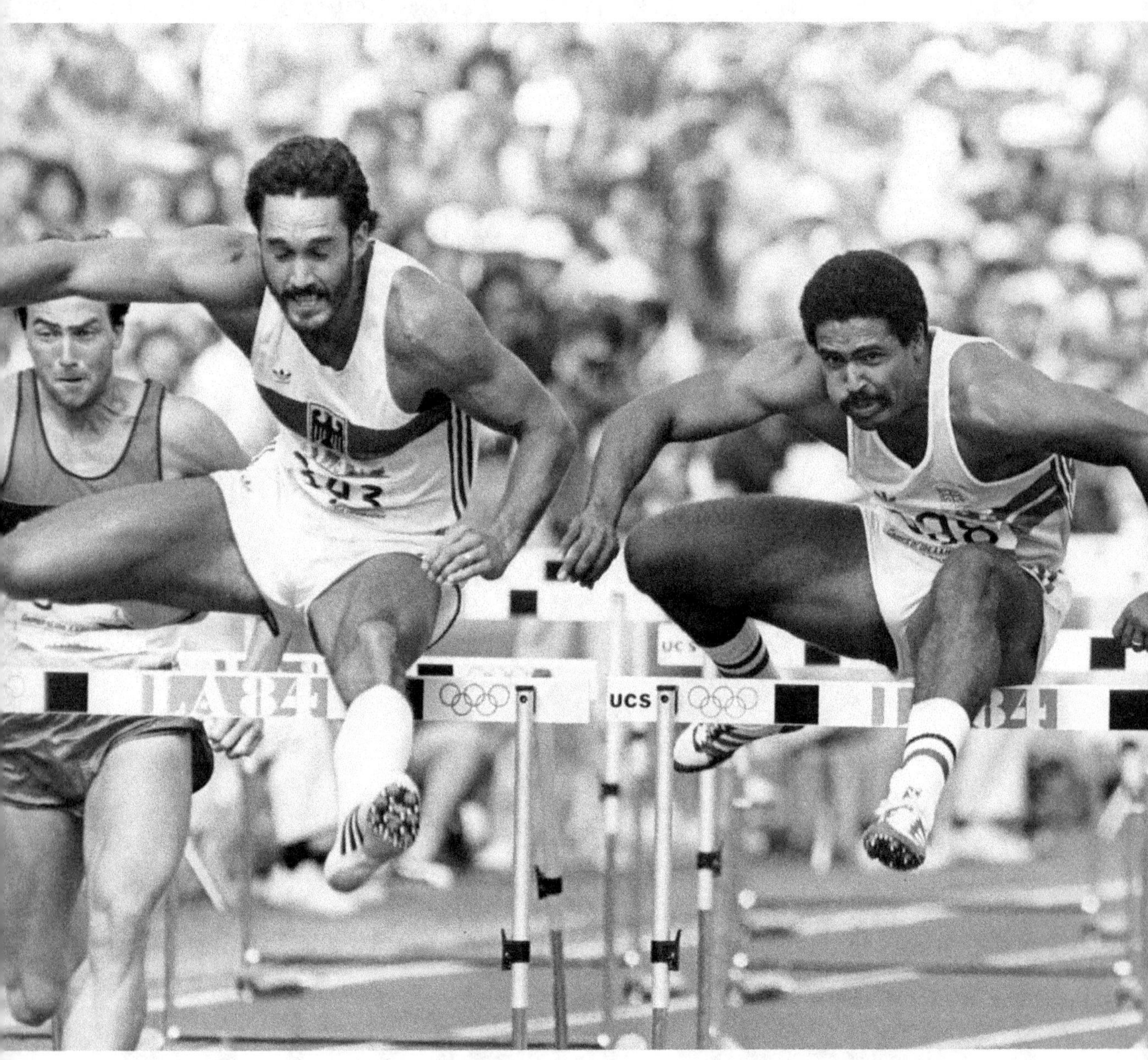

Great Britain's Daley Thompson (*right*) competed in the hurdles event en route to winning the decathlon gold medal. (Paul Chinn)

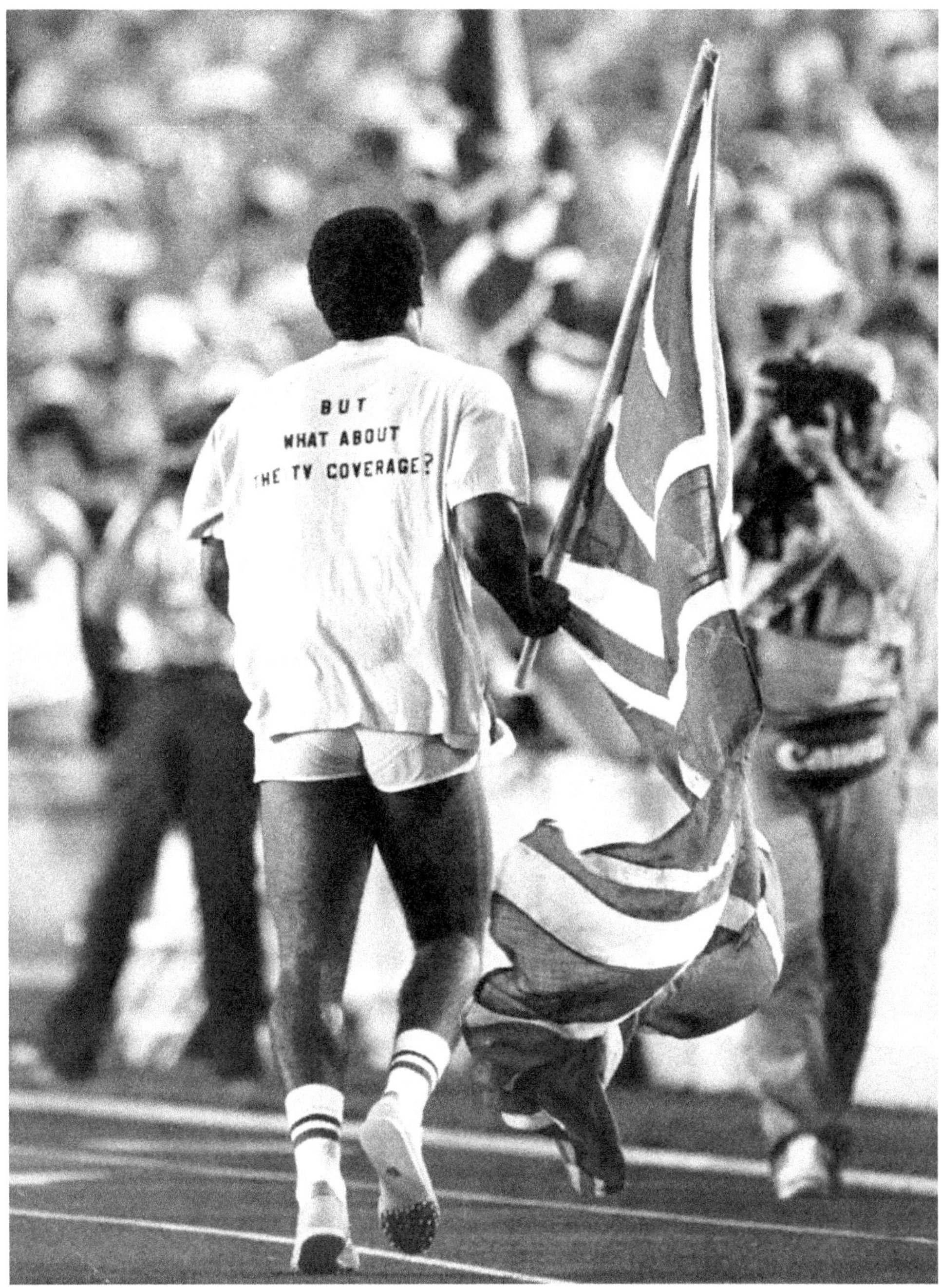

"Thanks America for a Good Games and a Great Time," read the front of Thompson's T-shirt, but it was the words on the back of the shirt mocking ABC-TV's coverage that caused controversy. (Paul Chinn)

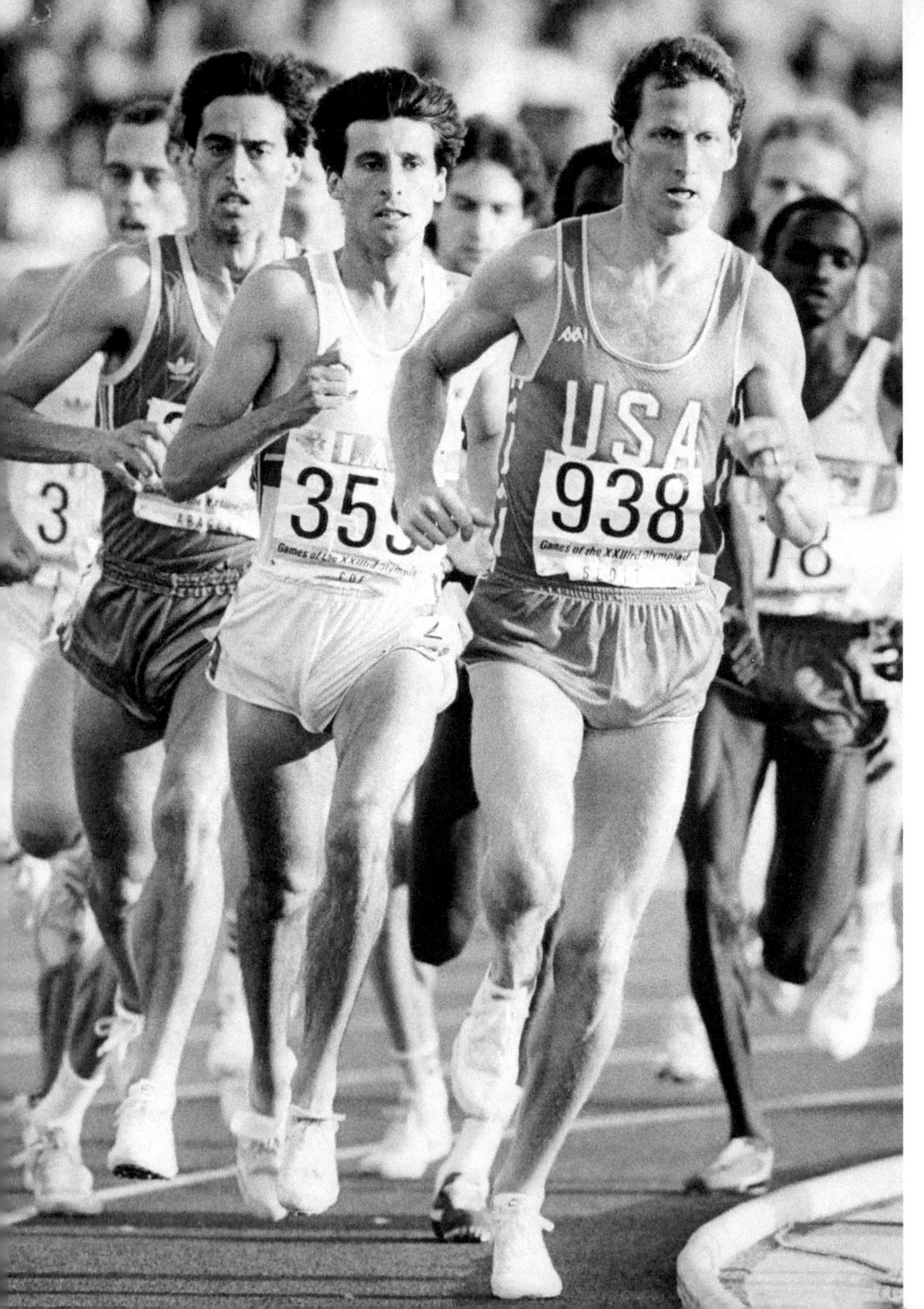
USA
938
Games of the XXIIIrd Olympiad

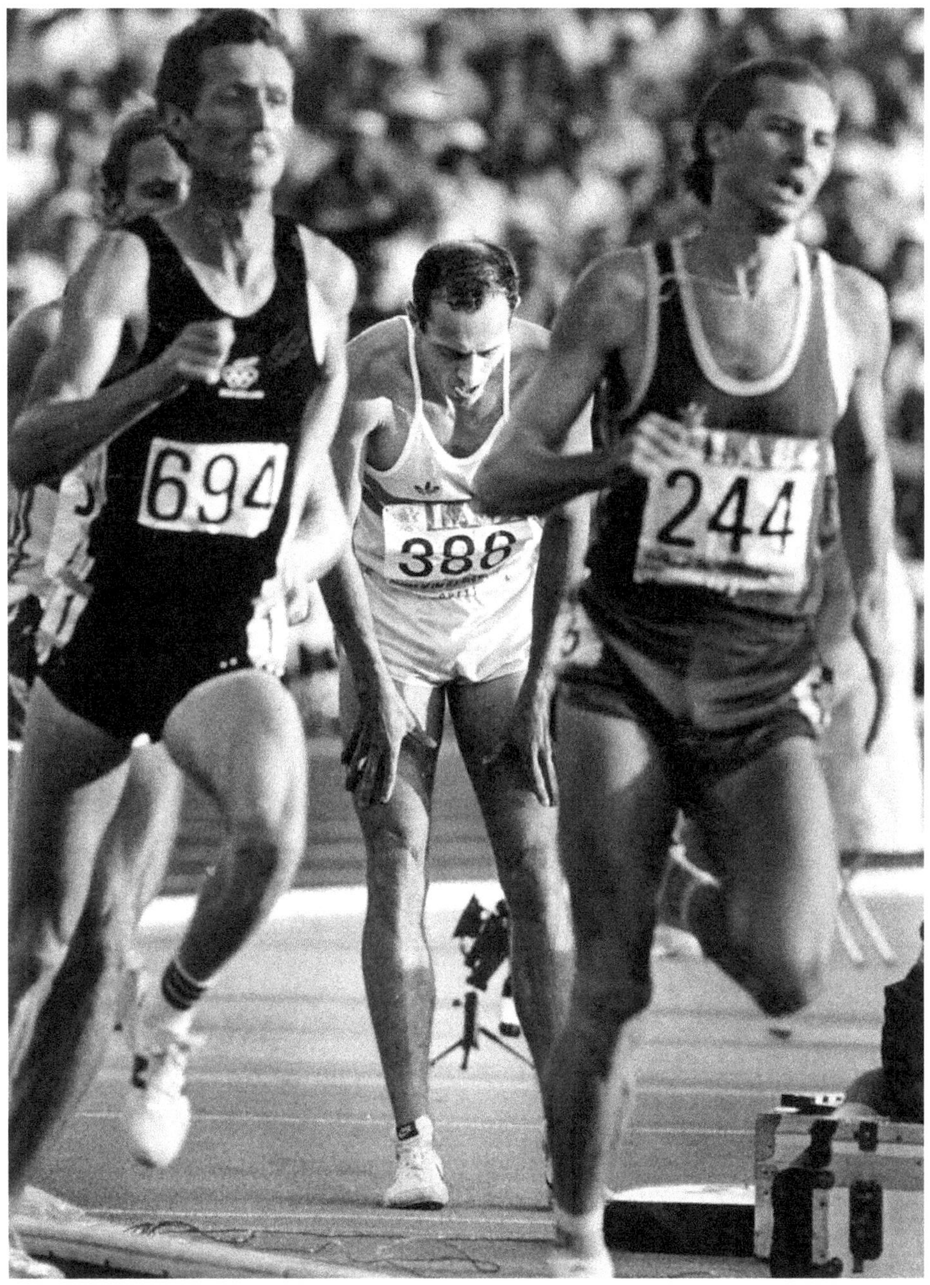

Above and opposite: **American Steve Scott led midway through the 1,500 meters, but Britain's Sebastian Coe (just behind Scott) rallied to win the race. The pace forced favorite Steve Ovett (*center*) to drop out. (Paul Chinn)**

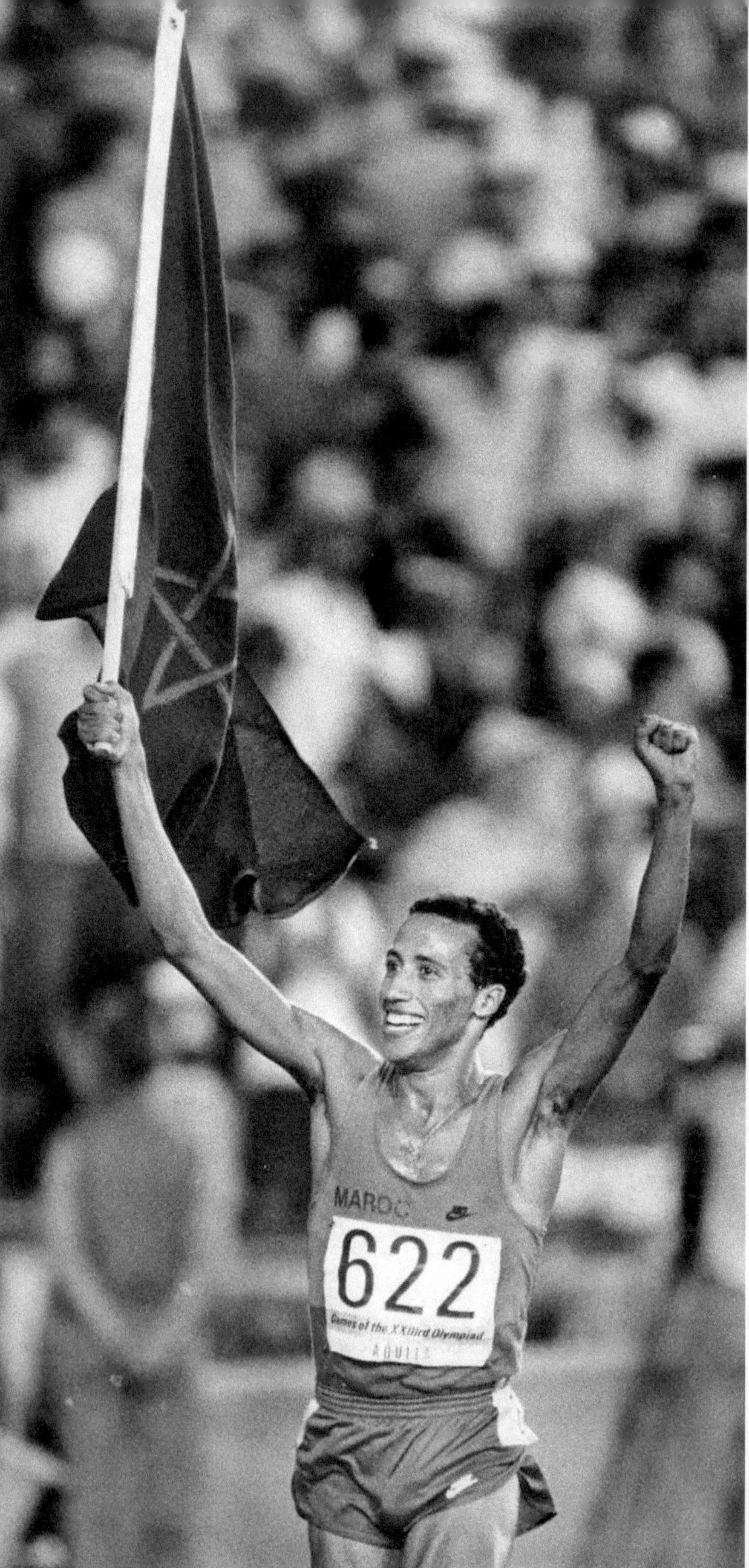
MAROC
622
Games of the XXIIIrd Olympiad

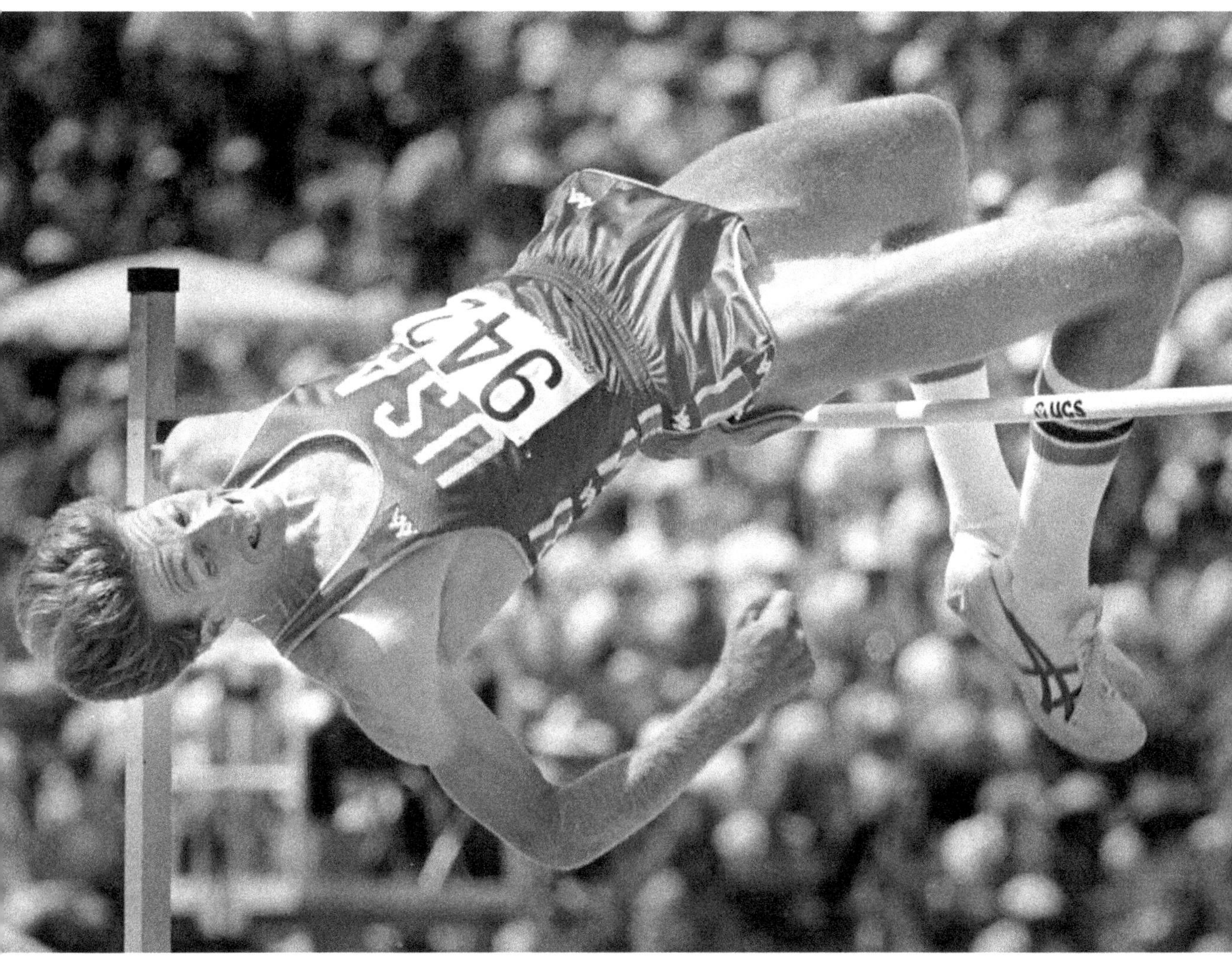

Dwight Stones finished fourth in the high jump. (Paul Chinn)

Opposite: **Morocco's distance great Saïd Aouita celebrated after winning the 5,000 meters in record time. (Paul Chinn)**

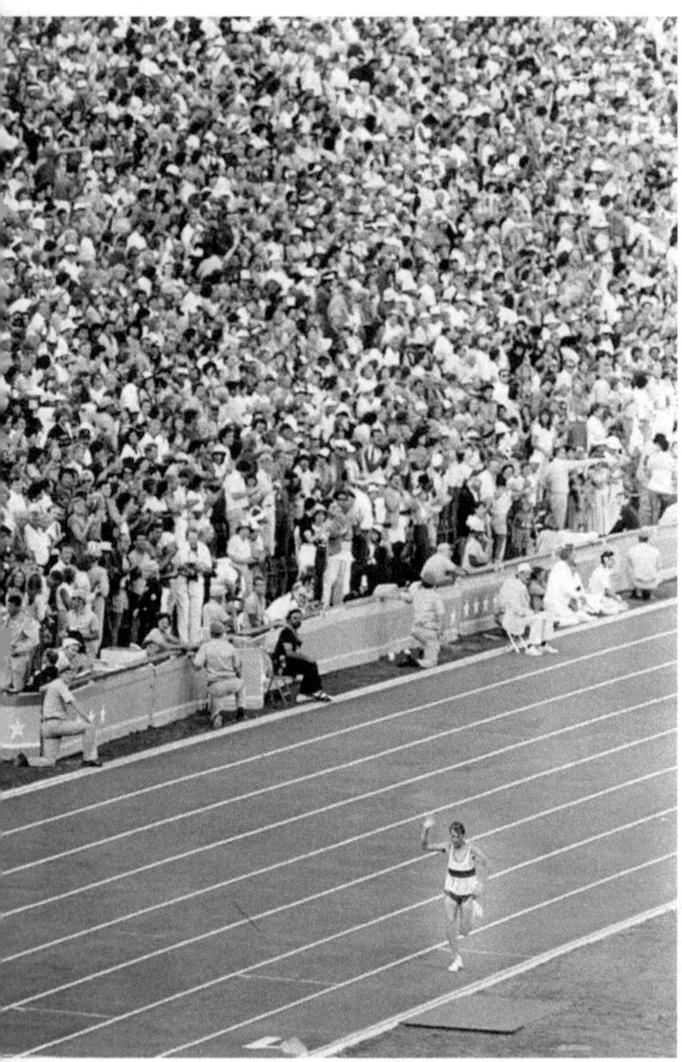

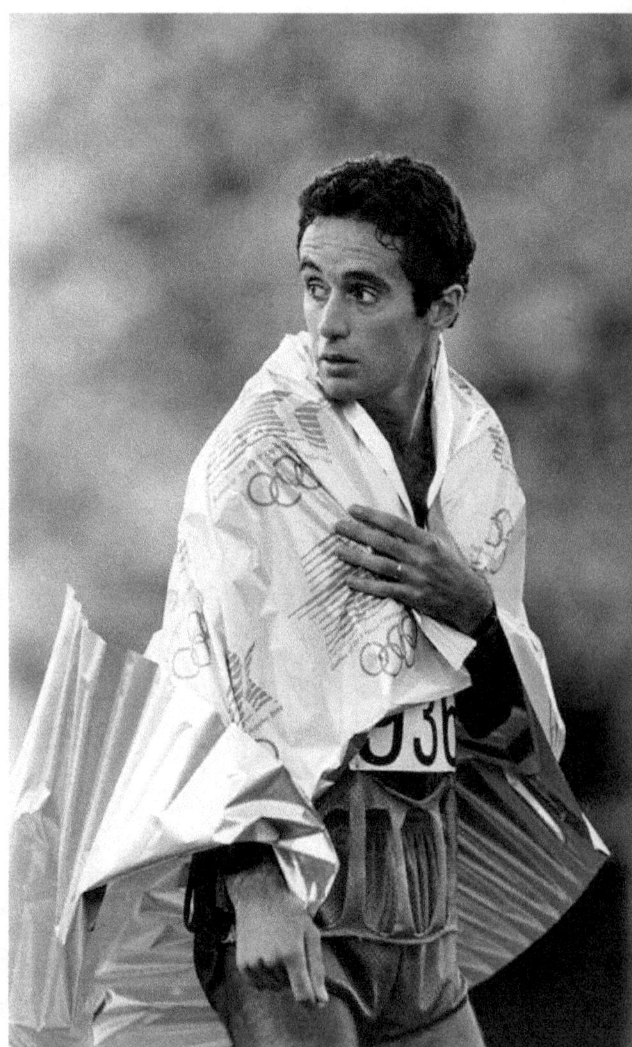

Left: **Portugal's Carlos Lopes (#723) won the men's marathon, defeating a top-notch field that included a disappointed Alberto Salazar (who finished 15th). (*Left,* Dean Musgrove • *Right,* Paul Chinn)**

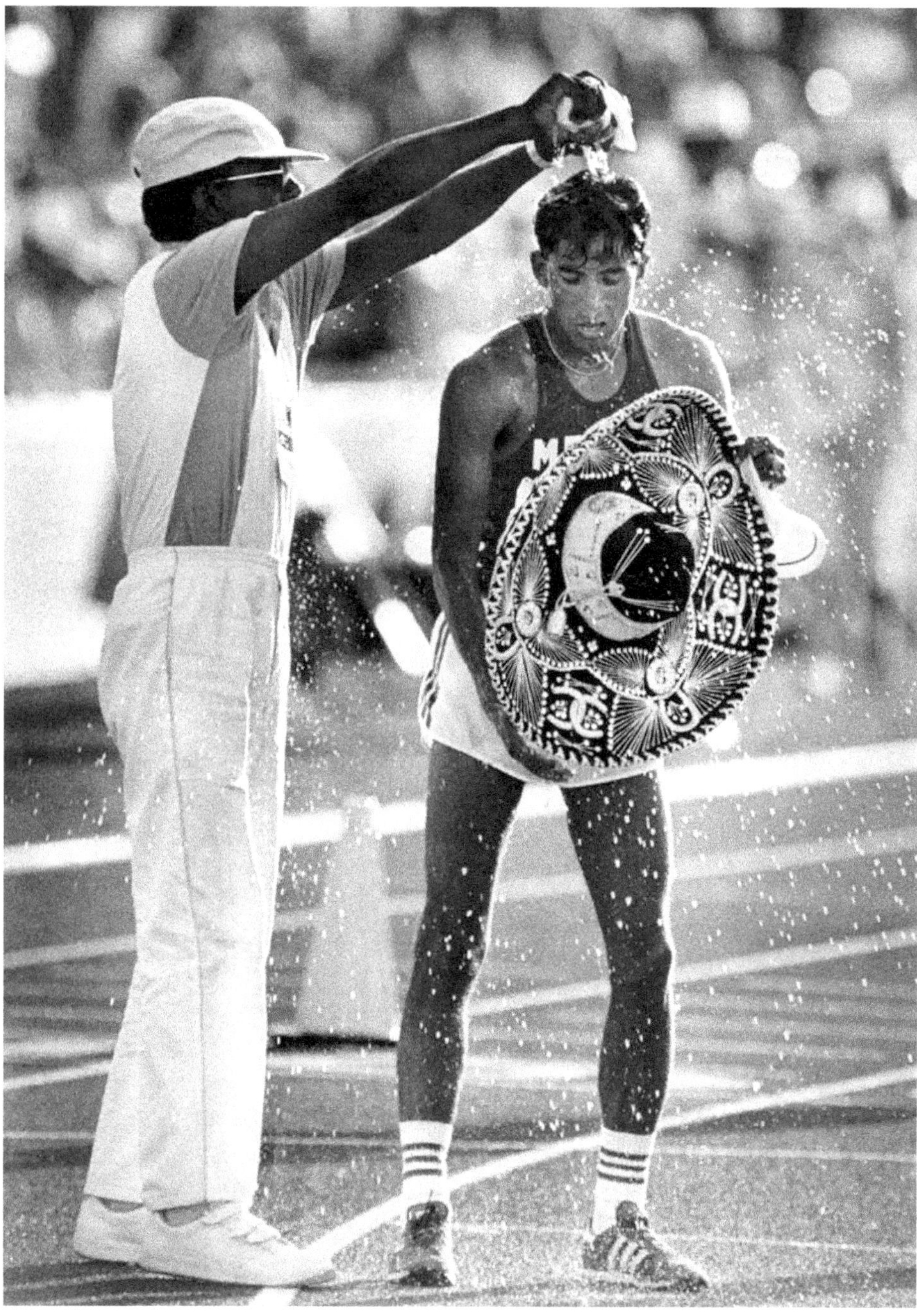

After Mexico's Ernesto Canto won the 20-kilometer walk event, an official doused him with water as he collected a victory sombrero thrown from the stands. (Paul Chinn)

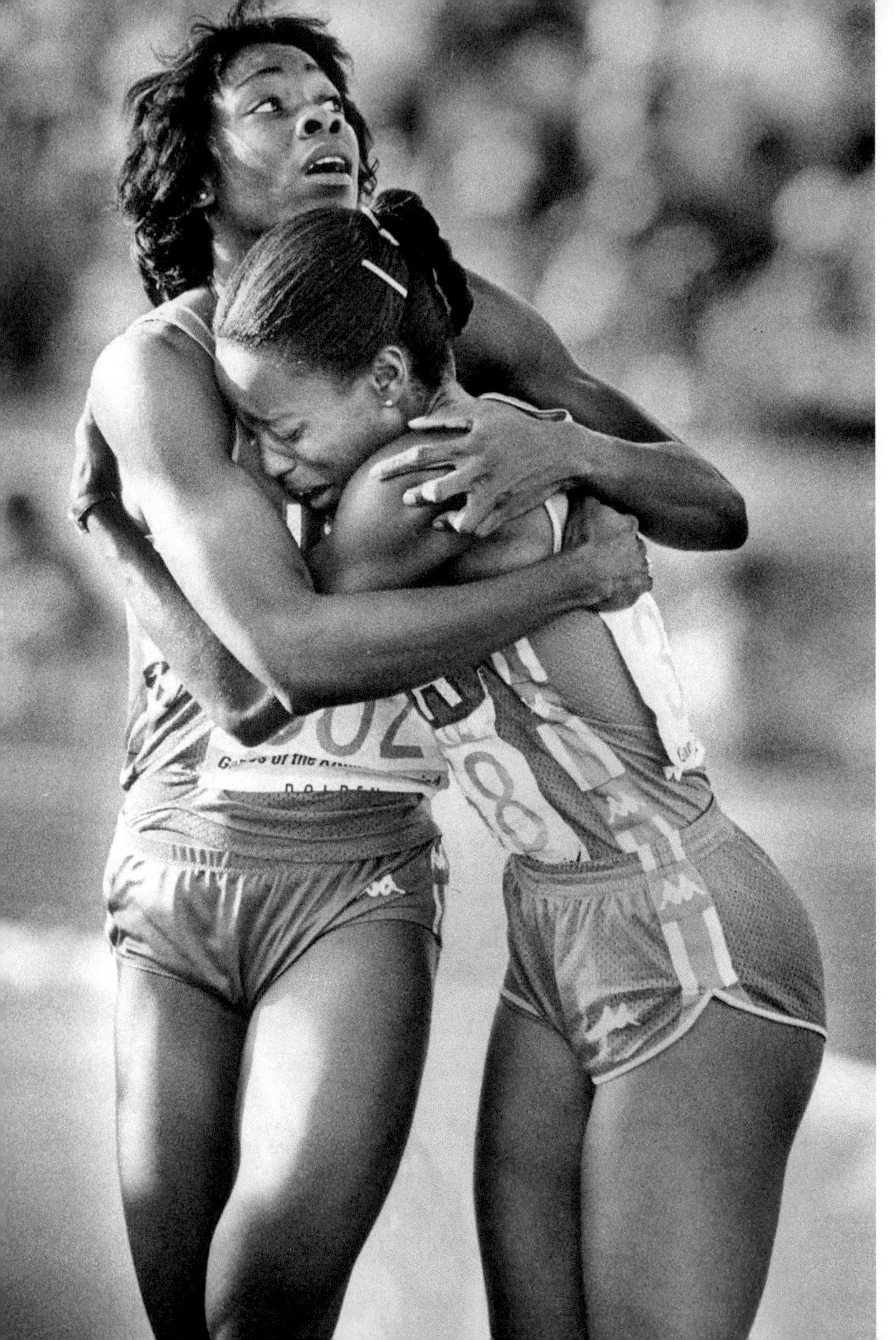

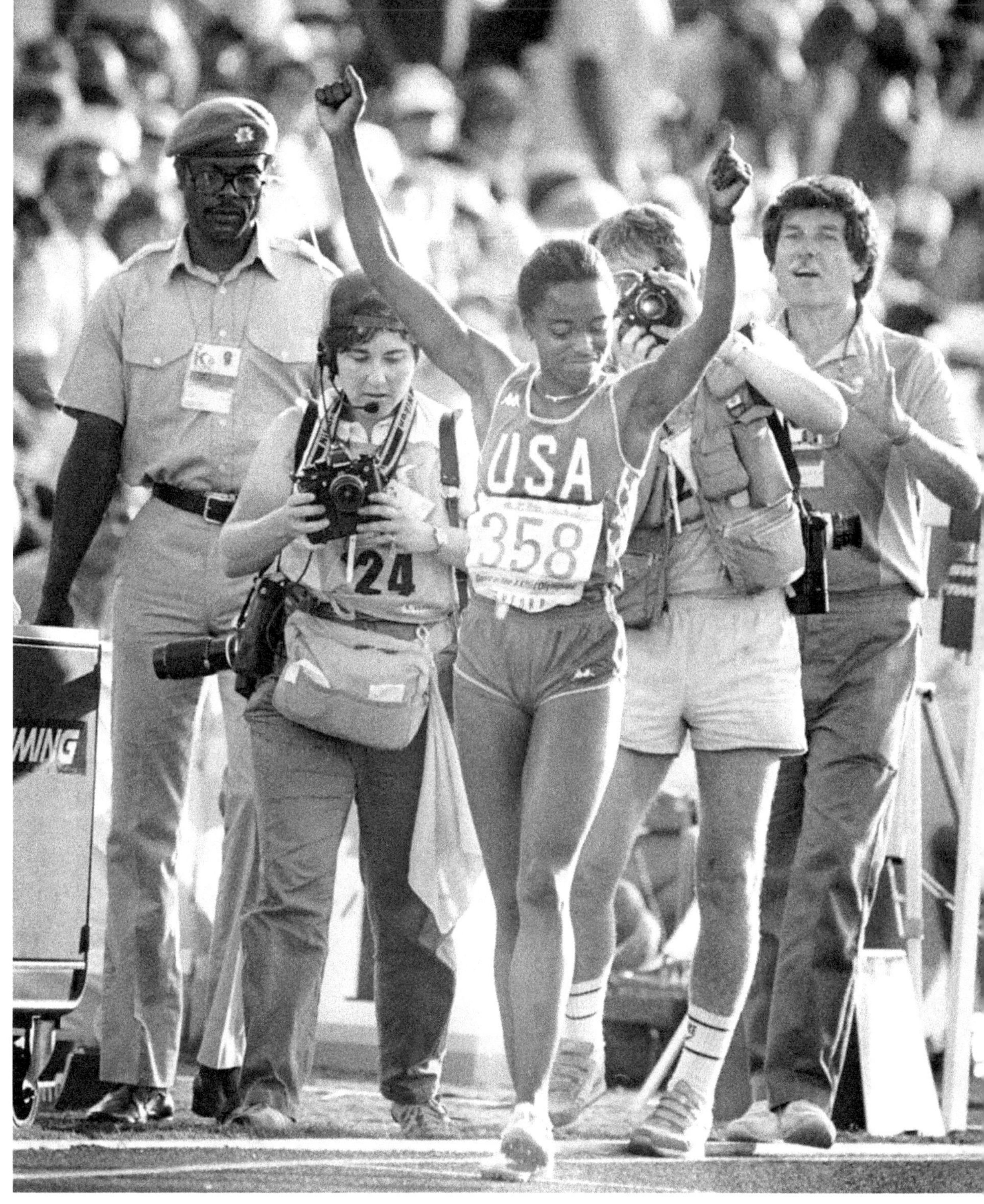

Above and opposite: **After winning the 100-meter race in a new Olympic record, Evelyn Ashford (*right*) hugged teammate Jeanette Bolden (who finished fourth). Ashford and Bolden were part of the triumphant 4x100-meter relay team. (Paul Chinn)**

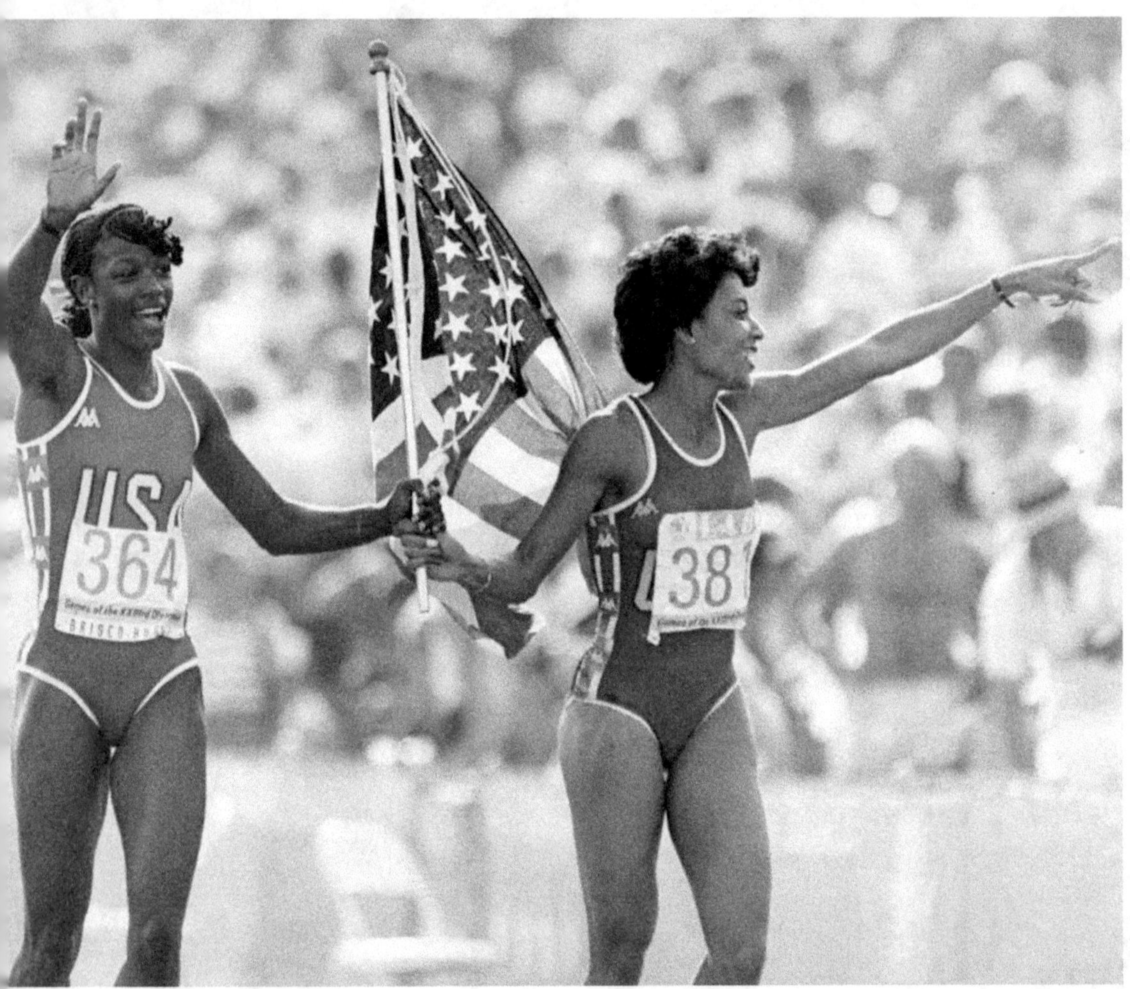

Valerie Brisco-Hooks (*left*) and Florence Griffith celebrated their one-two finish in the 200 meters. (Paul Chinn)

***Opposite:* Brisco-Hooks (holding her son during the Olympic Trials) became the first competitor to complete the 200-400 double at the same Olympics and also won a gold medal in the 4x400 relay. (Paul Chinn)**

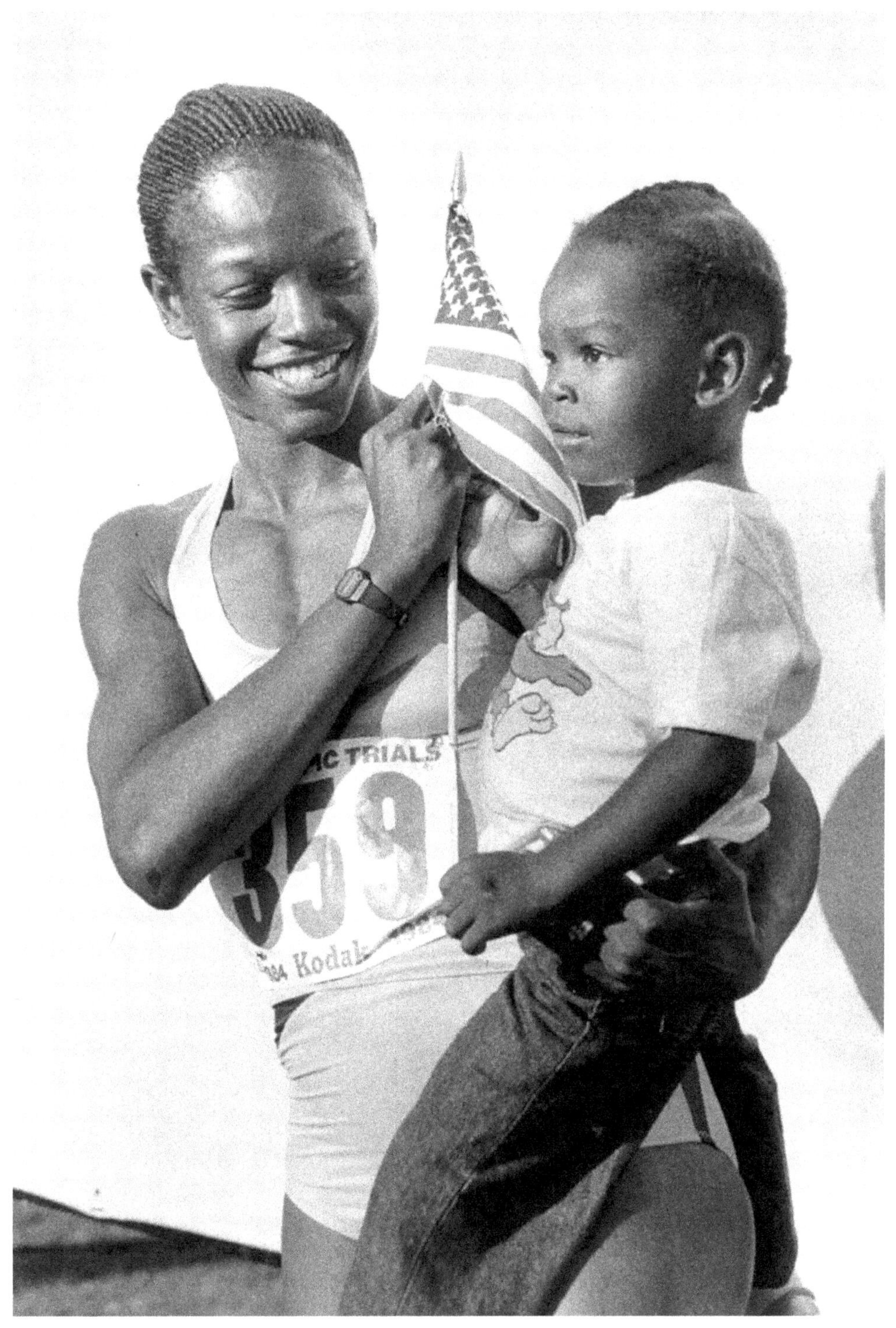
TRIALS
359

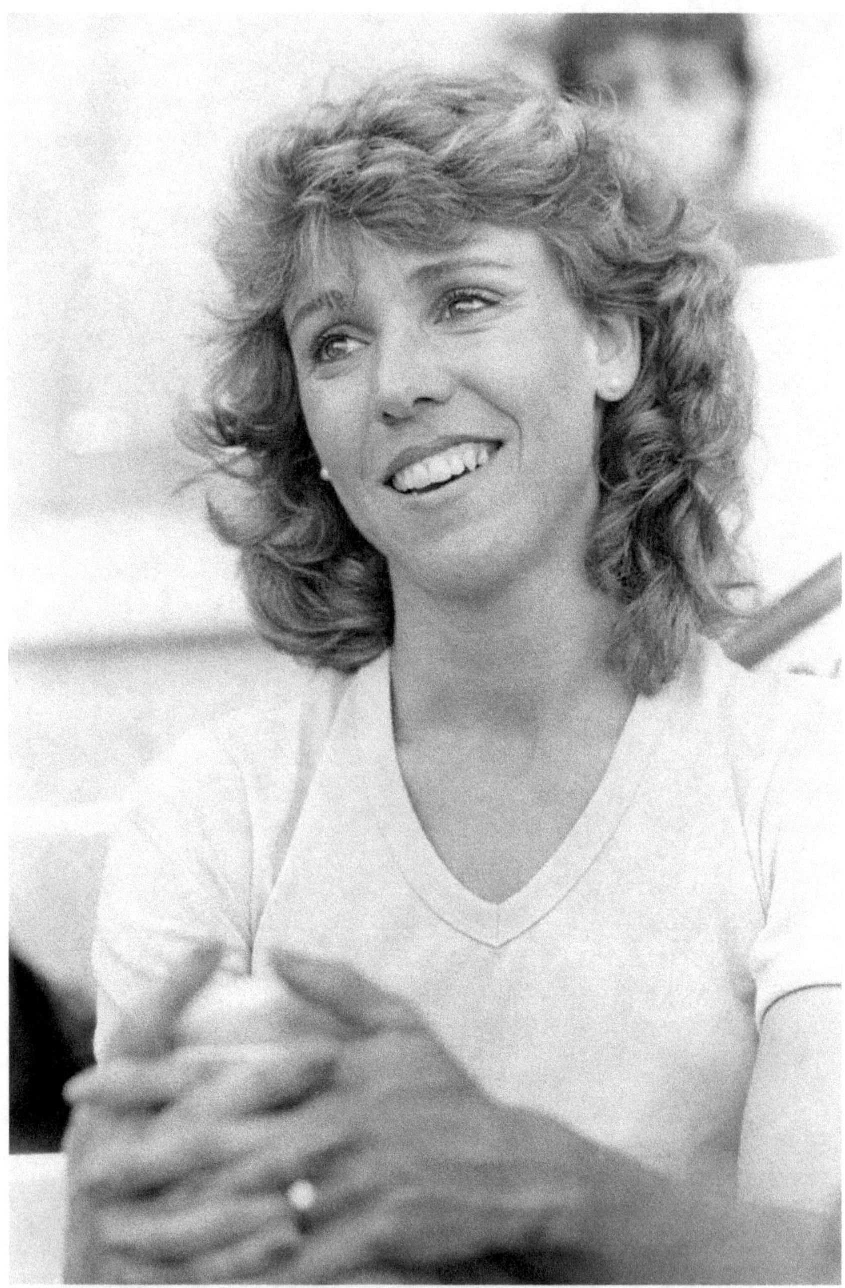

Above and opposite: **Mary Decker was America's premiere middle-distance runner, but injuries and the 1980 boycott prevented her from attaining her Olympic dream. Injury-free in 1984, she cruised to victory at the U.S. Trials in the 3,000 meters. (*Above,* Michael Haering • *Opposite,* Paul Chinn)**

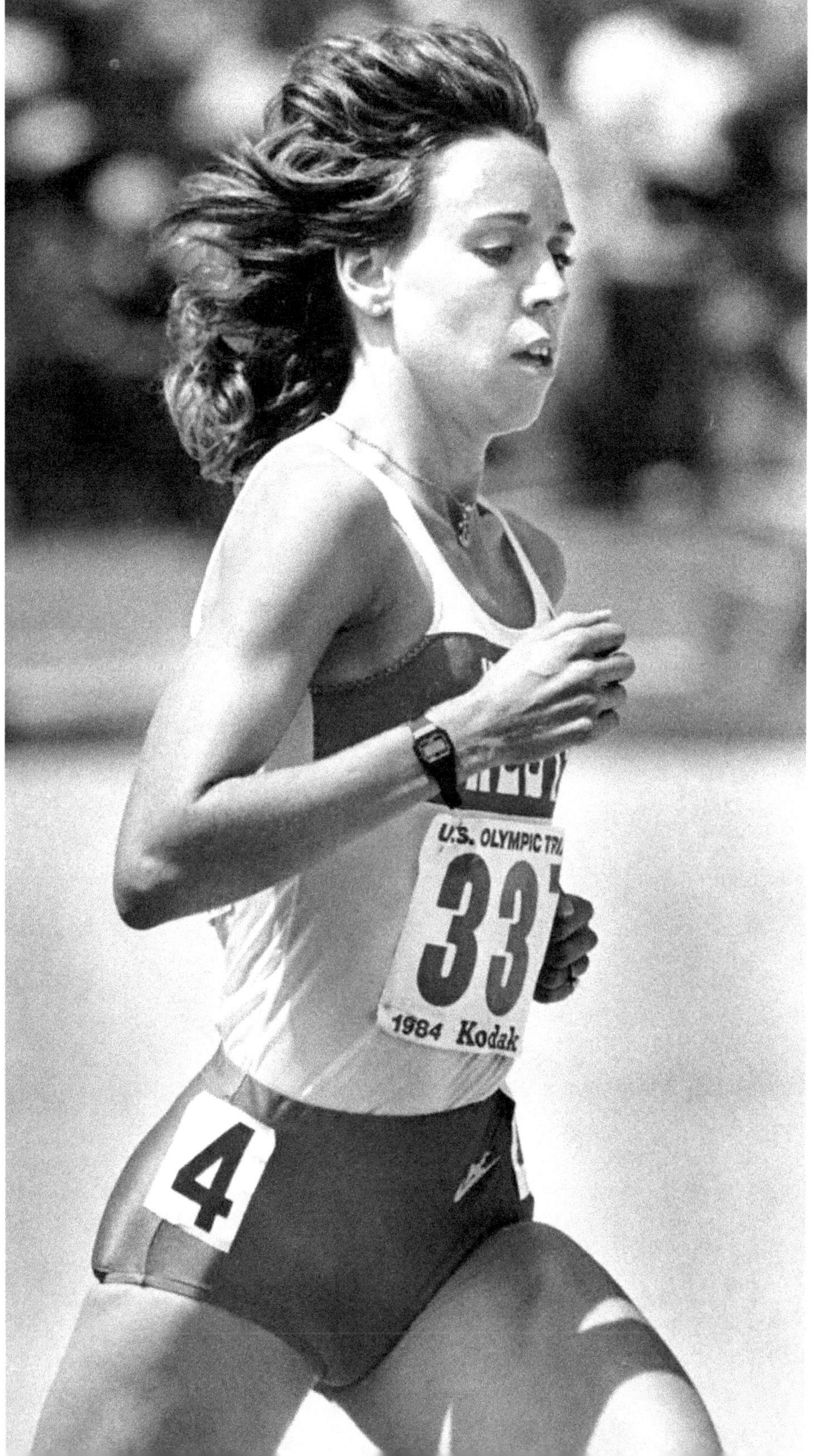
U.S. OLYMPIC
1984 Kodak
4

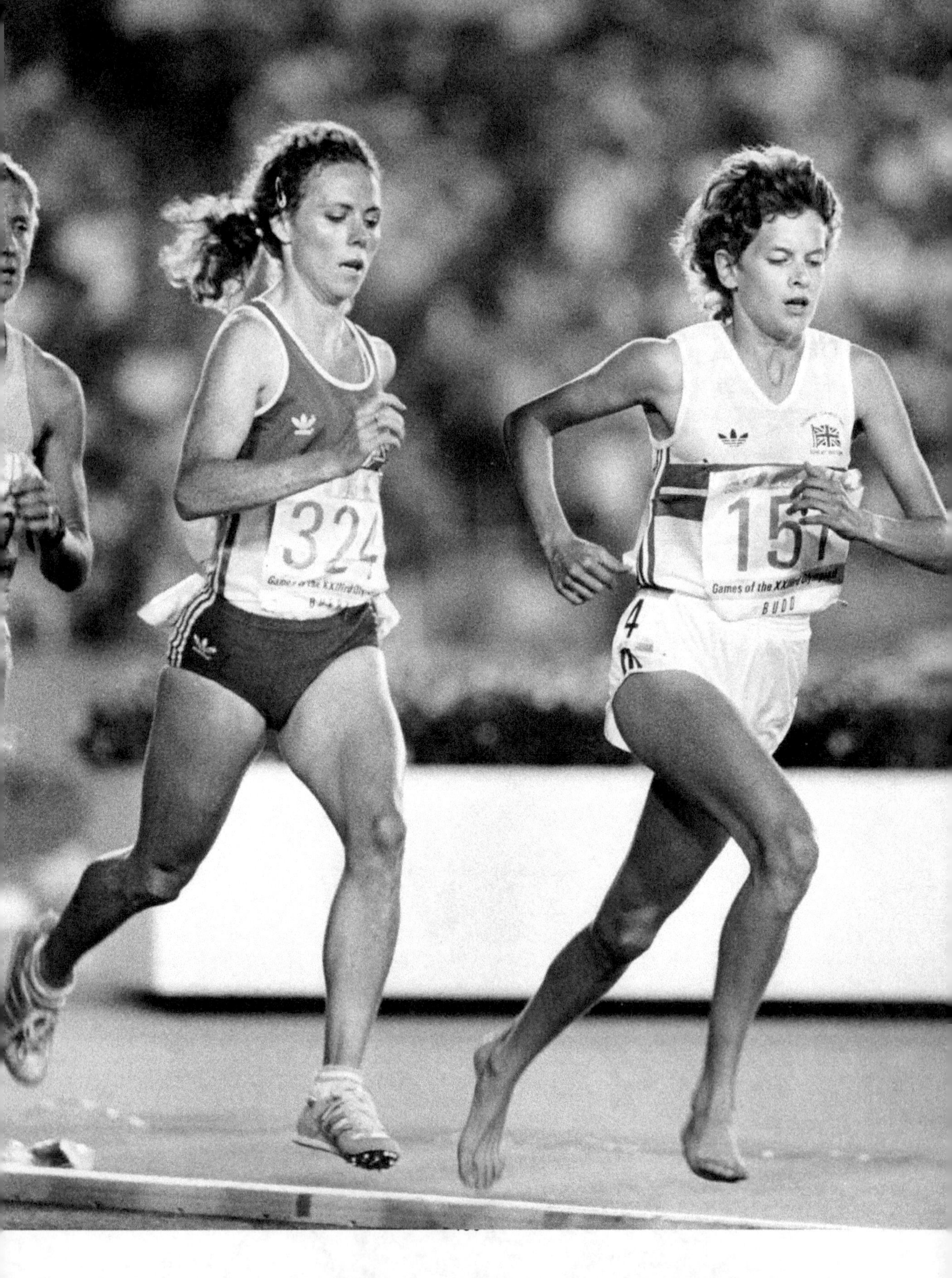
324
Games of the XXIIIrd Olympiad
BUDD

Opposite: **Mary Decker's main rival at the Olympics was Zola Budd, a diminutive 18-year-old barefoot runner who avoided the ban against South African athletes by using her family's ancestry to qualify on the British team. (Paul Chinn)**

Above: **In the highly anticipated final, Decker and Budd became entangled along the backstretch, causing Decker to fall awkwardly to the infield (her right leg is just visible, center, between the two judges) as the barefoot Budd and the pack continued. Behind Budd's right shoulder is Romania's Maricica Puica, who won the gold medal, with Budd seventh. The headline in the next day's** ***Her-Ex*** **screamed: "IS ZOLA GUILTY?" (Paul Chinn)**

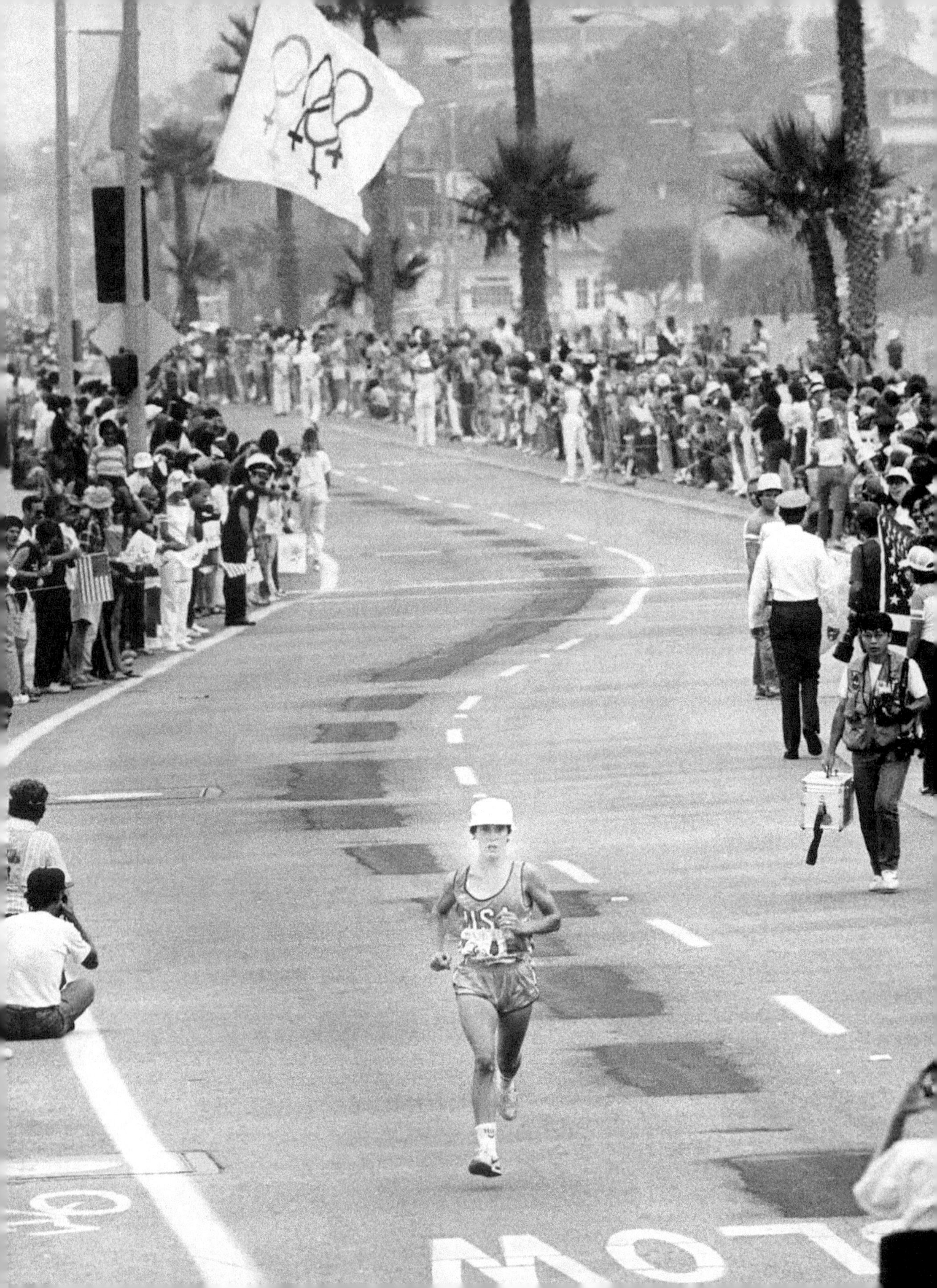
USA

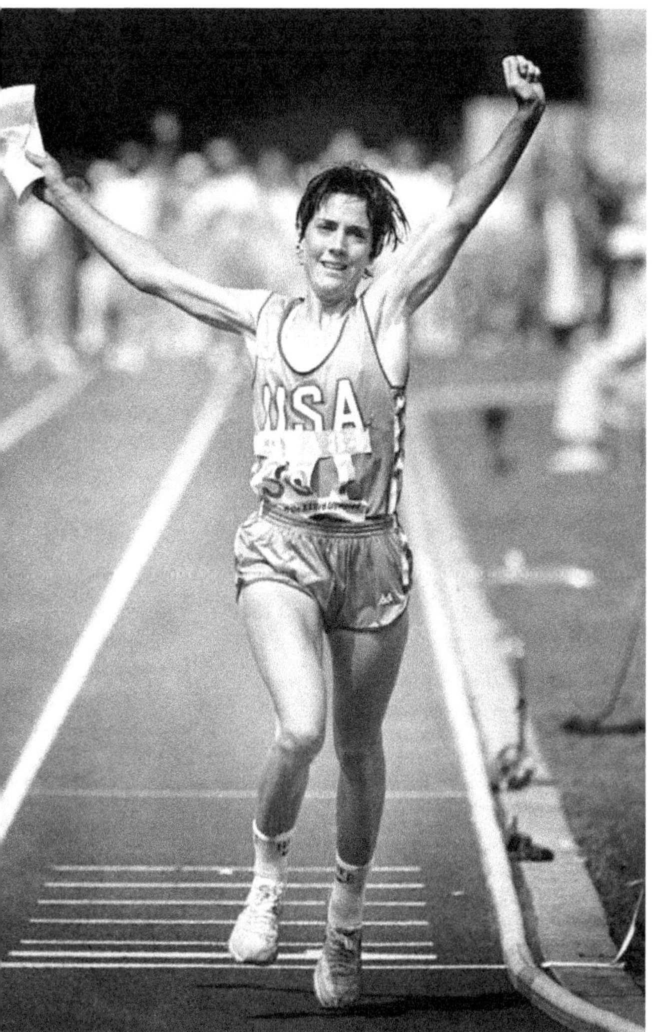

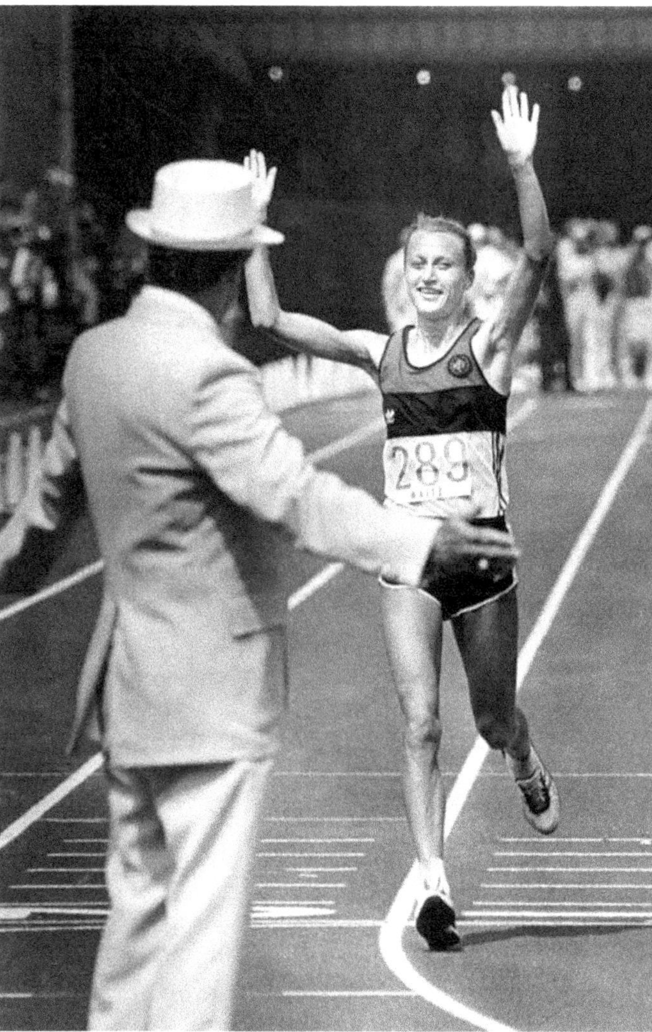

Prior to 1984, women were not allowed to compete in the marathon at the Olympics because of the sexist, outdated notion that their bodies were too fragile for such a distance. Joan Benoit squashed that myth in the inaugural Olympic women's marathon as she raced through the streets of L.A. and finished in 2:24.52, more than three minutes ahead of her chief rival, Norway's Grete Waitz. (*Above left and right,* Paul Chinn • *Opposite,* Chris Gulker)

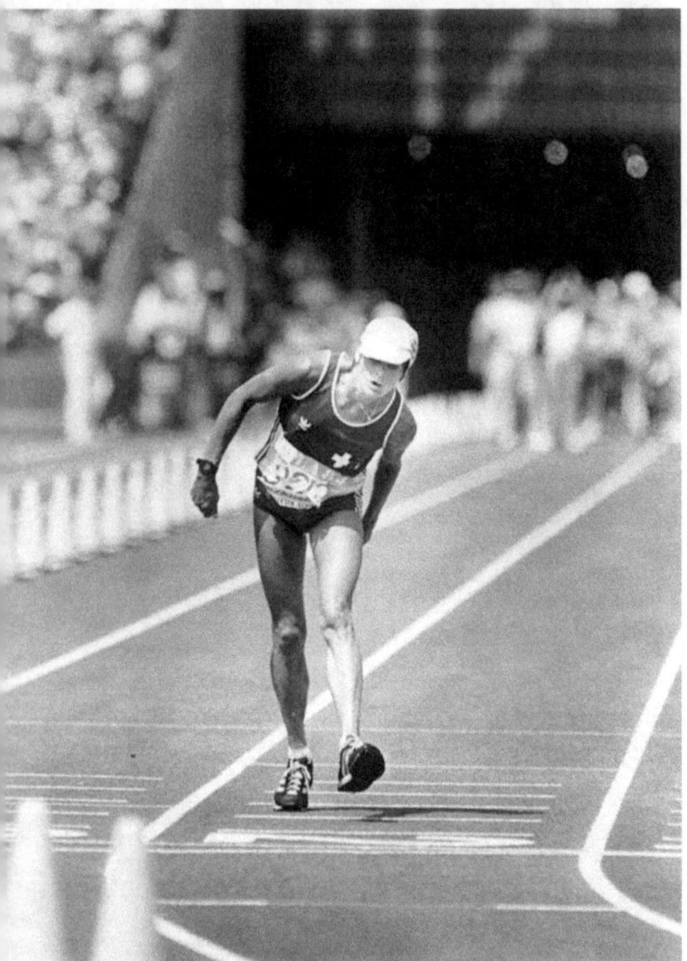

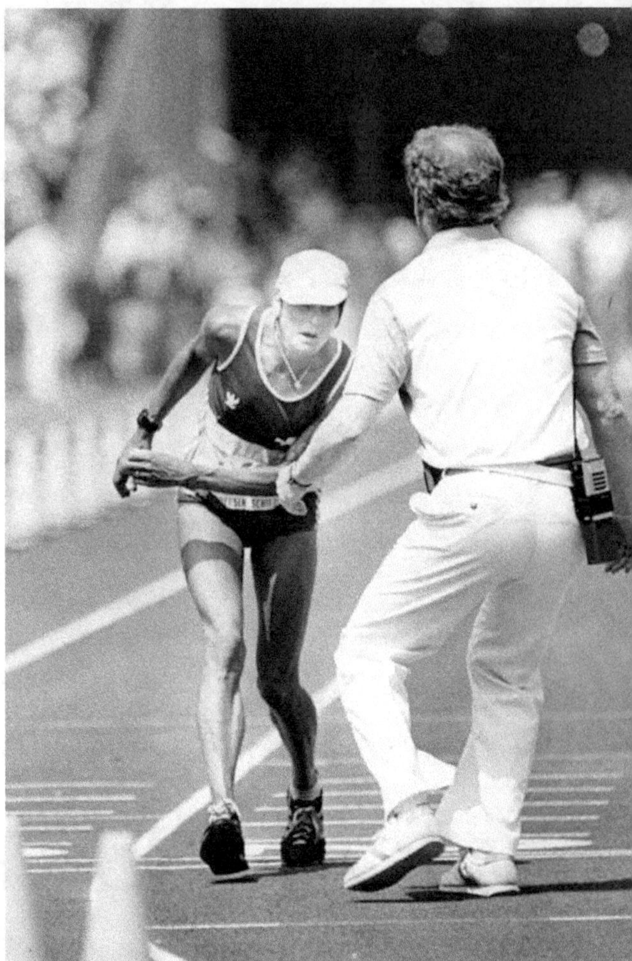

Above left and right and opposite left: **About 20 minutes after Benoit's historic victory, Switzerland's Gabriela Andersen-Schiess entered the Coliseum suffering from heat exhaustion. She refused medical assistance and staggered around the track until she finished, and collapsed, in 37th place. (Paul Chinn)**

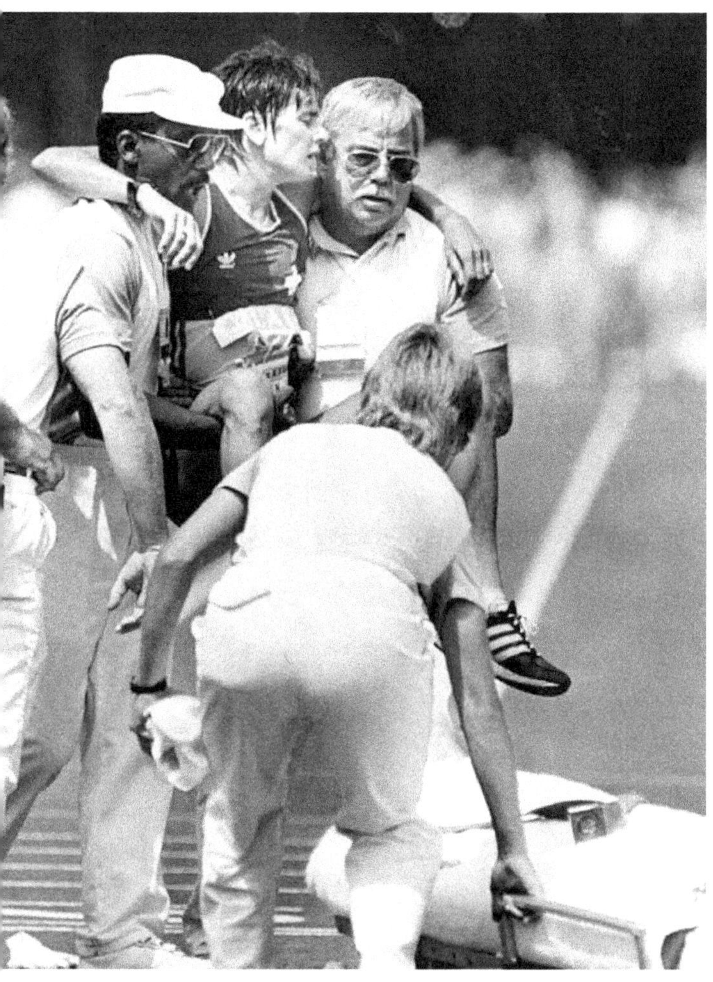

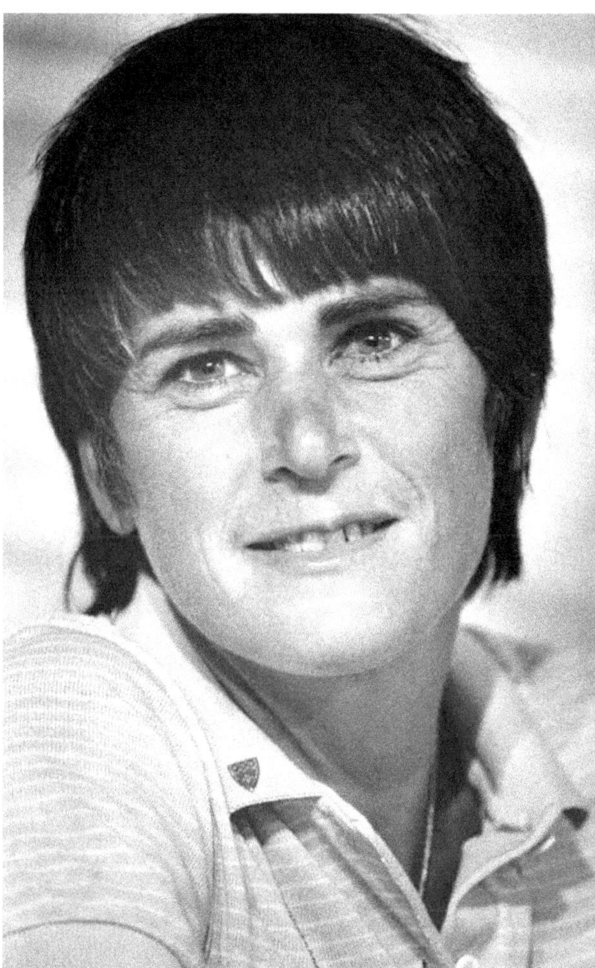

Right: **Andersen-Schiess was well enough to meet the media the next day. (Dean Musgrove)**

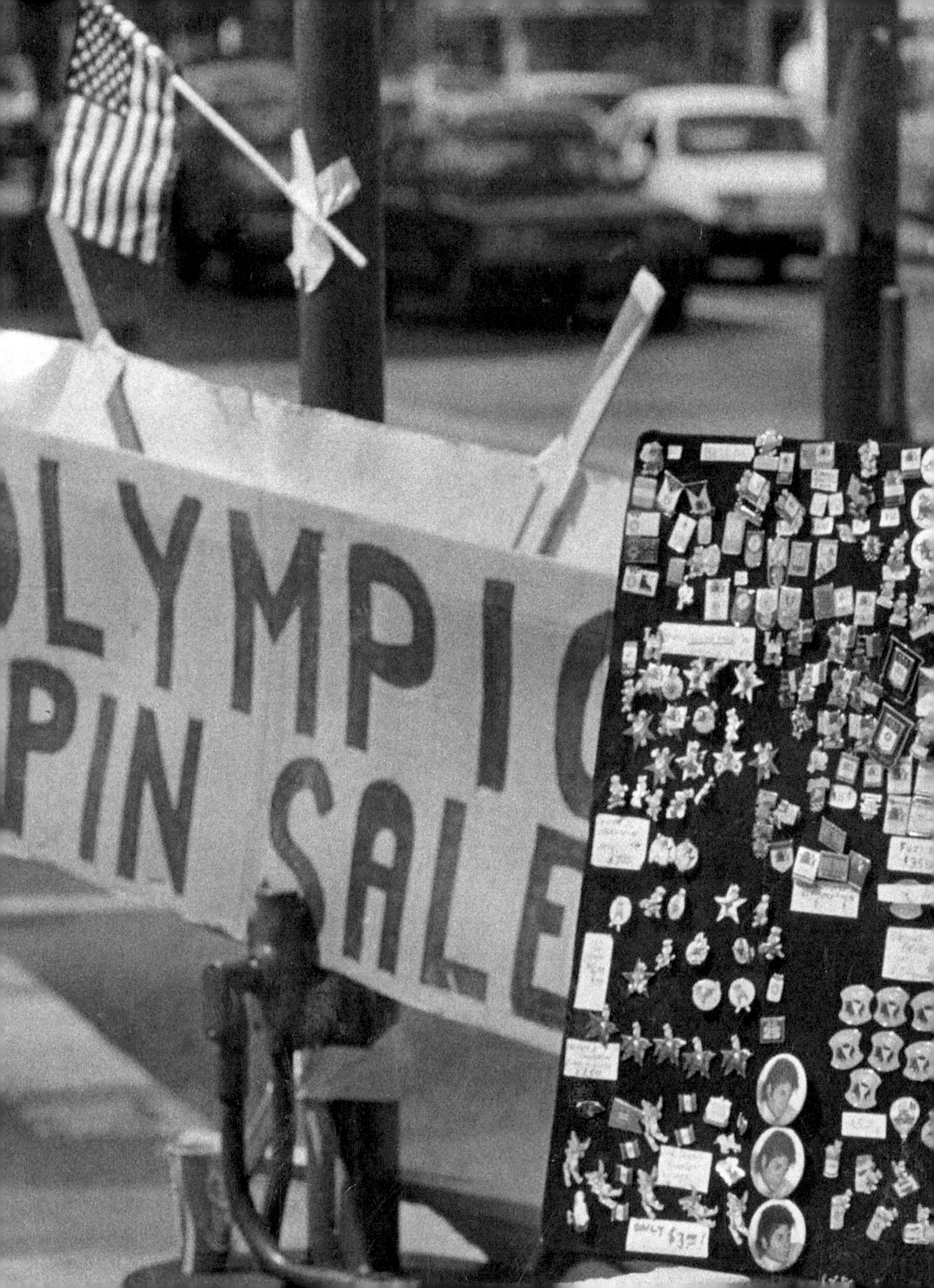

LYMPI
PIN SALE

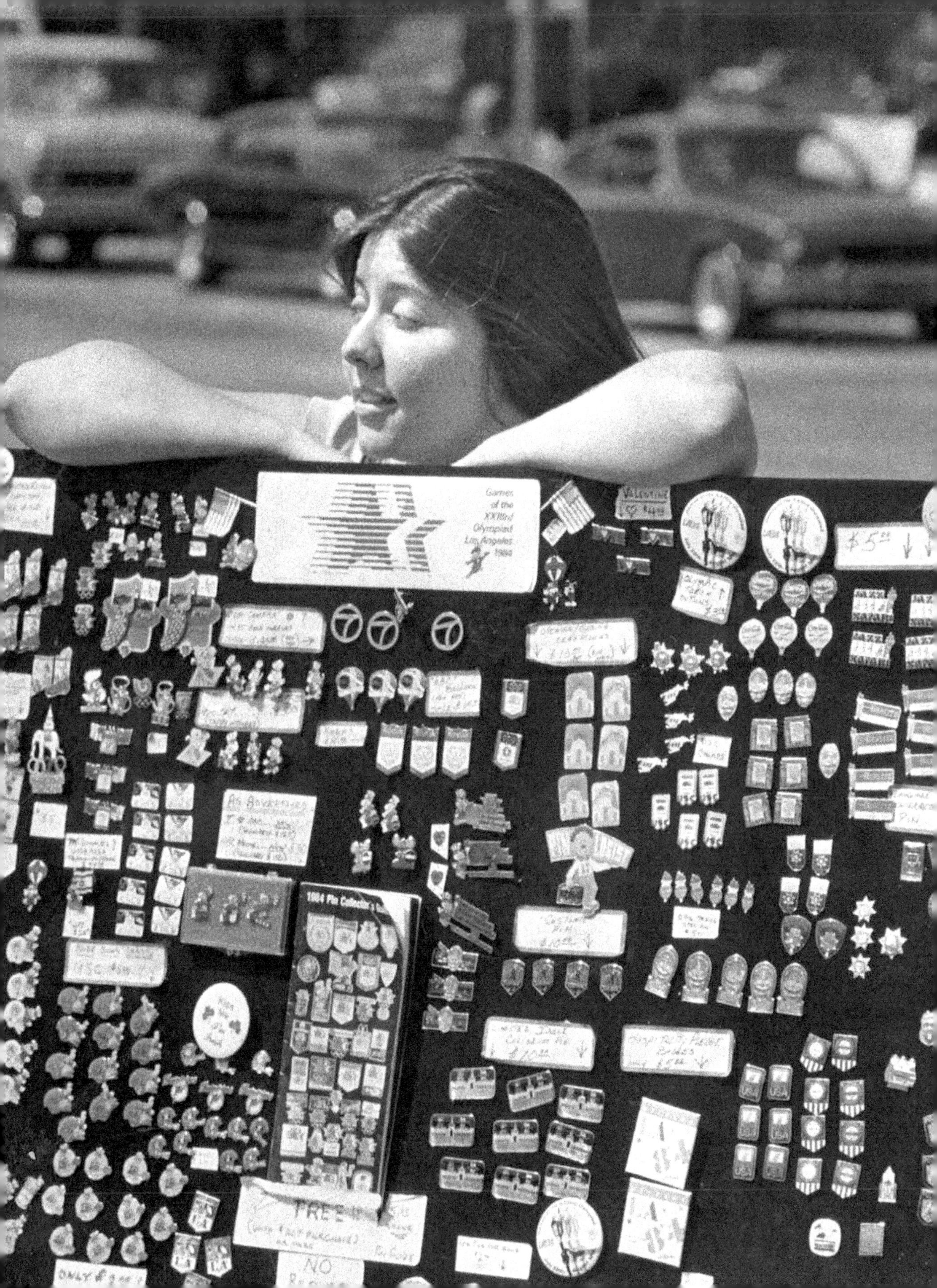
Games of the XXIIIrd Olympiad Los Angeles 1984
VALENTINE

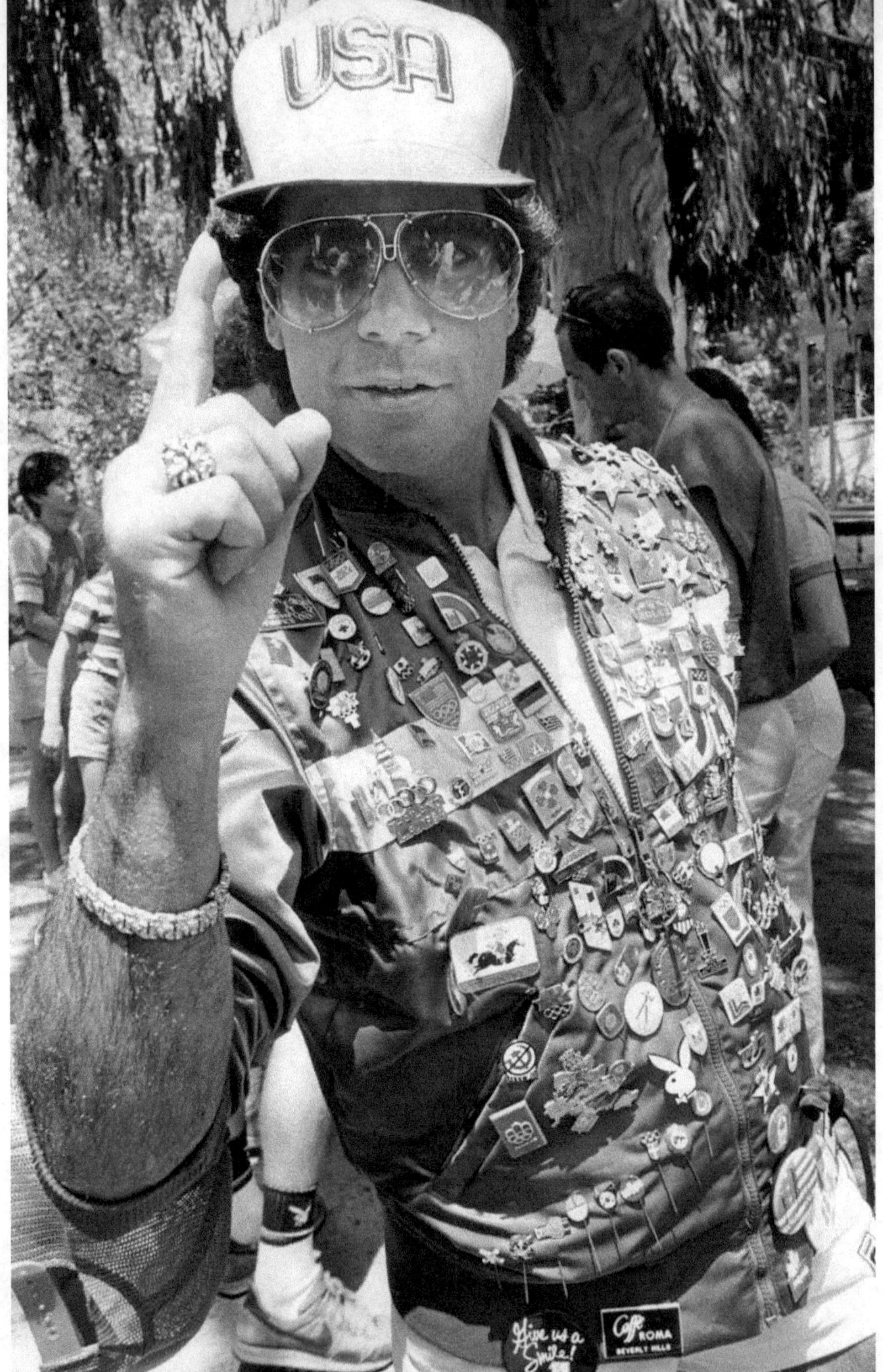

Above, opposite and overleaf: **Pin trading was a popular sport during the Games. (*Above,* Toru Kawana • *Opposite top,* Tom Zimmerman • *Opposite bottom,* Mike Sergieff)**

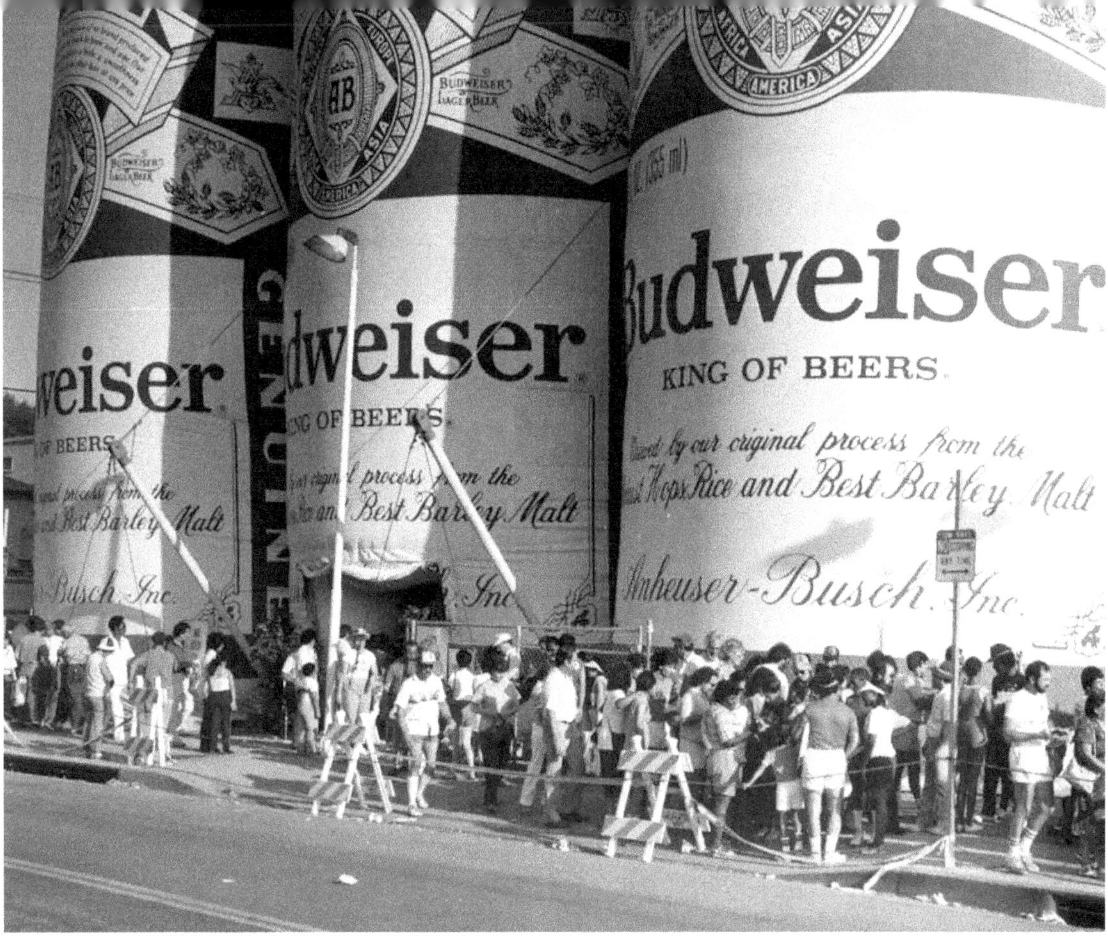
Budweiser
KING OF BEERS
Anheuser-Busch. Inc
GENUINE

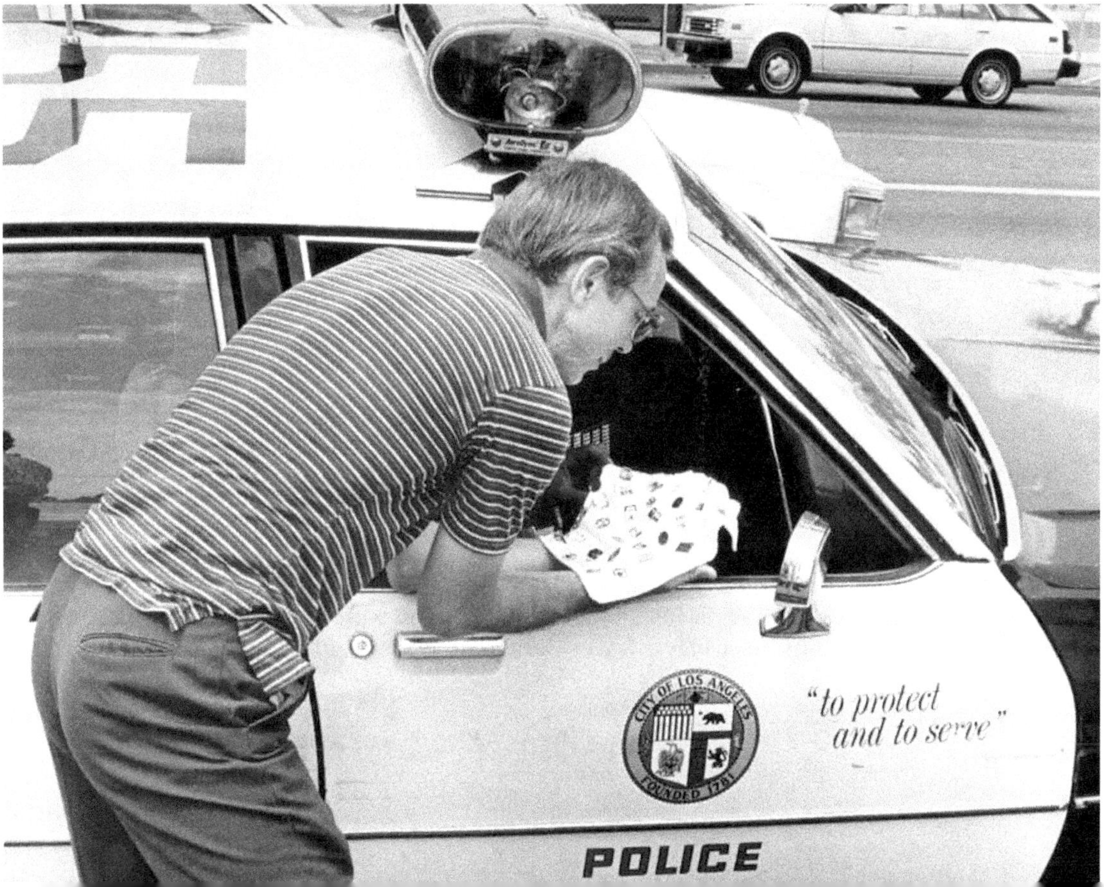
"to protect
and to serve"
CITY OF LOS ANGELES
FOUNDED 1781
POLICE

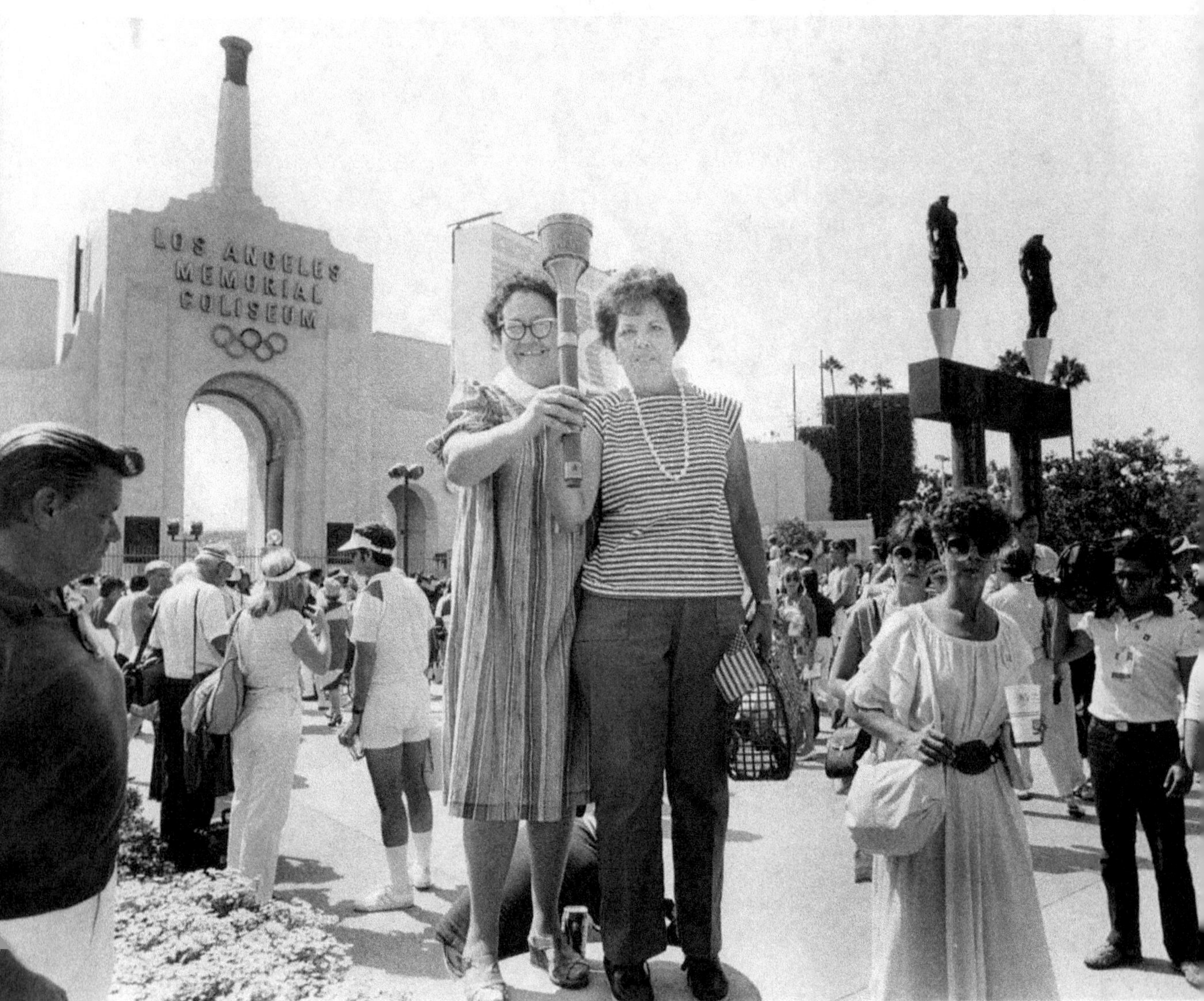

Above, opposite, pages 118-121: **Outside the Coliseum, and in the surrounding neighborhood, were crowds of spectators, break-dancers, fans watching the action on a miniature TV, people selling parking spaces and water, and a sneaker company hawking its wares. (*Above,* Javier Mendoza • *Opposite,* Chris Gulker)**

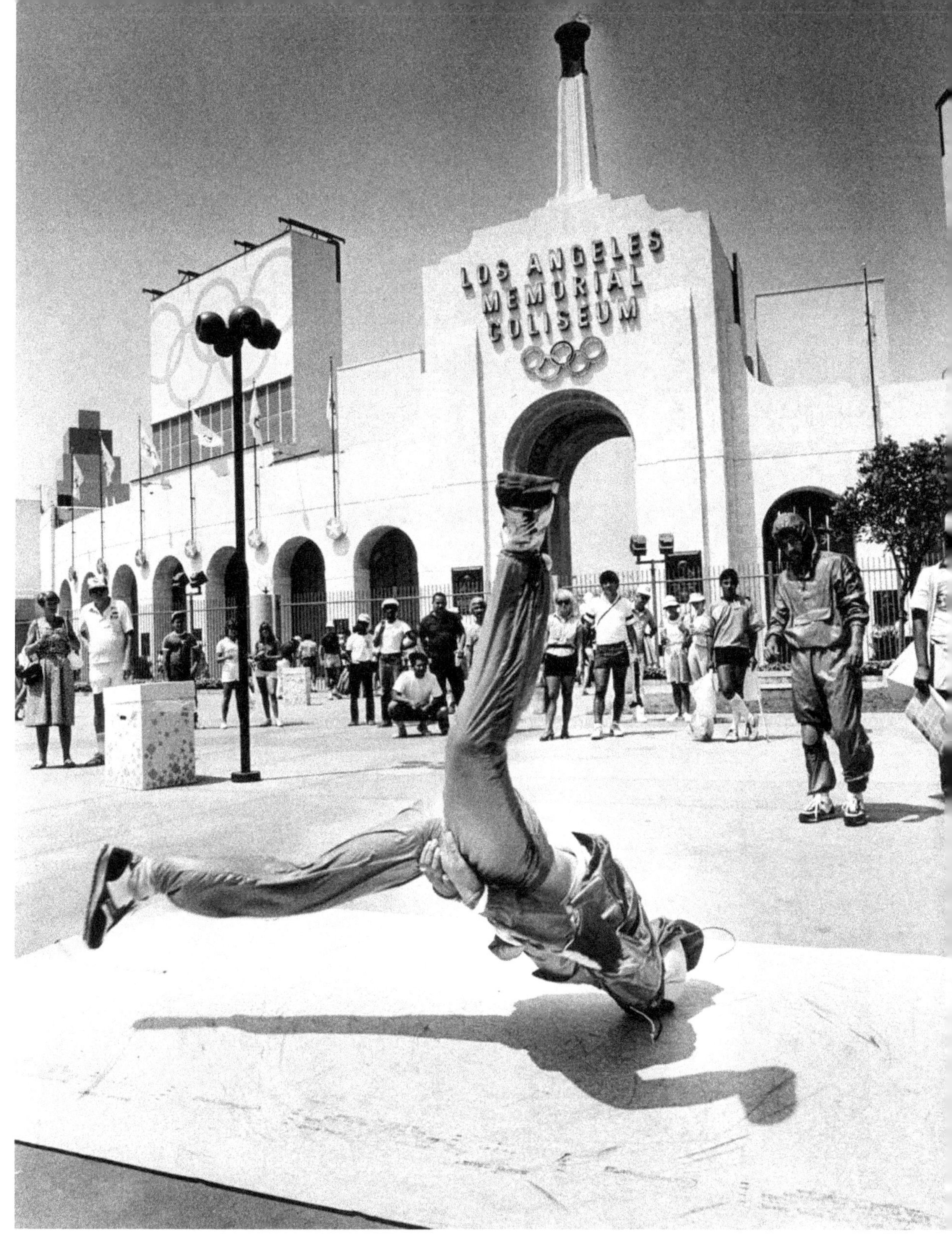
LOS ANGELES
MEMORIAL
COLISEUM

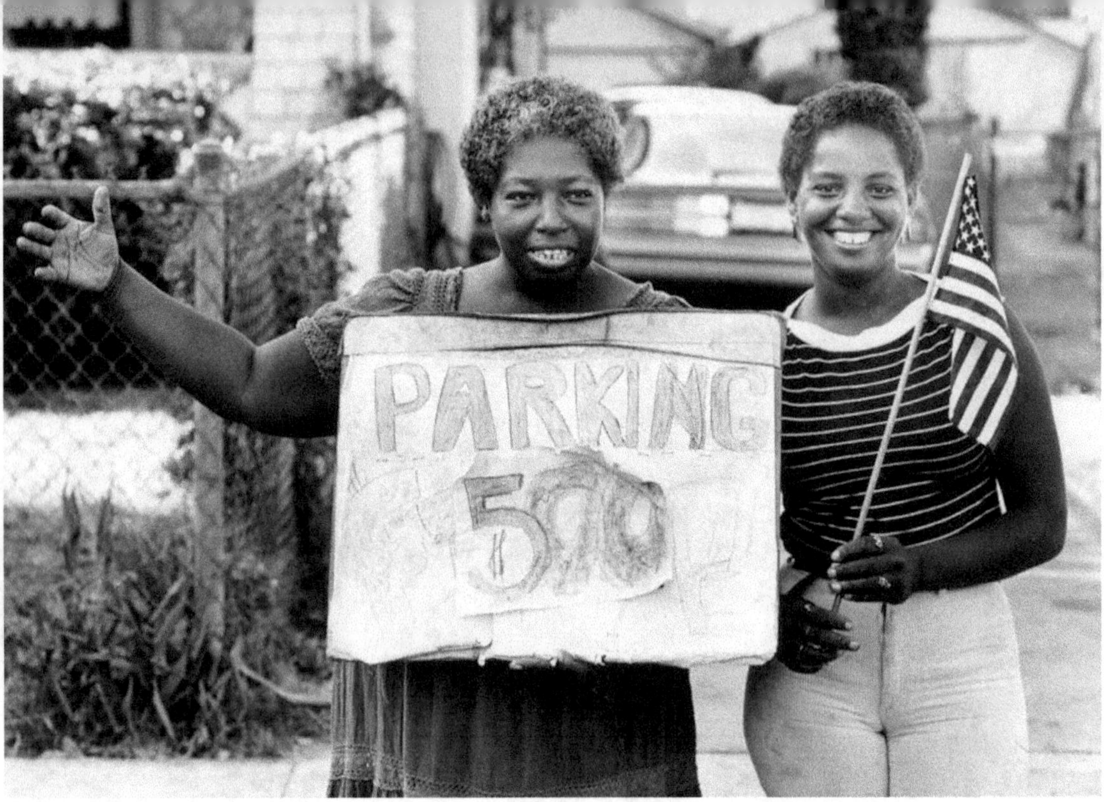

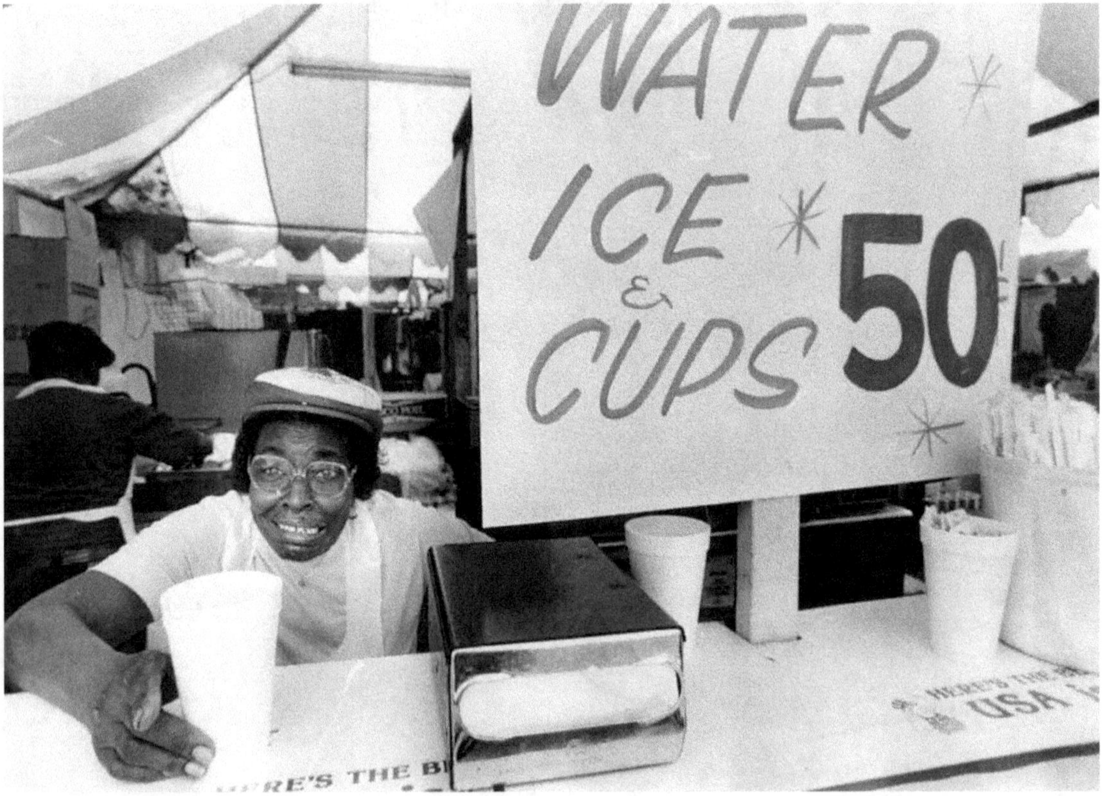

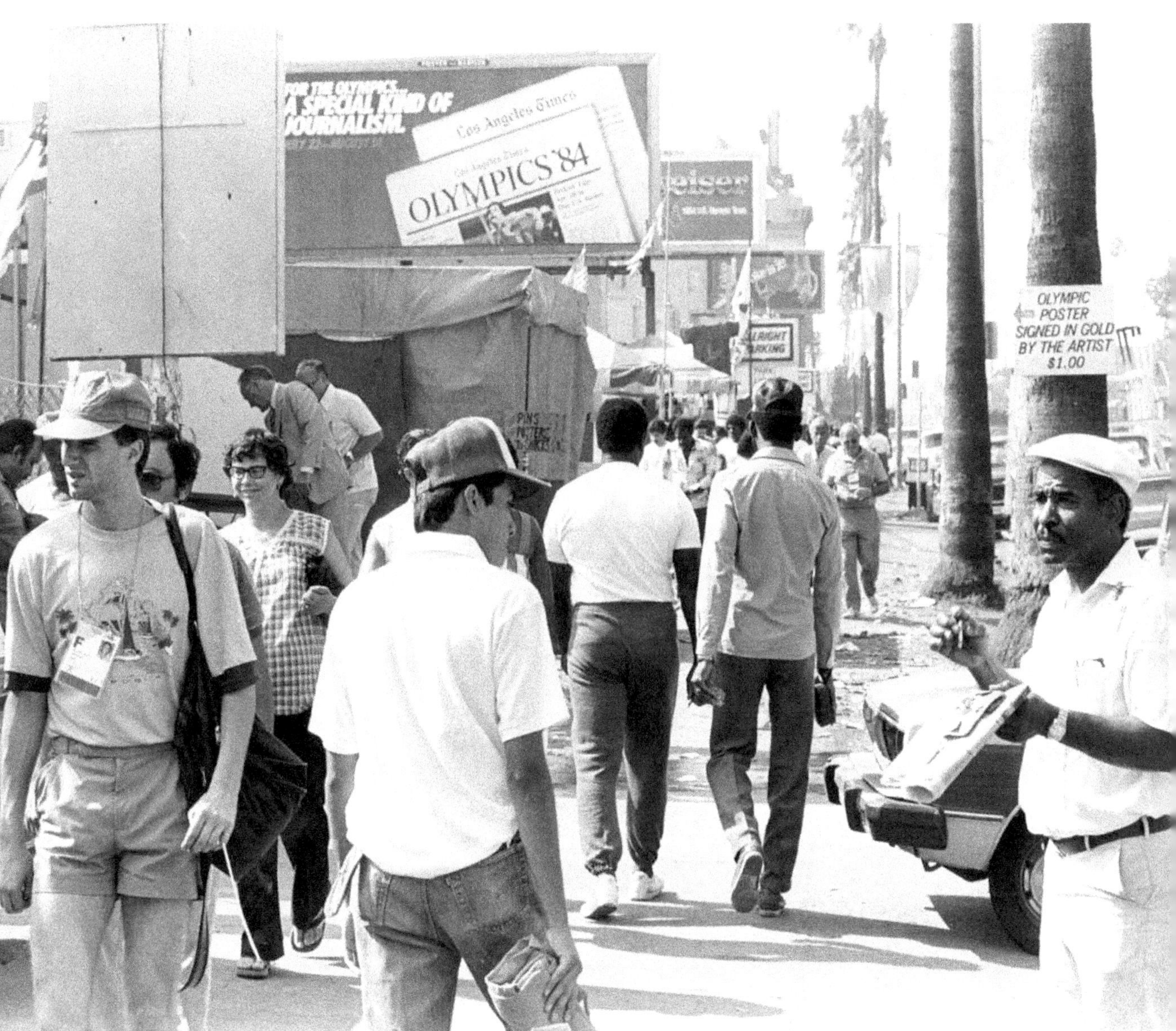

(*Above,* **Mike Sergieff** • *Opposite top,* **Tom Zimmerman** • *Opposite bottom,* **Michael Haering**)

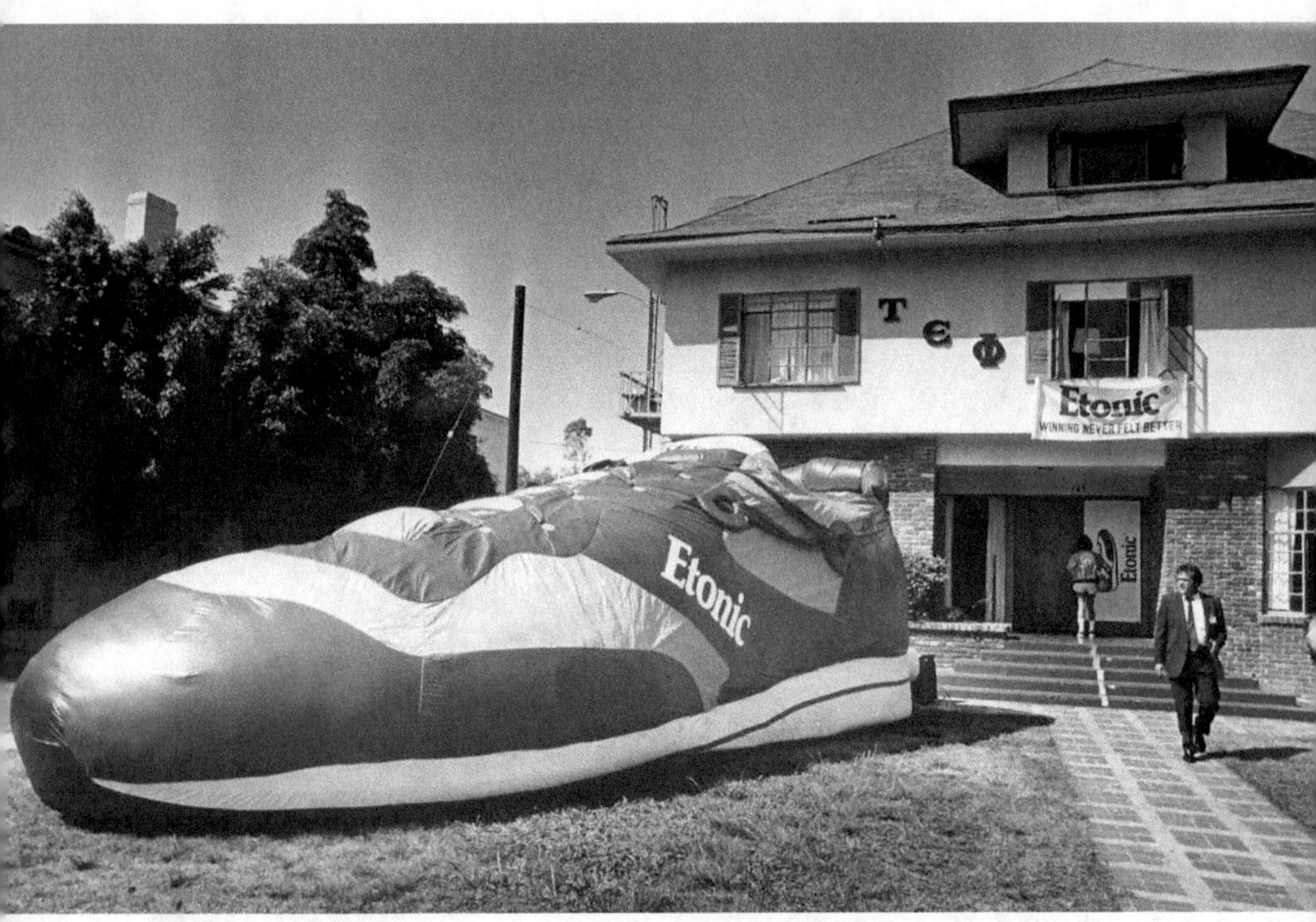

(*Above,* Chris Gulker • *Opposite,* Tom Zimmerman)

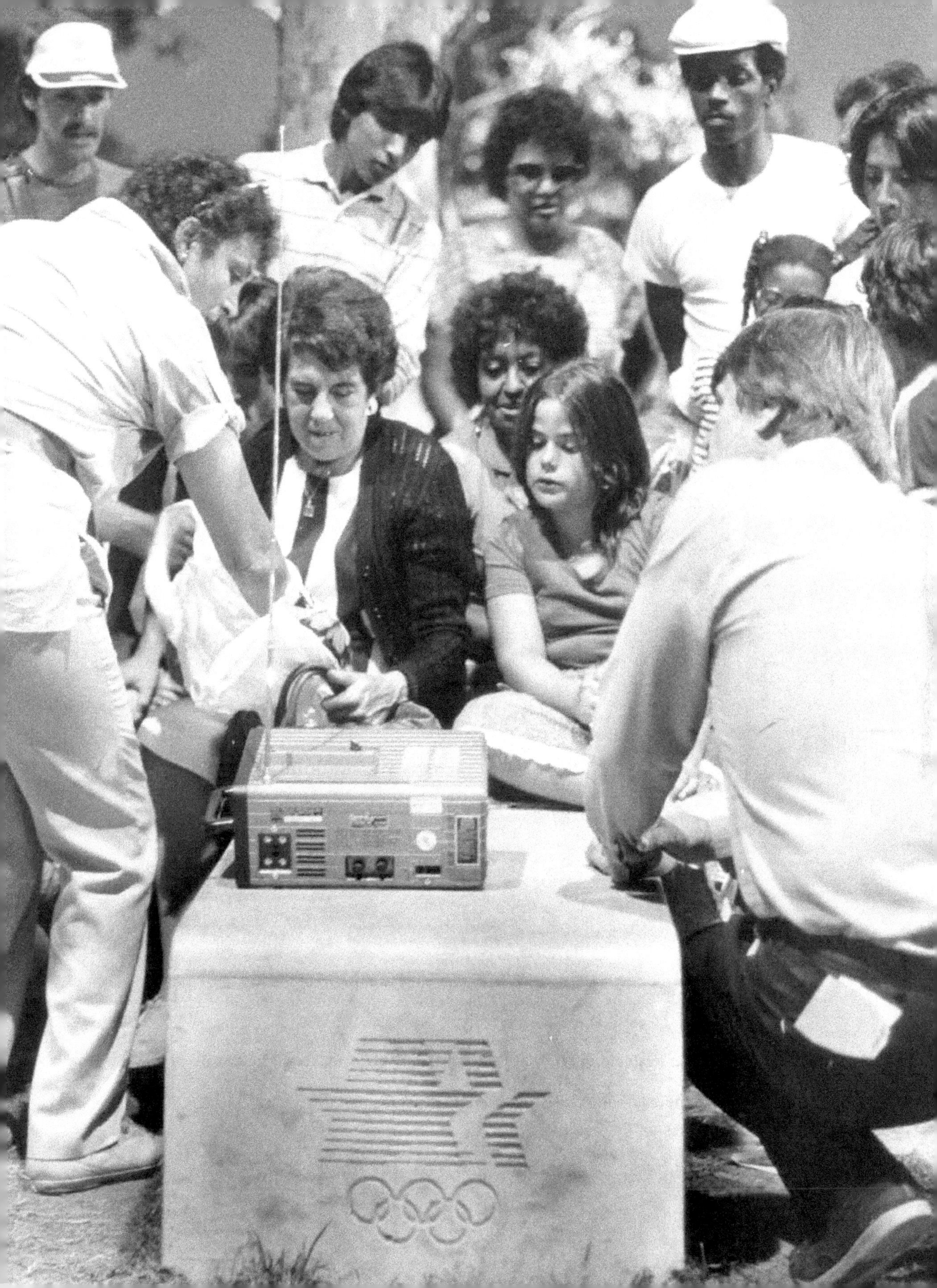

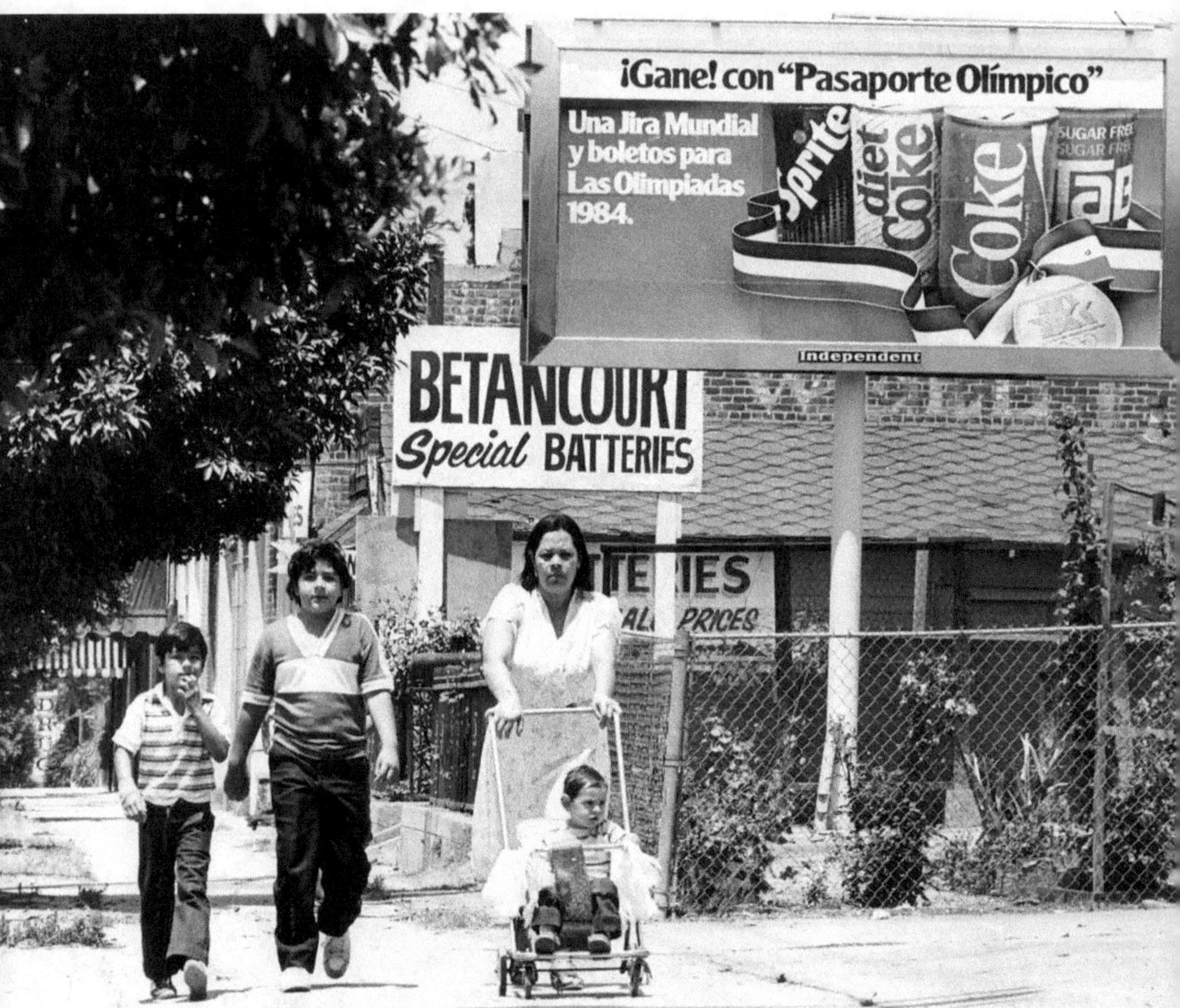

A billboard in Spanish along Whittier Boulevard in East L.A. (Javier Mendoza)

Opposite: The models from a billboard campaign re-enacted their kiss. (Mike Sergieff)

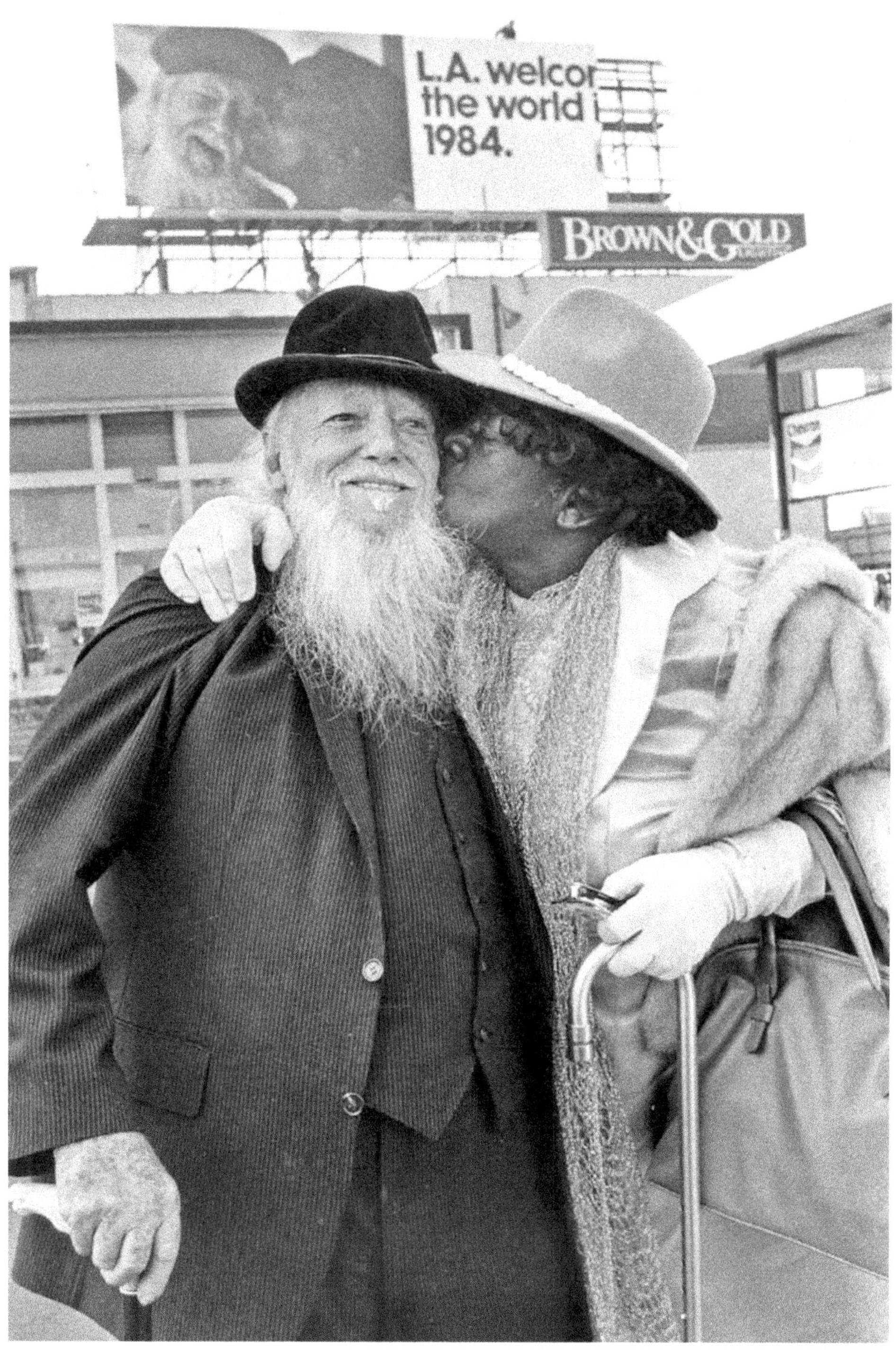
L.A. welcor
the world i
1984.
BROWN&GOLD

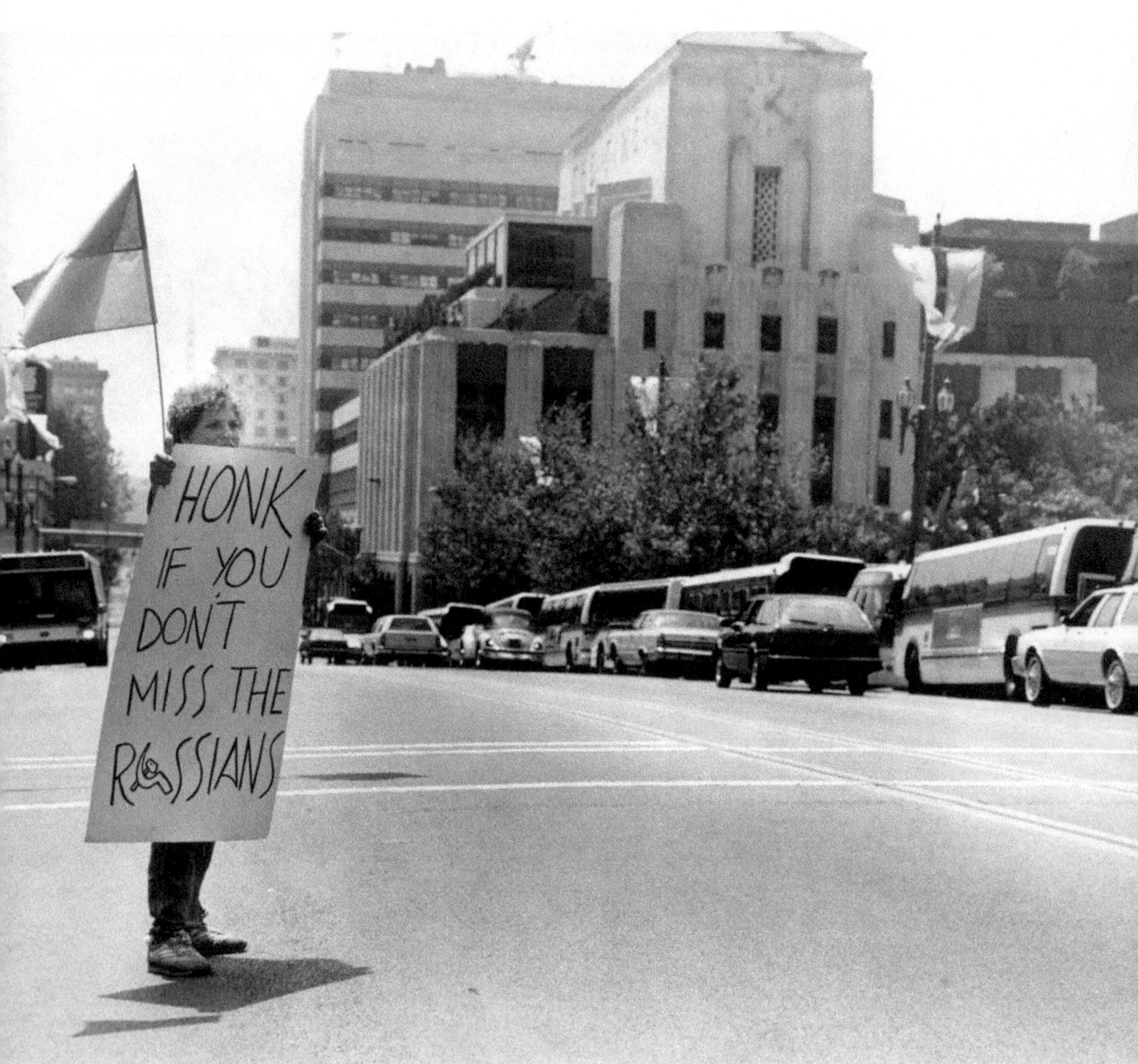

In downtown LA, a Ukrainian protester held up a sign mocking the boycott by the Soviet Union. (Tom Zimmerman)

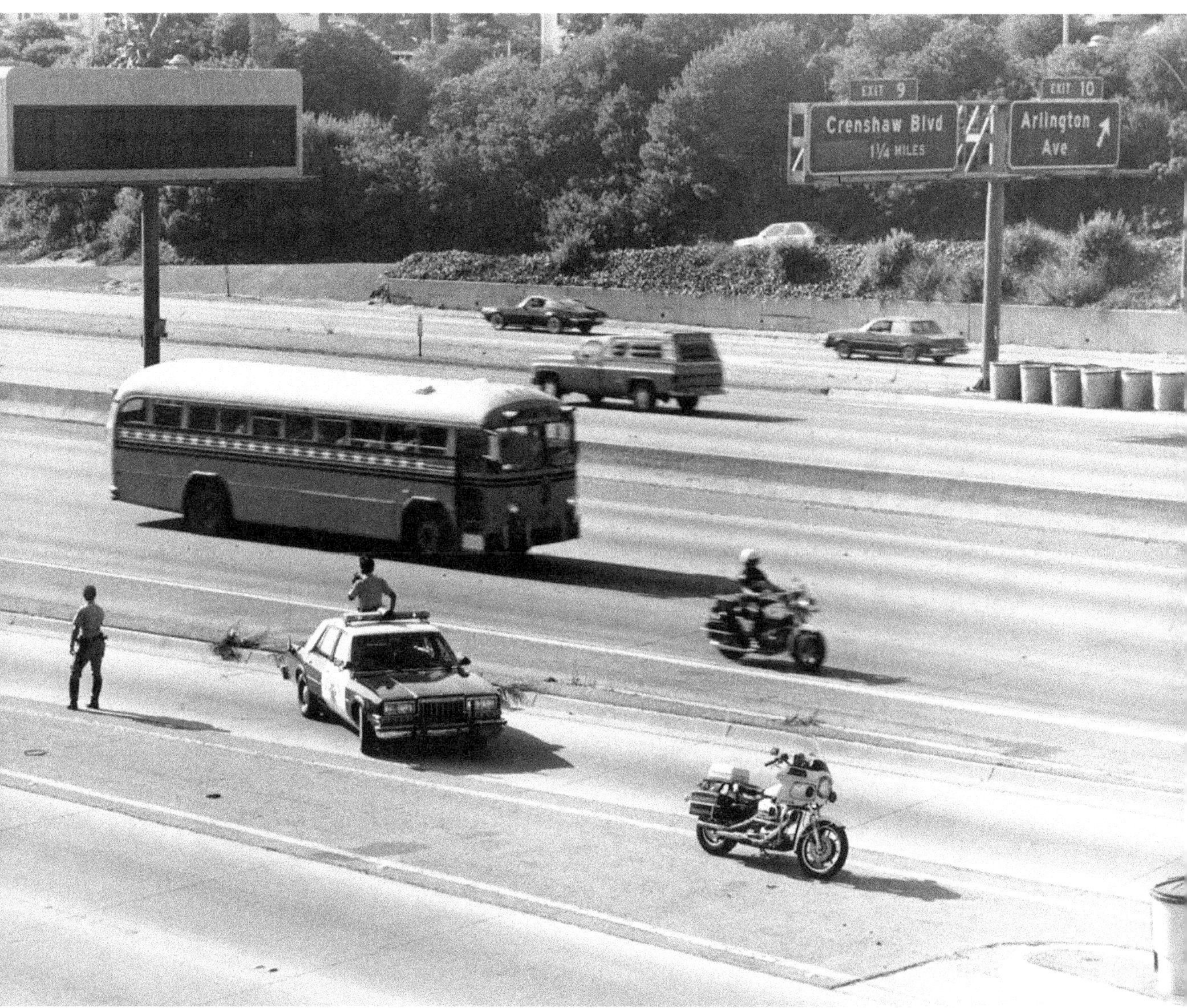

Traffic was lighter than usual during the Games, enabling buses to swiftly take the athletes to their events. (Tom Zimmerman)

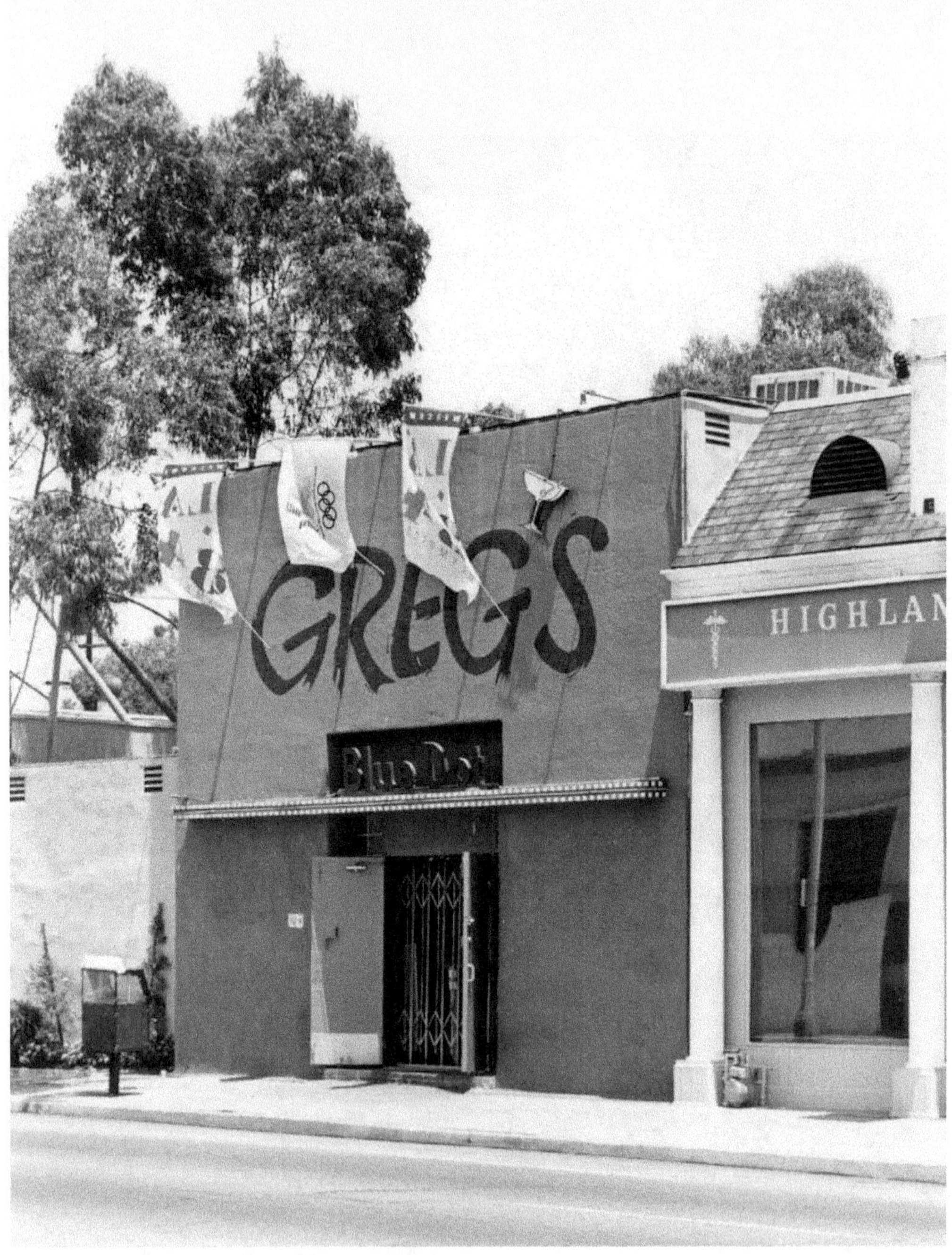

Greg's Blue Dot, a bar in Hollywood, was open for business during the Games (Tom Zimmerman), as was the Rialto Theater in South Pasadena (*opposite*). (Chris Gulker)

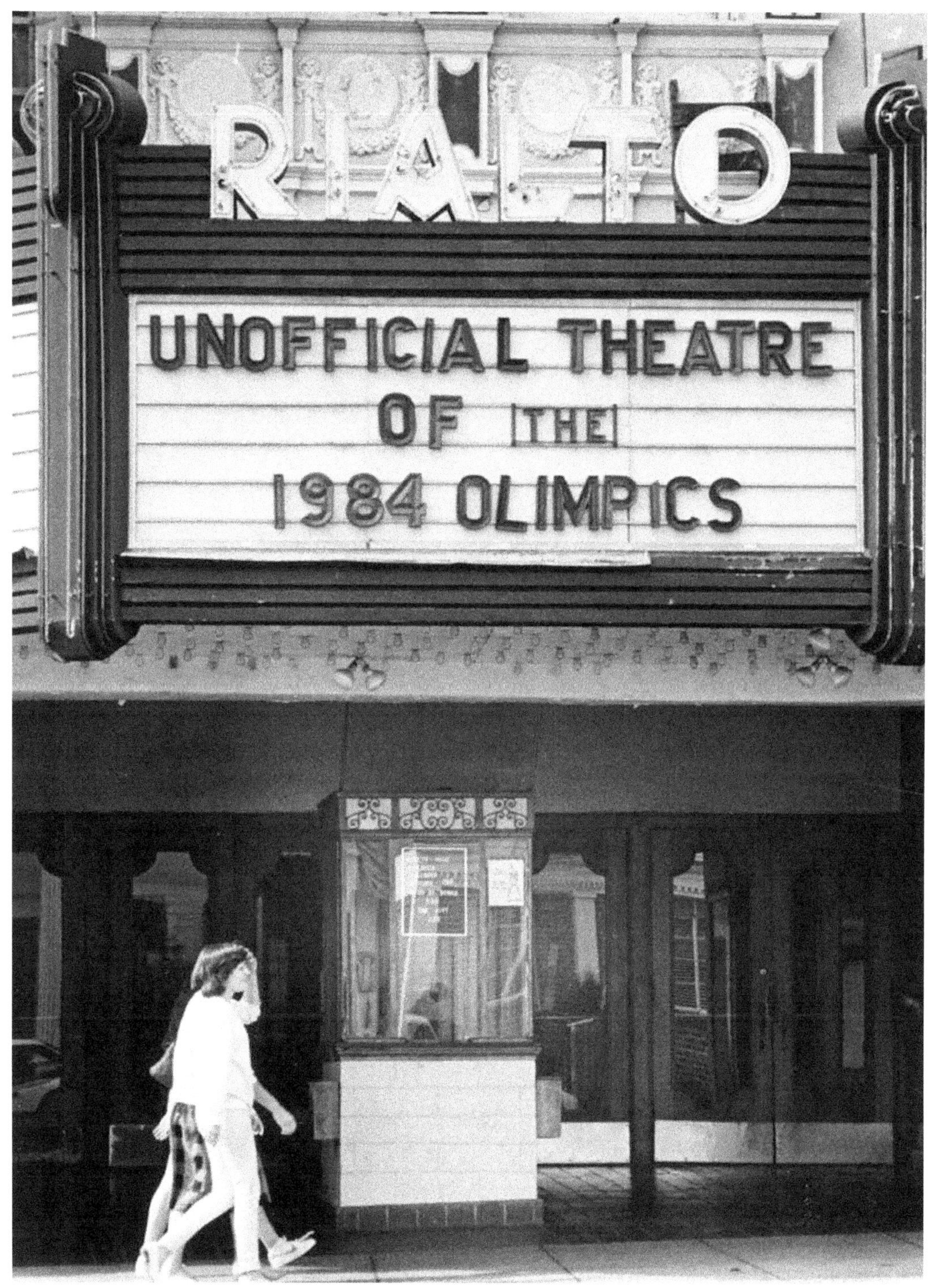
RIALTO
UNOFFICIAL THEATRE
OF THE
1984 OLIMPICS

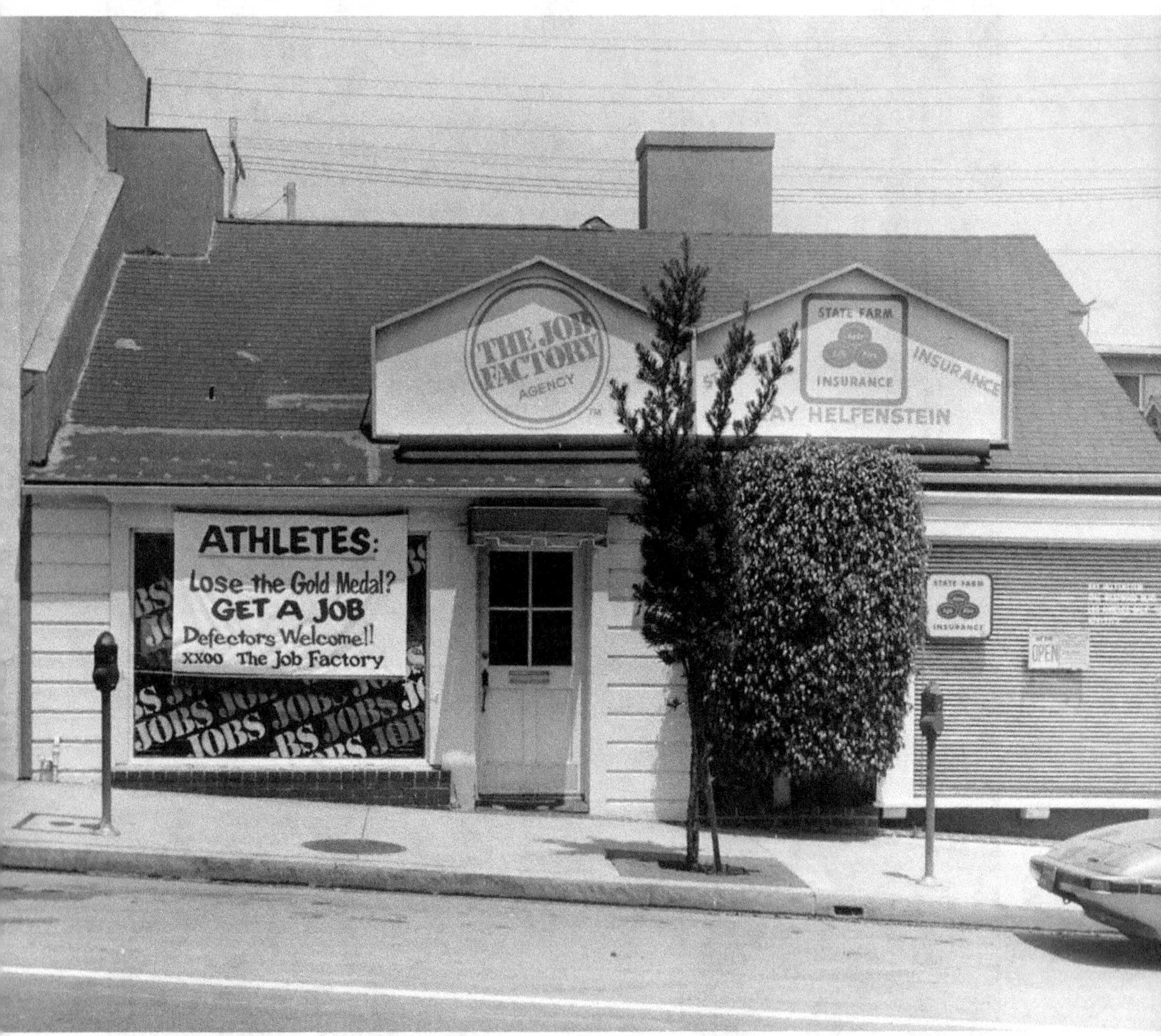

The Job Factory on Westwood Boulevard sought fresh talent, and a gas station at Highland and Melrose welcomed the world (*opposite*). (Tom Zimmerman)

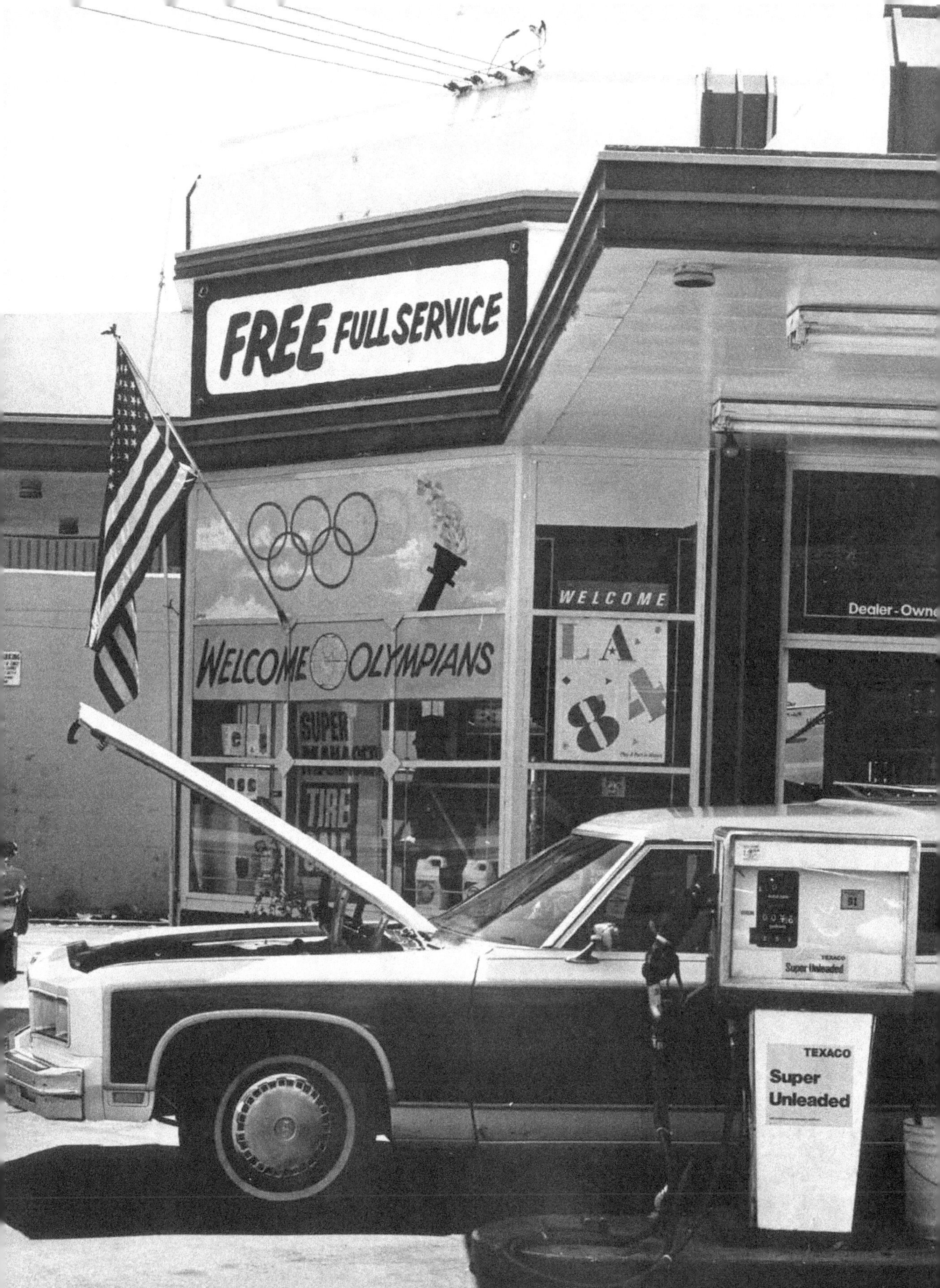
FREE FULL SERVICE
WELCOME OLYMPIANS
WELCOME
LA 84
SUPER
TIRE
Dealer-Owne
TEXACO
Super Unleaded
TEXACO
Super
Unleaded

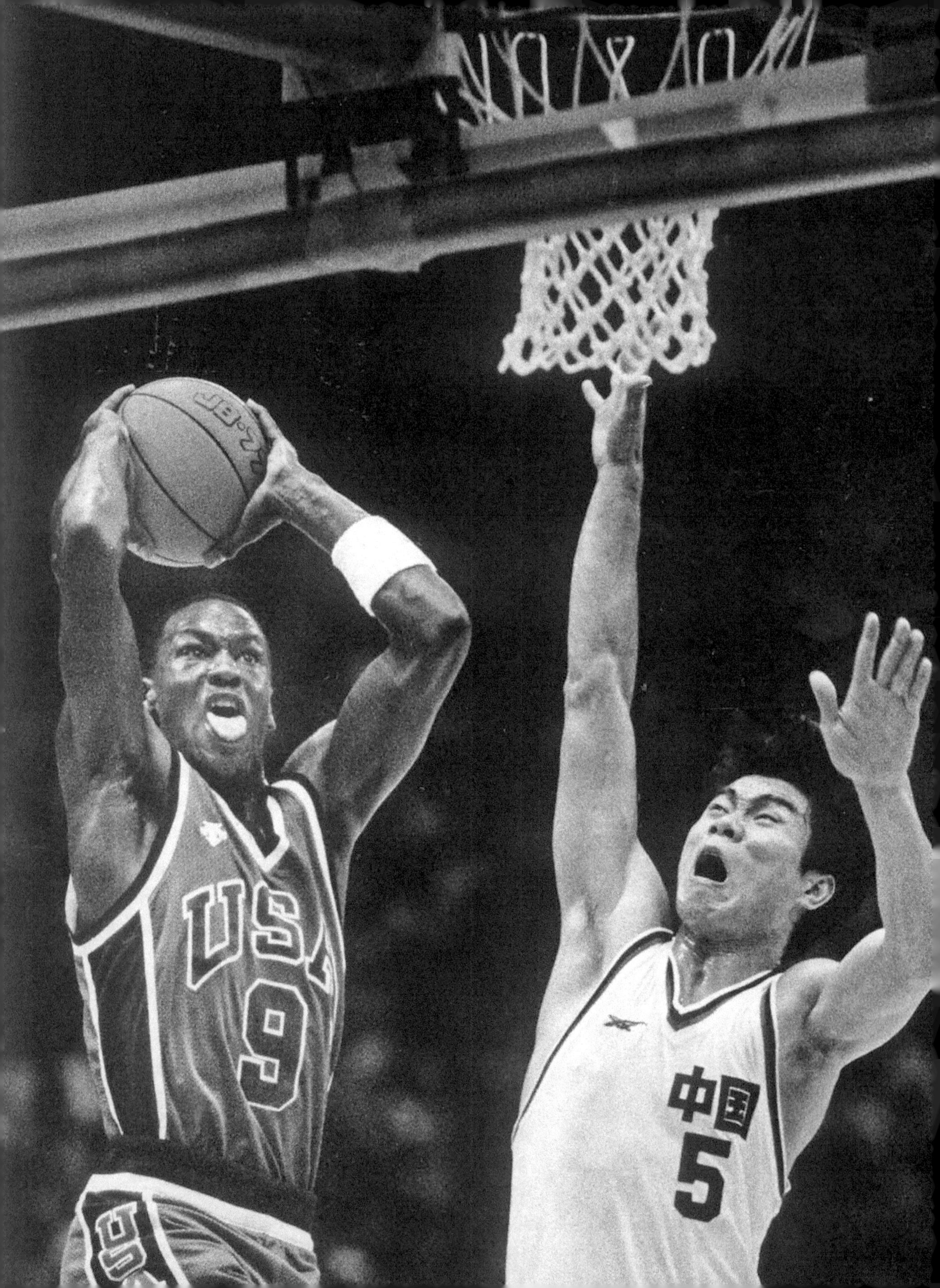
USA
9
中国
5

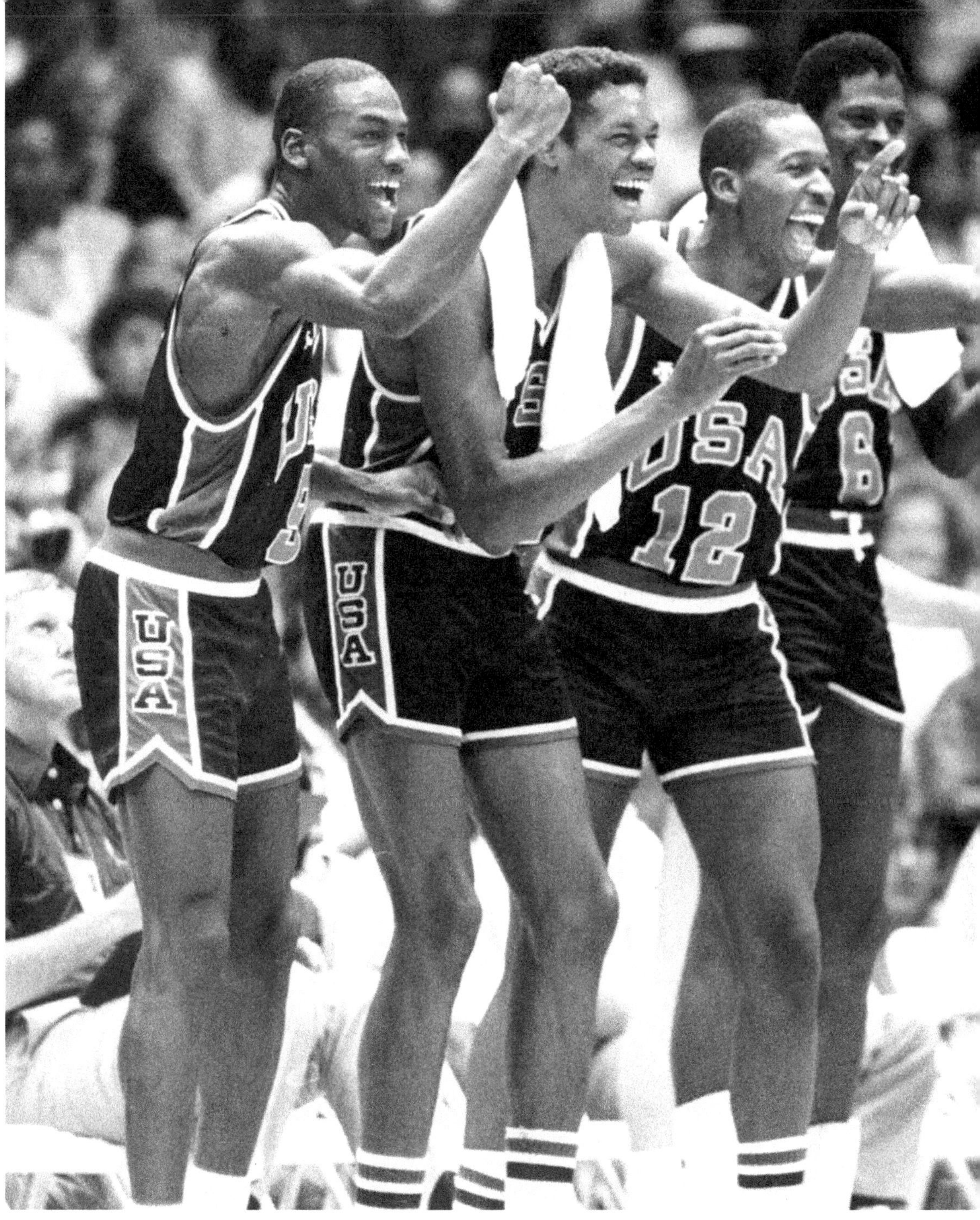

Michael Jordan rooted from the sidelines alongside teammates (*from left*) Sam Perkins, Wayman Tisdale, and Patrick Ewing—as he led a team of collegians to the gold medal. (James Ruebsamen)

Opposite: **At the Forum, Michael Jordan soared against an opponent from China. (James Ruebsamen)**

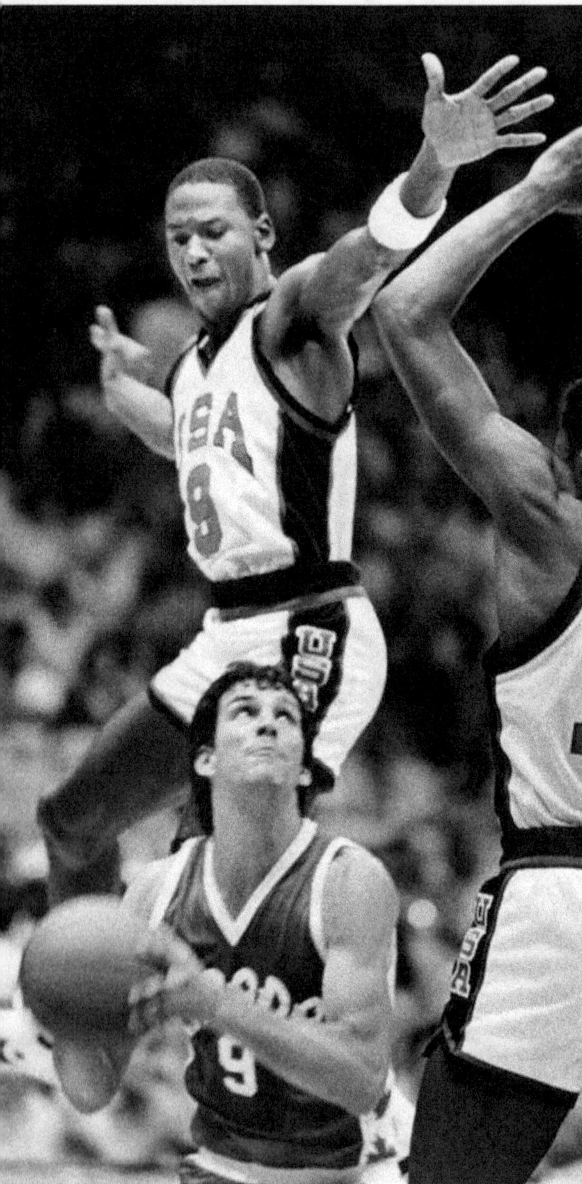

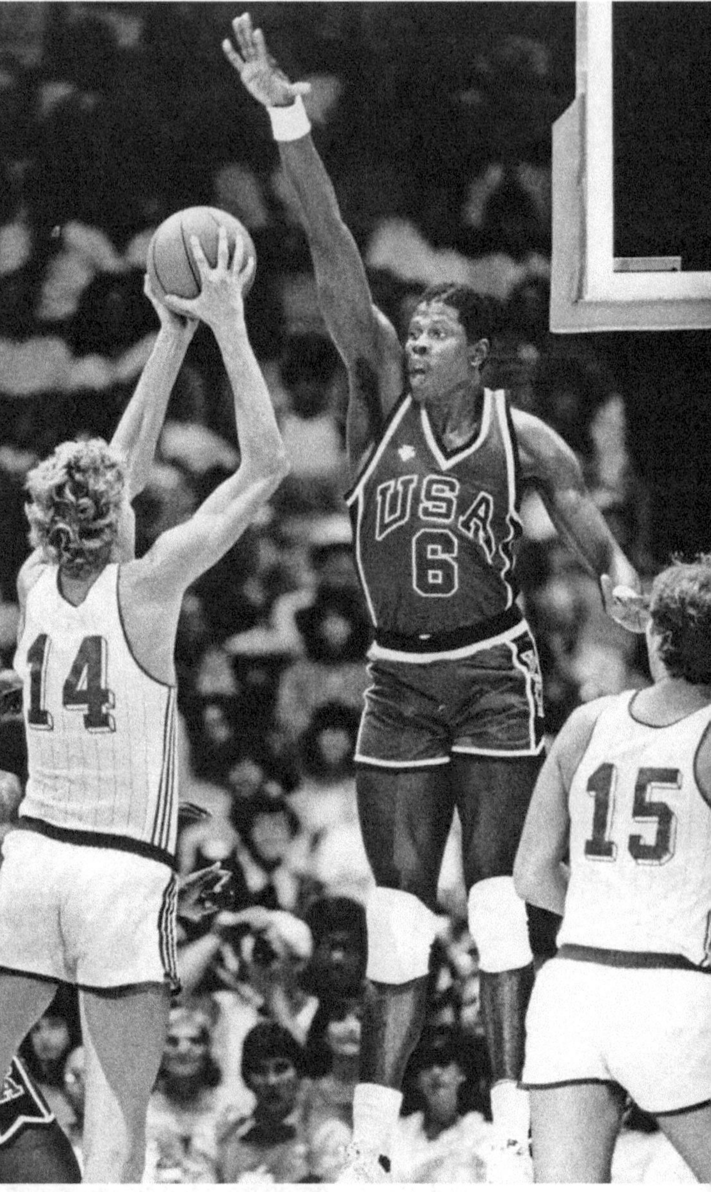

Left: **Defense by Jordan against Canada.** ***Right:*** **Against Germany, Ewing readied to reject this shot. (James Ruebsamen)**

Opposite: **Coach Bobby Knight argued his case against Uruguay. (James Ruebsamen)**

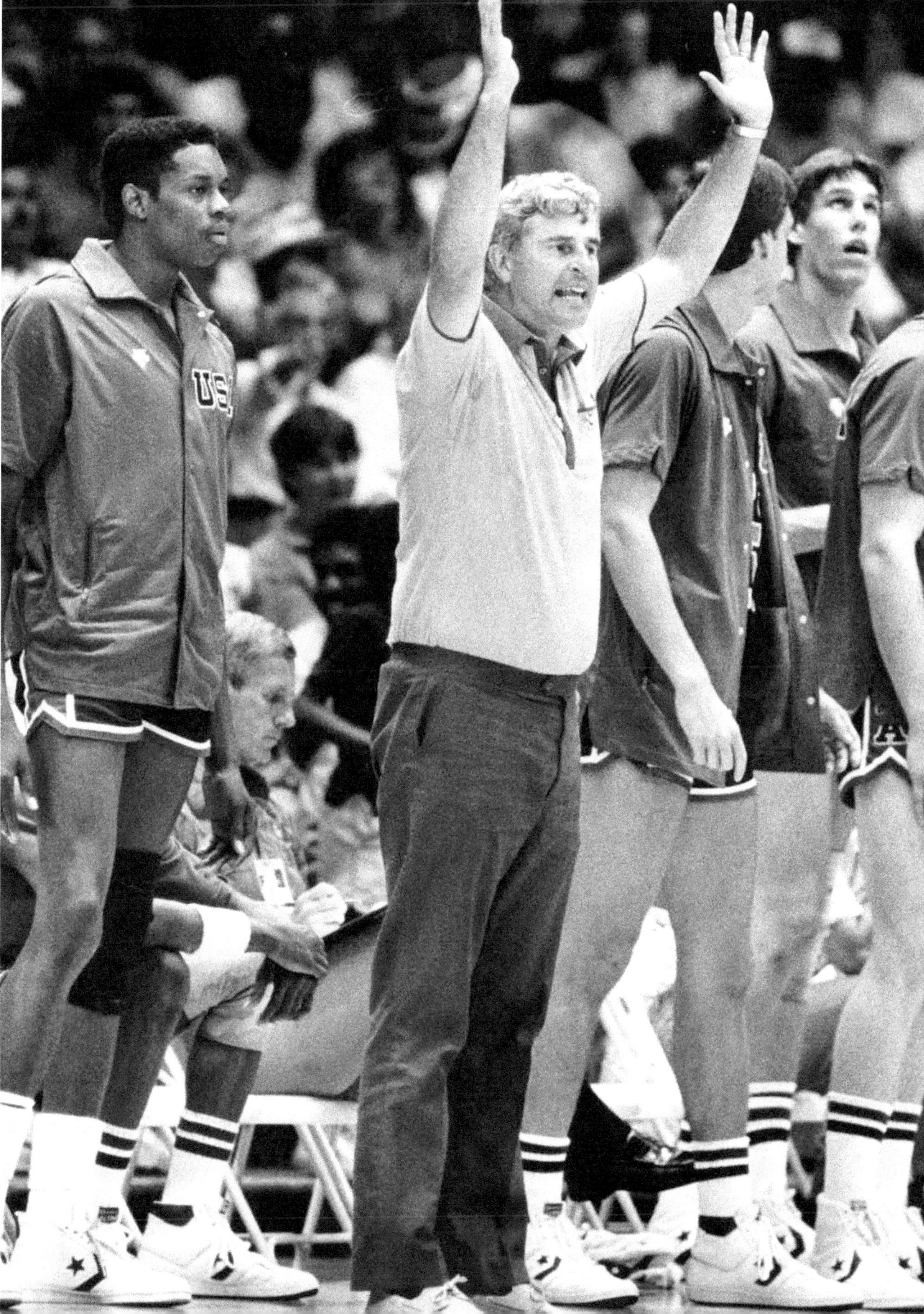

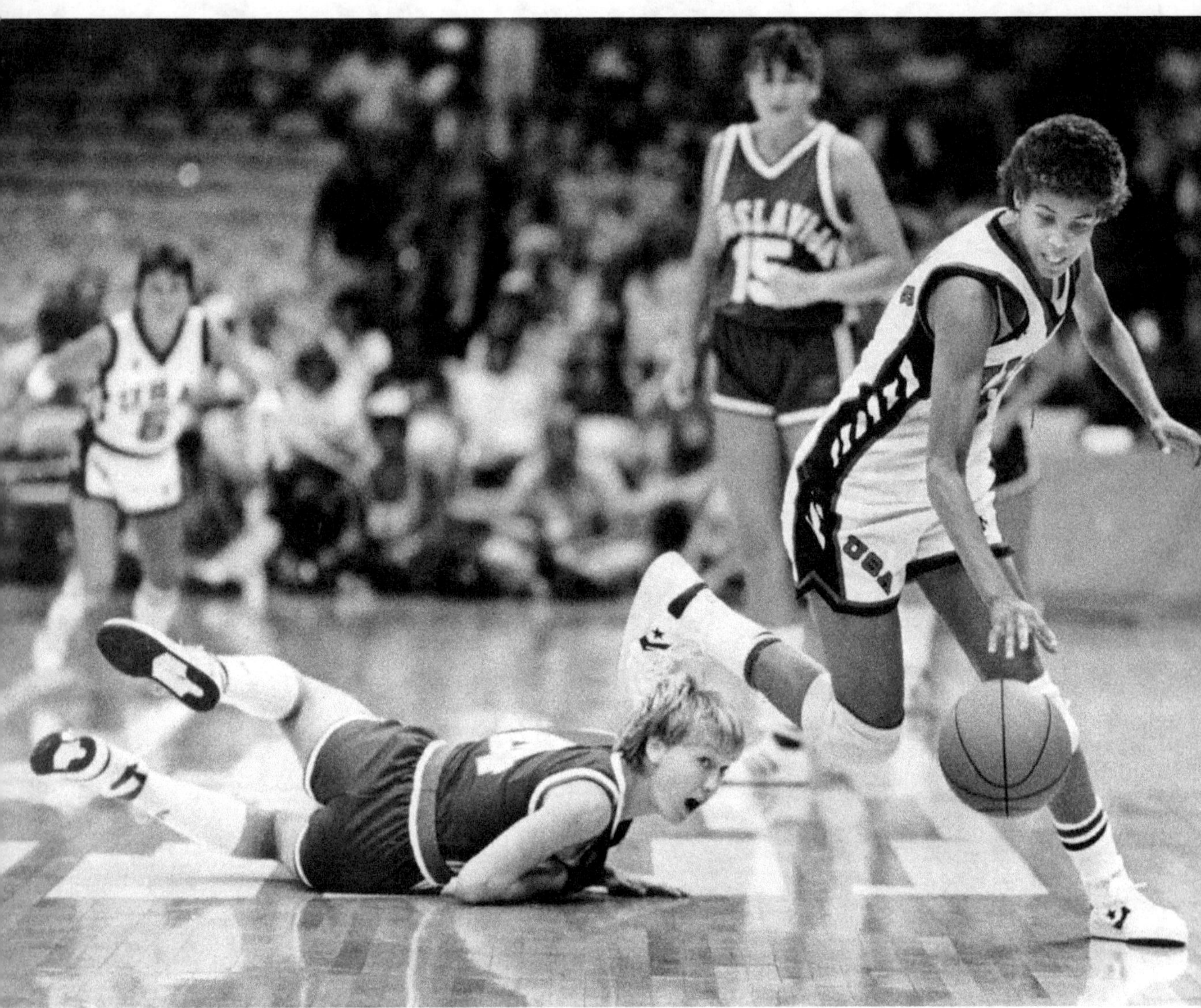

Above and opposite: **Local hero Cheryl Miller (Riverside Polytechnic High and USC grad) was a prime catalyst for the U.S. women's team. (James Ruebsamen)**

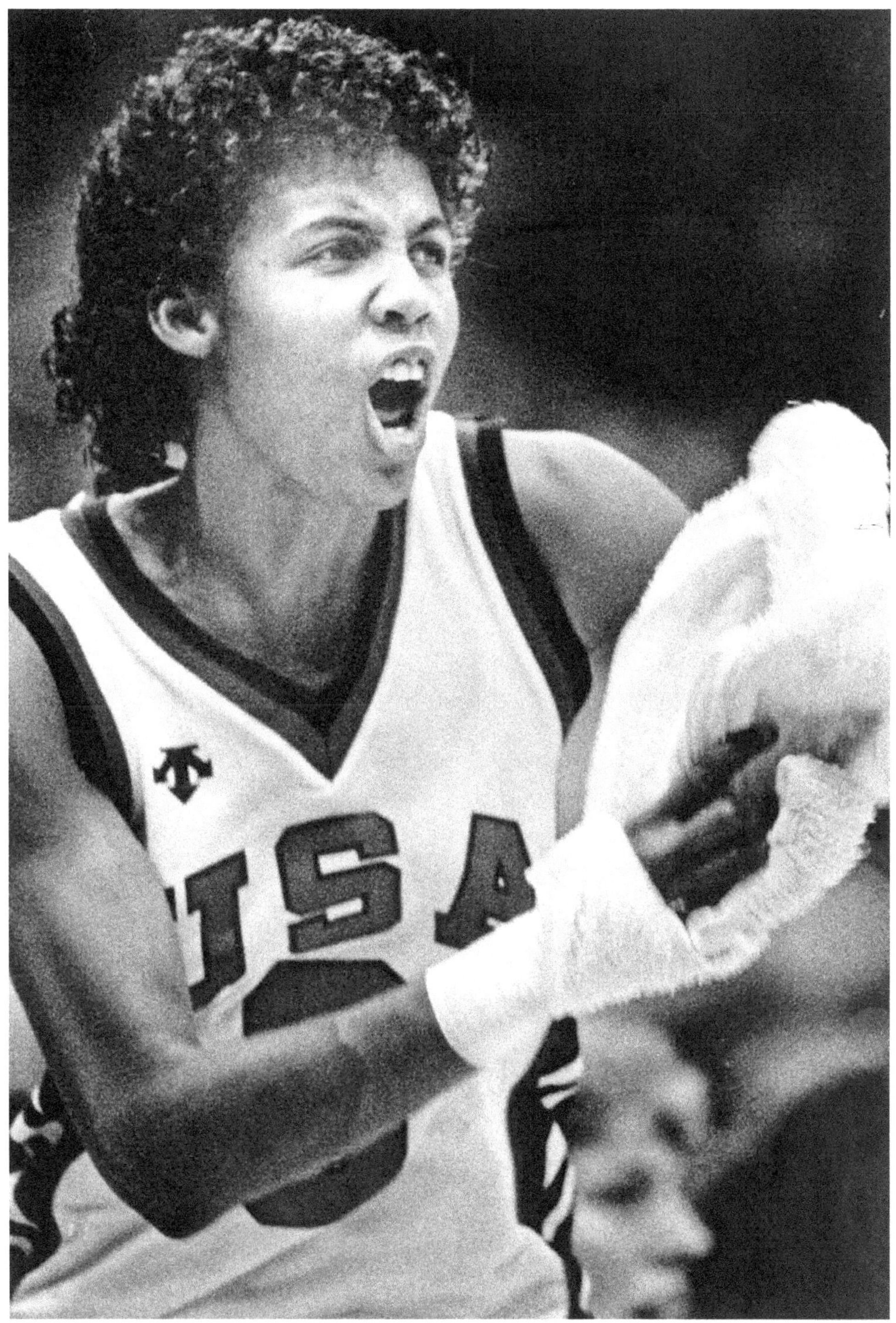

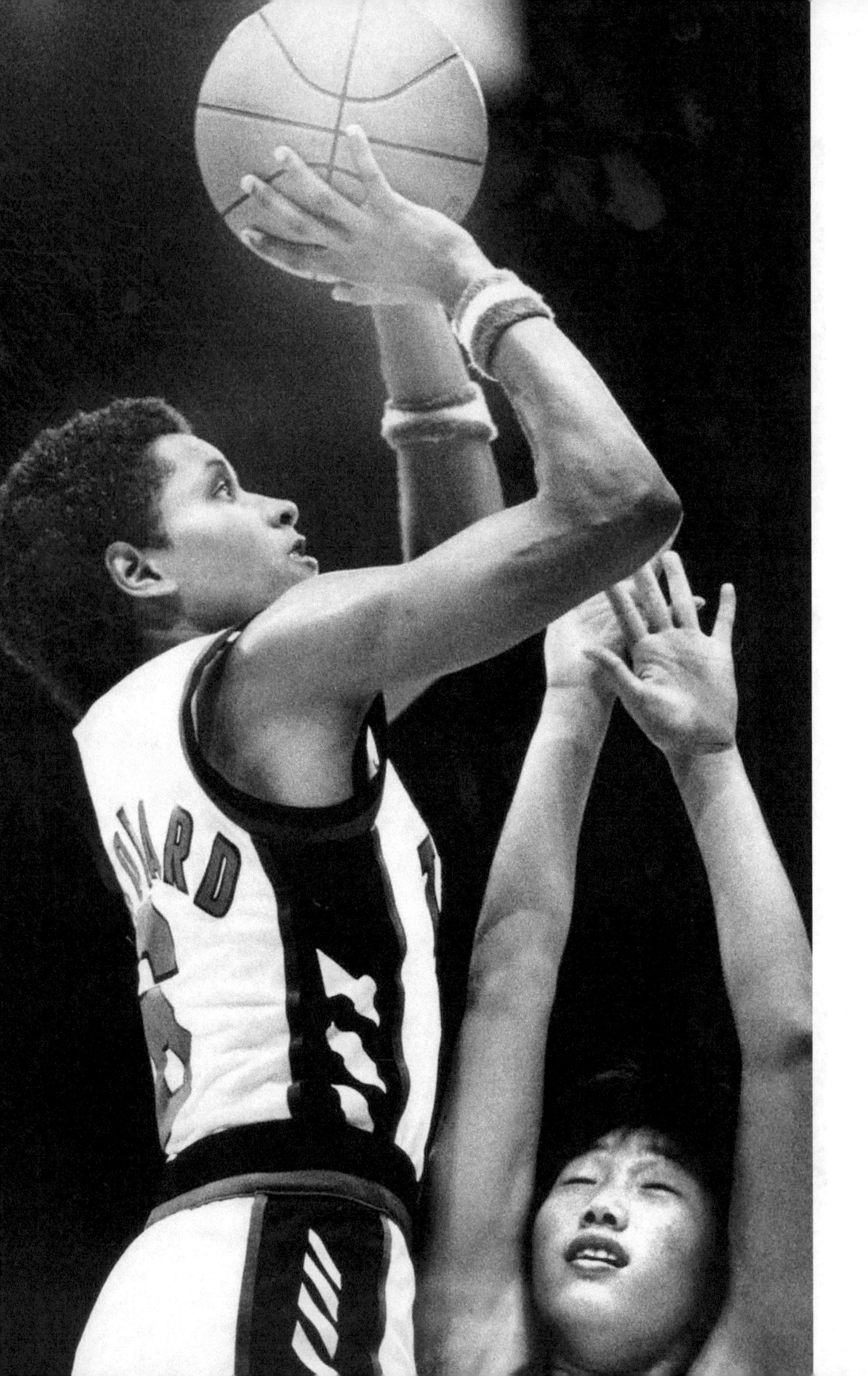

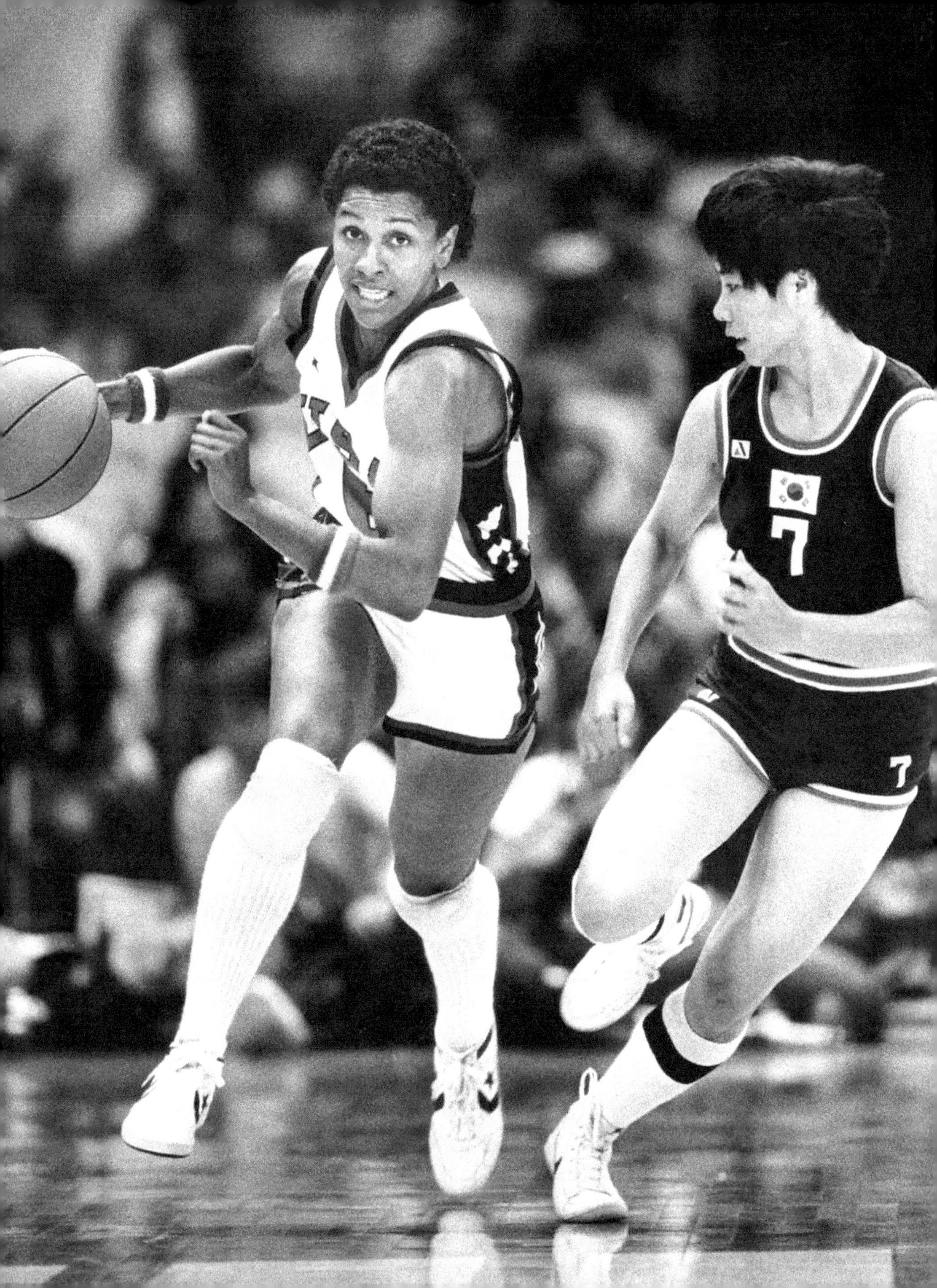
7
7

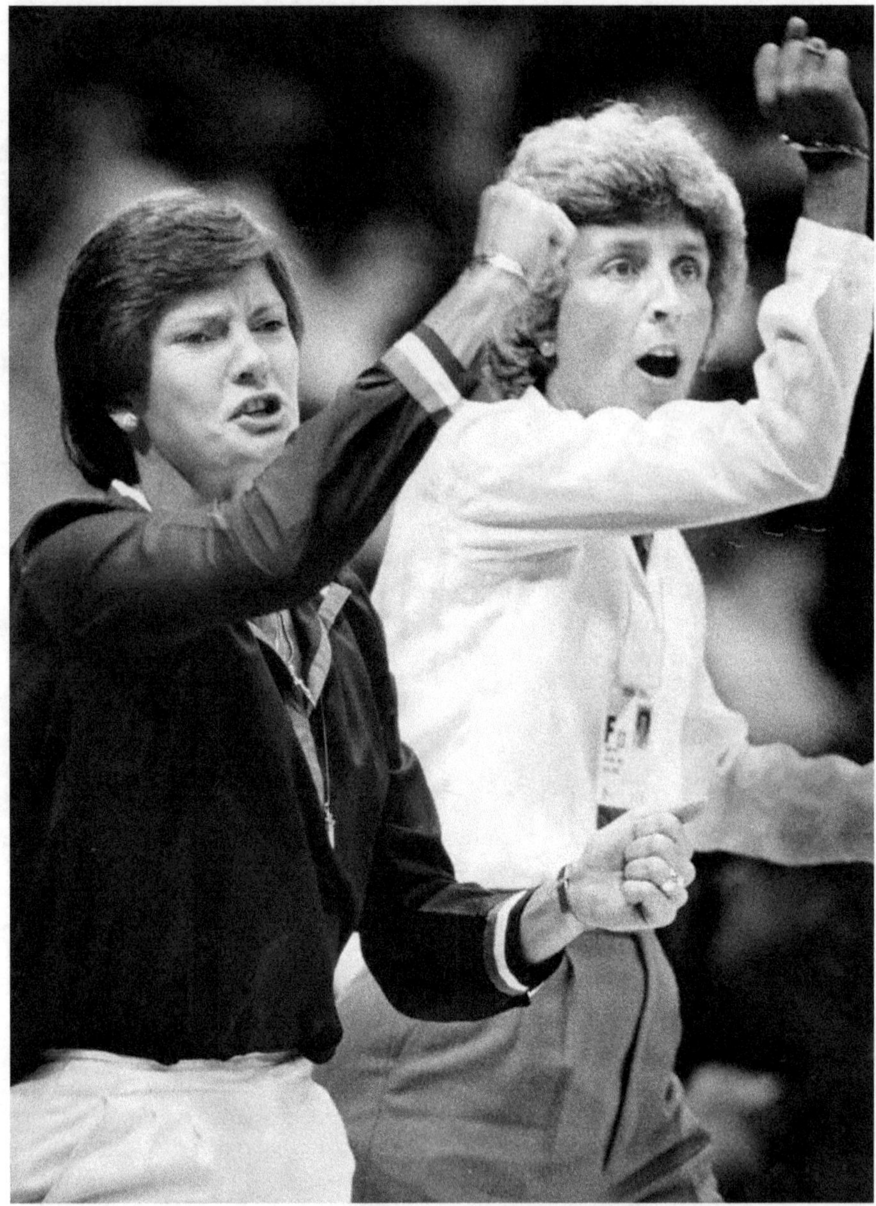

Coach Pat Summit (*left*) and assistant coach Kay Yow signaled to their team. (James Ruebsamen)

***Opposite:* Summit was carried aloft after the U.S. women won the gold medal. (James Ruebsamen)**

***Overleaf:* Lynette Woodard in action. (James Ruebsamen)**

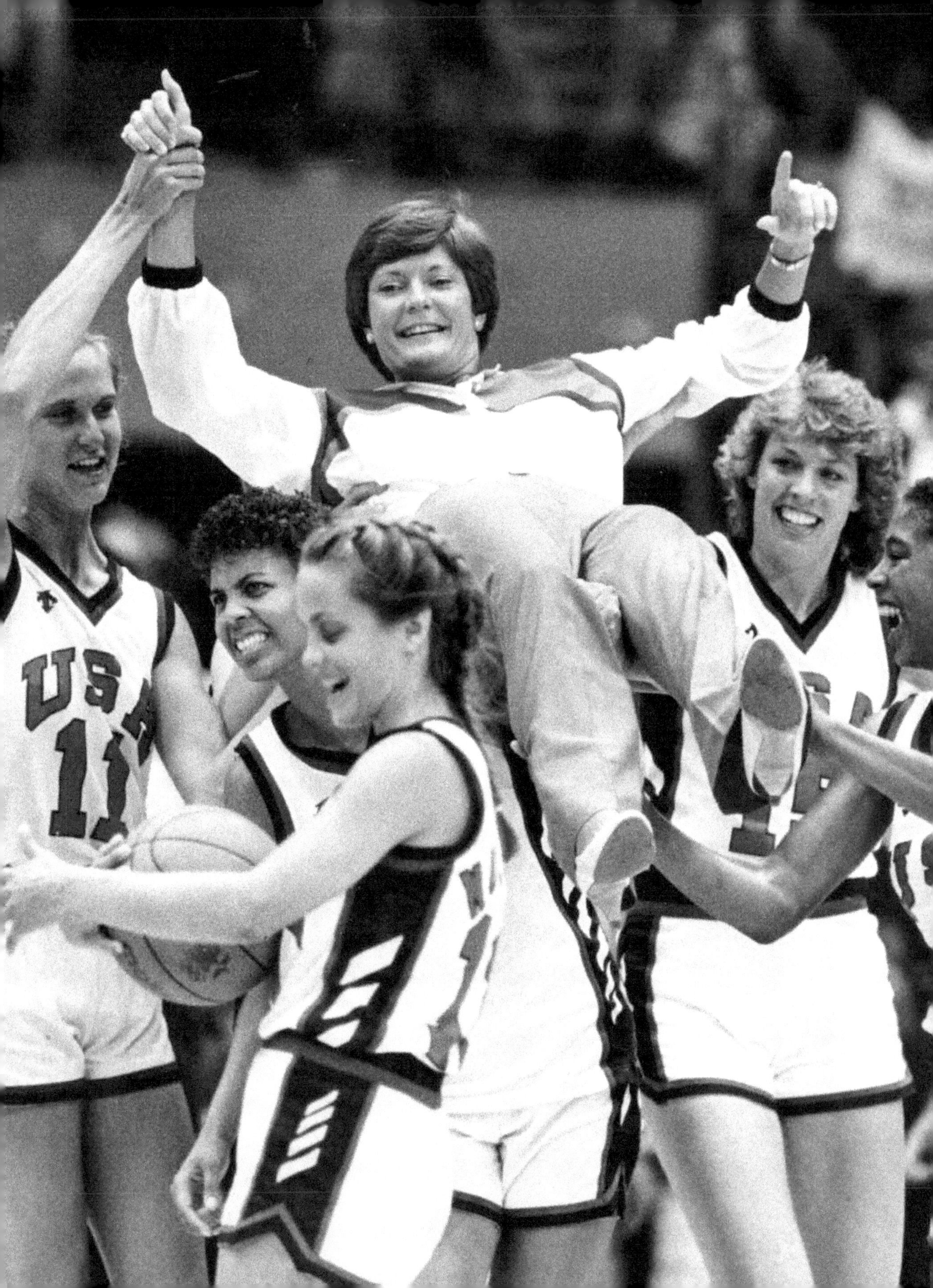
USA
11

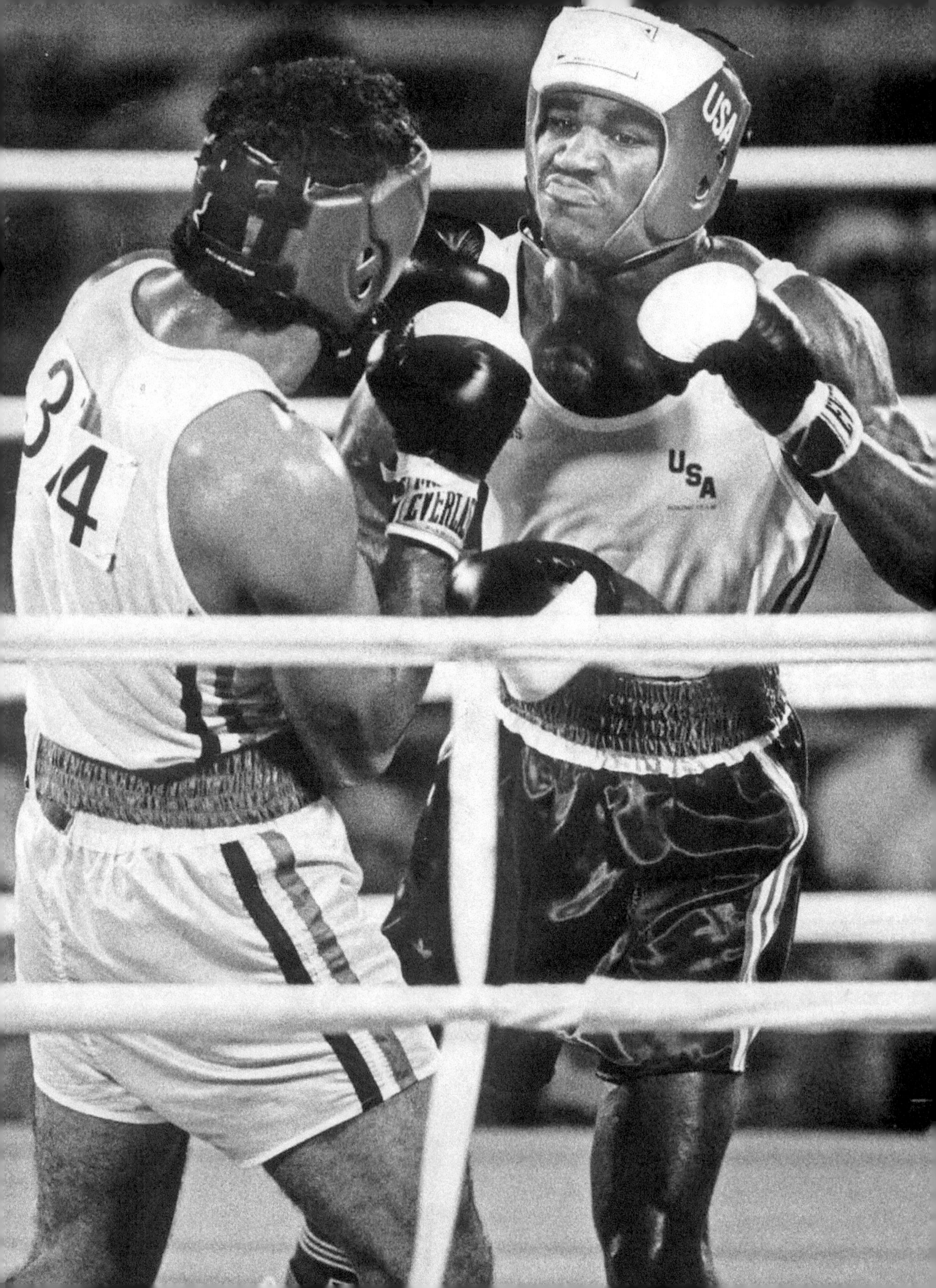
USA
USA

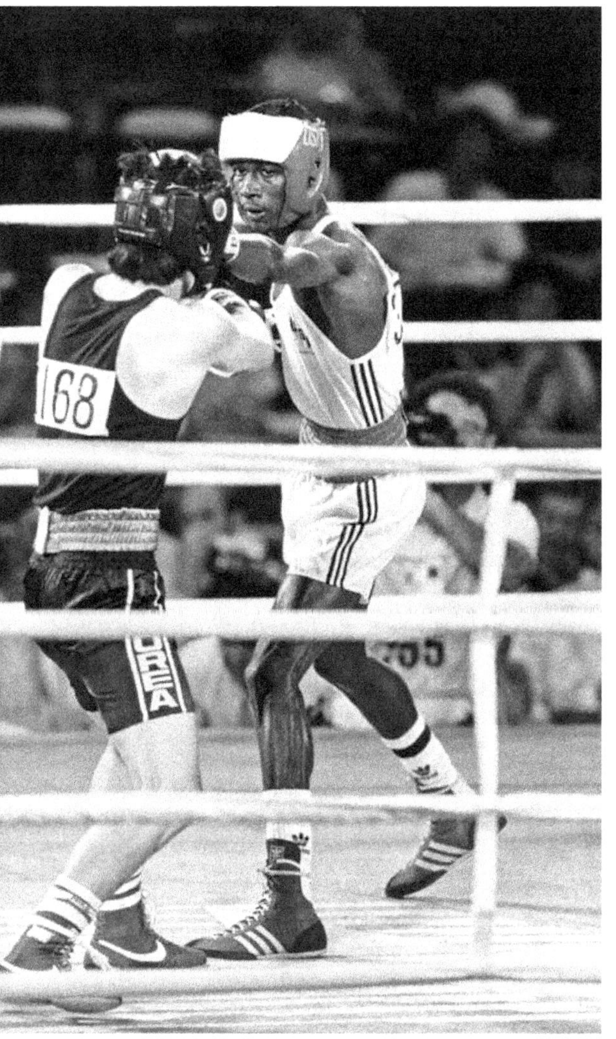

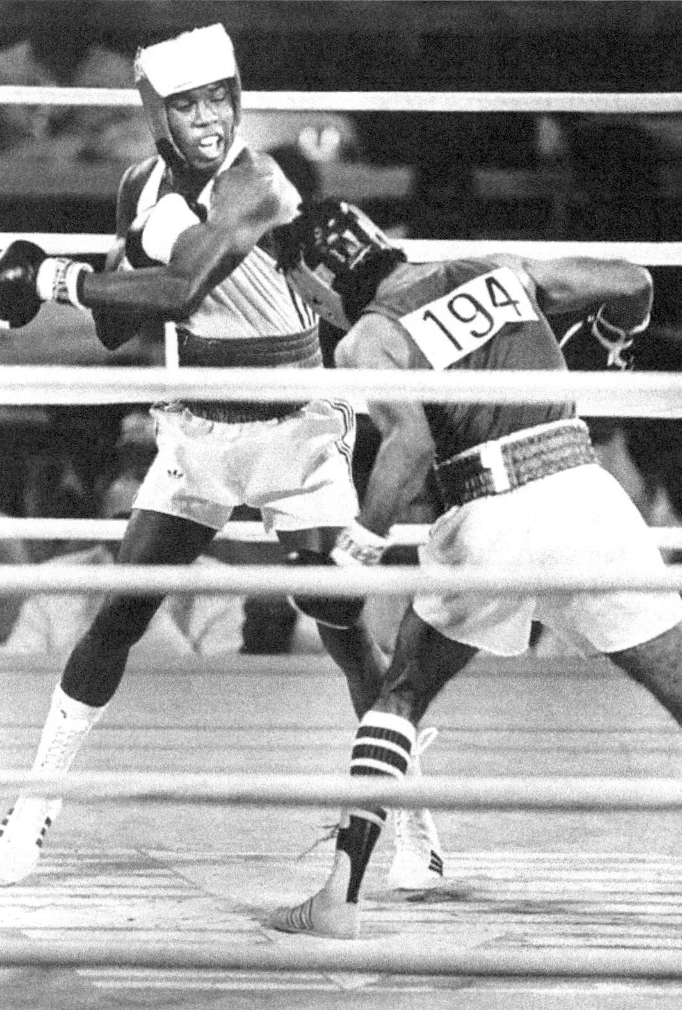

Left: **Welterweight Mark Breland won the gold medal by defeating South Korea's An Young-Su. (James Ruebsamen) •** ***Right:*** **Featherweight Meldrick Taylor, en route to the gold medal, defeated Mexico's Francisco Camacho. (James Ruebsamen)**

Opposite: **Light heavyweight Evander Holyfield attacked Iraq's Ismail Salman. Holyfield was disqualified in his semi-final bout on a disputed call and settled for the bronze medal. (James Ruebsamen)**

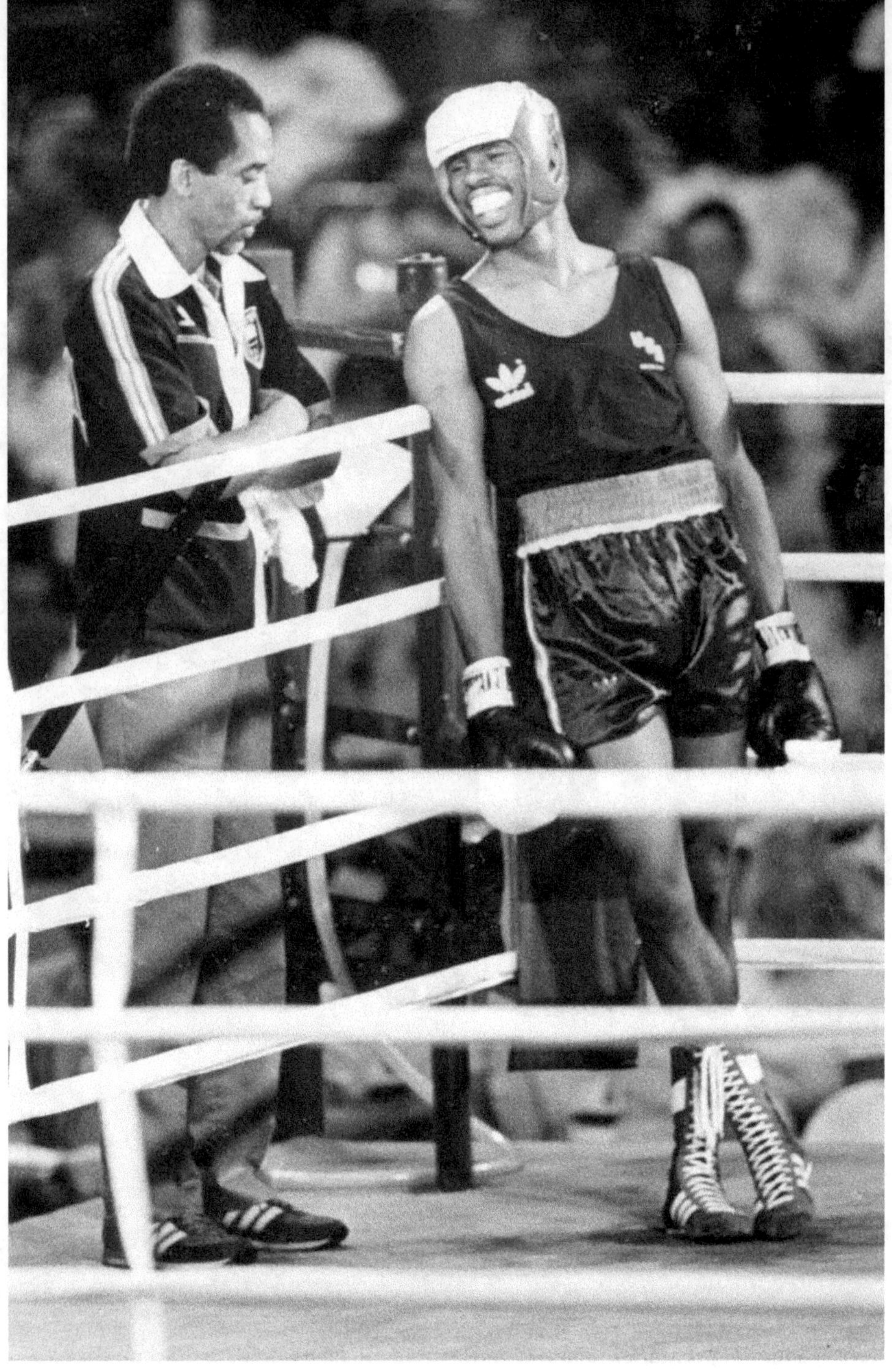

Frank Tate exulted after winning his semi-final match in a walkover; he captured the gold medal in the light middleweight division. (James Ruebsamen)

Opposite: **Pernell "Sweet Pea" Whitaker celebrated his victory in the lightweight division. (James Ruebsamen)**

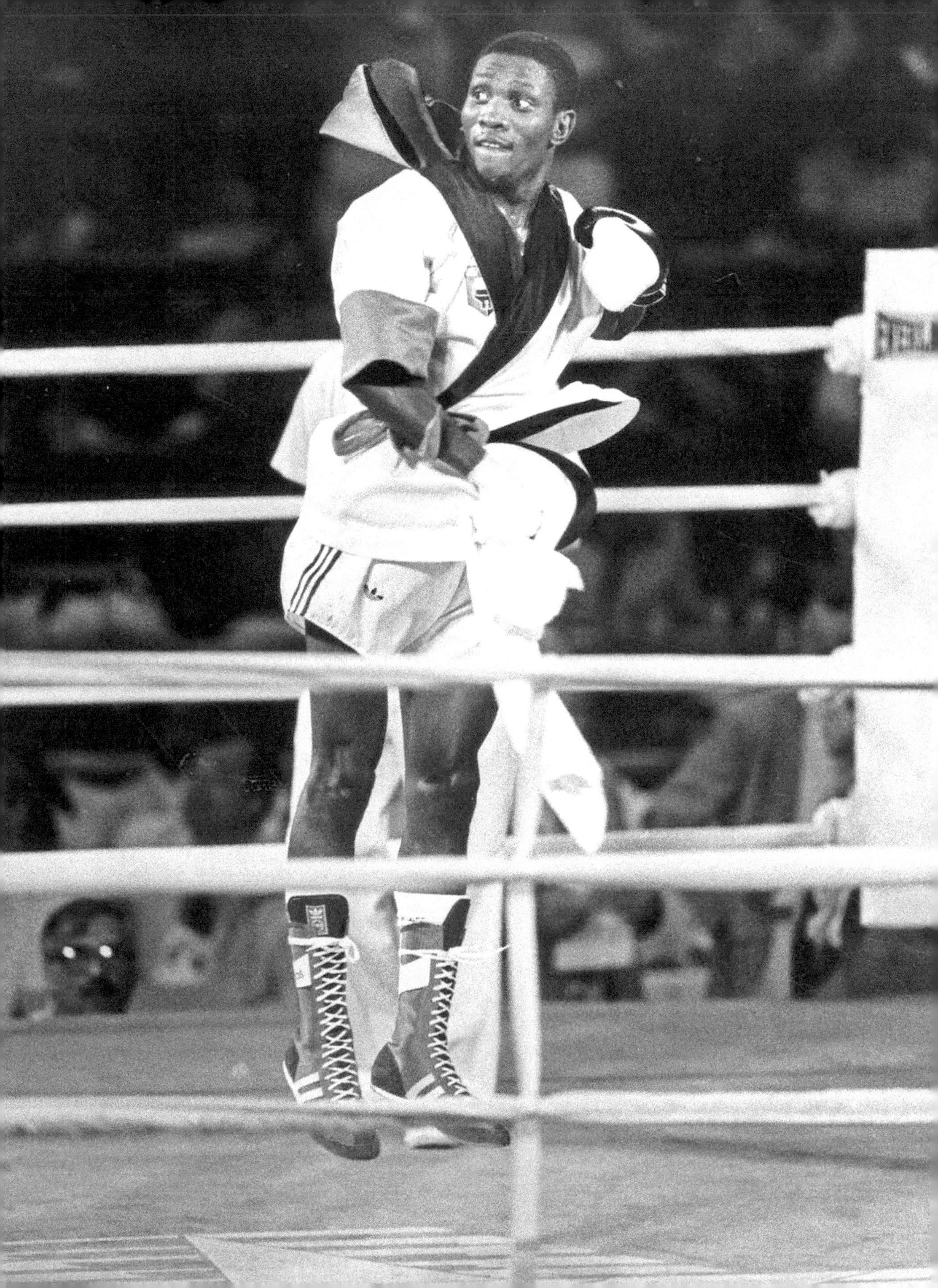

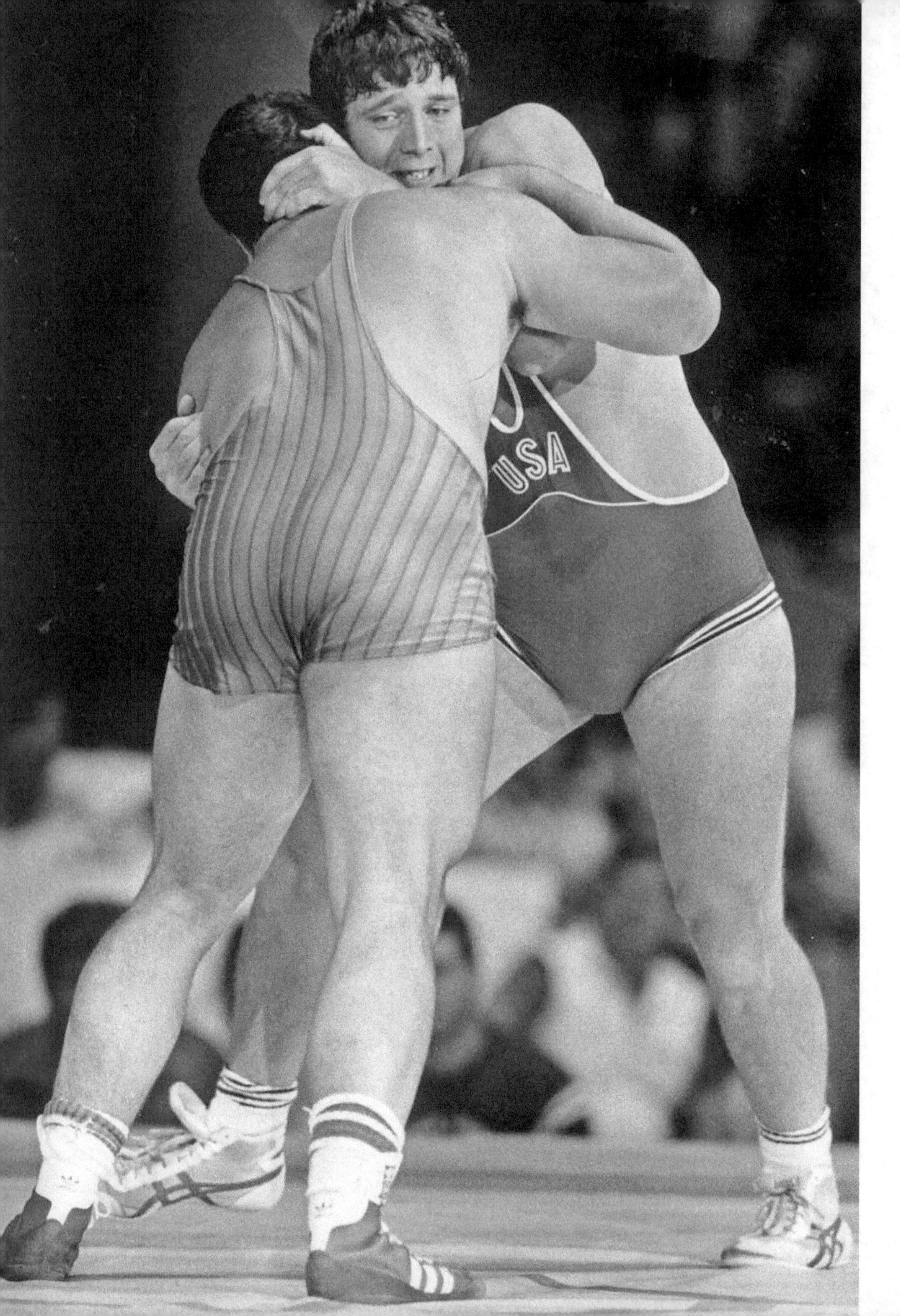
USA

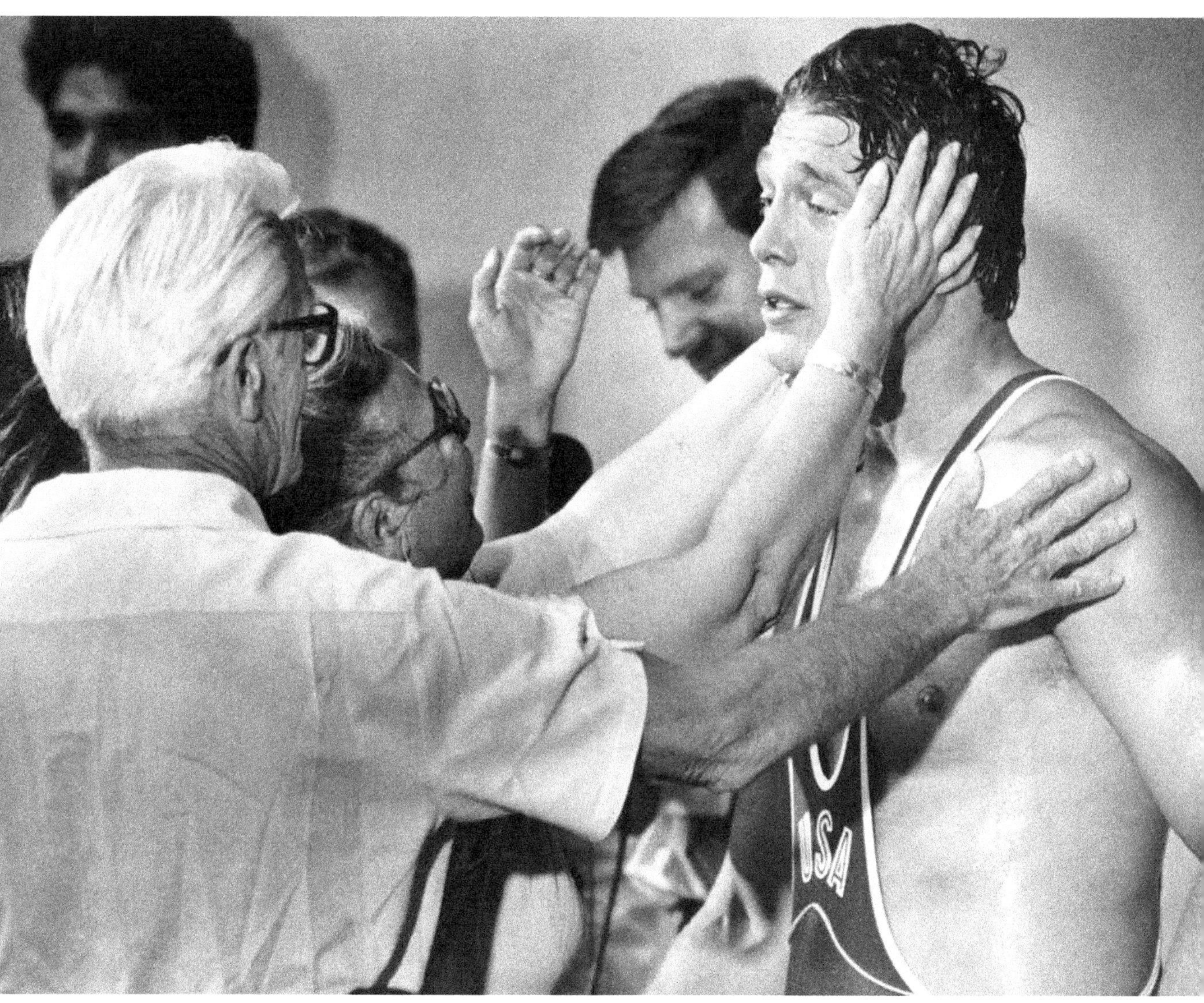

Above and opposite: **Super heavyweight Greco-Roman wrestler Jeff Blatnick overcame cancer to make the U.S. team, then defeated Sweden's Tomas Johansson to win the gold medal. He celebrated the emotional moment with his parents. (Paul Chinn)**

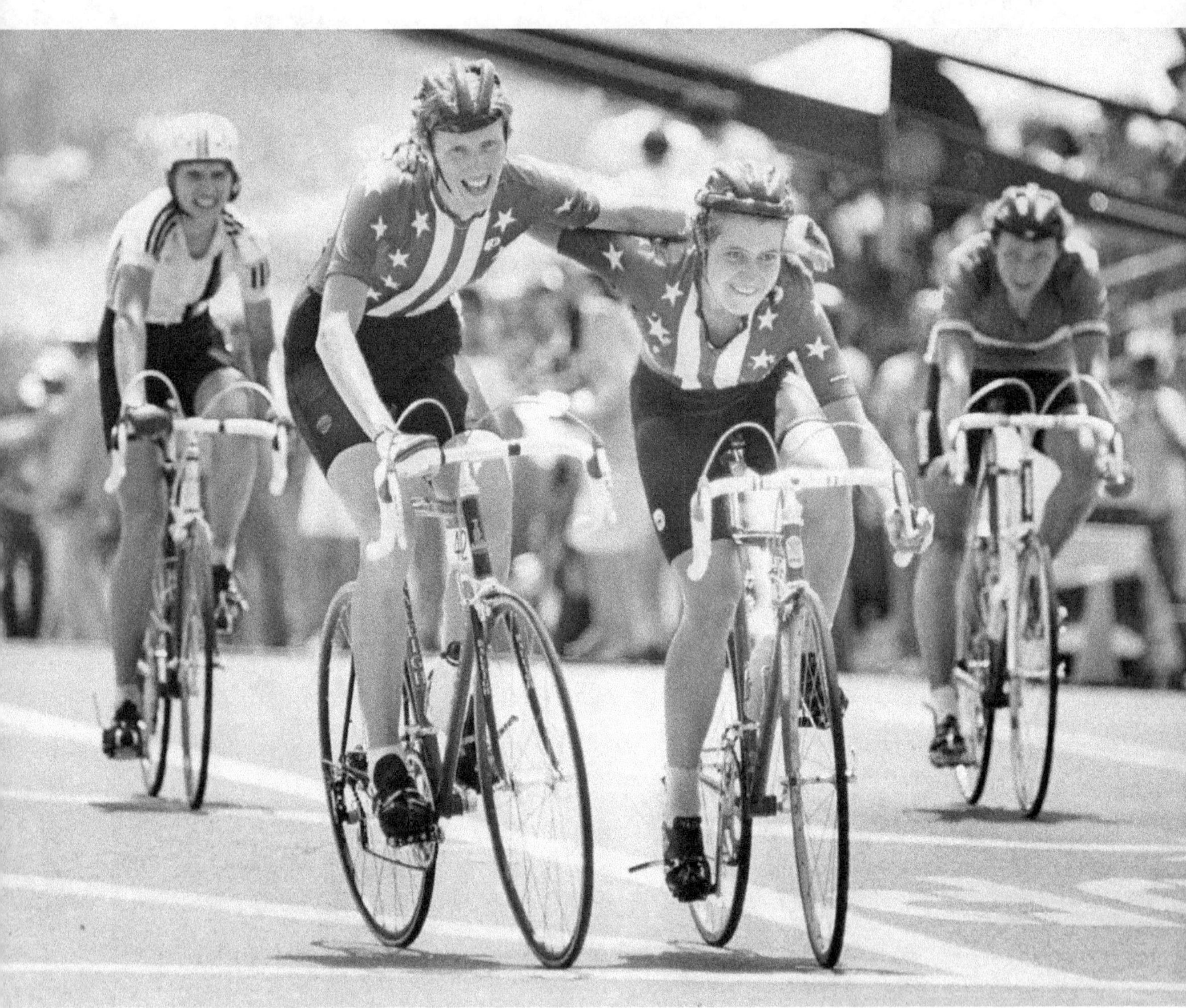

Connie Carpenter-Phinney (*left*) and runner-up Rebecca Twigg embraced after their one-two finish in Mission Viejo in the first women's Olympic road race. (Leo Jarzomb)

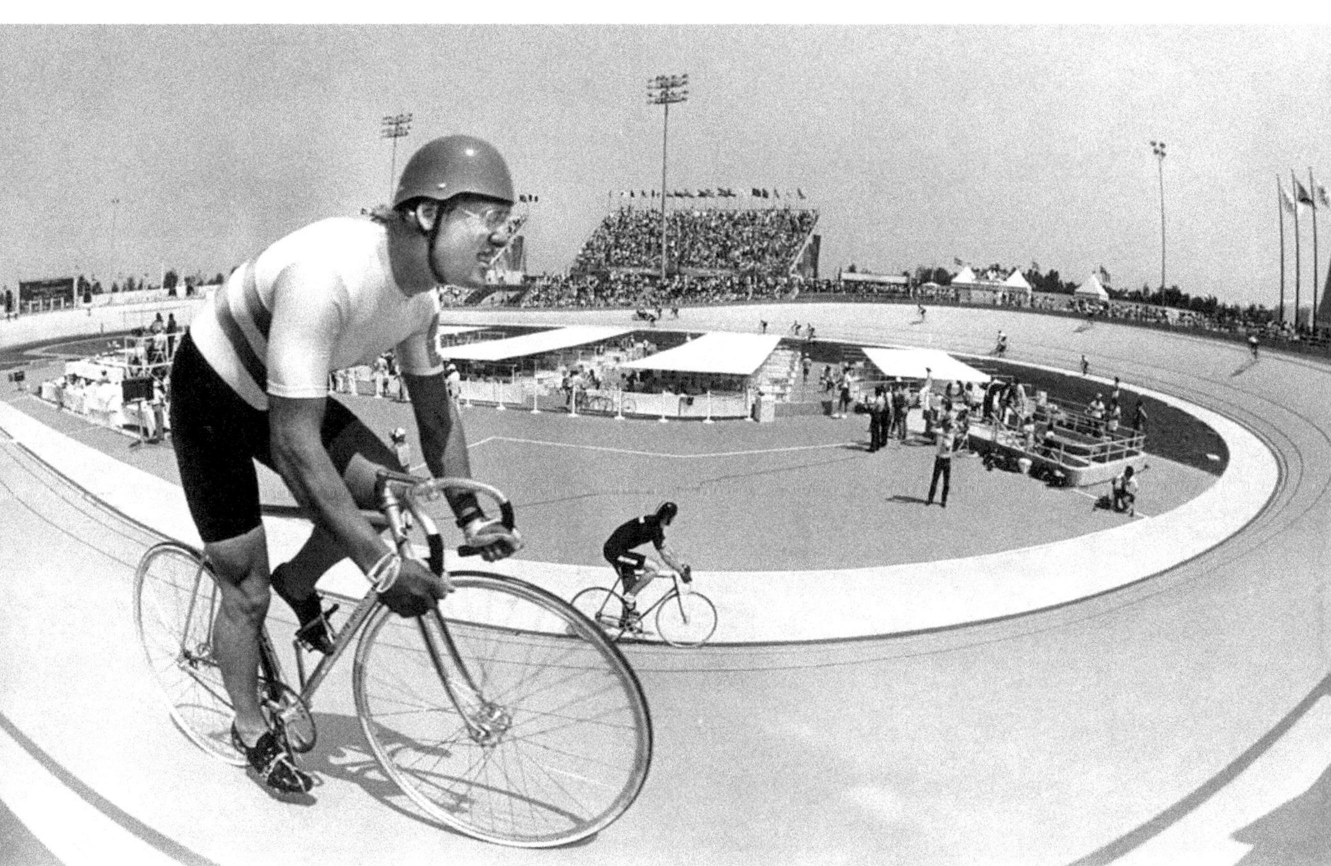

Cyclists warmed up at the Velodrome on the campus of Cal State Dominguez Hills, one of two facilities built specifically for the 1984 Olympics. (Paul Chinn)

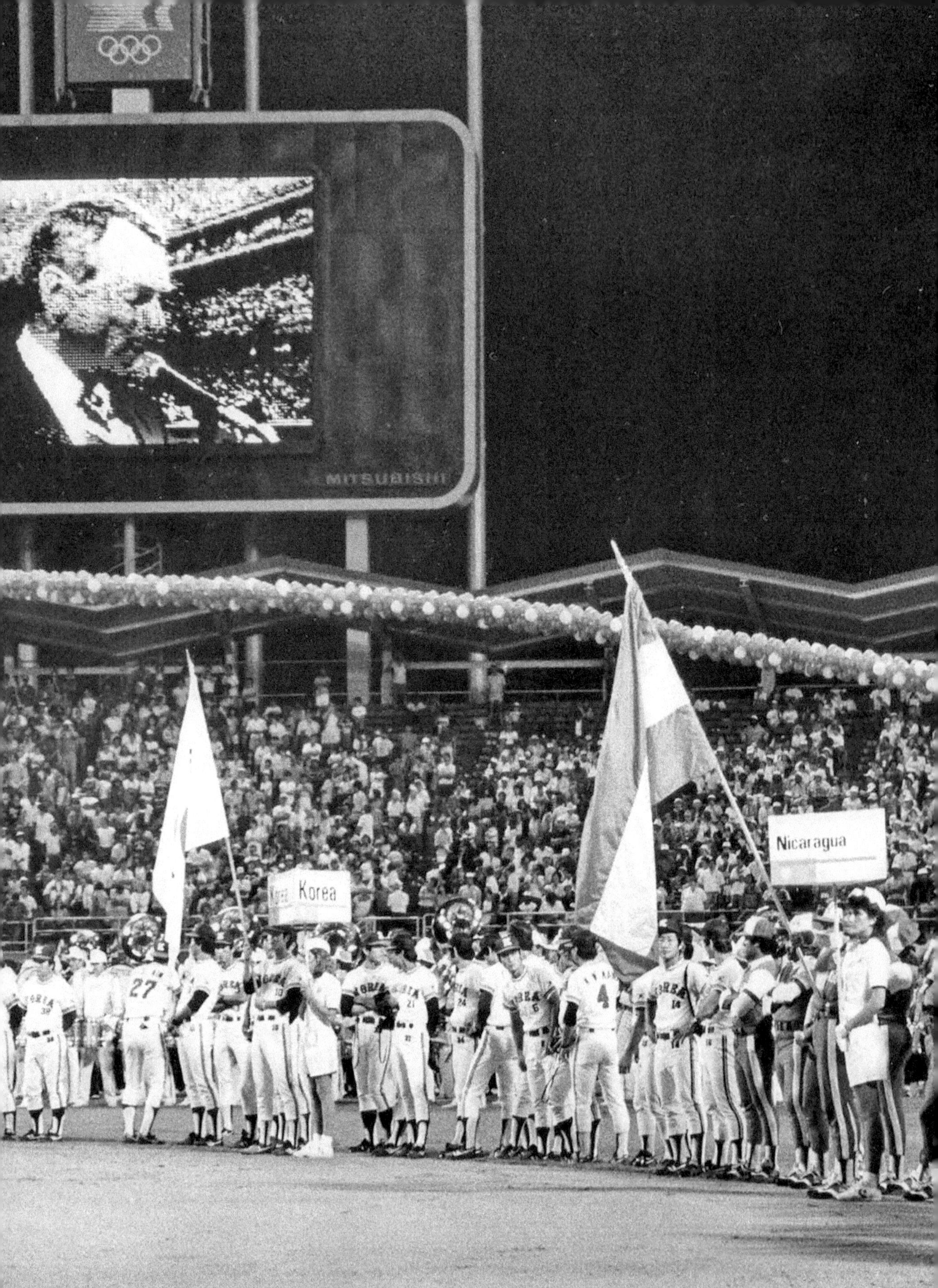
MITSUBISHI
Korea
Nicaragua

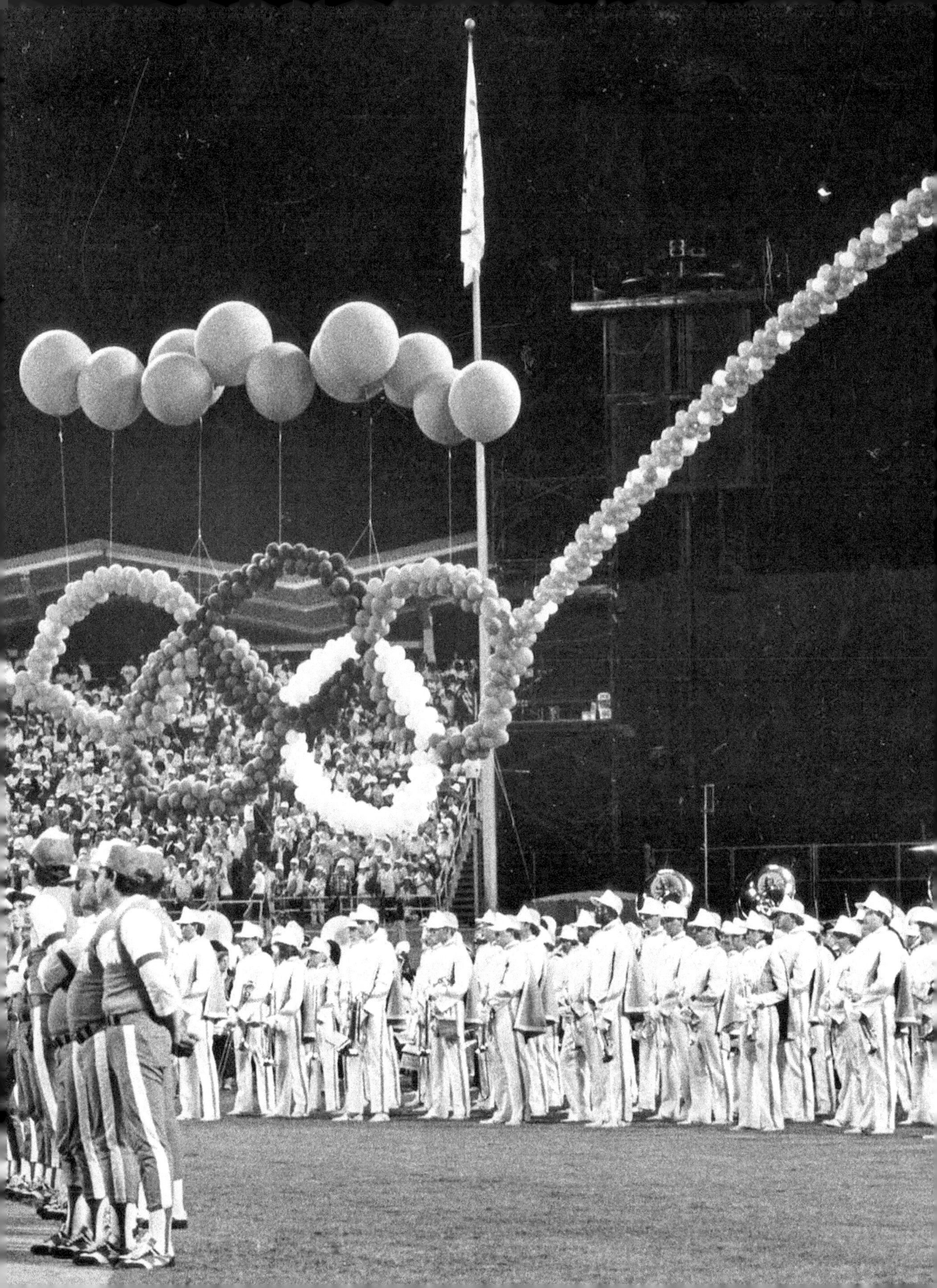

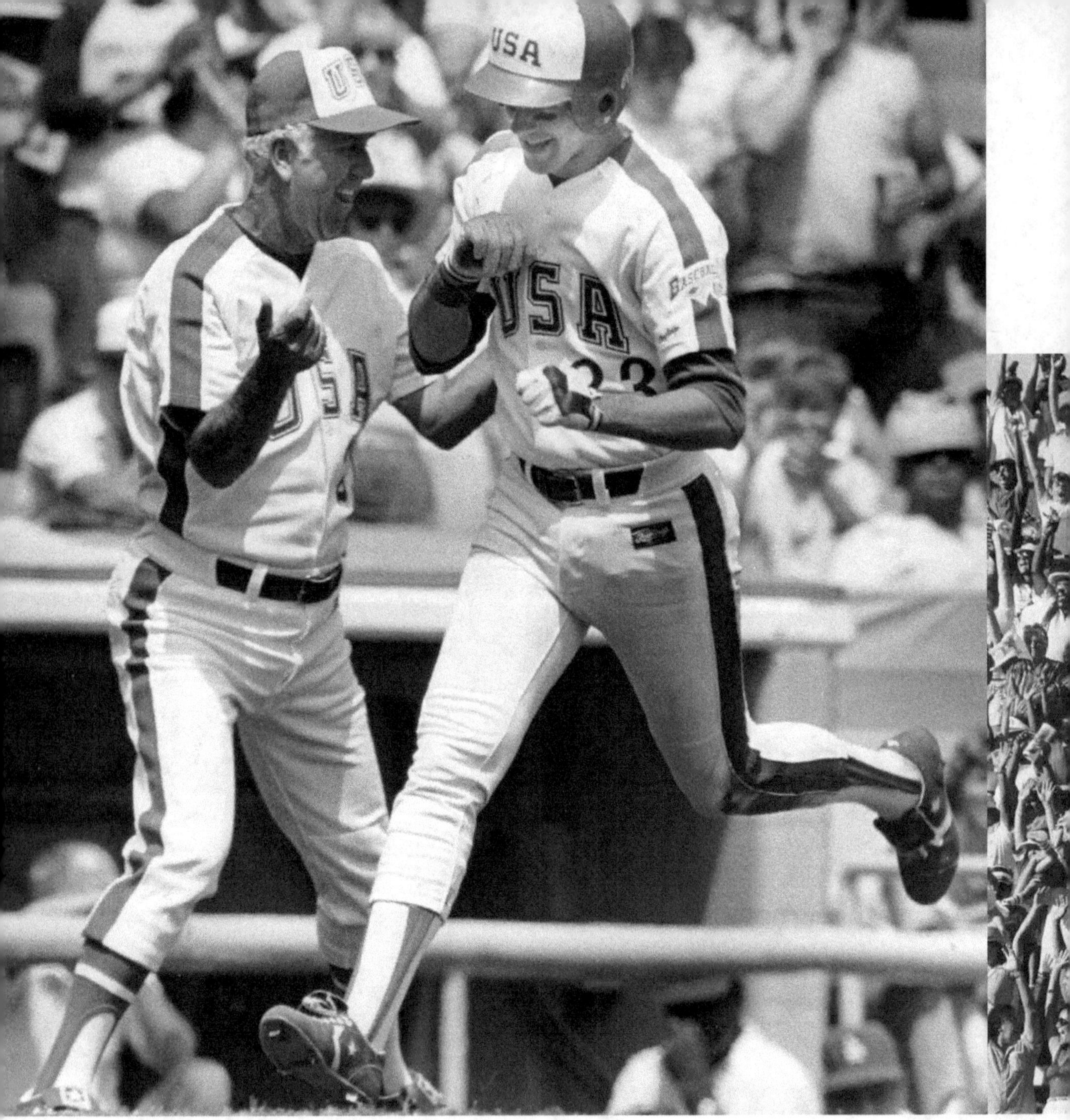

Future Major Leaguer Will Clark rounded third after hitting a home run against the Dominican Republic. (Toru Kawana)

Overleaf: **Baseball was a demonstration sport in 1984, complete with its own opening ceremony at Dodger Stadium. (Toru Kawana)**

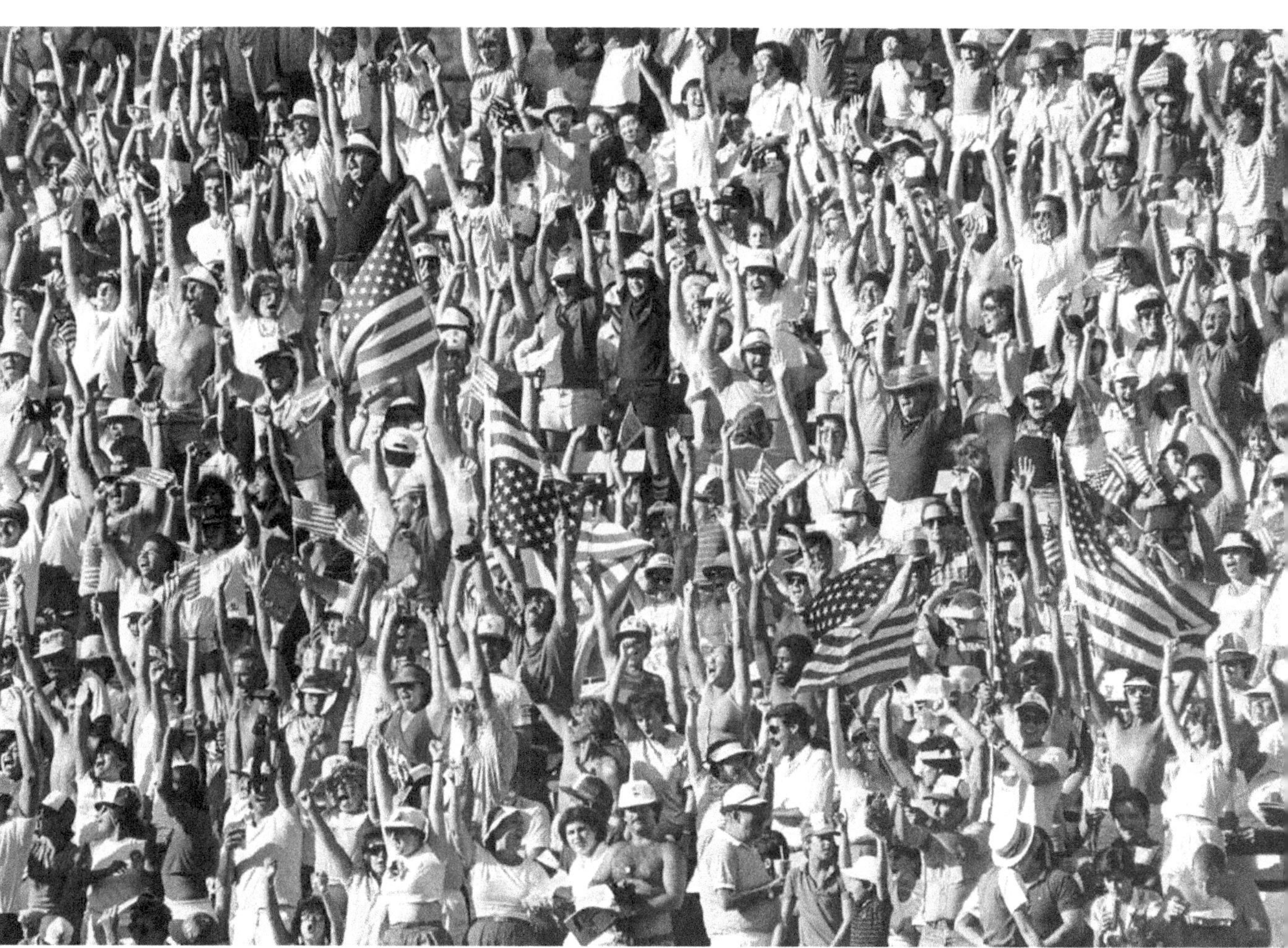

The U.S. baseball team finished second behind Japan as fans root-root-rooted for the home team. (Toru Kawana)

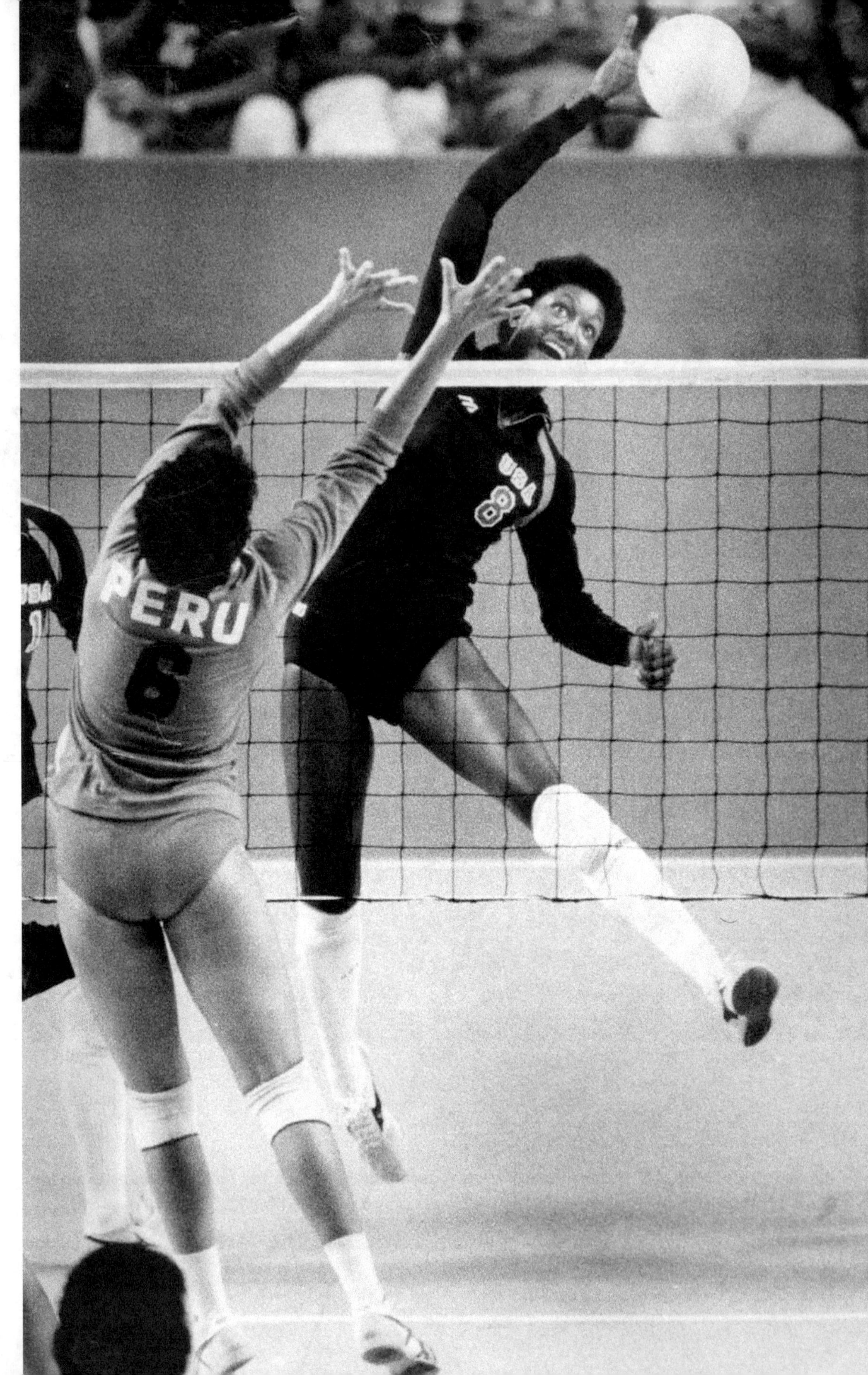
PERU
6
USA
8

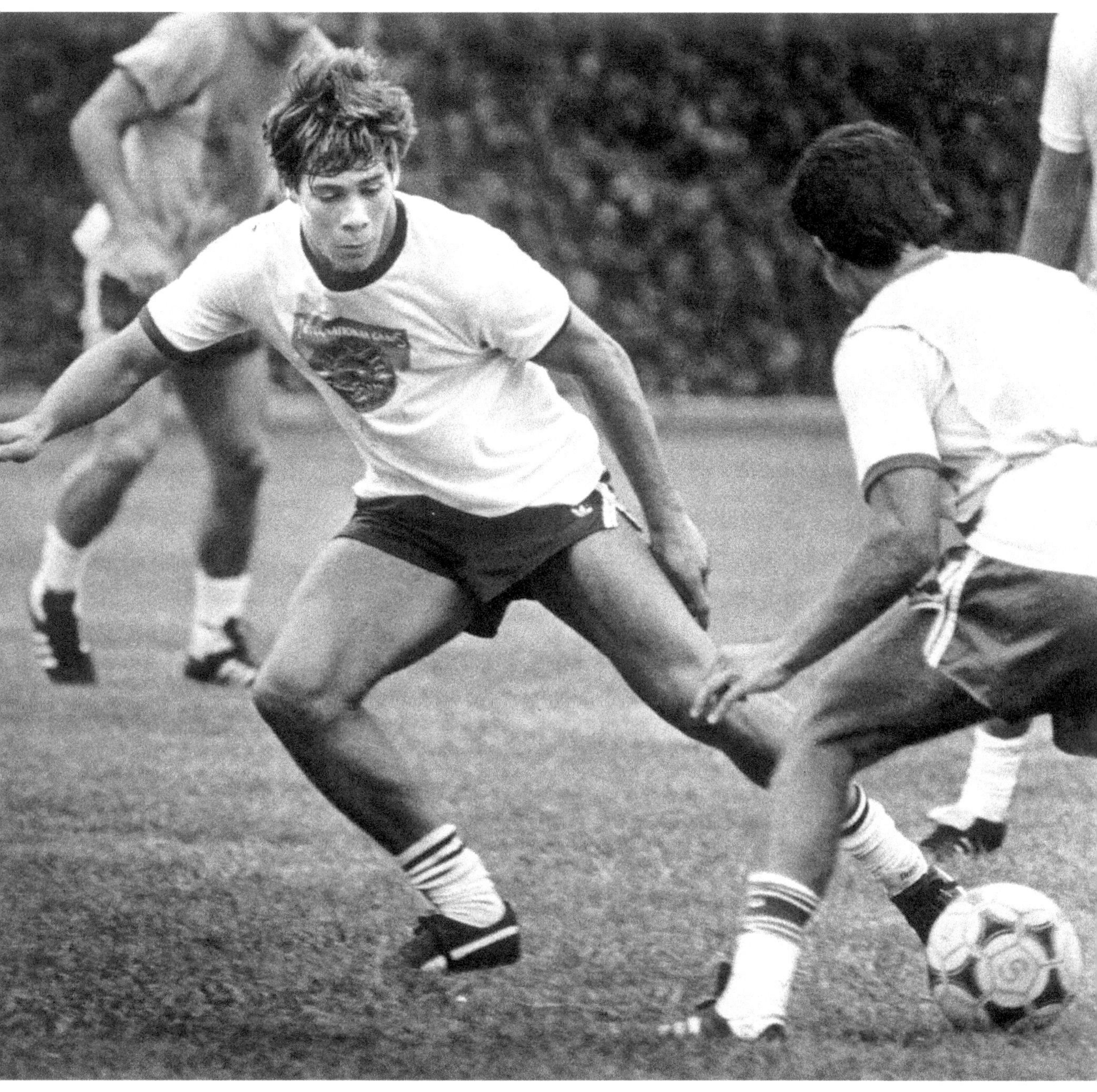

Paul Caligiuri and his U.S. soccer teammates practiced before the Olympics. France defeated Brazil in the gold-medal match at the Rose Bowl. (Leo Jarzomb)

Opposite: **Rose Magers spiked the ball versus Peru in the semi-final match at the Long Beach Arena. The U.S. women's volleyball team finished second behind China. (Javier Mendoza)**

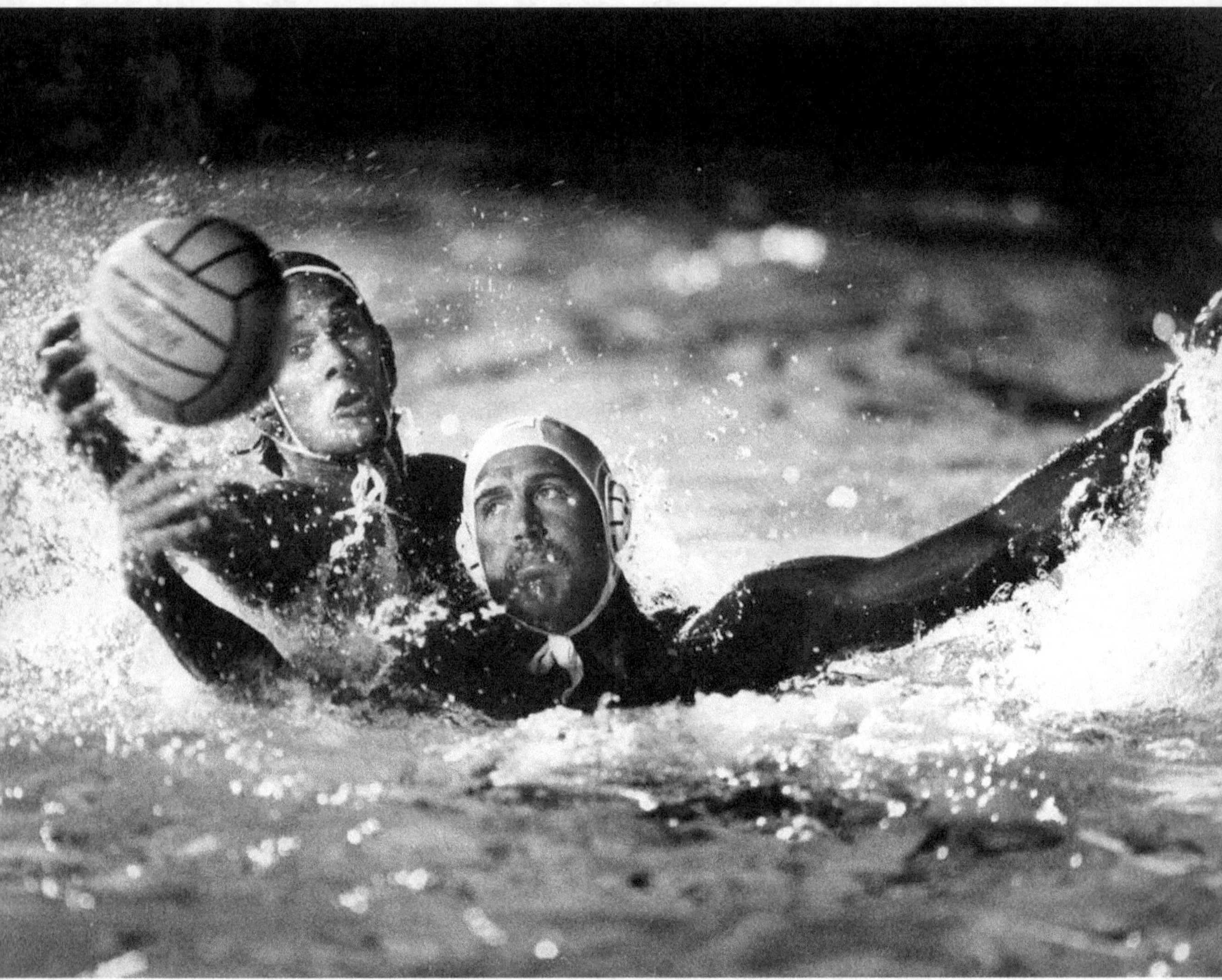

Yugoslavia's Igor Milanovic (*right*) battled American Peter Campbell in the water polo finals at Pepperdine University's pool. The match ended in a draw, but Yugoslavia was awarded the gold medal on goal differential. (Javier Mendoza)

***Opposite:* Jovica Elezovic soared to score as Yugoslavia defeated West Germany, 18-17, in the handball finals. (Ken Papaleo)**

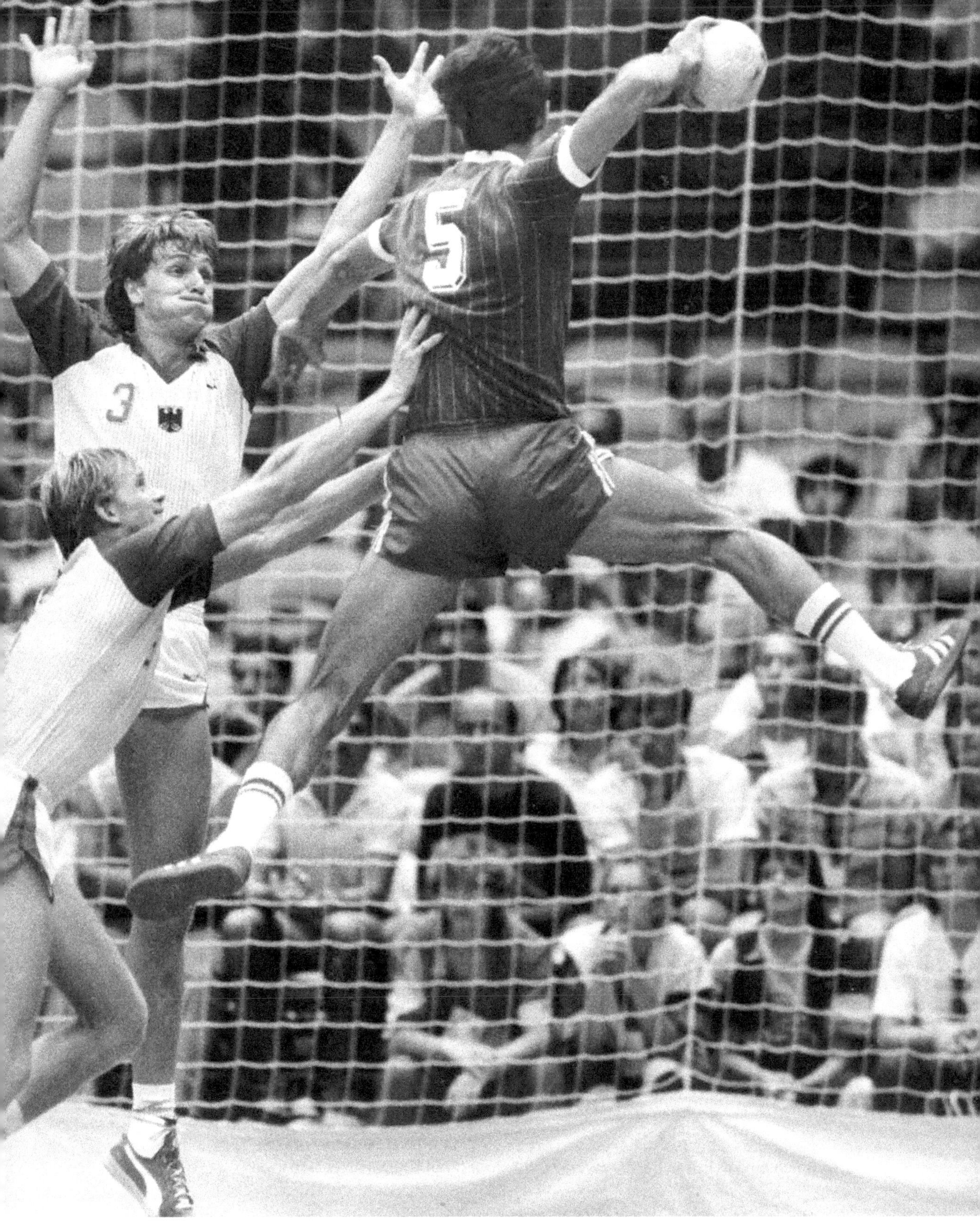

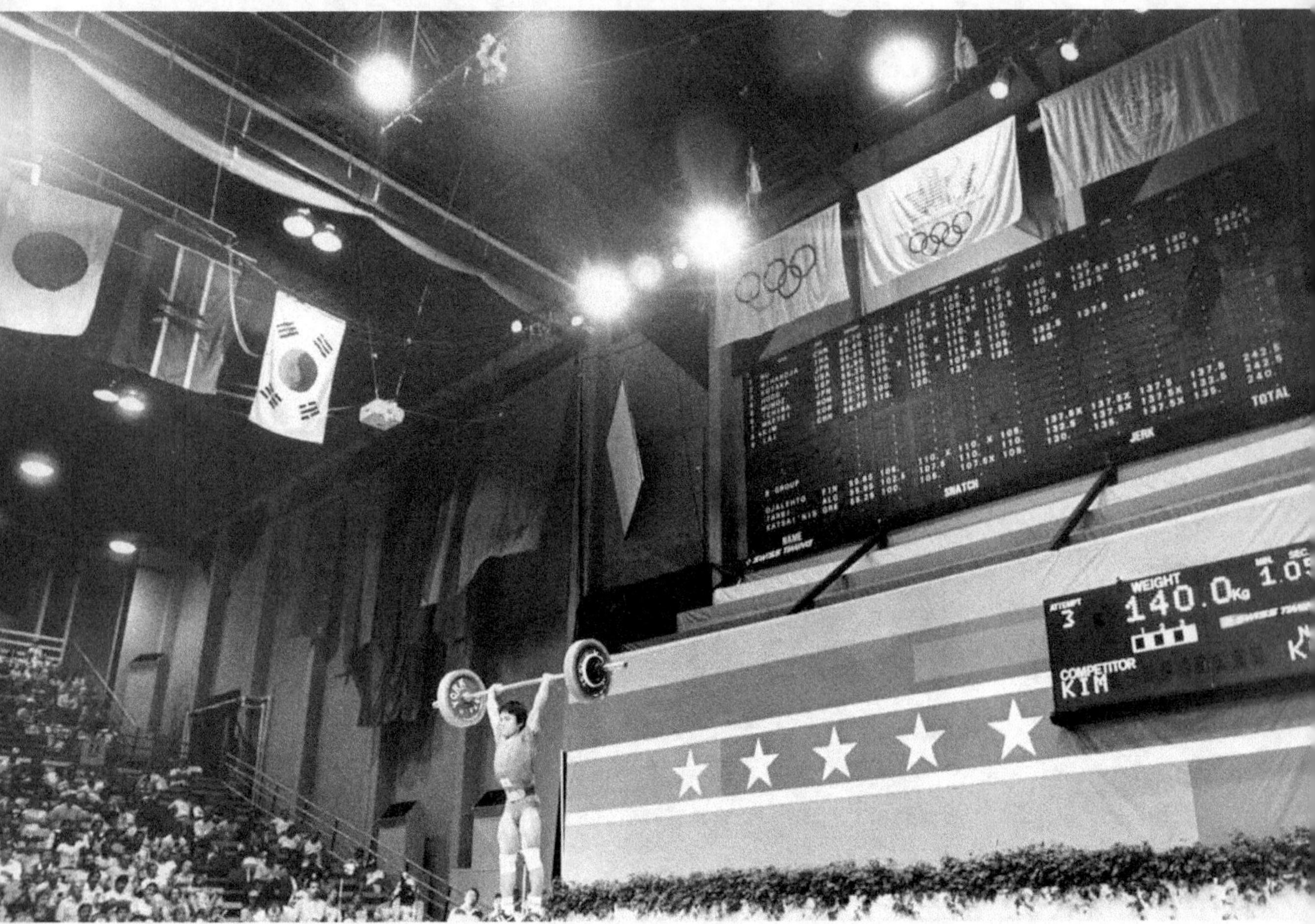

South Korea's Kim Chi-Bong in action at the Gersten Pavilion on the campus of Loyola Marymount University. (Paul Chinn)

Opposite: **Los Angeles' Albert Hood broke three national weightlifting records only to finish eighth in the bantamweight division. (Paul Chinn)**

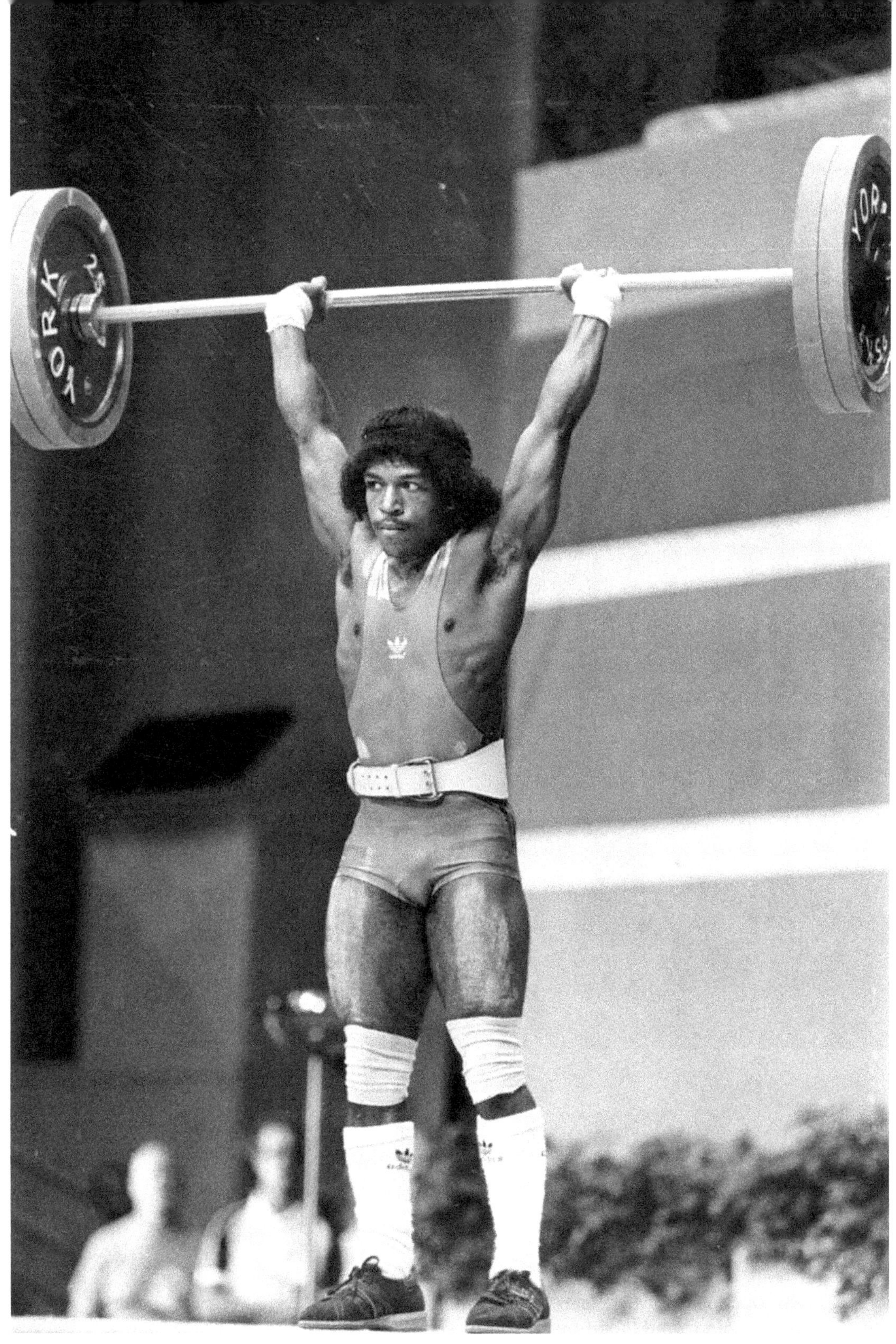
YORK

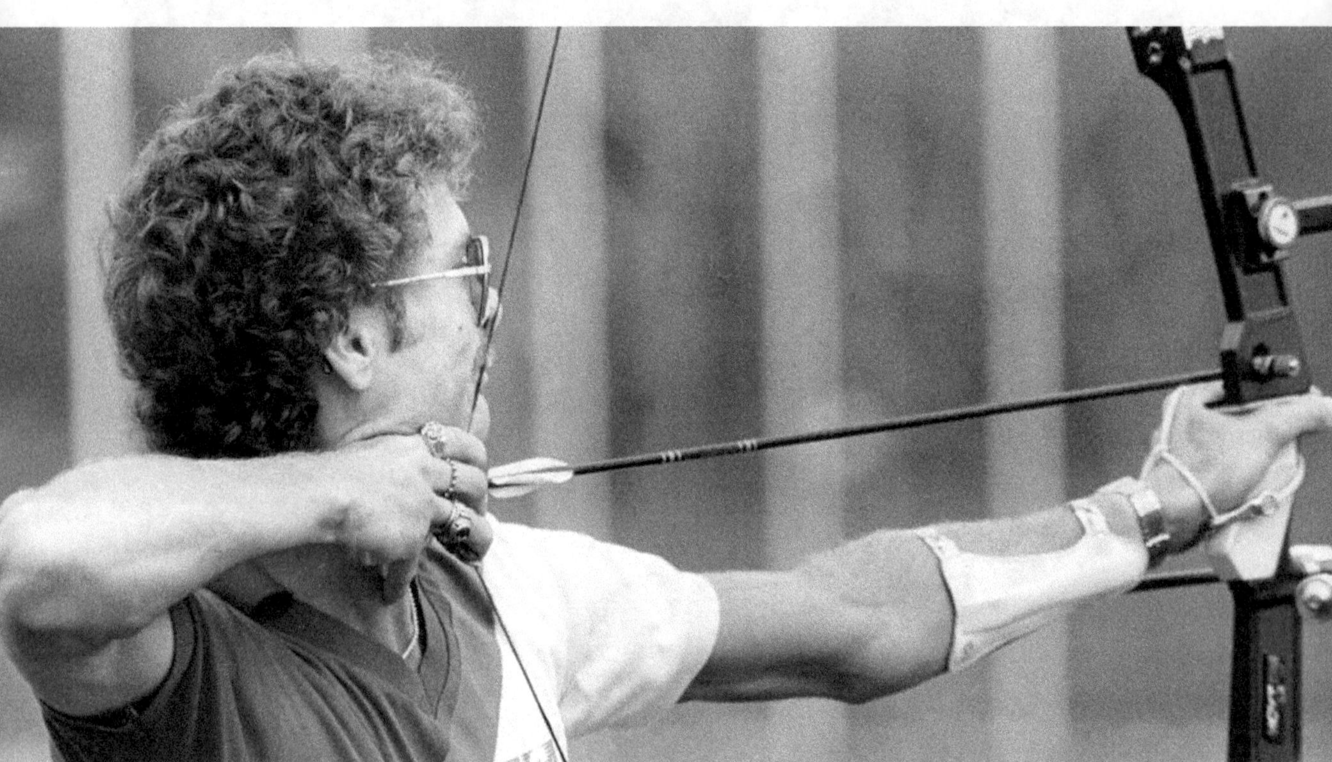

Above and opposite: **American Darrell Pace showed his gold-medal form as the other archers tested their bows at El Dorado Park in Long Beach. (Ken Papaleo)**

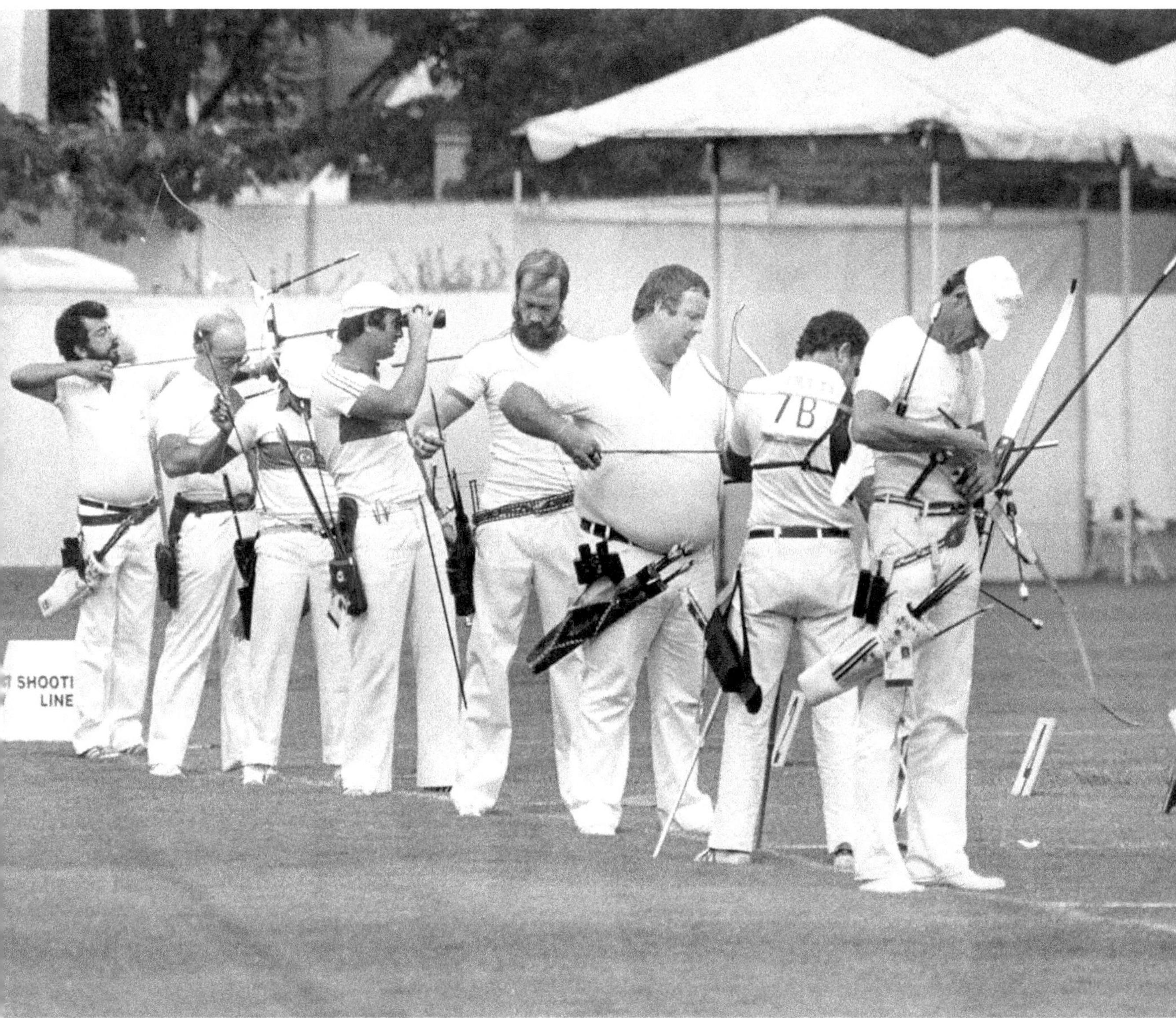
SHOOTI
LINE
7B

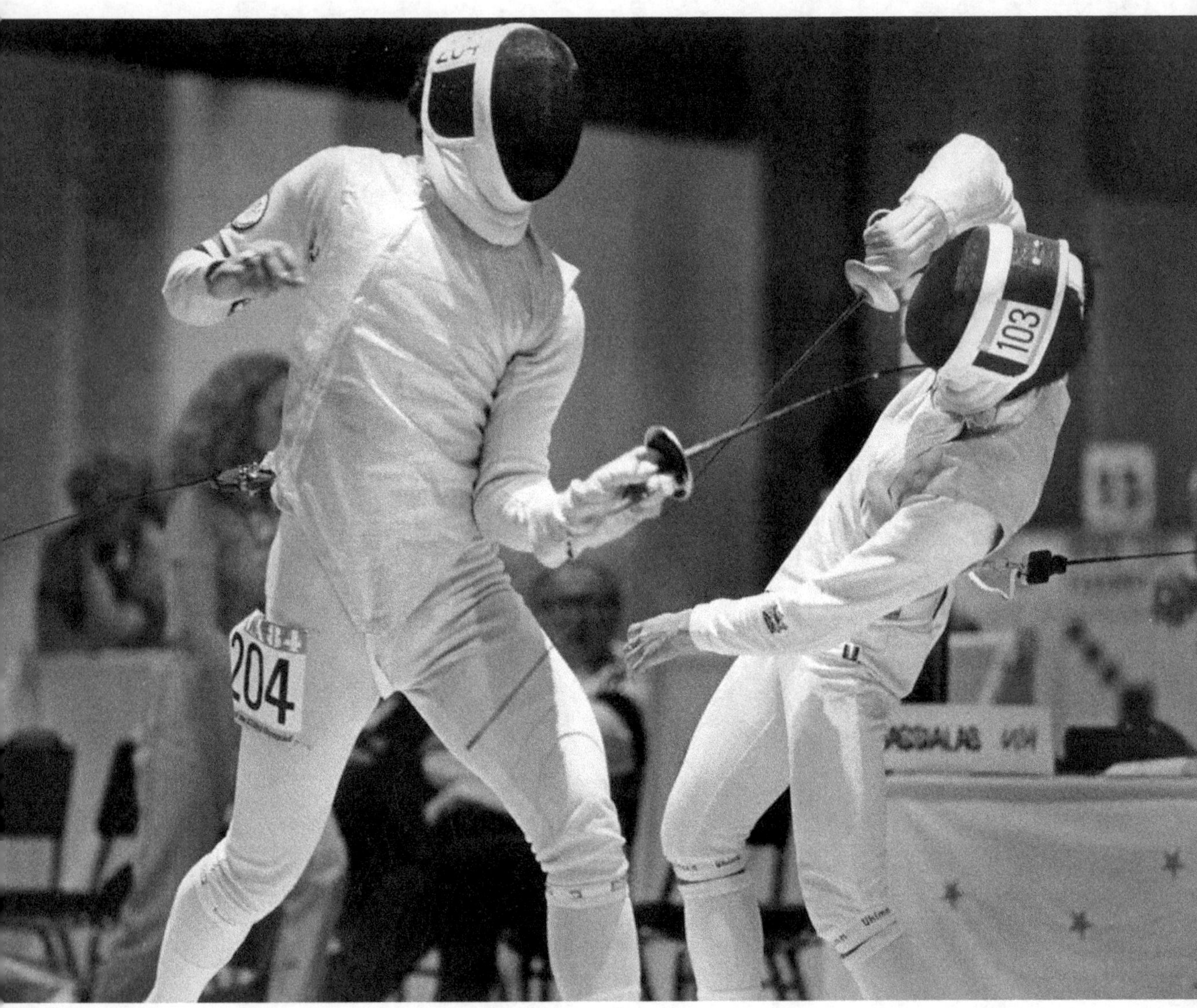

American Greg Massialas (*left*) defeated Hong Kong's Lai Yee Lap in a preliminary foil match at the Long Beach Convention Center. (Paul Chinn)

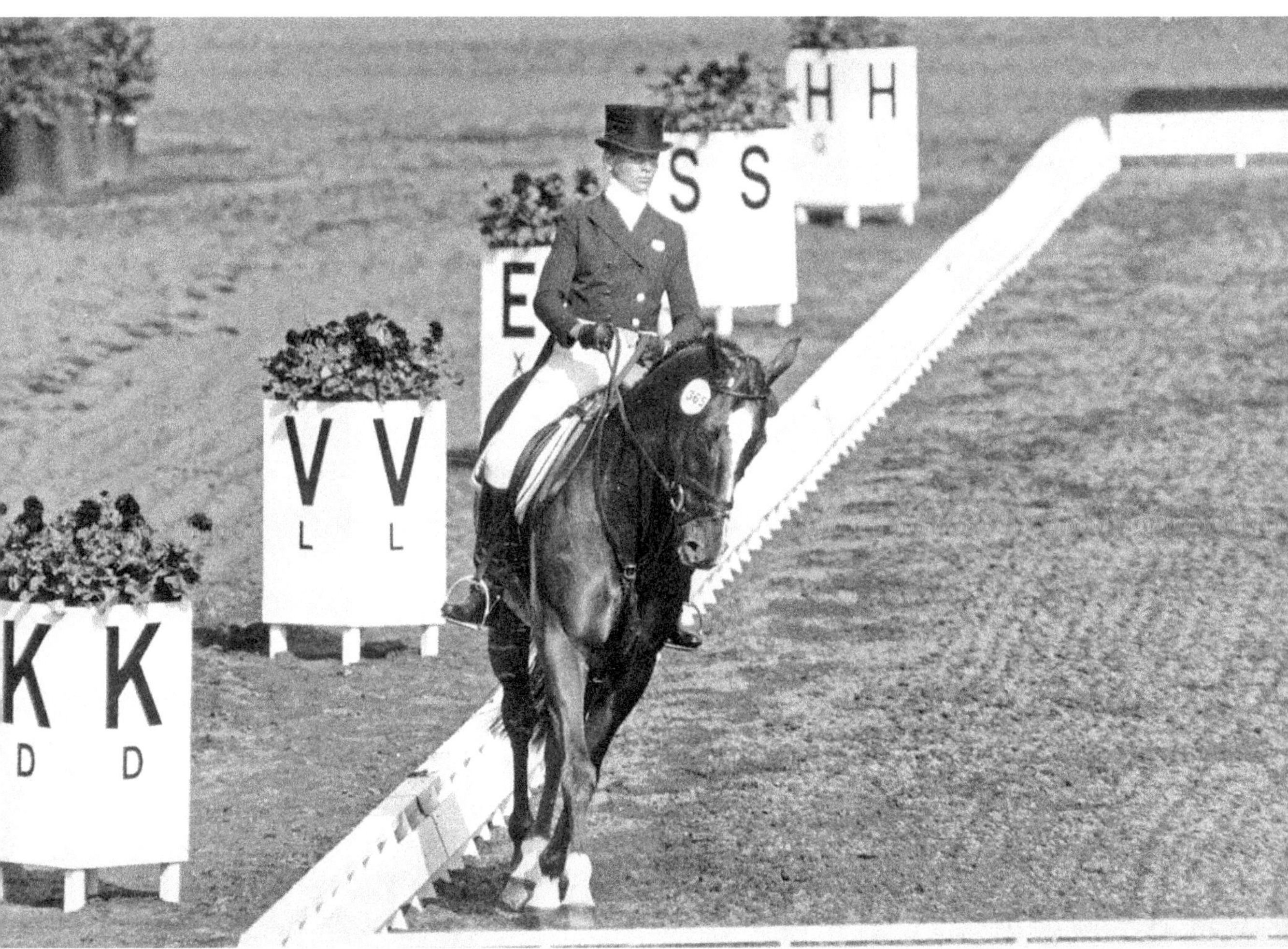

Torrance Watkins Fleischmann and Finvarra competed in the three-day dressage event at Santa Anita Park, helping the Americans win the team gold. (Ken Papaleo)

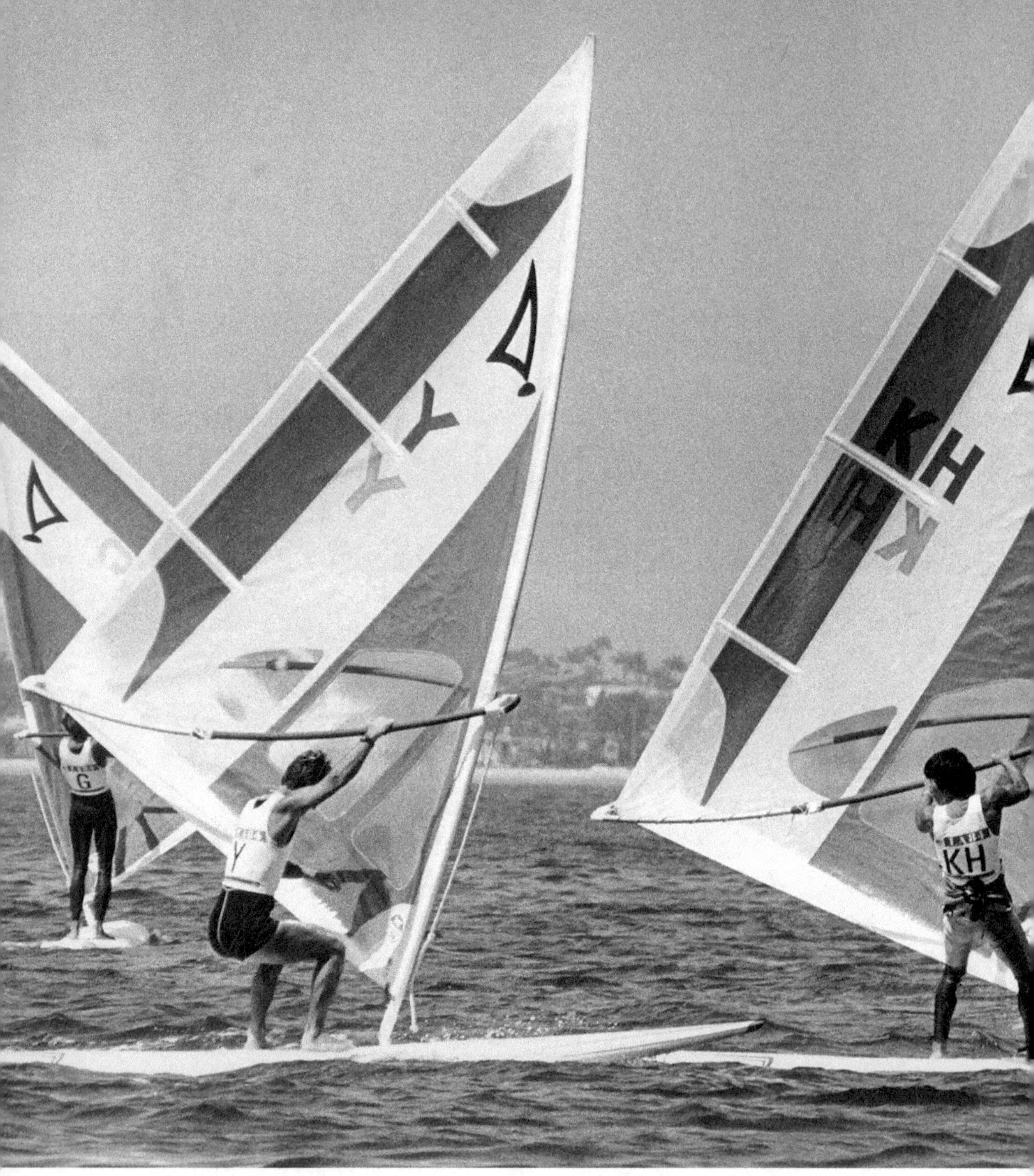

Windsurfing became an Olympic event for the first time in 1984, with seven races in Long Beach Harbor. (Ken Papaleo)

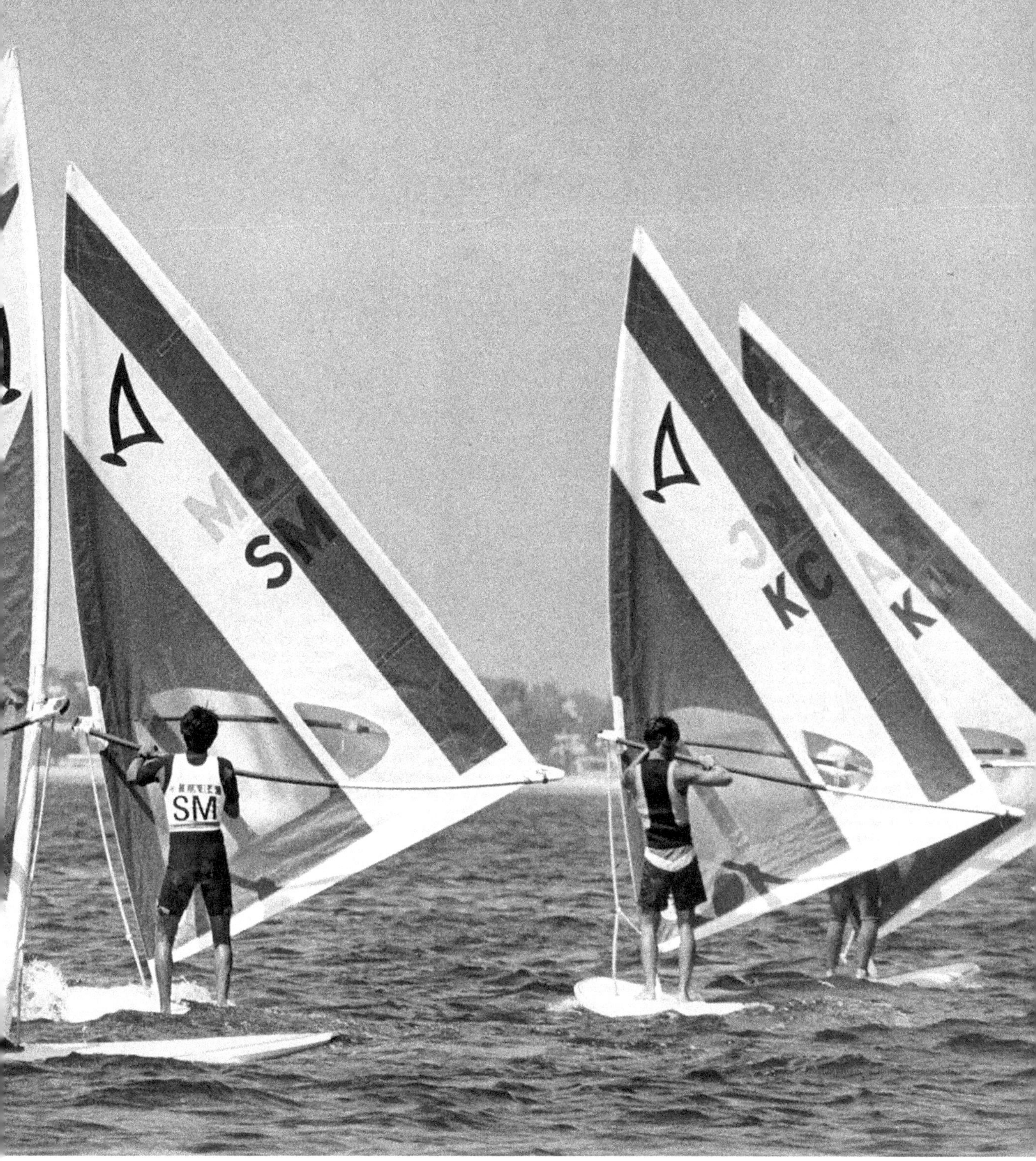
SM
SM
KC

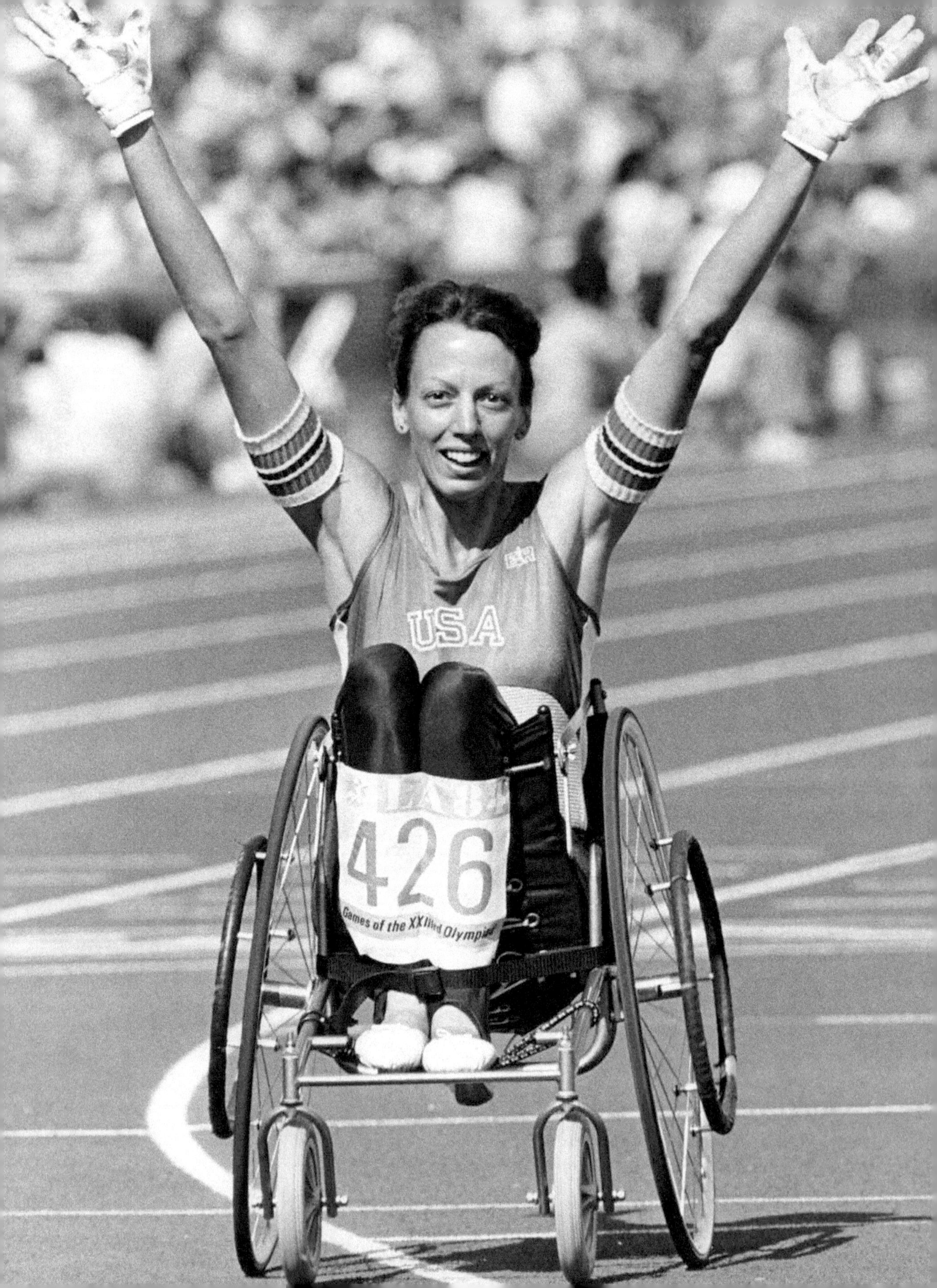
USA
426
Games of the XXIIIrd Olympi

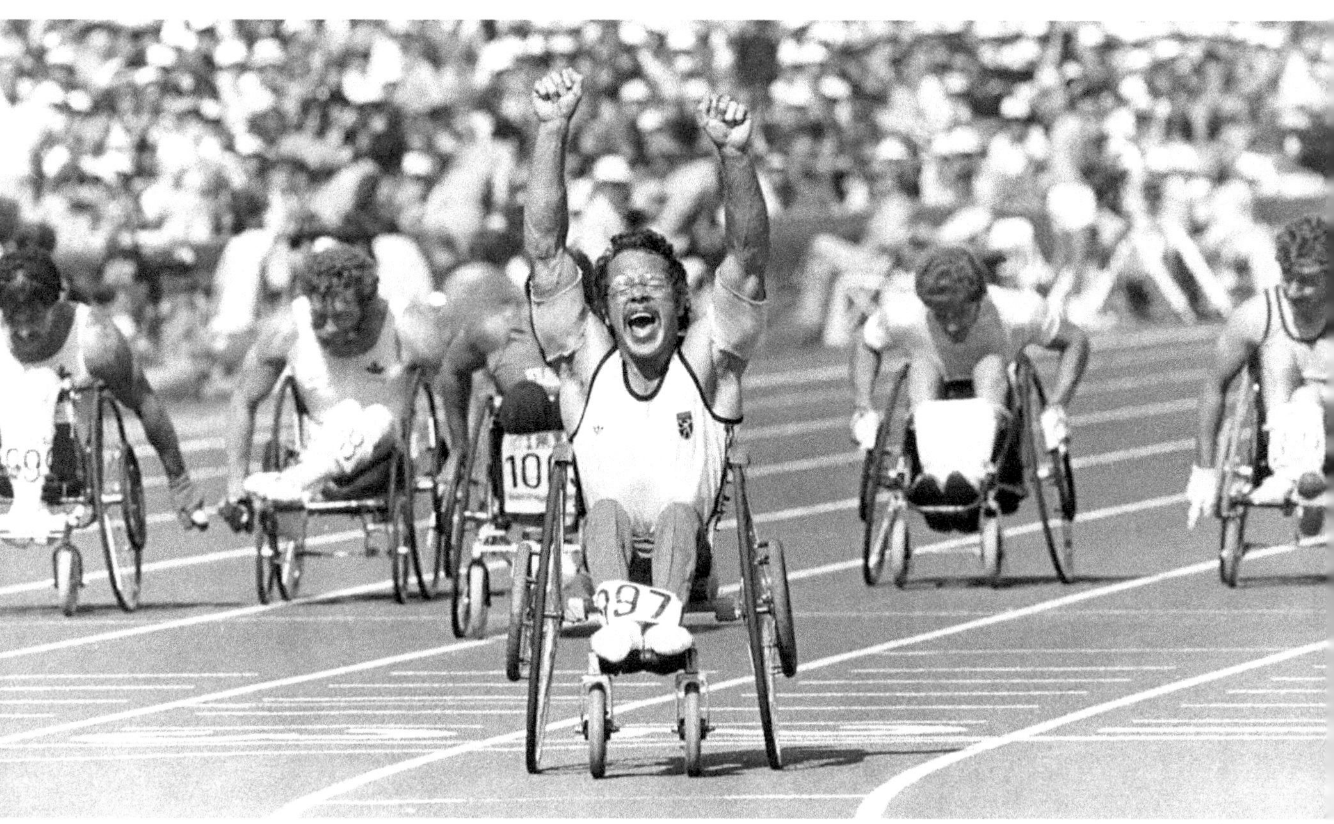

Two demonstration wheelchair races were held at the Coliseum, the first time that events for adaptive athletes were held in conjunction with the Summer Olympics. *Opposite:* American Sharon Hedrick won the 800-meter women's race (Anne Knudsen), while Belgium's Paul van Winkel (*above*) won the 1,500-meter men's race. (Paul Chinn)

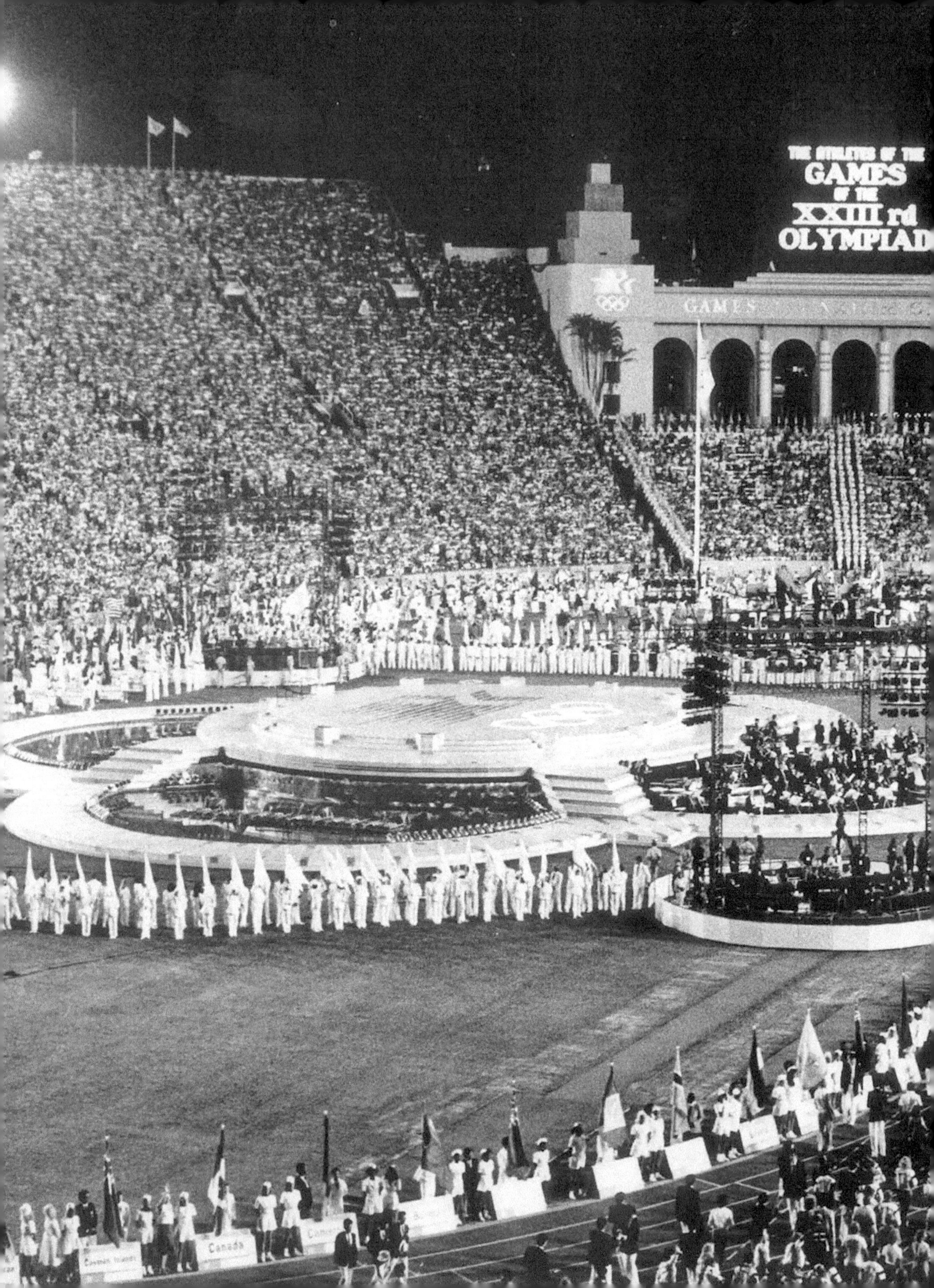

THE ATHLETES OF THE
GAMES
OF THE
XXIII rd
OLYMPIAD
Canada

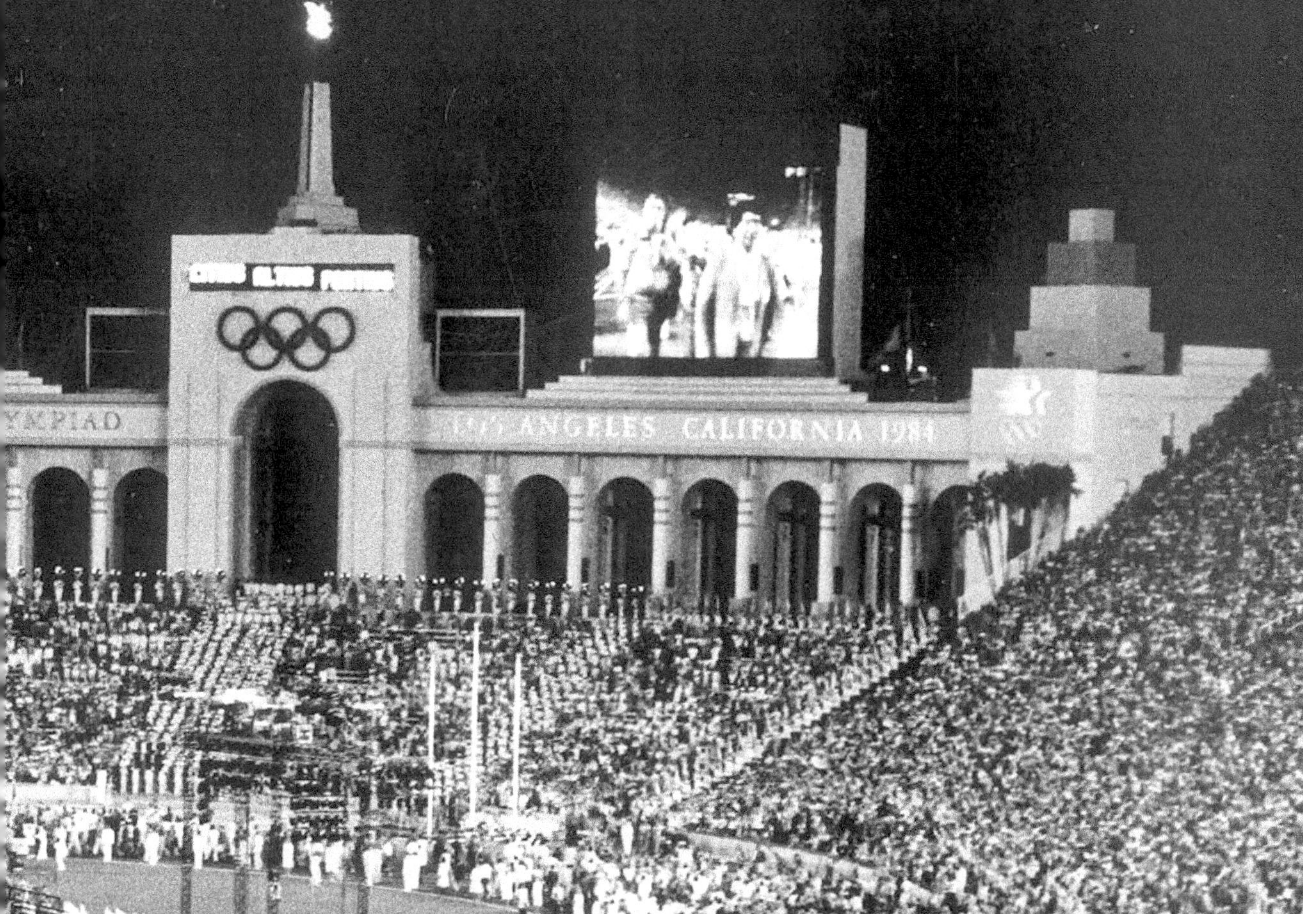
ANGELES CALIFORNIA 1984

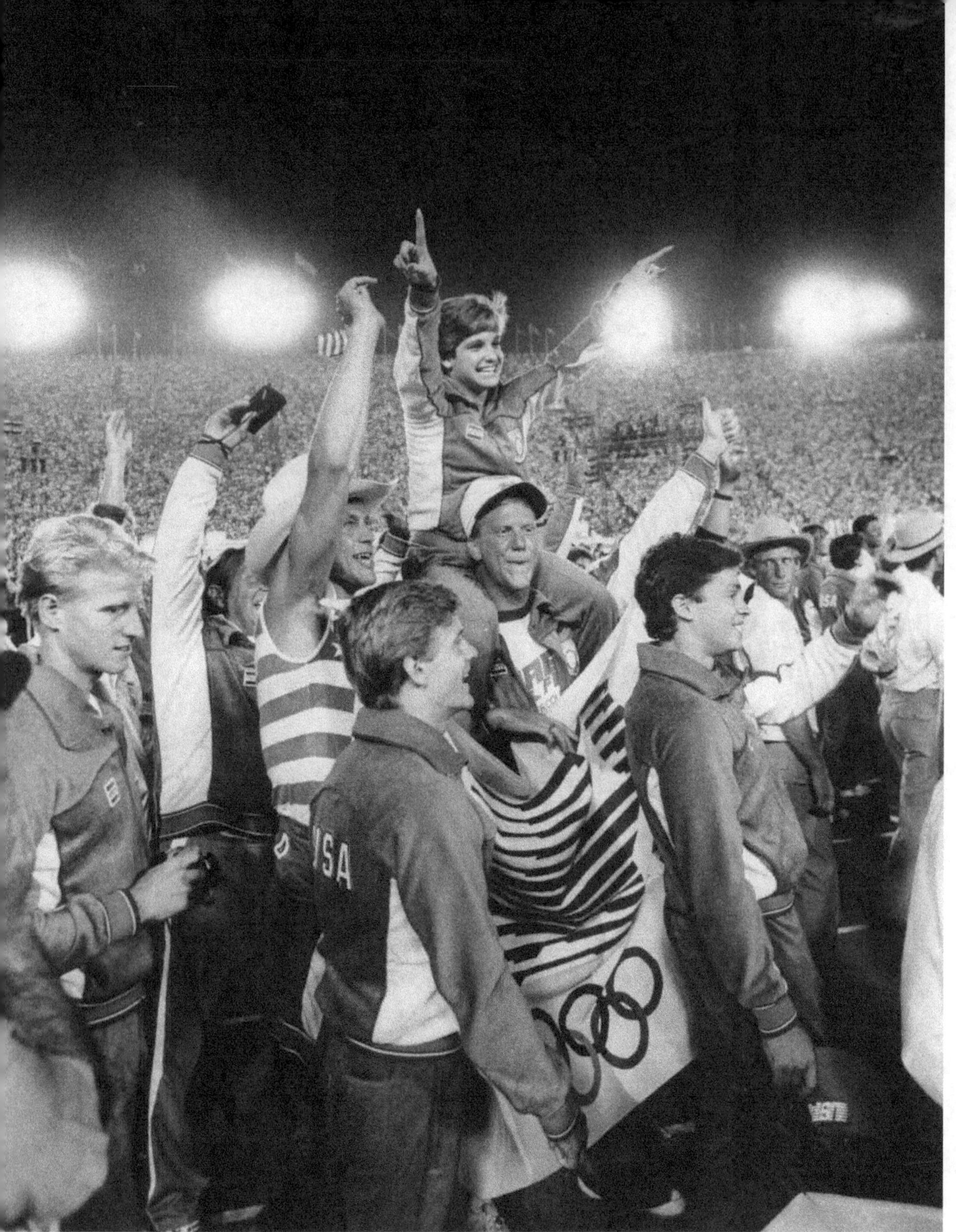

Above, opposite and overleaf: **The Closing Ceremony at the Coliseum featured fireworks, a performance by Lionel Ritchie, and a victory lap by the athletes, including Mary Lou Retton and fellow gymnasts. (*Above, Paul Chinn • Opposite,* Anne Knudsen • *Overleaf,* Dean Musgrove)**

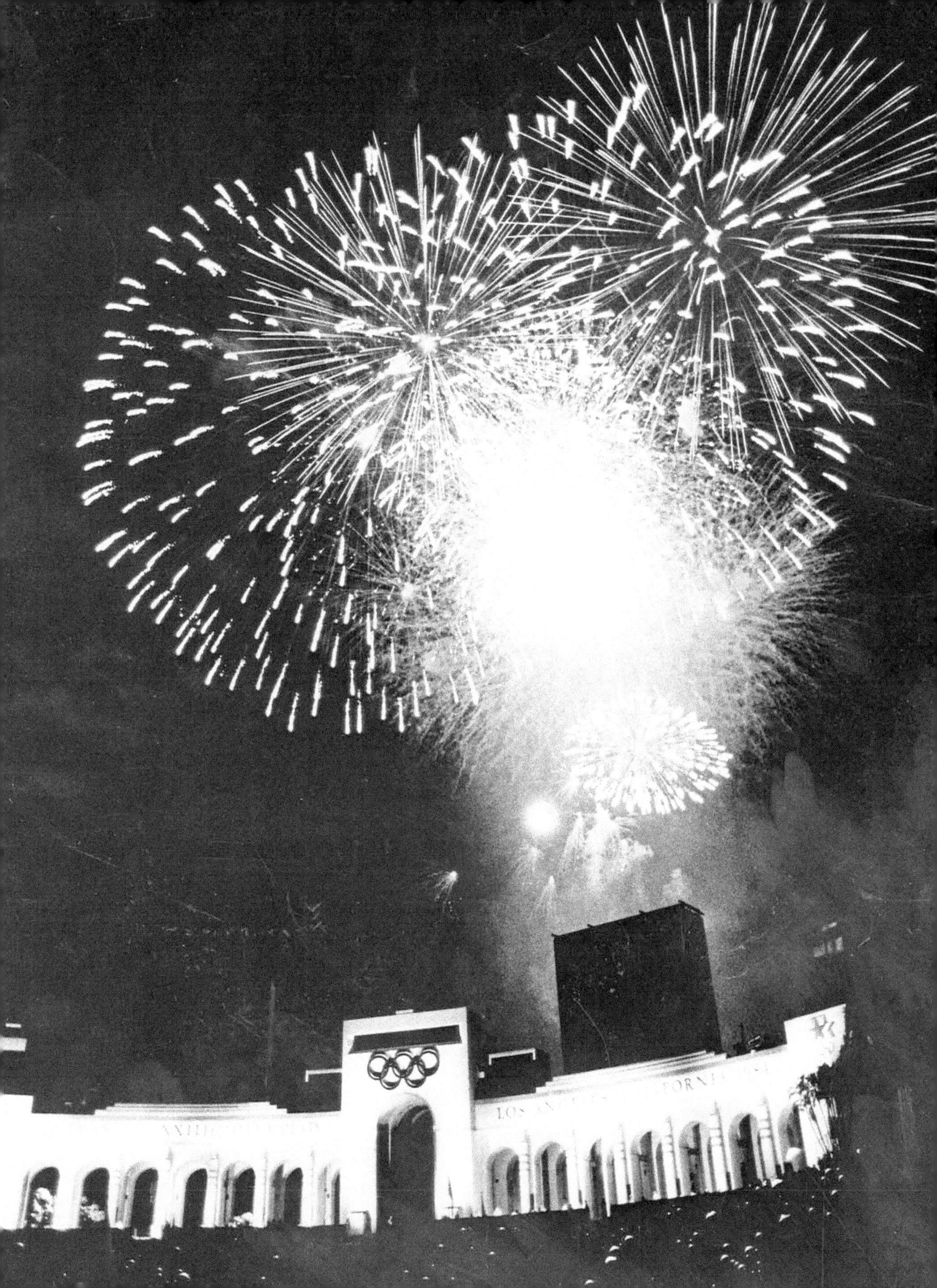
LOS

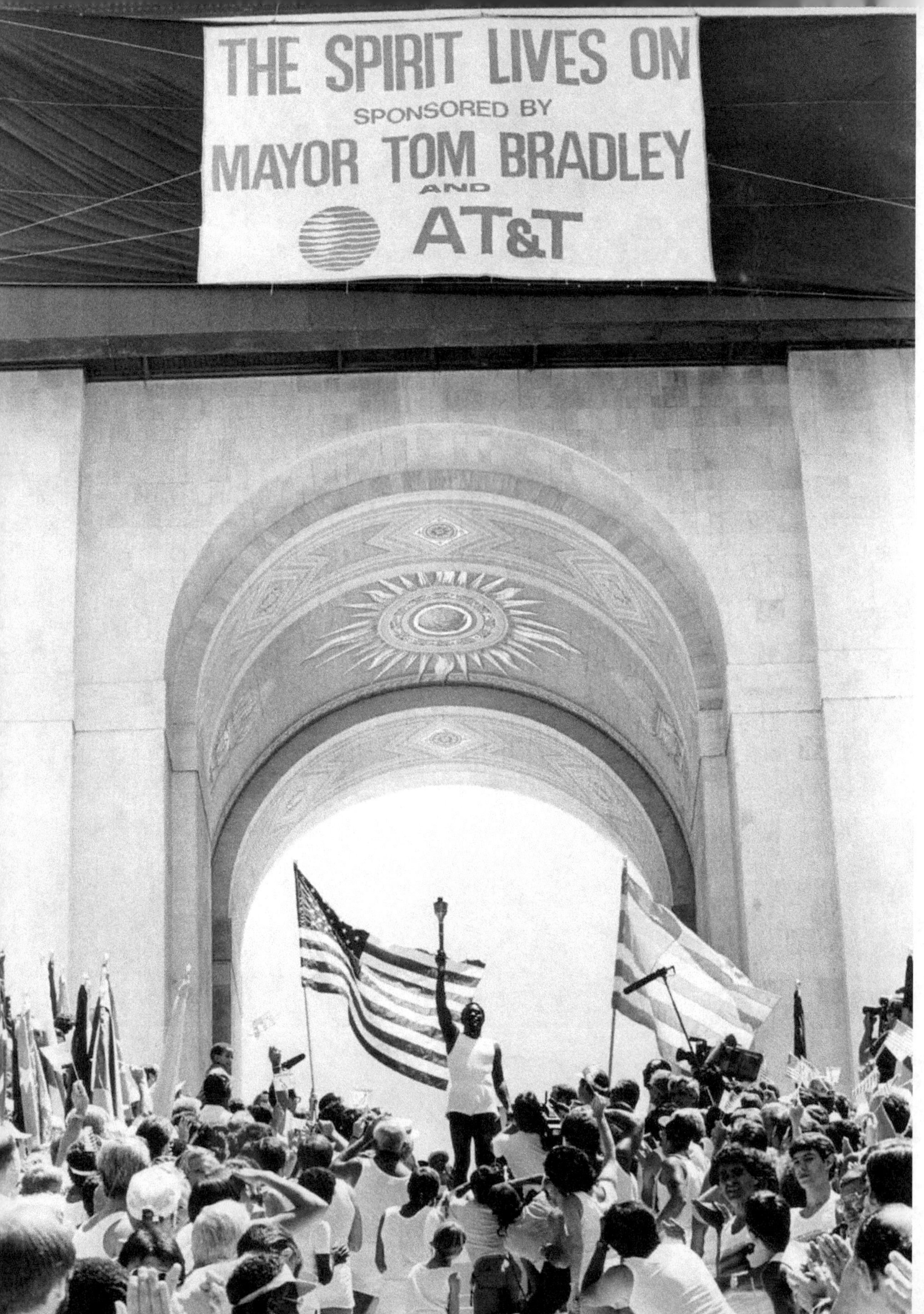
THE SPIRIT LIVES ON
SPONSORED BY
MAYOR TOM BRADLEY
AND
AT&T

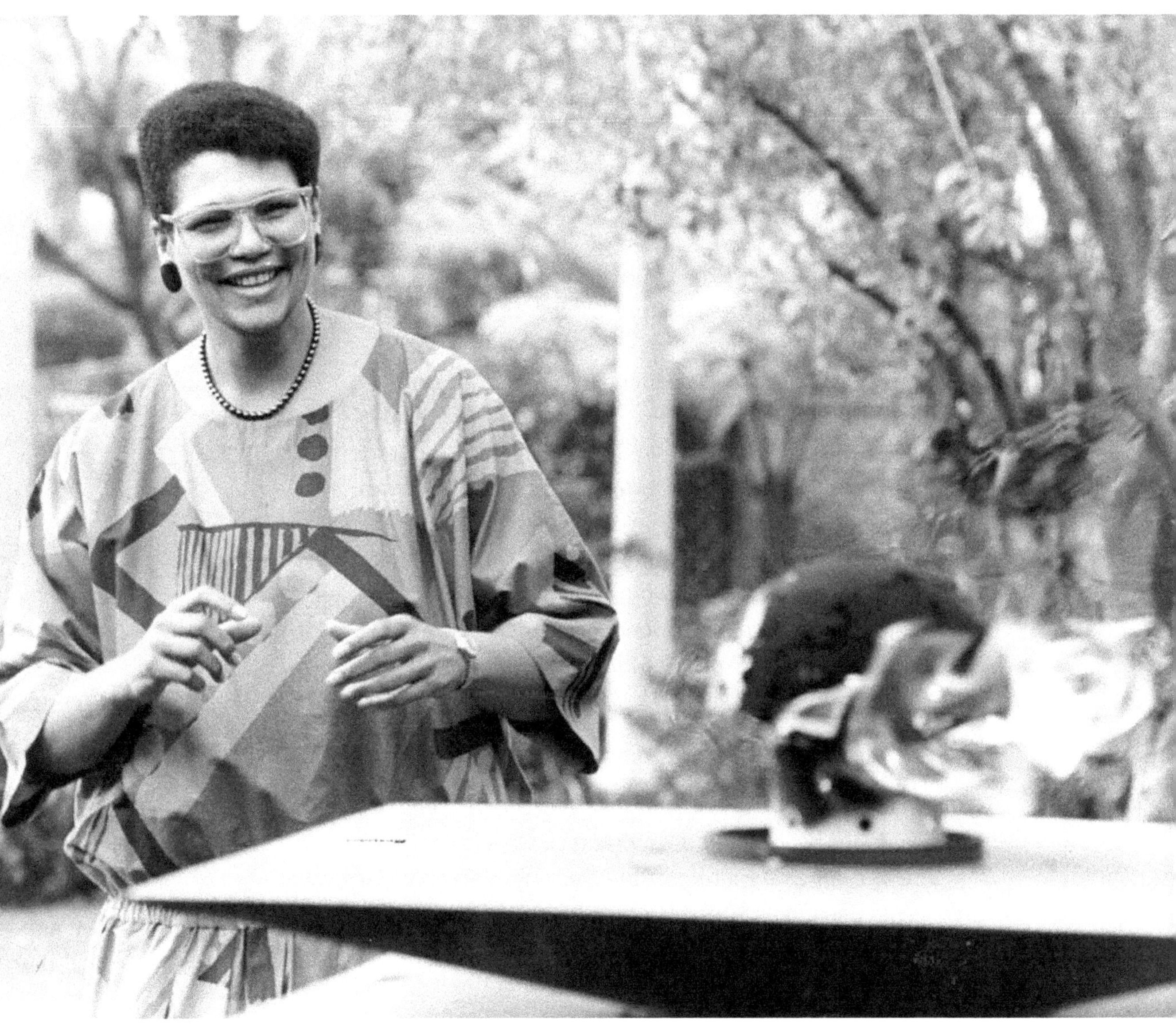

Opposite: Mayor Tom Bradley held a special ceremony to mark the one-year anniversary of the 1984 Olympics at the Coliseum. (Mike Sergieff)

Above: Attorney Anita DeFrantz, a bronze medalist in rowing at the 1976 Olympics, took charge of the LA84 Foundation (formerly known as the Amateur Athletic Foundation) after the Olympics. The LA84 Foundation continues to support youth-sports programs throughout Southern California, serving as a valued and enduring legacy of the 1984 Olympics. (Michael Haering)

Resources

Articles from the Los Angeles *Herald Examiner,* Los Angeles *Times, LA Weekly, Sports Illustrated, Time, Journal of Olympic History,* among other publications.

LA84 Foundation website: http://www.la84.org

Books

Breaking the Surface, by Greg Louganis and Eric Marcus.

The Complete Book of the Summer Olympics, by David Wallechinsky.

The Los Angeles 1984 Olympic Games, by Barry Sanders.

Los Angeles the Olympic City, edited by Delmar Watson, text by Paul Zimmerman.

Los Angeles Times 1984 Olympic Sports Pages, introduction by Bill Dwyre.

Making It Happen: Peter Ueberroth and the 1984 Olympics, by Kenneth Reich.

Official Report of the Games of the XXIIIrd Olympiad Los Angeles, 1984.

Official Report of the Games of the Xth Olympiad Los Angeles, 1932.

Olympic Arts Festival, text by Robert Fitzpatrick.

Olympic Collision: The Story of Mary Decker and Zola Budd, by Kyle Keiderling.

Olympic Retrospective: The Games of Los Angeles, edited by Richard Perelman.

Shooting for the Gold: A Portrait of America's Olympic Athletes, photographs by Walter Iooss, Jr., text by Dave Anderson.

Tales of Gold: An Oral History of the Summer Olympic Games, by Lewis Carlson and John Fogarty.

10 Photographers: Olympic Images, by Graham Howe, Howard Spector, and Edward Welch, essay by Peter Schjeldahl.

Films & Images

Los Angeles: Legacies of the 1932 Olympic Games, an exhibit of Historic Photographs from the Security Pacific National Bank Collection, Los Angeles Public Library.

Runner, from ESPN's "Nine for IX" series, directed by Shola Lynch.

16 Days of Glory, a documentary directed by Budd Greenspan.

Thank You

Thanks to the photographers from the gone-but-never-forgotten *Herald Examiner* newspaper who have been gracious enough to speak with me over the years. In particular, thanks to Paul Chinn, Javier Mendoza, Dean Musgrove, and James Ruebsamen for patiently answering my questions about the 1984 Los Angeles Olympics. Your photographs, as well as those of your late colleague Anne Knudsen, are extraordinary. Thanks also to Photo Friends board member Tom Zimmerman for his contributions. And, major thanks to Paul Gonzales for sharing his gold-medal memories.

Thanks to Photo Friends president Amy Inouye for her enthusiasm and her design expertise. Thanks also to Christina Rice, who so productively and creatively oversees the Los Angeles Public Library's Photo Collection and associated programming. Thanks to Photo Friends board members for their support of our book series and, especially, thanks to Kim Creighton for so ably preparing the images for digitization and publication. Thanks to Nicole Possert and librarian Wendy Horowitz for their assistance. A tip of the hat to PF founder and dear friend Carolyn Cole.

Thanks to Wayne Wilson, Michael Salmon, Shirley Ito at the LA84 Foundation – and thanks also to Patrick Escobar and Anita DeFrantz.

Finally, thanks to my family and friends. I can do nothing without your love.

About the Author

Award-winning journalist David Davis is the author of three books: *Waterman: The Life and Times of Duke Kahanamoku; Showdown at Shepherd's Bush: The 1908 Olympic Marathon and the Three Runners Who Launched a Sporting Craze;* and *Play By Play: Los Angeles Sports Photography, 1889-1989;* and one eBook: "Marathon Crasher: The Life and Times of Merry Lepper, the First American Woman to Run a Marathon." His work has appeared in *Sports Illustrated, Smithsonian, New York Times, Wall Street Journal, Los Angeles Magazine* and *Vice*; his writing has been anthologized in *The Best American Sports Writing* series. He has curated two photography exhibitions at the Los Angeles Central Library and has been a board member of Photo Friends since 2004. He lives in Los Angeles.

About the Photo Collection

The Los Angeles Public Library (LAPL) began collecting photographs sometime before World War II and had a collection of about 13,000 images by the late 1950s. In 1981, when Los Angeles celebrated its 200th birthday, Security Pacific National Bank gave its noted collection of historical photographs to the people of Los Angeles to be archived at the Central Library. Since then, LAPL has been fortunate to receive other major collections, making the Library a resource worldwide for visual images.

Notable collections include the "photo morgues" of the *Los Angeles Herald Examiner* and *Valley Times* newspapers, the Kelly-Holiday mid-Century collection of aerial photographs, the Works Progress Administration/Federal Writers Project collection, the Luther Ingersoll Portrait Collection, along with the landmark *Shades of L.A.,* which is an archive of images representing the contemporary and historic diversity of families in Los Angeles. Images were chosen from family albums and copied in a project sponsored by Photo Friends.

The Los Angeles Public Library Photo Collection also includes the works of individual photographers, including Ansel Adams, Herman Schultheis, William Reagh, Ralph Morris, Lucille Stewart, Gary Leonard, Stone Ishimaru, Carol Westwood, and Rolland Curtis.

Over 110,000 images from these collections have been digitized and are available to view through the LAPL website at *http://photos.lapl.org.*

About Photo Friends

Formed in 1990, Photo Friends is a nonprofit organization that supports the Los Angeles Public Library's Photograph Collection and History & Genealogy Department. Our goal is to improve access to the collections and promote them through programs, projects, exhibits, and books such as this one.

We are an enthusiastic group of photographers, writers, historians, business people, politicians, academics, and many others, all bonded by our passion for photography, history, and Los Angeles.

Since 1994, Photo Friends has presented a regular series called *The Photographer's Eye,* which spotlights local photographers and their work. In 2011, Photo Friends inaugurated *L.A. in Focus,* a lecture series that features images drawn primarily from the Photo Collection. We have presented programs on L.A. crime, the San Fernando Valley, Kelly-Holiday aerial photographs, and L.A.'s themed environments, among others.

With initial funding from the Ralph M. Parsons Foundation, Photo Friends sponsored *L.A. Neighborhoods Project* by commissioning photographers to create a visual record of the neighborhoods of Los Angeles during the early part of the 21st century (all now part of the collection). To ensure the library's collection will continue to reflect such an important part of Los Angeles's history, a generous grant enabled Photo Friends to hire five contemporary photographers to document present-day industrial L.A. These images have become part of LAPL's permanent collection and are available through the Library's photo database. Photo Friends also curates photography exhibits on display in the History Department.

Photo Friends is a membership organization. Please consider becoming a member and helping us in our work to preserve and promote L.A.'s rich photographic resource. All proceeds from the sale of this book go to support Photo Friends' programs.

photofriends.org

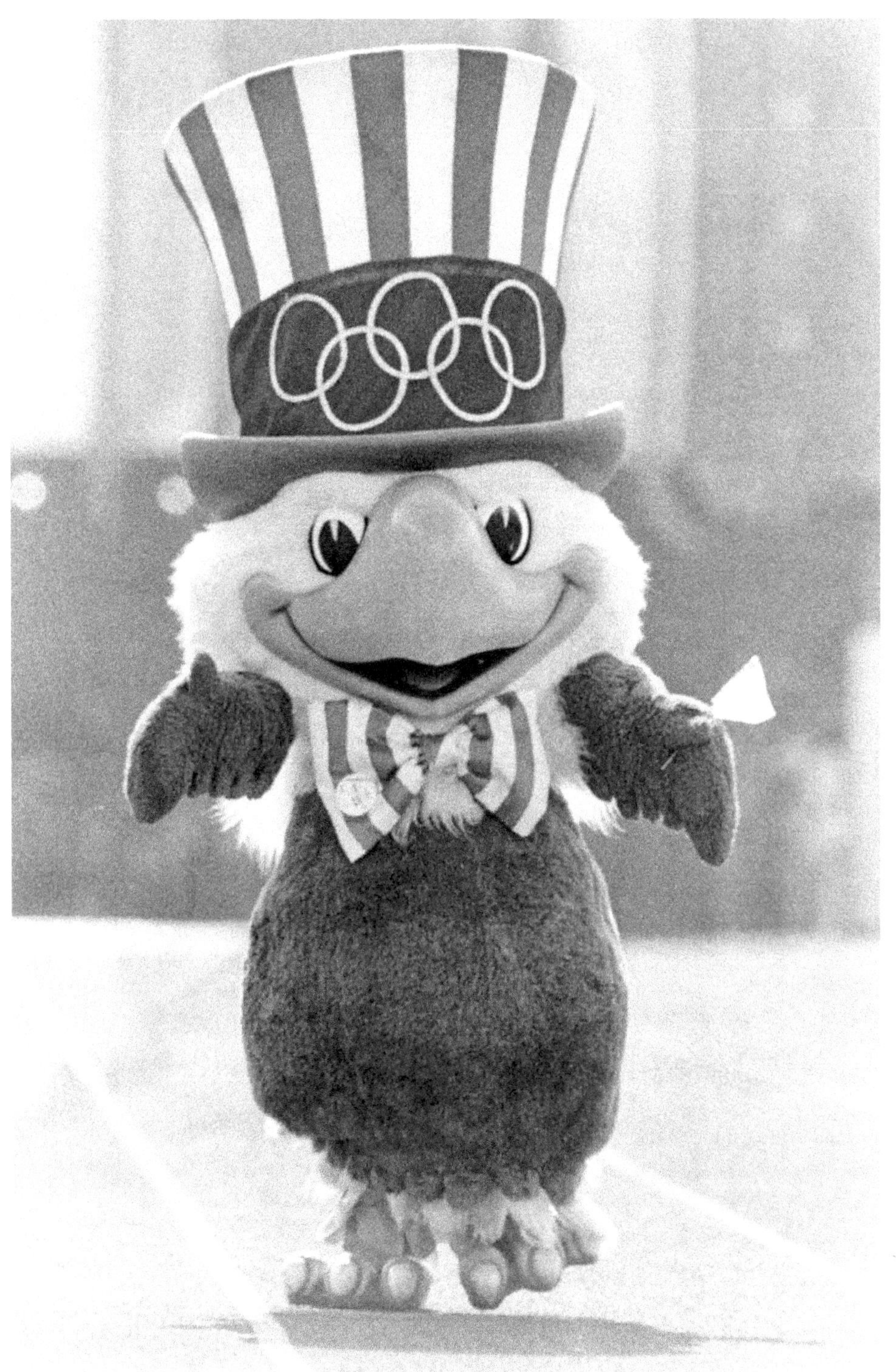

The development of Sam the Eagle, the official mascot, was credited to art director C. Robert Moore of the Walt Disney Company. (Paul Chinn)

One Golden Moment

The 1984 Olympics Through the Photographic Lens of the Los Angeles *Herald Examiner*

Published by:

Photo Friends of the Los Angeles Public Library
c/o Future Studio
P.O. Box 292000
Los Angeles, CA 90029
www.photofriends.org

Designed by Amy Inouye, Future Studio Los Angeles

Special quantity discounts available when purchased in bulk by corporations, organizations, or groups. Please contact Photo Friends at: photofriendsla@gmail.com

ISBN-13: 978-0-9978251-0-7

Printed in the United States

www.ingramcontent.com/pod-product-compliance
Lightning Source LLC
LaVergne TN
LVHW081324110826
845149LV00007B/1587

* 9 7 8 0 9 9 7 8 2 5 1 0 7 *